P9-BHT-711

BUDDHIST PRECEPT AND PRACTICE

BUDDHIST PRECEPT AND PRACTICE

Traditional Buddhism in the Rural Highlands of Ceylon

RICHARD F. GOMBRICH

KEGAN PAUL INTERNATIONAL
London and New York

First published in 1971

This edition published in 1995 by
Kegan Paul International
UK: P.O. Box 256, London WC1B 3SW, England
Tel: (0171) 580 5511 Fax: (0171) 436 0899
E-mail: books@keganpau.demon.co.uk
Internet: http://www.demon.co.uk/keganpaul/
USA: 562 West 113th Street, New York, Ny 10025, USA
Tel: (212) 666 1000 Fax: (212) 316 3100

Distributed by

John Wiley & Sons Ltd
Southern Cross Trading Estate
1 Oldlands Way, Bognor Regis
West Sussex, PO22 9SA, England
Tel: (01243) 829 121 Fax: (01243) 820 250

Columbia University Press
562 West 113th Street
New York, Ny10025, USA
Tel: (212) 666 1000 Fax: (212) 316 3100

© This edition Kegan Paul International, 1995

Printed in Great Britain by T.J. Press (Padstow) Ltd, Padstow, Cornwall

All rights reserved. No part of this book may be reprinted or reproduced or utilized in any form or by any electronic, mechanical or other means, now known or hereafter invented, including photocopying and recording, or in any information storage or retrieval system, without permission in writing from the publishers.

ISBN 0–7103–0444–7

British Library Cataloguing in Publication Data

Gombrich, Richard, 1937-
Buddhist precepts and practice.
I. Title
294.3

ISBN 0–7103–0444–7

Library of Congress Cataloguing–in–Publication Data

Gombrich, Richard Francis.
Buddhist precept and practice: traditional Buddhism in the rural highlands of Ceylon / Richard Francis Gombrich.
p. cm.
Originally published: Oxford: Clarendon Press. 1971
Includes bibliographical references and index.
ISBN 0–7103–0444–7
1. Buddhism—Sri Lanka
BQ356.G64 1995
294.3' 095493—dc20 95–18484
CIP

'In our opinion, the first condition for a sound development of a Sociology of India is found in the establishment of the proper relation between it and classical Indology.'

Dumont and Pocock

Preface

THIS book is a revised version of my thesis, 'Contemporary Sinhalese Buddhism in its relation to the Pali Canon', approved for the D.Phil. degree at Oxford University. The thesis was substantially written in the university vacations of 1966–7. On sabbatical leave in Ceylon in the latter half of 1969 I took the opportunity to make some changes, but although I hope to have eliminated some mistakes, I could not entirely bring it up to date, or profit by all the publications which have appeared since I started writing. Rather than delay publication still further I am letting it go forward now, for revision is a process which can never be completed. In particular, however, I must mention that Chapter 8 was written before I had read *Homo Hierarchicus* by Louis Dumont (Gallimard, Paris, 1966); I would formulate most of the first half of the chapter very differently today, but I have let it stand because I do not think that my conclusions have been invalidated. I regret also that the following reached me too late to be used: Heinz Bechert, 'Einige Fragen der Religionssoziologie und Struktur des südasiatischen Buddhismus', *International Yearbook for the Sociology of Religion*, vol. 4, 1968, pp. 251–95; S. J. Tambiah, *Buddhism* and *the Spirit Cults in North-East Thailand* (C.U.P., Cambridge, 1970).

The greatest pleasure in finishing the book comes from the opportunity it gives me formally to acknowledge the help and kindness I have received during its preparation. The field work on which it is based was undertaken in Ceylon from August 1964 to August 1965, a visit wholly financed by a Treasury Studentship from the British Government. My second visit, in 1969, was largely paid for by a Hayter travel grant awarded to me by Oxford University. The success of both visits was, however, entirely due to the material and moral support given me by friends, and to my wife, who both times accompanied me and kept house unaided in the village for a total of nearly two years. In England before I left, Professor Gananath Obeyesekere gave me invaluable advice about criteria on which to choose my village, as well as a great deal of academic advice and practical assistance when he had returned to Ceylon. The Rev. Walpola Rahula received me in Paris, answered a lot of questions, and has continued ever since to treat me with the greatest kindness. I owe my introduction to both these scholars to that renowned patron of Ceylon studies Professor E. F. C. Ludowyk. When we reached Ceylon we would never have found a suitable village had not Professor P. W. Vithanage devoted several whole days to driving us round and giving us the benefit of his geographical knowledge and geological wisdom. Our first steps in Sinhalese were guided by Mr. B. L. Fernando of St. Antony's College, Kaṭugastoṭa, who for two months took endless trouble in teaching us, and has never since lost interest in his pupils. These are my more strictly academic debts in Ceylon. I am not thanking a field assistant or interpreter because I had none.

On the more personal side, I wish to thank Major and Mrs. A. A. de Alwis, Dr. and Mrs. W. M. J. Bartholomeusz, Professor and Mrs. E. F. Bartholomeusz, Mr. and Mrs. F. Lobo, Professor and Mrs. G. Obeyesekere, Professor and Mrs. P. W. Vithanage, Proctor and Mrs. H. A. C. Wickremeratne, Mr. and Mrs. L. Y. Wickremeratne, and Mr. Jayatissa Yapa for hospitality such as non-Ceylonese can hardly conceive.

While the thesis was being composed Dr. Brenda Beck, Dr. K. Malalgoḍa, Professor Sir Karl Popper, and of course my supervisor, Professor R. C. Zaehner, read all or part of the work and made valuable suggestions. The typists involved were too many to name individually, but I would especially like to thank the first, Mrs. Sriani Fernando, and the last Mrs. Wendy O'Flaherty, for their sympathetic cooperation. Mrs. Heather Ion and my wife sacrificed much time to proof-reading when they both had better things to do.

The completed thesis was read by Dr. Bryan Wilson, Professor Obeyesekere, and my father, all of whom made just and stimulating criticisms from which I hope I have benefited. My intellectual debt to these three people and to

Professor Popper cannot be adequately conveyed by references in the text. Mr. C. H. B. Reynolds generously gave me Sinhalese lessons for a whole year without prospect of reward. My mother and my wife helped immensely with the mechanics of revision and production, and spotted many slips. Finally I thank the staff of the Clarendon Press for their encouragement and efficiency.

I dedicate this imperfect draft to my informants, with gratitude and respect.

සැමදෙනාවහන්සේට නිවන්සැප ලැබේවා

Note on the Revised Edition

For this edition the book has been corrected, not rewritten. I have made about a hundred changes in the body of the text, the great majority of them small corrections of misprints and slips. I owe most of the corrections to the Rev. Dr. Walpola Rahula, who has put me still further in his debt by the care with which he perused the book.

Oxford, May 1989.

Abbreviations

A.N.	*Anguttara Nikāya*
C.U.P.	Cambridge University Press
Dh.A.	*Dhammapada Aṭṭhakathā*
D.N.	*Dīgha Nikāya*
J.	*Jātaka*
J.A.S.	*Journal of Asian Studies*
J.R.A.S.	*Journal of the Royal Asiatic Society*
Mhv.	*Mahāvaṃsa*
M.N.	*Majjhima Nikāya*
O.U.P.	Oxford University Press
P.T.S.	Pali Text Society
R.A.S.	Royal Asiatic Society
S.N.	*Saṃyutta Nikāya*
Vin.	*Vinaya Piṭaka*
Vv.	*Vimāna-vatthu*
Vv.A	*Vimāna-vatthu Aṭṭhakathā*

Pronunciation and Transliteration of Sinhalese

(with remarks on Sanskrit and Pali)

The full Sinhalese alphabet contains all the letters used in Sanskrit (and therefore in Pali) with a few additions, but many of these letters occur only in words loaned from Sanskrit. The Sinhalese pronounce Sanskrit and Pali much as do European scholars. A given letter has generally the same phonetic value (pronunciation) in Sinhalese, Sanskrit, and Pali.

Sinhalese vowels follow a phonetic pattern close to English vowels minus the diphthongs. Sinhalese *a, ä, e, ā, ǟ, ē*, approximate respectively to the vowels in English *bun, ban, Ben, bard, bad*, and the first element in *bane*; however, in an unstressed syllable *a* is a central vowel, just as happens in English (compare the vowels in *man* and *postman*), and *ā* is pronounced short. Stress is very light and is as far back as English pronunciation would tolerate, tending to fall on a long syllable (i.e. on a long vowel or a vowel followed by more than one consonant). The Sanskrit vowel *ṛ* is pronounced as in American *cur*, long or short. In Sanskrit and Pali the vowels *e* and *o* are not marked for length because there is no ambiguity: in Sanskrit they are always long, in Pali short before a double consonant and long elsewhere.

Of the consonants, *g* is always hard, *c* is like English *ch*, *j* as in English, *ñ* (palatal *n*) like English *ny* (as in *onion*). *Ṭ* and *ḍ* are pronounced further back than English *t* and *d*, but not as the true retroflexes found in other Indian languages; *t, d* are true dentals, like those letters in French and Italian. The distinctions between Sinhalese *ṇ* and *n*, *ḷ* and *l* are historical only. *Y* is as in English *yes*. *Ś* and *ṣ* occur only in Sanskrit loanwords; in Sanskrit they are pronounced much like English *sh*, but in Sinhalese this is ignored (except by pedants) and both are pronounced as *s*. *H* after another consonant denotes aspiration, not a change in quality (English *hothead* not *bother*); this too occurs only in Sanskrit loanwords, and tends to be ignored in Sinhalese pronunciation. *Ň, ň, m̆* are pronounced very lightly indeed. *Ṃ* is a pure nasal like standard English *ng* in *singing*; in colloquial Sinhalese any final nasal is so pronounced.

The letter which is here transliterated sometimes as *v*, sometimes as *w*, may strike the English ear as either, but falls in between English *v* (a labiodental fricative) and English *w* (bilabial semi-vowel): it is a bilabial fricative. The exception to this is that in final position it is pronounced as a semi-vowel, i.e. *pav* is pronounced like the first syllable in English *power*. By scholarly convention the transliteration is *v*, but the English administration represented the letter as *w*, which is the custom in Ceylon to this day.

The scholarly system of transliteration which is standard for all three languages has been consistently used so far as is feasible without undue pedantry. Apparent inconsistencies may be due to switching between languages, espccially in the reproduction of orally gathered material, since speakers tend to make free use also of parallel Sinhalese forms (e.g. Pali: *Mahāsena*; Sinh: *Mahasēna* or *Mahasen*).

Contents

ABBREVIATIONS xi

PRONUNCIATION xiii

Introduction: Aims and Scope of this Book 1

I. The Problem: Religious Change 1
II. Why Ceylon? 20
III. The History, Geography and Economy of Ceylon 23
IV. Field-work and Presentation 43

1. Sinhalese Buddhism—Orthodox or Syncretistic? 47

2. The Basic Vocabulary of Buddhism 67

3. The Buddha 95

I. The Buddha's Biography 95
II. The Buddha as worshipped: Man or God? 121

4. A Sketch of the Universe as seen from Mīgala 169

I. Causation 169
II. The Contents of the Universe 180
III. Attempts to influence non-human Beings 224
IV. Summary 246

5. Total Responsibility in Theory and Practice 251

6. The Ethics of Intention 285

7. The Monastic Ideal and the Decline of Buddhism 314

8. Caste in the Monastery 343

9. Conclusion 372

APPENDIX 383

GLOSSARY 395

BIBLIOGRAPHY 406

INDEX 414

Introduction: Aims and Scope of this Book

I. The Problem: Religious Change

> ...in case it be said that we have only described the facts in relation to a theory of them and as exemplifications of it and have subordinated description to analysis, we reply that this was our intention.[1]
>
> Evans-Pritchard

THIS is intended as a contribution to the empirical study of religion, and in particular to the study of religious change.

Religion is studied in many different ways, characteristic of different academic disciplines. Theologians customarily study their own religion, which they accordingly meet on its own terms, and discuss problems posed by and within this historically given framework of ideas. When they carry the study of other religions beyond polemics the result is usually called comparative religion. This vague term can of course always be applied to studies of any type which compare two or more religions, but the study which is now called comparative religion is practised and organized principally by theologians. Philologists study the texts which form the basis of at least the most famous religions, and speculate about their origins and what the authors meant. Religious historians study past religious doctrines and institutions where these are accessible through documentary or perhaps archaeological evidence. Sociologists and anthropologists of religion describe and discuss, usually with some stress on their behavioural aspects, existing religious practices and institutions; if any difference is made between the two disciplines it is usually held to be that sociologists study literate, social anthropologists illiterate societies, or that sociologists study

[1]E. E. Evans-Pritchard, *The Nuer* (Clarendon Press, Oxford, 1940), p. 261.

larger or more differentiated communities than anthropologists, or that sociologists are more likely to concentrate on formal organization, anthropologists on more informal behaviour. Social psychologists who work on religion are like sociologists and social anthropologists in that they too study the religions of contemporary social groups; but they probably concentrate more on the ideas and attitudes of their subjects. Other psychologists of religion deal with the religious attitudes of individuals in various ways; at one extreme are behaviourists, who will study only religious behaviour, with a marked disinclination to include in this category verbal utterance. At the other extreme are psychoanalysts and other more philosophically oriented psychologists, who are very interested in the words and notions of their subjects, but share with the behaviourists a reluctance to use their subjects' terminology or indeed conceptual framework in the discussion of religion—unless of course the subject should happen to hold the same views as they do themselves.

It may be objected that this classification by subject matter is naïve, because I should have classified these studies by method, certain methods being typical of the humanities (e.g. the philologists) and others of the social sciences. I have not done so because I believe that scholarly research advances by only one method, shared by the humanities, the social and the natural sciences: the method of hypothesis and falsification, of theory and test, of conjecture and refutation; the method which has been formulated and explained by K. R. Popper.[2] Metaphysics, with which theologians are concerned, are not usually amenable to this method; at the other end of my list, the theories of

[2]Originally in *Logik der Forschung* (Julius Springer, Vienna, 1935), republished (translated and amplified) as *The Logic of Scientific Discovery* (Hutchinson, London, 1959). For a simple and succinct statement see also Popper's paper 'Science: Conjectures and Refutations', republished in *Conjectures and Refutations* (Routledge and Kegan Paul, London, 1962). On classification by subject matter see the remarks in Popper's paper 'The Nature of Philosophical Problems and their Roots in Science', republished in the same book, pp. 66–7.

psychoanalysts and psychiatrists tend to wander over the border into philosophical speculation or degenerate into technological rules of thumb; but the method of conjecture and refutation is characteristic of all the disciplines listed in between; and in so far as studies in them are duly characterized by this method they constitute what in the first line I called the empirical, or might call scientific, study of religion. The method, then, is only one; the means—documents, interviews, experiments—are infinite, whatever the researcher can lay his hands on as he does his best to test his old hypotheses and to formulate new and better ones which may lead him towards the truth.

Again, it may be objected that my classification is jejune and uninteresting. With this objection I agree; indeed, to elicit it was one of my reasons for drawing up the list. Academic boundaries are artificial: the realities are the problems. Problems have a way of crossing these boundaries; while chasing one the hapless researcher may wander, alone and unarmed, into the territory of a foreign and possibly hostile discipline. If he keeps quiet he may escape unobserved; if he is fool enough to raise his voice he will be apprehended, and must throw himself on his captor's mercy. I am in this unfortunate position. By education a philologist, far less of a historian, and devoid of anthropological training, I have been chasing the problem of religious change, and found myself far from home, deep inside the territory of the social sciences, far from Oxford libraries in a village in central Ceylon. The bulk of this book consists in the presentation of a year's field work, the very stuff of anthropology; and my problems and conjectural explanations are of the type which hitherto have interested mainly those trained in the social sciences.

In extenuation of my presumption let me plead that some eminent anthropologists of religion say that they are dissatisfied with the limitations of much work in their field, limitations imposed by the tradition that anthropologists study only what they can observe at first hand. This especially hinders the study of social change: an anthropologist who goes out to observe a society naturally produces what is called a synchronic study in which the society, including its religion, has its picture taken at one moment and is thus presented as if static. Very rarely can an anthropologist revisit a society to see for himself how it changes; moreover anthropology itself is still so young that few communities have been systematically observed twice even by different people. Further, as Professor Evans-Pritchard has pointed out in a series of lectures at Oxford,[3] by an unfortunate chance most of the people who have had interesting ideas about the anthropology of religion were not themselves field-workers and lacked detailed and accurate knowledge of any society on which they might have tested their hypotheses: Tylor, Durkheim and Lévy-Bruhl are celebrated examples. Even Radcliffe-Brown and Malinowski, who did field-work themselves, did not possess comparable data collected in one society at different times, and so lacked material for diachronic studies; this lack may have decisively influenced their own lines of interest, which virtually ignored the problem of social change. In the absence, then, of data collected in the field, the student of social change must rely on glimpses of the past to be found in myths and folklore, and on the more conventional written sources. Professor Evans-Pritchard has invited anthropologists to become historians; and this gives heart to the philologist turned anthropologist.

Let me now return to my list of approaches to religion. Another reason I had for drawing it up was indeed heuristic. There are several distinct senses in which a religion may be described; some of these correspond to the academic distinctions made in my list, and some do not. 'Jesus Christ is the son of God' is a theological or metaphysical statement. 'According to the Bible Jesus Christ is the son of God' is a philological statement; a still more precise one would be to quote the Bible in Greek. 'People have believed Jesus Christ to be the son of God' is a historical statement, and in a sense '85 per cent of the present

[3]See also his *Theories of Primitive Religion* (Clarendon Press, Oxford, 1965).

inhabitants of Cremona believe that Jesus Christ is the son of God' could be called a historical statement too. Where does this leave the other social sciences? The academic distinctions between sociology, anthropology, and psychology do not accurately correspond to different ways of talking about religion; yet within the subject-matter of these disciplines logical distinctions can and should be made.

The distinctions I propose to make, and use throughout this book, are between what people say they believe and say they do, and what they really believe and really do. These are simple categories which I have chosen because I find them heuristically useful; in themselves they, and the words I have chosen to express them, of course explain nothing. What people really do I shall call simply religious behaviour. What they say about their beliefs and practices I shall call 'cognitive'. What they say may of course vary according to circumstances, but though this point is of great practical importance in field-work, it is not theoretically important. For our present purposes I will assume that people who say what they believe are speaking the truth; yet there may still be something more to find out about their beliefs. What people really believe I am aware to be ultimately unknowable; but this does not mean that it is nonsense to talk about it. Only a pure behaviourist refrains from making inferences from what people really do to what they are thinking or feeling. If a lapsed Roman Catholic states that he has lost all belief in God, and yet is seen to cross himself at a moment of crisis, we infer from his actions that he is operating on an ideological system which differs from his explicit or conscious beliefs: he behaves *as if* he still believed in God. In old-fashioned terms it is the religion of the heart, not the head. So I propose to call it 'affective'[4] religion. However, whatever my terminology, behaviourists and other adherents of scientistic creeds may still balk at my entertaining such a category at

[4]'Affective...2. Pertaining to the emotions, opp. to intellectual...1623'. *Shorter O.E.D.* Unfortunately I cannot use the word 'intellectual' instead of 'cognitive' for what people state about their religion, because it has misleading overtones.

all. In answer I would remind them that most religions include ethics, which involve a value system, which I wish to study: and in ethics the tensions between the cognitive and the affective belief system and value system are notoriously acute. Someone may tell us quite seriously that he esteems a certain virtue, and yet act in a contrary manner without apparent sense of guilt or incongruity. In such cases we speak of unconscious hypocrisy, or say he is deceiving himself (all concepts unacceptable to a behaviourist, who is plainly, though unconsciously, not at home in politics). Nothing depends on terms, and I shall be glad to use such everyday words as 'hypocrisy', but by using also the expression 'affective ethics' I shall try to keep their logical standing clear.

Much confusion has arisen from statements which ignore these distinctions. Let us take an example. A Catholic[5] theologian may make the statement, 'The souls of the dead do not return to this world, but are in Heaven, Hell or Purgatory'; and other theologians may concur: i.e. the statement is theologically correct. A corresponding empirical statement which looks correct is, 'According to Catholic doctrine the souls... Purgatory'; the philologist could produce chapter and verse. All too often, however, 'According to Catholic doctrine... ' is taken as equivalent to 'Catholics believe that...'. But if this substitution is made we have to ask, 'Which Catholics?' Our interlocutor may be a historian and correctly specify a certain group. But if he is merely a non-specialist, or even a theologian, he may rashly answer, 'All Catholics.' Then we have to jog his memory and ask, 'What about ghosts?' Undoubtedly many Catholics admit to a belief in ghosts. This is their cognitive position. Others may say they do not believe in ghosts, but tell stories of experiences they declare to be inexplicable in any other terms; the cognitive position of these people is inconsistent. Other professed unbelievers may refuse to sleep in what they are told is

[5]This term covers of course not only Roman Catholics, but also the many Anglicans who would accept it.

a haunted bedroom—in that case their behaviour is inconsistent with their cognitive position, and we may say that affectively they believe that ghosts exist or at least might exist. Having reminded ourselves of the importance of ghosts to many Catholics, we may look back at the doctrinal position of Catholic theology, and see that things are not quite so simple. There are no ghosts in the Bible in the sense of spirits of dead people,[6] so those who consider the Bible to be the foundation of their religion, and yet believe in ghosts, are unorthodox or inconsistent by this criterion. Yet members of some major Christian denominations still occasionally perform a ceremony for exorcism, and I have established by questioning that Anglicans generally consider the entities exorcised to be not devils, as happens in the New Testament, but ghosts, euphemistically known as 'spirits of the departed'. I have just mentioned the inconsistent position of a Catholic who in effect states that he does and does not believe in ghosts: is there a parallel inconsistency in doctrine, in Anglican theology? Being no theologian I put this question to the Archbishop of Canterbury at a public meeting in Oxford in December 1963. Referring to a recent exorcism performed by the Bishop of Exeter which had been reported in *The Times*, I asked His Grace whether Anglicans believed in ghosts. He replied that belief in the spirits of the departed and their return to this earth was neither accepted nor rejected by Christian doctrine. So even the theological statement at the beginning of this paragraph was not so impeccably correct as it seemed.

The Archbishop's reply illustrates another point: while individuals are frequently inconsistent in their statements of beliefs, the theologies of the highly organized religions are rarely if ever inconsistent on matters of importance. There are two ways, apart from critically arguing through

[6] Except the ghost of Samuel, summoned by the witch of Endor (1 Samuel 28). But this passage is theologically contentious, especially among Catholics, who are not committed to a literal interpretation of the Old Testament. Certainly ghosts are not part of the general biblical scheme of things.

the matter to a (possibly negative) conclusion, in which they avoid contradictions at difficult points. One way is to declare the matter a mystery inaccessible to human reason: this is a solution beloved of Protestants, but in contrast not available to Theravāda Buddhists, who claim, as the Buddha claimed, that their doctrines are founded mostly on reason and that anyone can test their truth. The other way is to ignore the problem altogether, either silently or by explicitly stating that it is not their concern to come to a decision. Inevitably there must be problems of which any system of thought takes no cognizance; but these are more likely to concern the philosopher than the empirical inquirer whose subjects have never heard of them. Refusal by a religion to come to a decision on certain points is a more important phenomenon in our present context. The Archbishop's comment on ghosts is one example. *Mutatis mutandis* the same reply might have been made by a Buddhist cleric: whether or not you believe in ghosts is irrelevant to whether you are a 'good' or orthodox Buddhist, and the same incidentally is true of whether you believe in gods (see Chapter 1). Perhaps the most celebrated exponent of the undecided question was the Buddha himself. On one occasion[7] he refused to answer a monk who asked him whether the world was eternal, whether it was finite, whether the soul and the body are identical, and whether an enlightened man in any sense existed after death. The Buddha replied that he had never promised to answer these questions; anyone who refused to lead the religious life till they were answered would be like a man wounded by an arrow who refused to have it removed till he knew the name and caste of the man who shot it; his teaching was merely the practical way to release from misery. At another time[8] he condemned as idle speculation a far longer list of metaphysical questions.[9] This refusal to pontificate on what he

[7] *M.N., Sutta* 63 (*Cūḷa Mālunkya Sutta*).

[8] *D.N., Sutta* 1 (*Brahmajāla Sutta*).

[9] Whether the soul or the world was eternal, whether the world was spatially finite, whether there were other worlds, whether the

regarded as inessentials was what we might expect of a man who asked his listeners not to take any doctrine on trust or authority but only to accept what they themselves found reasonable; it certainly has been very influential in the history of Buddhism, and goes far to explain why Buddhists vary so much in some areas of belief and take little interest in others: they are not covered by the Buddha's doctrine. Religion provides a framework for interpreting reality. On certain points a religion is specific; these we usually call dogmas; other points are undecided. Religions are dogmatic on different matters, and Buddhism has rather few dogmas altogether.

I have so far discussed religion in general terms without attempting to define it. This does not really matter, because everyone knows what I have been talking about, and problems of definition are essentialist problems, essentially trivial.[10] But I cannot entirely fail to mention a matter so controversial. For a long time it was stated or assumed that religion was essentially characterized by belief in God or

soul or the world arose without cause, whether there were beings who originated without natural causes (i.e. gods and spirits), whether good and bad actions (*karman*) entail good and bad results, whether the soul (Skt.: *ātman*; Pali: *attan*) existed after death and in what form, whether a *Tathāgata* (man who is 'thus-gone', i.e. as dead—enlightened?) existed after death, and whether and in what form 'salvation' (*nirvāṇa*) is possible in this life. For a fuller account see E.J. Thomas, *The History of Buddhist Thought* (Routledge and Kegan Paul, London, 1933), pp. 74–5. Not all of these questions are in fact left undecided elsewhere in the Pali Canon; it is stated that the soul does not exist, that ethical actions do entail appropriate results, and that *nirvāṇa* is possible in this life if one follows the Noble Eight-fold Path leading to the cessation of suffering. On the undecided questions see Ninian Smart, *Doctrine and Argument in Indian Philosophy* (Allen and Unwin, London, 1964), pp. 33–7. Smart shows that the Buddha rejected these questions not only as 'tactically unwise' but also as 'wrongly put' in that their formulation was misleading.

[10]For an explanation and repudiation of essentialist definitions see especially K. R. Popper, *The Open Society and its Enemies* (Routledge and Kegan Paul, London, 2nd ed., 1952), chap. 11 sec. II.

gods, but it was then objected (e.g. by Durkheim)[11] that Buddhism, or at least Theravāda Buddhism, lacked this belief, so on empirical grounds another definition seemed to be needed. Moreover, on theoretical grounds sociologists wished to broaden the definition to include institutions. With this I have some sympathy. It seems to me an unnecessary duplication of terminology to focus on the belief or ideological aspect of religion and so to define it that it coincides with theism, the first meaning of which given in the *Shorter O.E.D.* is 'Belief in deity or deities'. So far as concerns Buddhism the whole controversy has illustrated the confusion caused by not observing the logical distinction between the cognitive and the affective level. It is probably (arguably) not true that Theravāda Buddhism as a philologist sees it, as a set of doctrines found in texts, involves belief in gods. Although the Buddha himself believed, so far as we can tell,[12] that supernatural beings exist, it can certainly be argued, and is indeed believed by Sinhalese Buddhists, that this is not a part of his teaching, any more than the proposition that, say, animals exist. If we now inquire what Buddhists believe, we find that most of them do indeed believe in supernatural beings. But my landlord, a Sinhalese Buddhist villager, emphatically stated that he believed in neither gods nor demons, nor did he ever behave in such a way as to make me doubt his assertion. But he called himself, and was admitted to be, a Buddhist. He believed in the Buddha. What this involves will be discussed at greater length in Chapter 3, where I will suggest that for Sinhalese the Buddha is cognitively human but affectively divine. Unfortunately even this does not settle the matter finally, because in this context the categories of human and divine do not correspond

[11]E. Durkheim, *The Elementary Forms of the Religious Life*, trans. J.W. Swain (Collier Books, New York, 1961), pp. 45–7.

[12]The case is not clear-cut. See J. Masson, *La Religion Populaire dans le Canon Bouddhique Pâli* (Bureaux du Muséon, Louvain, 1942), especially pp. 11–12. *Vide contra* H. von Glasenapp, *Buddhism: a non-theistic Religion*, trans. I. Schloegl (Allen and Unwin, London 1970), p. 19.

to those of natural and supernatural; it is not I think possible to translate 'supernatural' precisely into Sinhalese, for the Buddha is believed to have had superhuman attributes which we, but not the Sinhalese, would consider contrary to the laws of nature. Whether a definition which equates religion with theism holds on the cognitive level is therefore controversial; the only level on which I think it certainly holds is the affective: Sinhalese Buddhists behave, at least with regard to the Buddha, as if they believe in a supernatural being.

Faced with these complications I for my part am content to leave the definition of religion to the practitioners themselves. Sinhalese Buddhists do call Buddhism (*Buddhāgama*) a religion (*āgama*), so I will not gainsay them;[13] similarly I would allow that there was a religion wherever a group claimed *bona fide* that it had one. (This seems to be the logical result of adopting conventionalism as distinct from essentialism.) I would merely note that a religion combines certain systems, or structured sets of associated phenomena, of which some systems are more important in one religion and some in another. Dr. Percy Cohen's list seems exhaustive: (1) cognitive system[14] (2) moral system (3) ritual system (4) symbolic system (5) affective system (6) social system. None of these systems are peculiar to religion (as Ruth Benedict pointed out in her slightly different analysis), but their concurrence is probably shared only by a few political creeds, e.g. Communism, which, apparently for this very reason, some desire to call 'religions'.

What religion, however, does not include is magic, and I had better explain here how I propose to demarcate magic from religion on the one hand and science on the other. Very simply. Science admits of falsification, which reli-

[13]What they mean by this is explained in Chapter 2.

[14]Dr. Cohen's lucid uses of the words 'cognitive' and 'affective' are of course slightly different from my own, as I have been concerned to express a different type of classification. My 'cognitive religion' I might call in Dr. Cohen's terminology the 'expressed cognitive system', my 'affective religion' I might call the 'implied cognitive system'.

gion and magic do not. The difference between magic and religion is that between a spell and a prayer: magic is a technique or technology, which is to say that if correctly performed it must effect the desired result; religion requires aid which must be asked for and cannot be compelled. Let me reiterate that this is no definition or exhaustive description of religion, but merely an *ad hoc* distinction—a statement of where I consider magic to stop and religion to begin: the Sinhalese Buddhist monk in his own language does not consider that it is 'religion' to ask for anything.

Since writing the above I have read with admiration Professor Melford Spiro's sensible and witty paper, 'Religion: Problems of Definition and Explanation'.[15] Spiro is led by his acquaintance with Theravāda Buddhism in Ceylon and SE. Asia to remark that Buddhists are not in fact usually atheists. Moreover he points out that even if they—or other large groups of people—were atheists, this need not debar us from defining religion in theistic terms, as there is no *a priori* reason for making the definition so broad as to cover everyone. In fact a narrower definition may be more interesting, and prompt research. Spiro thinks it useful to have a working definition of religion—and for his purposes it is, as he wants to discuss religion in general. (He shows himself to be, like Popper but unlike most famous anthropologists, both a deductivist and a conventionalist.) He finally (p. 96) defines religion as 'an institution consisting of culturally patterned interaction with culturally postulated superhuman beings', a more precise, if less elegant, reformulation of the old-fashioned view. If a definition of religion is called for I am glad to accept this one, with the small modification that I would except magic by the criterion explained in the previous paragraph.

Having explained my own concepts I had better say why I am interested in religious change (and, as a corol-

[15] In Michael Banton (ed.), *Anthropological Approaches to the Study of Religion* (Tavistock Publications, London, 1966), pp. 85–126.

lary, in religious conservation), and how I propose to deal with it. It is difficult to establish causality within the field in which the social sciences are interested, because chicken-egg situations are so often cropping up; the association of two phenomena is noted, but in the absence of controlled experiments it is hard to say which has causal primacy. Perhaps this is one reason why theoreticians of the social study of religion have been much preoccupied with the problem of the origin[16] of religion itself. Unfortunately the origins of most religions, and therefore of religion itself, are lost in the past, so that answers to this historical question must be speculative and untestable. Thus the problem seems to be insoluble; the apparently divergent answers have really been answers to different questions. Intellectualist answers like Tylor's have in fact been attempts to explain the origins of belief systems; sociological answers, like those of Durkheim and Malinowski, have been attempts to explain the origins of moral and social systems; etc. True, each theoretician laid claim to explaining religion as a whole by asserting the causal primacy of the system they had explained; Ruth Benedict, for example, inherited from Marx and Durkheim the theory that beliefs were mere rationalizations of, i.e. caused by, religious behaviour. All these claims were demonstrably exaggerated, and there seemed to be no reason for giving one system any primacy over the other; rather they came to be viewed as potentially completely independent, as in Cohen's formulation above. Recently, however, there has been a resurgence of intellectualism in a tradition which owes most to Tylor among anthropologists and Weber among sociologists. This tradition focuses on the idea that people often really do things—perform ceremonies, found and support institutions, undertake moral acts—because of what they believe to be the case. At the same time researchers have realized that while we cannot get back to the origins of

[16]For those who work with the hypothesis that social institutions (e.g. religion) owe their origins to the need for them, investigating religion's function is much the same as investigating its origin.

religion itself, we can look at the origin of bits of religion, i.e. *religious changes*. When we have historical evidence for beliefs in former times, we may be able to document changes in a belief system; and when we know about a change in a belief system we can speculate on its causes. This is why it seems important to study religious change and why such change can best be studied in societies long literate, and best of all in societies following religions based on books.

It may seem paradoxical that the social study of religion should concentrate on the rational, but Popper, the begetter of what he calls the 'rationality principle', has shown that there is no other way. The rationality principle is the zero principle, the basic assumption of the social sciences; it is the principle that in so far as behaviour is amenable to social study, it is the behaviour of people acting in what they conceive to be their best interests. Its application to the sociology of religion has been expounded by I. Jarvie in his interesting and provocative book *The Revolution in Anthropology*.[17] If we see a man in an agricultural comunity oppressed by a drought enter a special building (called, maybe, a church), get on his knees, fold his hands and start muttering, we may assume that he is insane, in which case we can offer no further testable explanation of his conduct, or that he thinks his actions may bring rain. And if that is what he thinks, we must assume that he thinks some entity is capable of giving him rain, and that that entity, which begins to look rather human in its emotions, will be placated by his suppliant posture and humble gesture, and listen to his words. The rationality principle refers to rationality in behaviour in a situation (which includes a set of given beliefs). It does not apply

[17]Routledge and Kegan Paul, London, 1964. This paragraph and the next I owe mainly to Jarvie's book, especially to section 4 of Chapter 4 (i.e. pp. 111–14). Jarvie in turn is developing some of Popper's ideas. The ideas which I am conscious of owing are the rationality principle (alias situational logic), methodological individualism, and social change as unintended consequences. The example of the man praying for rain is also taken from Jarvie's book.

directly to the situation, or to the beliefs included in the situation, although the question of the rationality of those beliefs may be raised: a belief is rational if it is a good solution, in a given intellectual situation, of some problem it tries to solve. Conduct is rational if it consists in using what seem appropriate means to attain given ends: the man praying for rain is acting rationally. What are given to him are the beliefs that make those means seem appropriate and the ends he wishes to attain; in this case that rain should fall. The sum of all the ends a man considers desirable is his value system; the sum of his beliefs is his belief system. Ultimately values cannot be derived from facts (nor facts from values); but frequently a man's beliefs about facts and his values have a common historical origin. Some of his beliefs about facts he gained from his own experience, and many of these he holds critically. The rest of his beliefs, both about facts (what is the case) and about values (what is desirable) he derived from other people, usually his parents and teachers; this of course applies also to his beliefs about mundane and trivial things, but important for us are only his beliefs about metaphysics and ethics, which together constitute his religious belief system, and which are all untestable.

Social changes come about as the unintended or the intended consequences of the actions and utterances of individuals. Religious change is not often an intended consequence: when it is, the individual who brings it about is usually said by sociologists to have charisma, a term invented by Weber which stands in lieu of an explanation. However, even these 'charismatic' individuals bring about many changes which they do not intend, and the greater their influence the more unintended consequences of their actions there are: Jesus Christ is surely not accountable for the whole of Christianity. Most social changes therefore are the unintended consequences of other social changes. Moreover, the exceptions just mentioned need not worry us unduly, for people only become charismatic *a posteri-*

ori, because their ideas have affected other men.[18] (This shows that the sociological concept of charisma is quite distinct from the Christian theological concept of a special favour vouchsafed by God,[19] which is the original meaning of the word. The theological concept is unaffected by my argument, as the grace of God does not depend for its existence on human recognition.) Even a religious innovator must offer people something they want; a man who preaches suicide will only be listened to in times of exceptional misery. This shifts the question back to what people want, their ends, aims, or values, the sum of which we call a value system.

The relation to each other of values in a value system may be hierarchic or preferential. In a hierarchy of values only certain things are desirable for their own sakes; and other things are good or desirable as means to these higher-level values.[20] Preferences, on the other hand, have no rigid structure (there is an infinite number of possible preferential choices), and, especially at the lower levels, tend to be *ad hoc*. Just now I prefer strawberries to raspberries, an *ad hoc* preference which may change by the next meal; but unless I am unusually gluttonous or misanthropic I always prefer friendship to good food. Even among hedonists only the very sophisticated will claim that they value friendship only as a means to happiness, and in practice it is highly doubtful whether anyone goes through life making these calculations (i.e. 'If I help that friend will I increase my happiness?'), so the value attached to friendship in our society does not seem to be hierarchically subservient to any

[18]What I am saying does not in any way imply that the ideas of charismatic leaders are not true or good—it is a matter of common experience that the truth or excellence of an idea has never been a guarantee of its acceptance. If someone accepts a true or good idea this fact as such requires congratulation, not explanation.

[19]*Shorter O.E.D.* under 'charism', which is merely the anglicized form of the Greek word Weber adopted.

[20]I owe the entire structure of the argument in the ensuing paragraph to a conversation with Karl Popper, though for its expression I take full responsibility.

higher-level aim or value. Therefore it is safe to say most contemporary western intellectuals have a plurality of values. However, the value systems of most religions are doctrinally, and perhaps cognitively, hierarchically structured, at least at the higher levels. A Christian may express the view that the attainment of Heaven is the *summum bonum,* the one highest level aim to which all other aims are subservient. Below Heaven in this hierarchy he might put the three cardinal virtues, faith, hope, and charity, and all other values would be subservient under these. (A modern Protestant might say that these virtues too are valued 'for their own sakes'; but as the practice of these virtues must by Christian doctrine invariably lead towards Heaven this does not destroy the hierarchy.) This forms an interesting contrast to Buddhism. A cornerstone of Theravāda Buddhist doctrine is that *nirvāṇa* is the *summum bonum.*[21] As *nirvāṇa* is a kind of extinction it precludes the practice of virtues (it is beyond good and evil) such as charity, which is admitted as a means, a subsidiary goal, but not as part of the end itself. Some early Buddhists obviously found this unsatisfactory: they developed the doctrine of the Bodhisattva ideal. In contrast to the Pratyekabuddha ('Enlightened singly'), who seeks *nirvāṇa* for himself alone, the Bodhisattva takes a vow to attain *nirvāṇa* only as a Buddha, who first attains every moral perfection over a vast series of lives and preaches his wisdom to others to save them. Out of his infinite compassion he denies himself the supreme bliss, but works in the world to bring others towards it. Love has replaced *nirvāṇa* as the ideal. This at least is the accepted view of the distinction between Theravāda and Mahāyāna ethics; whether it

[21]This doctrine is curiously up to date in my part of the world. In *An Atheist's Values* (Clarendon Press, Oxford, 1964), Richard Robinson writes (p. 17) of our search for 'the good': 'So we come to hope for a panacea, something that will permanently remove all misery for ever...Alas! There is no such panacea. Or, rather, there is, but it is death. Death is the only permanent cure for dissatisfaction and misery. While we live we are liable to them.' In Buddhist cosmology to attain *nirvāṇa* is the only possible escape from rebirth i.e. death.

is correct will be considered in the last chapter.

The high-level aims shared by members of a community we call the ethos of that culture. (Like the aims of which it is constituted, the ethos may be discussed on either the cognitive or the affective level.) Unfortunately ethos is so general a thing that it is difficult to observe it in the field and perhaps impossible to describe it in testable and refutable statements. The best we can usually do is to characterize it by negative example: an English gentleman would never kick a dog or a lady. At this point anthropology has become an art rather than a science; but that need not deter us.

We can now see *what* changes when a religion changes. A religious action is based on a belief about facts and directed to certain aims. Either the belief or the aims may change. What does not change is the relation between these two: that the action based on the beliefs and directed to the aims follows the rationality principle. If it does not it is not amenable to systematic study. We can also see *why* the religion changes: as the consequence, usually unintended, of the changed situation which has been brought about by individuals. The types of explanation I am therefore looking for will become plain if I quote, as briefly as possible, three examples from my field-work.

The first is an example of changing beliefs. There is a widely held hypothesis, to which I also subscribe, that many of men's beliefs about the invisible world mirror their experience of this world. This applies especially to the power structure. Central Ceylon a couple of hundred years ago had, in the precise sense, a feudal social structure, and numerous political divisions and subdivisions. The gods were conceived on the same pattern: each god was the main god, i.e. overlord of a certain territory, and had a retinue of lesser gods who were in charge of lesser territories within his; these in turn had their retinue, and so on down to village level. When the British conquered central Ceylon in 1815 they at first left the structure of authority unchanged at all but the highest levels, merely substituting government officials for local noblemen, and imposing a far more comprehensive central control. The correspondence between the divine and the human political structure is explicitly recognized by some Sinhalese themselves—in the modern terminology: an old monk with no western-style education told me in so many words that a certain god was like the Government Agent (G.A.), a lesser one like the District Revenue Officer (D.R.O.), etc. However, an unintended consequence of the British conquest, with its abolition of feudalism and its centralization of authority, as well as of improved communications within the island, is that local gods are losing their authority, i.e. their interest for the villagers, to the extent that some of their shrines are falling into disuse; and even of the four gods who were said to have jurisdiction over the island three are greatly declining, one greatly increasing in authority, so that political centralization may eventually bring about a local monotheism. This trend has probably been hastened by the fact that since Independence politicians have deprived the administrative civil service of much of its power and autonomy; even the G.A. (the senior administrator of a province) counts for less than he did under the British. A more up-to-date villager, telling me of the gods' arrangements, said that they have a sort of parliament.

My second example is one of changing aims. It was the aim of the Buddha to attain *nirvāṇa*, a mystical release from normal states of consciousness; it is attained in life, and someone who has attained it is not reborn: he escapes from the wheel of rebirth, to which all creatures are tied. Rebirth the Buddha considered misery; the peace of *nirvāṇa* was the only good worth having. But most Sinhalese villagers do not want *nirvāṇa*—yet. They are like St. Augustine who prayed 'Make me chaste and continent, O Lord—but not yet.'[22] They say they want to be born in heaven; some of them would even like to be reborn in a favourable station on earth. They fear, as their Teacher did not, the extinction of sensation, and want to

[22]'Da mihi castitatem et continentiam, sed noli modo.' *Confessions*, VIII, 7.

go on feeling. Moreover, though they will probably utter the impeccably orthodox sentiment that life is suffering, most of them plainly do believe—and say so when they are not speaking in a religious context—that people with wealth and power are happy. This shifting of an aim, from *nirvāṇa* to heaven or even to earth, is thus explicable in terms of higher-level changed aim—wish to go on living, and a changed belief—that rich people, or at least gods, are happy. The next step is to inquire why the higher-level aim and the belief have changed; but this would take me too far afield just now. An unintended consequence of the Buddha's teaching might be that it made life seem worth living!

My third example is an illustration of what might be a changing ethos; it is very similar to one given by Jarvie (p. 114). Many Sinhalese with the aim of temporal advancement have changed their religion in the last 500 years. They became Catholics to avoid being murdered by the Portuguese, Protestants to placate the Dutch, Protestants again to please the British. Recently many Christian Sinhalese have been changing back to Buddhism for similar reasons. However, once a man has changed his religion, he and his children are exposed to the whole ideology of that religion, so that gradually the entire ethos of the family may change. In this case a man's ethos, i.e. highest-level aims, changed as the unintended consequence of his, or his father's, have changed as a result of his, or his father's, rational pursuance of lower-level aims.

II. Why Ceylon?

I have said why I think religious changes are worth studying, what they are, and in what terms I propose to explain them; but I have not yet said why I chose to study Sinhalese Buddhism. The methodological reasons are these. I mentioned a while back that to study religious change we have to be quite sure what the present religion, which we can now see, has changed from; and as the detailed and systematic observations of social scientists are a recent event in history our best hope lies in studying religions based on books, i.e. scriptures. I am not confusing history with philology: I do not claim that these books tell us what the mass of adherents to the religion at that time believed. But they do tell us what their authors believed. In some celebrated cases, e.g. the Bible, the authors of the scripture were unfortunately not the founders of the religion, but for our problem this does not matter too much, as it is Jesus Christ's doctrine as reported in the Bible which has been influential. All the religions usually reckoned as 'world religions' have been founded on books. Further, a great number of splinter groups within religions, known to sociologists as sects, have been founded on books, especially in western society. Some of these, notably Protestant sects, have been admirably studied by sociologists since Weber: Bryan Wilson's book *Sects and Society*[23] is an illustrious example. However, the study of sects has its own problems, which are not mine: I am interested rather in the broader religions, which sociologists call churches, which are found in societies at large. The problems of studying Christianity in any given society are especially complex, as no religion has moved through so many cultures and undergone so many upheavals. I do not know Hebrew, Arabic, or Chinese, so I cannot adequately study the doctrines of Judaism, Islam, Taoism, or Confucianism. The problems of Hinduism are again peculiar: although there are scriptures the authority of which all must acknowledge, namely the Vedas, they are so ancient, their scope is so limited—for they are a collection of hymns and sacrificial formulae—and their interpretation so obscure that their relevance to what people believe is negligible; moreover, only a minority of Hindus have been allowed access to them. There are innumerable other texts, but some, like the Upanishads,[24] are esoteric, while only a

[23]Heinemann, London, 1961.

[24]The Upanishads are properly part, the latest part, of Vedic literature, and therefore must be acknowledged by all to be divinely inspired; but the study of their metaphysics is vouchsafed to few, their comprehension maybe to fewer.

very few possess an authority not confined to certain sects or strata of the population;[25] to make matters worse, the chronology of Hindu scriptures is totally obscure.

Buddhism however has the advantage of a well-established chronology. We know that the Buddha lived in NE. India and died there at the age of 80 after preaching for forty-five years. It is fairly certain that he died in 486 or 483 B.C., which would mean that his Enlightenment, which is when Buddhism can be said to have started, took place in 531 or 528 B.C. The Buddhist era, however, is dated from the Buddha's death. But by the Buddhist era, used in Ceylon and thence adopted by other Buddhist countries, the Buddha died in 544–3 B.C., some sixty years earlier. The discrepancy is believed to have arisen in the eleventh century, the dark ages of Ceylon, when Tamil invasions smashed the ancient civilization and many cultural traditions were lost. Of the two kinds of Buddhism, Theravāda and Mahāyāna, the latter is very heterogeneous: moreover the only Mahāyāna country in which fieldwork is now practicable is Japan, the furthest from the Indian sources and the last to be converted. Theravāda Buddhism has the further advantage of a unitary body of acknowledged scripture, the Pali Canon; Pali is an ancient Indian language closely related to Sanskrit. Three countries, Ceylon, Burma and Thailand, are the principal bearers of the Theravāda tradition. Of these Burma and Thailand were once Mahāyāna countries; they adopted Theravāda through contact with Ceylon, notably in the eleventh and twelfth centuries.[26] Ceylon has further advantages from my point of view. It is an island, so that the influences which have entered it can be comparatively well isolated and identified. It has a written chronicle, of varying but sometimes considerable excellence, which

[25]The scripture with most influence on Hindu society has undoubtly been the Laws of Manu.

[26]These contacts continued up to the reverse borrowings by Ceylon which resulted in the founding of the modern Ceylonese orders in the eighteenth and nineteenth centuries. See Kenneth E. Wells, *Thai Buddhism*, p. vi.

enables us to follow the fortunes of the Sinhalese people from the very start, or at least from their conversion to Buddhism in the third century B.C., and which, being the work of monks, contains much information on Buddhism. Most of the commentaries on the Pali Canon were composed in Ceylon, which in ancient times was a centre of Buddhist learning. (The chronicle and commentaries will be discussed in Chapter 1.) The Sinhalese, who form the great majority of the inhabitants, have always been preponderantly Buddhists, so that in an important sense there is an uninterrupted tradition of over 2,000 years.[27] Finally, Sinhalese is a language descended from Sanskrit and Pali, so that any conceptual shifts of terms used in the texts in those languages should be fairly easy for me as a Sanskritist to spot, being undisguised by translation; moreover, I expected I could learn Sinhalese more easily than Burmese or Thai, which are structurally unrelated to Sanskrit. So Ceylon it was; and this work is about Ceylonese Buddhism.[28] To explain why I chose to study it on the ground in the way I did, I must first give a brief sketch of Ceylonese history, geography and economy, which will further serve as a background to my findings.

III. The History, Geography and Economy of Ceylon

The history of Ceylon can conveniently be divided into

[27]My learned (though partial) predecessor, Bishop R.S. Copleston, wrote in the opening chapter of his *Buddhism Primitive and Present in Magadha and Ceylon* (Longmans, Green, London, 1892), p. 4, '. . . the Ceylon branch of [Buddhism], though small, is perhaps the best [the student] could study, or at least the one to study first. For it is confessedly among those which have least diverged from the primitive stock, and it has a far longer continuous history than any other.'

[28]Ceylon, an English corruption of the word *Siṃhala*, is the name of the island and the modern nation. Sinhalese is the name of a language and of the people who speak it. There are Ceylonese who are not Sinhalese (see the next section); excepting only a few individuals they are not Buddhists, so that Ceylonese Buddhism effectively coincides with Sinhalese Buddhism.

two main periods, ancient and modern, with the dividing line drawn at 1505, when the Portuguese arrived in the island as the first European colonial power. The ancient period can then be subdivided into two unequal parts, the Anurādhapura and Poḷonnaruva periods, which are named after the capital cities of the time. The Anurādhapura period is from the fourth century B.C. to the late ninth century A.D.; the Poḷonnaruva period properly ends in the thirteenth century, after which there is another period of political instability, the capital shifting from place to place. Although the Anurādhapura period is always recalled as the golden age of the Sinhalese nation and Sinhalese Buddhism, many of the distinctive institutions of modern Sinhalese Buddhism came into being during the Poḷonnaruva and immediately subsequent periods.[29] For most of the modern period the island was politically divided in two, and the political division acquired cultural importance. The European powers ruled only in the coastal areas, and were based on Colombo on the west coast, with important ports at Jaffna and Galle, at the northern and southern ends of that coast. The Portuguese were ousted by the Dutch in 1658, the Dutch by the British in 1796. Meanwhile in the mountainous interior the Kandyan kingdom maintained its independence till it surrendered to British treachery in 1815. The British restored independence to a unified Ceylon in 1947.

Independent Ceylon has preserved the British administrative division of the island into nine provinces, each divided into two or (usually) three districts. Most of these divisions, even down to district level, are good approximations to the boundaries of subcultures in this amazingly diverse island, but only a few need concern us here.

The four principal cities are still Colombo, Kandy, Galle and Jaffna. The Central Province, in the centre of which is Kandy, was the core of the Kandyan kingdom, which comprised roughly this province and the four provinces ad-

[29]For instance the Daṁbadeni Katikāvata of 1266 outlines the principles on which the Sangha is still organized.

joining it. Kandy is called in Sinhalese simply 'The City' (*Nuwara*). The English name is a corruption of the Sinhalese phrase 'On the mountain' (*kandē* or *kandē uḍa*). It lies at 1,600 feet above sea level in the midst of very hilly country. To the south of Kandy the mountains are far higher; the plateau at Nuwara Eliya, only 25 miles as the crow flies and 48 miles by road, is at 6,000 feet. The passes down to the coastal plain from this eminence are precipitous and spectacular; those to the west and east of Kandy are hardly easier—hence the city's impregnability. To the north, however, the hills decline rather more gradually till they give way to the plains of the North Central Province, in which lie both Anurādhapura and Poḷonnaruva. This area was the principal seat of the ancient civilization, but after its devastation by the Tamils it relapsed into sparsely populated and malarial jungle, in which condition it remained till this century, when archaeological interest, nationalist sentiment, and above all the need for cultivable land led to systematic jungle clearance and restoration of the ancient irrigation system. Although the Europeans made Colombo the focal point of all communication systems, so that the east coast is now the most backward and inaccessible, in ancient times this was not so: it was on the east coast that Mahinda landed when he brought Buddhism to Ceylon in the third century B.C. Perhaps the last famous visitor to arrive from that side was Robert Knox (see below) in 1660, when the west coast was already developed, but in European hands. A lesser centre of the ancient civilization was in the now totally undeveloped south-east: it was to here that the Sinhalese had to retire when beaten by Tamil invasions, and from here that the Sinhalese national hero, Duṭugämuṇu, marched up the east coast, some way inland, to defeat the Tamils—a march he would have difficulty in repeating today.

Village agriculture is concerned mainly with the growing of rice, locally known as paddy, which is the staple food. In the five months which it takes to grow, rice requires to stand in nonstagnant water. There are two monsoons, the SW. from May to September and the NE. from October to

January. Little rain from the SW. monsoon clears the central mountain massif, so that the north, the eastern coast and the south-east depend on the rain which falls in three months. The Sinhalese who lived in these areas in ancient times built huge reservoirs (*väva*), locally known as tanks, and irrigation canals (*äla*), which are justly considered a wonder of the ancient world: modern technology cannot improve on them. The type of paddy cultivation which depends on such a tank has been exhaustively described by E. R. Leach in his study of a village in the North Central Province.[30] In the west, southwest and centre of the island, where there is a likelihood of rain for nine or ten months in the year, no such system of water conservation is necessary, although there used to be some tanks of unknown antiquity, even in the hills round Kandy; one in the village where I worked had its bund (dyke) permanently breached in the eighteenth century. Much of the land in this wetter half of the island is now used as plantations of tea, rubber and coco-nuts, the cash crops on which the country's exports depend. Rubber and coco-nuts are commoner in the low country, while the higher the hills the better the tea. Most of the higher land in the centre of Ceylon was appropriated by the British in the nineteenth century to plant first coffee and then tea; as a labour force they imported Tamils from South India, whose descendants and relations still work on them today. The cultural isolation of the plantations on the slopes from the villages in the valleys is amazing, though it has been exaggerated by politicians: I found few Sinhalese villagers in the area who could not speak at least a little Tamil, and no doubt the reverse is also true.

Most of the hills in the Kandy District of the Central Province, where I worked, are not so high nor the valleys so steep as in the most famous tea country, but there is hardly an inch of flat ground. This and the lush vegetation amid which the houses stand make for rather diffuse settlements, in which often one house can barely glimpse the

[30] E.R. Leach, *Pul Eliya* (C.U.P., Cambridge, 1961).

next through the trees; sometimes a small group of cottages forms a little hamlet, maybe even with its own shop, as a distinct unit within the larger village. Since the British eradicated malaria in the Second World War population pressures have been very severe—3½ per cent per annum growth for the country as a whole. Thus the rice-growing villages of farmers, some landless and all under-employed, sprawl out so that the boundaries between one and the next are often hard to discern, and political or administrative units may not coincide with traditional parish limits. A village (*gama*) is therefore capable of various definitions, but by traditional criteria it consists of an area of land, an estate, all of which originally, in fact or fantasy, belonged to the families of the founders of the village. It still consists in a fairly compact body of land holdings (with bits taken out by estates, roads, or government colonies), but many of these are nowadays owned by absentee landlords. These holdings are part rice fields (*kum̆buru*)[31] and part dry land (*goḍa*), which is usually known in English under the rather misleading title of 'village gardens'. In fact this *goḍa* is not cultivated, but on it grow all the types of fruit a villager uses; on it the livestock graze, and houses are built. The commonest plants provide coco-nuts (*pol*), which are the basis of all local curries, king coco-nuts (*täm̆bili*), many kinds of bananas (*kesel*), jak fruit (*kos*), bread-fruit (*del*), betel leaf (*bulat*) and areca nut[32] (*puvak*) which are chewed together, limes (*dehi*), pineapple (*annāsi*), various condiments and spices which are in daily use, and finally the kitul palm. From the sap of its flower is made a delicious brown sugar called jaggery (*hakuru*); no wonder the villagers despise the sugar-cane (*uk gas*) which also grows wild. (Nowadays it is cheaper to buy ordinary imported

[31] Also called wet land (*maḍa bim*, literally 'muddy ground'), as the opposite of *goḍa bim*.

[32] This is often known in English as betel-nut, which confuses foreigners. It grows on the areca palm, but is used wrapped in a betel leaf. Villagers, especially men, tend to add a smear of (the mineral) lime (*hunu*), which besides being very caustic combines with the other ingredients to produce a red dye which stains the mouth.

sugar.) This same sap, like that of the ordinary coco-nut palm, can be drunk at various stages of fermentation, as toddy (*rā*) or arack (*arakku*). Very rarely a house may have a cultivated vegetable garden, but most vegetables are grown in a *hēna*, a casual cultivation of otherwise unused land, which is usually cleared by burning. The *hēna* used to be cultivated—illegally—on Crown lands, but the scope for this is nowadays much restricted, and there is very little unused land to be had even for rent, so most vegetables are bought at the market, by those who can afford them. The most important vegetables, from the villagers' point of view, are chillies (*miris*), onions (*lūṇu*), and lentils (*parippu*). The livestock in a Kandyan village is mostly chickens (which supply eggs and meat) and goats (which are eaten but not milked); water-buffaloes are used to draw ploughs and are never killed, but their milk is sometimes used for making curd, and is served with jaggery to monks and other honoured guests. Other cattle are rare (on beef-eating see Chapter 6, pp. 305), and for milk, which is always used in tea, most depend on tins of milk powder, or government supplies. Cheese is not eaten, butter an exotic luxury. Pigs are almost unknown in the hill country, and most villagers have never seen a horse or a sheep. Nearly every house has a dog, and cats are common; those who can afford to feed their domestic animals tend to give them rice and other human foods. A rich man in the village where I stayed owned an elephant, which was tethered to a tree outside his house when not working for hire.

Most houses are solidly built of cemented bricks covered with plaster and whitewash. They have cement floors. Windows are always barred, usually have shutters and occasionally glass. Roofs are of red tiles or corrugated iron sheeting; ceilings are rare. There are internal walls, partitioning the building into three or four rooms; older or grander houses may have an open or half-open verandah in front. Almost all houses are bungalows. Kitchens are usually in a lean-to against the back of the house; cooking is on wood fires, and there are no chimneys. Every house has a separate earth privy in a building of its own. The very poorest houses are of wattle and daub, with roofs of cadjan (plaited palm fronds). (This is much commoner in the dry zone.) There are cemented wells which the local council builds for drinking water, and more informal unwalled wells for bathing, though river bathing is preferred as more fun.

The rice fields are terraces formed from the hillside; each step is surrounded by a low mud dyke (*niyara*) just wide enough to walk along. Small gaps (*vakkaḍa*) in these dykes keep the water moving down the hillside. The rice is a cheerful light green. The valleys with streams sparkling through them; above these the dark and varied vegetation dotted with red tile roofs; above these again the hills terraced in shimmering yellowy green, lined with mud paths along which move a few figures in white and bright colours; further up still the higher hills, their redder earth almost hidden by dark green tea bushes; and at the back of all the mountains blue in the distance: this vista, combining natural grandeur and comprehensible humanity, is the most beautiful I know. A small but important feature of such a landscape is likely to be a cluster of buildings round a huge peepal tree and an object shaped like a dome with a spire, between 10 and 40 feet high, washed white or pale blue. The Bo tree, under which the Buddha attained Enlightenment, and the stupa, which contains a relic, indicate the presence of a Buddhist monastery, where dwell one or more monks and novices, dressed in bright robes of yellow, orange, or even red. These people and institutions are representatives of an ancient religious tradition; let me now attempt to summarize its history.

The main primary source for the history of Ceylon in general and the Sinhalese in particular is the *Mahāvaṃsa*, a Pali verse chronicle composed in four instalments, the first in the sixth century (Anurādhapura period), the second in the thirteenth, the third in the fourteenth and the last in the eighteenth century.[33] In the European edition (ed. Wilhelm Geiger)[34] only the first part is called the *Mahāvaṃsa*: the three latter parts form the *Cūlavaṃsa*; but the consecutive numeration of the chapters is preserved. The whole work is written by Theravāda monks, so naturally it is especially concerned with religious history; indeed, its identification of the fortunes of the Sinhalese with those of Buddhism is the main intellectual source of modern Sinhalese Buddhist nationalism. The quality varies, especially with the distance of events described from the times of writing, but archaeological corroboration fills us with admiration for the oldest part; although it contains many miraculous incidents these are mostly to be regarded as embellishments of the true events. For the ancient period there are many other literary sources in Pali and Sinhalese, notably histories of relics; also much epigraphic and other archaeologic al evidence. For the modern period there are also literary sources by Europeans; justly the most celebrated is the first book ever written on Ceylon in English, maybe still the best and certainly the most entertaining: Robert Knox's *An Historical Relation of the Island of Ceylon*, first published in 1681.[35] Knox (1641–1720) was a merchant seaman whose ship put into harbour on the east coast of Ceylon after a storm late in 1659; in 1660 he was captured with his father the captain, and several companions by King Rājasiṃha II (1635–87), who collected European prisoners, whom he maintained in comfort and honour in various villages—probably over a thousand of them in the course of his reign. Knox made

[33]The work has been continued since, but for modern times there are many other and in part more reliable sources.

[34]*Mahāvaṃsa*, 1908, *Cūlavaṃsa*, vol. 1, 1925, vol. 2, 1927, all published by the Pali Text Society, London. The same publishers produced Geiger's translations: *Mahāvaṃsa*, 1912, *Cūlavaṃsa*, vol. 1, 1929, vol. 2, 1930.

[35]Reprinted MacLehose, Glasgow, 1911, with an introduction by James Ryan, and Maharagama, 1958, as vol. VI of the *Ceylon Historical Journal*, with a valuable introduction by S. D. Saparamadu. Both editions include Knox's short *Autobiography*.

good but never settled down, and escaped in 1679. Religion is the facet of Sinhalese culture he seems to have understood least well—he always kept his Bible with him—but even so his information is invaluable to us.

The outstanding secondary source for the history of Ceylonese Buddhism is the Rev. Walpola Rahula's *History of Buddhism in Ceylon*,[36] but unfortunately, as the subtitle tells us, this covers only the Anurādhapura period. Space does not allow me to discuss this invaluable work, which should be consulted by all serious students of Buddhism. The Rev. Rahula reports the conclusions of two articles on heterodox traditions by the highest authority on Ceylonese antiquities, Professor S. Paranavitana, 'Pre-Buddhist Religious Beliefs in Ceylon'[37] and 'Mahāyānism in Ceylon'.[38] He also makes full use of Professor G. P. Malalasekera's *The Pali Literature of Ceylon*,[39] which deals with this aspect of Buddhism up to modern times. Unfortunately there are no other secondary sources of comparable usefulness available for the post-Anurādhapura period, i.e. the last thousand years; Wilhelm Geiger's *The Culture of Ceylon in Mediaeval Times*[40] (which appeared posthumously, edited by Heinz Bechert), is a fine harvest of facts gleaned from the chronicles, but its synchronic approach obscures the course of development, and on Buddhism it is altogether disappointing.

The Sinhalese nation was allegedly founded by Vijaya, the grandson of a lion (Skt.: *siṃha*), a ne'er-do-well from NW. India who landed in Ceylon on the day the Buddha died. The island was at that time inhabited only by spirits and demons. More prosaically, it was probably inhabited by Väddas, a people anthropometrically and culturally distinct from the Sinhalese; a few Väddas can still be distinguished among the inhabitants of the jun-

[36]Gunasena, Colombo, 1956.

[37]*J.R.A.S.* (*Ceylon Branch*), vol. XXXI, no 82, 1929, pp. 302–27.

[38]*Ceylon Journal of Science, Section G*, vol. ii, 1928–33, pp. 35–71.

[39]R.A.S., London, 1928.

[40]Harrassowitz, Wiesbaden, 1960.

gles of eastern Ceylon. Anurādhapura was founded by Paṇḍukābhaya[41] in the fourth century B.C. His grandson, Devānaṃpiya Tissa, was a contemporary of the emperor of India, Asoka (ruled *c.* 269–230), who was a convert to Buddhism. Asoka sent religious ambassadors to countries as distant as Egypt and Macedonia, and after the third Buddhist council (according to Theravādin reckoning) monks were sent to all the outlying regions and border countries round India to preach Buddhist doctrine. To Ceylon was sent one of Asoka's own sons, Mahinda. According to the chronicle he was accompanied by four other monks, a novice, and a lay disciple. A single monk performs the lower ordination ceremony, by which a layman enters the Order as a novice, but five monks are the quorum needed to perform the higher ordination ceremony (*upasampadā*) by which a novice becomes a monk; if such a quorum cannot be mustered no ordination can take place, the line of succession is broken, and after a time there are no more monks. Mahinda's group was therefore the smallest possible paradigm community of male Buddhists. The Buddhism which Mahinda brought was of the Theravāda school, which has its scriptures in Pali; these scriptures, the Pali Canon, were at that time not yet written down, but Mahinda and his followers presumably brought them in their heads. Tradition has it that they thus brought the commentaries too, and that Mahinda translated these into Sinhalese. Mahinda received as a gift from the king, who was the first Ceylonese convert, a park in Anurādhapura in which to found the Mahāvihāra ('Great Monastery'); he then ploughed a furrow round the city as a parish boundary (*sīmā*), and by this token established Buddhism in Ceylon.[42] The Mahāvihāra was to become the bastion of

[41]The names of historical figures in the ancient period are given in Pali, except where otherwise stated.

[42]Monks within a *sīmā* regularly perform certain ceremonies together, notably the *uposatha*, a mutual confession which should take place every fortnight. Normally a *sīmā* encloses only the grounds of a monastery, and has no further relevance to the laity; but in this case the king said the city should be included, so he had something like a

Theravādin orthodoxy for more than a thousand years, and it is in this tradition that Ceylonese monks, especially those of the Siyam Nikāya (see below), stand today. The commentaries and chronicles which survive from the Anurādhapura period were probably all written there (see Chapter 1). Mahinda had his sister Sanghamittā, who was a Buddhist nun, bring from India a branch of the sacred Bo tree under which the Buddha attained Enlightenment, and it was planted with great ceremony, and saplings distributed over the island. Sanghamittā also es-

parish boundary in mind. By establishing a *sīmā* Mahinda was establishing the *Sangha*, the Buddhist community of monks, and establishing Buddhism in this very precise sense. Rahula (op. cit., p. 54) is of course quite right to say, 'The idea of the "establishment" of Buddhism in a given geographical unit with its implications is quite foreign to the teaching of Buddha... Nowhere had he given injunctions or intructions regarding a ritual or a particular method of "establishing" the *Sāsana* (Buddha's doctrine). Buddhism is purely a personal religion.' Some confusion has arisen because the *Mahāvaṃsa*, which was composed after the rise of Sinhalese Buddhist nationalism, refers here (XV, 180) and elsewhere to the establishment of a *sāsana*, a broad term; but in the *Dīpavaṃsa* passage (XIV, 22) on which this is based it is the establishment of a *saṅghārāma* (monastery) which is discussed. Another source of similar date, Buddhaghosa's introduction to the *Samantapāsādikā*, varies the story further in the nationalist direction, for it has Mahinda tell the king (I, 102) that the roots of the *sāsana* would go deep in Ceylon only when a son born in Ceylon to Ceylonese parents studied the Vinaya monastic rule-book in Ceylon and recited it there, and has such a ceremony of establishment performed later on in the shape of a Vinaya recitation by the king's nephew. The fact that texts of the fifth century A.D. tend in their presentation to ignore the point that Buddhism (like any other religion?) is 'purely personal' does not allow us to assume that Mahinda 700 years earlier was going beyond the impeccably orthodox procedure for setting up a monastery, and does not necessitate the Rev. Rahula's hypothesis that 'This notion of establishing the Sasana or Buddhism as an institution in a particular country or place was perhaps first conceived by Asoka himself' (op. cit., p. 55). (His corroborative statement that Asoka 'was the first king to adopt Buddhism as a State religion' is dubious.) As he goes on to say, 'Although the two versions differ in the letter they agree in the spirit...the establishment of the *Sasana* is ultimately reduced to the establishment of the Sangha which is not possible without a *sīmā* and the recital of the *Vinaya*.'

tablished in Ceylon the Order of nuns, for only a nun can admit a woman to the Order. Asoka sent as relics the Buddha's begging bowl and various of his bones, of which the right collar-bone was enshrined in Ceylon's first stupa, the Thūpārāma. Both the tree and the stupa stand in Anurādhapura to this day.

In the second century B.C. Tamil invaders from South India ruled in Anurādhapura over the Sinhalese, who were apparently already Buddhists. There was a Sinhalese kingdom in western Ceylon, called Dakkhiṇadesa,[43] and a third in the south-east, called Rohaṇa. From Rohaṇa a national revival was led by Duṭṭhagāmaṇī (101–77 B.C.), who proclaimed that he was fighting not for a kingdom, but for Buddhism and put a relic in his spear; monks were in the army, though they left the Order for the occasion, and the war ended when Duṭugāmuṇu, as he is known in Sinhalese, slew the Tamil king in single combat at the gates of Anurādhapura. These events are the recorded beginning of Sinhalese Buddhist nationalism. From now on Sinhalese kings were regarded as defenders of the faith, and Buddhism acquired official trappings. Duṭugāmuṇu erected in honour of Buddhism enduring monuments of his reign. But within forty years of his death Ceylon suffered civil war, invasion, and a famine so severe that people resorted to cannibalism. The Mahāvihāra was abandoned and many monks fled to India. Those who were left feared that the oral traditions would be lost, and so about 30 B.C., for the first time in history, they wrote down the Pali Canon, with commentaries (presumably in Sinhalese). King Vaṭṭagāmaṇī-Abhaya (27–17 B.C.), who reconquered Anurādhapura from the Tamils, gave a new monastery called Abhayagiri to a monk from another part of the country who had helped him; but this distressed the monks of the Mahāvihāra, who expelled the monk. However, he

[43]Later called Māyā. See Geiger, *Culture of Ceylon*, p. 9. My statement is an over-simplification, but far less of one than Rahula's map (end-paper, op. cit.), which includes the western lowlands in Malaya; Geiger shows that Malaya was a geographical name for the hill country, not a political division.

and his followers refused to accept the expulsion, and thus arose the first schism in the Ceylonese Sangha. Within a few years this schism acquired a doctrinal rationale: the Abhayagiri monks accepted the teachings of Dhammaruci, a monk of the Vajjiputra sect in India, who taught for instance that there is a personal entity (*puggala*) peculiar to each individual over and above the five elements accepted in the Theravādin analysis of the phenomenal person. Abhayagiri monks then studied both Theravāda and Mahāyāna, while the Mahāvihāra monks were conservative and regarded them as heretical. Kings favoured now one, now the other, often both and occasionally neither. Late in the third century Mahāyāna monks came to Ceylon from India. Their teachings[44] were suppressed, but found favour at Abhayagiri in the reign of King Mahāsena (334–61), who was himself converted to them. At one point he even had the Mahāvihāra demolished and the premises sown with beans, but he later repented. In his reign is the first mention of a Bodhisattva image, which the king had made by his son, who was skilful at carving ivory; in his reign too the famous tooth relic was sent from India, though it arrived only after the king's death. This relic became the palladium of Sinhalese royalty till the British conquest of Kandy in 1815, and it was worshipped by Dudley Senanayake on his election as Prime Minister in 1965. Under Mahāsena also was crystallized a further division in the Sangha. A group of monks including one Sāgala had in the reign of Mahāsena's father left the Abhayagiri Vihāra, disturbed by the introduction of Mahāyāna. After a revolt against the Mahāyānists Mahāsena built for a follower of Sāgala the Jetavana Vihāra. For the rest of the Anurādhapura period the Sangha was divided into these three Nikāyas: Mahāvihāra, Abhayagiri, and Jetavana. A

[44]Pali: Vetullavāda; Skt.: Vaitulyavāda. For a discussion of the term and a summary of the probable nature of these teachings, which seem to have been based on scriptures in Sanskrit, see Rahula, op. cit., pp. 87–9. For a collection of all evidence concerning Mahāyāna in ancient Ceylon the above-quoted article by S. Paranavitana, 'Mahāyānism in Ceylon', is still not superseded.

Nikāya does not correspond to a sect or a denomination: the institution is clerical only, and its characteristic is that monks of more than one Nikāya will not perform ceremonies (ordination, *uposatha,* etc.) together; customs and teachings (Sinh. *sirit virit*) may also differ but need not do so. In ancient times, however, the doctrines of the Nikāyas usually did differ: after Mahāsena the Mahāvihāra was Theravāda, the Abhayagiri Mahāyāna, and the Jetavana alternated. Ceylon was naturally influenced by Buddhist developments in India. Indian chronology is uncertain, but Mahāsena's reign must have been roughly contemporaneous with the rise of the Yogācāra school of Buddhism in India. In the sixth century, when the great Buddhist logicians lived and disputed in India, a Theravādin monk came from India and defeated the Mahāyānists in public debate. In the seventh century, when the Chinese traveller Hiuen Tsiang recorded great veneration in India for Buddhist learning, there was so much interest in Ceylon in the *Abhidhamma* (Buddhist systematic philosophy) that one king before setting out for war 'asked his general to request his queen to study the *Abhidhamma,* preach it and transfer its merit to him'.[45] In the middle of the ninth century Indian Buddhist Tantrism (Vājiriyavāda) came to Ceylon, and though its esoteric doctrines diverged very widely from Theravāda it seems to have been influential even at the height of the Poḷonnaruva period, over 300 years later.[46] There are other telling signs of Mahāyāna influence on the official religion of the later Anurādhapura period, culminating in a tenth-century inscription[47] which declares that the Buddha promised that none but Bodhisattvas could become kings of Ceylon.

In the second century B.C. and fifth century A.D. there were periods when Tamil invaders ruled in Anurādhapura, but even they professed Buddhism, or at least followed

[45]Rahula, op cit., p. 106, referring to *Mhv.*, XLIV, 108–9.

[46]P.E.E. Fernando, 'Tantric Influence on the Sculptures at Gal Vihara, Polonnaruwa', *Univ. of Ceylon Review*, vol. XVIII, nos. 1 and 2, 1960, pp. 50–66.

[47]The Jetavanārāma slab inscription of King Mahinda IV (956–72).

Buddhist customs, and they do not seem to have occasioned any cultural discontinuity. However, with the rise of Pāṇḍyan power, invasions from South India became more frequent and more severe, and the Sinhalese and Tamils were repeatedly at war. Poḷonnaruva, further from India, was a royal seat for the first time in the late seventh century, and the capital gradually shifted to there; the last king to rule in Anurādhapura died in 896. Already the Tamil Hindus must have been exerting cultural influence, for in the late eighth century King Mahinda II feasted brahmins and gave them sweetened milk to drink, a Hindu practice. Similar activities are recorded in the ninth century. This is not surprising, as by no means all relations with Tamils were hostile: already in the seventh century there were Tamil ministers, who are recorded to have built Buddhist monasteries. There were peaceful Tamil colonists who intermarried with Sinhalese families, probably at all social levels; some Sinhalese kings had Tamil wives. Moreover the Sinhalese kings themselves used Tamil mercenaries called *Velakkāras*. Finally in A.D. 1001 the Coḷa dynasty from South India, at the height of their power, having already held Anurādhapura for some years, captured and ruled in Poḷonnaruva. The Sinhalese were confined to the mountains and the south, squabbling among themselves, while the Tamils sacked all the monasteries, and pillaged and destroyed the premises of luxury and religion. In this period much of ancient Ceylon was lost. When Vijaya-Bāhu I reconquered the throne in 1065 it was no longer possible to hold a higher ordination ceremony, as there were not five monks left to form a quorum, so he had to send to Burma for some monks to establish a new line of succession. The Order of nuns had died out completely, and this could not be reinstated, as there were no Theravādin nuns elsewhere, so that Order became extinct in Ceylon. Even after Vijaya-Bāhu's restoration the *Velakkāras* were so powerful that not only did they mutiny and sack Poḷonnaruva, but under one of his successors they were in control of the Temple of the Tooth there, probably operating a 'protection racket'.[48]

Parakkama-Bāhu I (1153–86), known as the Great, decisively defeated the Tamils and even invaded the Indian mainland. The cultural activity of his reign has led Malalasekera justly to dub it an Augustan age. The buildings both religious and secular erected by him and his successor still astound the visitor to Poḷonnaruva. There was great production of scholarly literature in Sanskrit, Pali and Sinhalese. The twelfth and thirteenth centuries were probably the only period when Sanskrit was used in Ceylon. Its rise, due perhaps to Mahāyāna influence within Buddhism and Tamil influence on society, had a lasting effect on the Sinhalese language, which since this period has been the prevailing literary medium. Modern Sinhalese is full of Sanskrit loanwords (i.e. *tatsamas*) with Sinhalese grammatical endings, but has, so far as I know, no Pali loanwords at all. This applies equally, and most remarkably, to the religious terminology, which is either 'pure Sinhalese'[49] (i.e. the mediaeval, un-Sanskritized language, also called *Eḷu*) or Sanskrit, also known as 'mixed Sinhalese'.[50] Linguistically almost the only thing which is Pali about Sinhalese 'Pali Buddhism' is the sacred texts, which are still normally used in the original.[51]

Parakkama-Bāhu held a council to reform the Sangha and establish the true doctrine. The *Mahāvaṃsa*[52] records that at this time 'In the villages belonging to the Sangha the good morals of monks consisted only in their supporting their wives and children.' Senior monks of the three

[48] A. L. Basham, 'Background to Parakkamabāhu', *Ceylon Historical Journal*, vol. IV, 1954-5, pp. 19–20.

[49] I shall refer to it, more accurately, as 'old Sinhalese'.

[50] e.g. a monk's official title in Sinhalese is *Sthavira*, the Sanskrit form; or *Terunnanse, tera* being the same word in Eḷu; only when speaking or writing English does a Sinhalese person use the Pali equivalent *Thero*.

[51] Pali is also used in certain categories of proper names having a connection with religion, e.g. monk's given names (Dhammaratana, Ñāṇatiloka) and names of sacred places (Anurādhapura, Nāgadīpa).

[52] *Mhv.*, LXXVIII, 3–4.

Nikāyas were convened, and after much discord the king himself, with the aid of three learned monks, decided the points at issue in favour of the Mahāvihāra; he accordingly suppressed the other two Nikāyas in 1165. The Sangha was thus organizationally unified for the first time in more than a thousand years. Poḷonnaruva fell in 1215. Under the pressure of Tamil attack and internal discord the Sinhalese kings of the next three centuries moved their capital from place to place, generally down the west side of the island and into the mountains. Parakkama-Bāhu II (1236–71) imported monks from the Coḷa country in South India 'and established harmony between the two teachings (*ubhayasāsanaṃ*)',[53] so we infer that though the Abhayagiri and Jetavana Nikāyas had formally been extinguished some monks still held to Mahāyāna doctrine. This, however, is the last occasion on which we hear of them. It is interesting that Theravāda Buddhism flourished in South India at this period. Parakkama-Bāhu IV (*c.* 1302–46) appointed as his teacher a monk from the Coḷa country, who taught him all the *Jātakas* (stories of the Buddha's previous births), which were then translated from Pali into what is still the standard Sinhalese version; the translation is ascribed to the king himself.[54] In 1411 the Chinese invaded the west coast and carried off the king. This was probably the last Sinhalese contact with Mahāyāna Buddhists till recent times. The Chinese installed Parakkama-Bāhu VI (1412–67), who ruled at Koṭṭē, near Colombo, and was the last king (till George III) to rule the whole of Ceylon.

When the Portuguese arrived in 1505 the island was politically divided in much the way that was to persist till reunification came under the British: one king ruled at Koṭṭē, another at Kandy. King Dharmapāla of Koṭṭē[55] was converted to Catholicism and became Don Juan Dharmapāla; he lost all power, and at his death in 1597 the line was

[53] *Mhv.*, LXXXIV, 9–10.

[54] *Mhv.*, XC, 80–3.

[55] From this date on the names of historical figures are given in Sanskrit.

finally extinguished, and with it all pretence of political independence for the low country. The Kandyan kingdom, after the brief reign of Rājasiṃha I (ruled 1580–91), who though a Sinhalese made Śaivism the court religion and persecuted Buddhism,[56] remained independent till 1815, and preserved a Sinhalese Buddhist cultural identity, but till the reign of Kīrti Śrī Rājasiṃha (1747–81) Buddhism does not seem to have prospered. In the intervening period no noteworthy works of Sinhalese or Pali literature were written. Moreover, within just over 150 years Kandyan kings sent abroad three times for monks to come and re-establish the higher ordination in Ceylon. The first two missions, received by Vimala Dharma Sūrya I (1592–1604) in 1596[57] and by Vimala Dharma Sūrya II (1687–1707) in 1697,[58] came from Burma and had curiously short-lived effects. According[59] to an eighteenth-century source[60] these two missions were invited not in order to initiate a genuine religious revival, but to legitimize the claims of incumbents to their temple lands. These incumbents, who had taken the lower ordination, claimed thereby the status of novices, but some of them kept their lay names and many were not even celibate. During the captivity of Robert Knox (1660–79) those who thus made no pretence of observing the monastic rules were known as *ganinnānsēs,* and wore not yellow but white. This class, half-way between monk

[56]His motives were probably not religious but political: monks had been plotting against his life. See P. E. Pieris, *Ceylon and the Portuguese*, 1505–1658 (American Ceylon Mission Press, Tellippalai, 1920), pp. 94–5.

[57]See *Mhv.*, XCVII, 8–15 and P.E.E. Fernando, 'The Rakkhanga-Sannas-Curnikava and the Date of the Arrival of Arakanese Monks in Ceylon', *Univ. of Ceylon Review*, vol. XVII, nos. 1 and 2, 1959, *n.* 46.

[58]See *Mhv.*, XCIV, 15–22 and D.B. Jayatilaka, 'Sinhalese Embassies to Arakan', *J.R.A.S.* (Ceylon Branch), XXXV (1940), 1–6.

[59]I owe much of the rest of this paragraph and of the next to Dr. Kithsiri Malalgoḍa's D.Phil. thesis entitled 'Sociological Aspects of Revival and Change in Buddhism in Nineteenth-century Ceylon', Oxford, 1970. The thesis was published in 1976—see the Bibliography.

[60]Gammullē Ratanapāla, *Siṃhala Vimānavastu Prakaraṇaya* (1770).

and layman, was a phenomenon unique in Ceylonese history.

In 1697 only one monk could be found to converse in Pali with the visiting monks from Burma. It was a pupil of both of this monk's pupils who instigated the revival of Buddhism in the mid-eighteenth century. Välivița Saraṇaṃkara[61] founded a renaissance of Pali and Sinhalese literature; he was soon the most learned man of his time, and he rapidly became the most influential, and deserves to be called the father of modern Sinhalese Buddhism. His patrons, oddly enough,[62] were members of a Tamil royal line from Madurai who ruled Kandy after 1739. Applications for monks were this time made to Siam; two embassies failed, but the monks who arrived in response to the third held a great ordination ceremony in Kandy in 1753 at Malvatta, Saraṇaṃkara's monastery. They made a *sīmā* there and a new *sīmā* at Asgiriya, Kandy's other main monastery, and then toured the country on similar errands. Saraṇaṃkara received the title of *Sangharāja* ('King of the Order') and founded the current lines of pupillary succession at Malvatta and Asgiri. Shortly afterwards the king put these two monasteries formally in charge of all other monasteries in the country, and ordered that only they could hold higher ordination ceremonies. They are still the headquarters of the Siyam Nikāya throughout the hill country, which is to say of the largest body of monks. Many Siyam Nikāya monks in the low country have headquarters elsewhere, but this is purely a matter of convenience. The founding in the nineteenth century of the other two Nikāyas of today, the Rāmañña and the Amarapura, will be discussed in Chapter 8.

[61]On Saraṇaṃkara the main source in English is Koṭagama Vāchissara, 'Välivița Saraṇaṃkara and the Revival of Buddhism in Ceylon' (unpublished Ph.D. thesis, London, 1961), which uses the two contemporary biographies.

[62]Kīrti Śrī Rājasiṃha (1747–81), to the praise of whose religious works the last two chapters of the *Cūlavaṃsa* are devoted, remained a Śaivite all his life. Clearly his patronage of Buddhism had strong political motivation.

When the British acquired Kandy in 1815 Buddhism ceased at last to be the State religion, but by the Kandyan Convention it was guaranteed that 'Buddhism and the Agama [religion] of the Devas [gods] were inviolable' and monasteries were allowed to retain their property and exemption from tax. In 1848 a Buddhist monk was executed by the British for allegedly taking part in an abortive revolt, but this was an isolated incident. In 1880 Col. H.S. Olcott of the Theosophical Society, intrigued by newspaper reports of a public disputation in 1874 in which a Buddhist monk had defeated a Methodist missionary, visited Ceylon and founded the Buddhist Theosophical Society, which set up its own schools in competition with Christian schools and started a new stream of Buddhist development—but this is another story, best left to Chapter 1.

There are at present some 17,000 Buddhist monks in Ceylon, in a population of $10\frac{1}{2}$ million of whom $7\frac{1}{2}$ million are Sinhalese and 7 million Buddhists. Almost all the Buddhists are Sinhalese. The other Sinhalese, except for a small Protestant minority, are Roman Catholics whose ancestors were converted under the Portuguese; almost all of these live along the west coast. Of the Sinhalese, $2\frac{1}{2}$ million are officially classed as Kandyans. The other elements of the population are as follows. There are over a million Tamils known as 'Ceylon Tamils' or 'Jaffna Tamils' whose ancestors came over in ancient and mediaeval times; they live mainly in the north of Ceylon and along the east coast, and the great majority are Śaivite Hindus. There are about a million Tamils known as 'Indian Tamils' or 'Indians' whose families were imported by the British to work on tea plantations; they mostly live in the hill country and are predominantly Śaivite Hindu, though a sizeable minority has been converted to Christianity, mostly Roman Catholicism. There are half a million Muslims, also known as 'Ceylon Moors', who are scattered throughout the island—mostly engaged in trade; their origin is not quite clear, but their ancestors were probably Arab merchants in the Middle Ages, and some of them at least must have arrived via South India, as they speak a dialect of Tamil; but they have intermarried a great deal with the local population, and in Sinhalese areas are usually bilingual. Of the smaller minorities, the Burghers, of mixed European and Ceylonese descent, are Christians, and live in towns (mainly Colombo) where they have white-collar jobs, or on estates as planters; there is a sprinkling of Malay Muslims, descendants of mercenaries employed by kings of Kandy; other Indian immigrant groups pursue trade in Colombo; and the few remaining Väddas, speaking their archaic Sinhalese dialect, live in the jungles on the eastern side of the mountain massif, where no doubt their relations have imperceptibly merged with the rest of the population.[63]

IV. Field-work and Presentation

> I wished to be a spectator of their sports and told them so; but finding they did nothing but look at me, I retired to a neighbouring house to take some refreshment . . .[64]
>
> John Davy

The raw material on which this book is based consists principally of some three dozen interviews with monks in the area, between ten and twenty miles from Kandy, where I lived for most of the year August 1964–August 1965. These interviews were conducted without interpreters, with bilingual friends present through three of them. I was able

[63]The figures for the main religions in 1891 were: 1,877,043 Buddhists; 723,853 Hindus; 302,127 Christians; 211,995 Muslims. This shows no great change in proportion, but notice how the population has exploded over the last seventy-five years. According to the same census there were 9,598 monks; of whom about half belonged to the Siyam Nikāya. The preponderance of the Siyam Nikāya today is even more pronounced.

[64]John Davy, *An Account of the Interior of Ceylon* (Longmans, etc., London 1821), p. 376. Davy had just come upon a Buddhist ceremony in my area.

to check dubious points and make a few revisions on a second visit to Ceylon in the latter half of 1969; in particular I used this opportunity to broaden my knowledge of lay opinion on religious questions. Let me briefly explain the reasoning behind my procedure.

In asking people their opinions I was always very much aware of two dangers. The more obvious one is that people will tell you what they think you like to hear. The Sinhalese are deeply courteous, and do not consider it a virtue to tell unpleasant truths. The answer to any leading question is therefore likely to be 'Ov' ('Yes'). This word, *ov*, which we translate 'yes', in effect has rather the meaning, 'I have heard'; it must not be taken as an answer to a question without further probing and corroboration. The less obvious danger is to force people to give an answer to something they would otherwise never think about. It is not that the question may be inappropriate, or phrased in the wrong terms; what I have in mind is rather that a question may unnaturally enlarge a man's cognitive position by forcing upon him a new thought. Such a question would be, 'What god or sort of god would you like to be reborn as?'; for although most villagers say they want to be reborn as gods, they have never thought about it more specifically. If the man X replies, 'As Kataragama', this is certainly of interest, but it would be misleading to record 'X wants to be reborn as Kataragama', unless the question—and indeed the whole assessment of the situation—were recorded too. This difficulty is to some extent unavoidable, as no field-worker can sit around for ever waiting for people to bring up subjects spontaneously and display the contents of their minds before him unasked; but one must exercise caution. Sitting around would be ideal; but it is too slow in practice. I had to conduct interviews. I did, however, feel that I should sit around for a time till I got some idea of what would be the right questions to ask about religion. After living for some seven months in the village which I shall call Mīgala I drew up a list of questions I thought I could profitably ask of monks, and these became the backbone of my set interviews. I added some questions as I went along, as I hit on interesting points of controversy; other questions I came to spend very little time on—though for the sake of uniformity I did not entirely drop them—as I perceived that the answers were standardized. Why did I choose to interview monks? Firstly, because this was considered a much more natural activity than to interview laymen, who would have wondered what I was up to; monks were not surprised that someone should want to talk to them about religion, and indeed some of them were quite flattered that an Englishman should have come so far to do so. Connected with this is the more important and rather obvious second reason: monks have many more opinions on religious topics than do most laymen. The list of religious questions I could have asked a layman which he might himself have asked, leaving aside those to which answers would be completely standardized, would be very short. Thirdly, monks are a clearly definable class, so that if I interviewed all or nearly all the monks in a certain area my study would be exhaustive in at least one respect, and even if I failed in my wider aims I would have done one thing thoroughly. Finally, interviewing the monks gave me a pretext not merely for travelling round the area in general, but in particular for visiting all the temples and thus making without too much extra effort a survey of local religious art and iconography. It was plainly convenient to interview monks in an area roughly centred on Mīgala; I made it my goal to interview all the monks, or rather all the incumbents, in the same parliamentary constituency, as this seemed to be about the number I would have time for. In the event I nearly succeeded in this aim. Altogether I visited thirty-nine local temples (including temporary establishments) and conducted reasonably full interviews (sometimes in more than one session) with thirty-four local monks, conversing at least briefly with all but two of the incumbents.

At first it seemed to me that my book should consist of this interview material, and the descriptive notes which go with it. However, they would be rather meaningless to readers of a cultural and intellectual background so far from that of a Kandyan monk unless I explained the assumptions on which the questions and answers rest. To do this would require a large part of the book as it now stands (especially Chapters 2 and 4). Moreover, the work would become unduly descriptive, with too little connection to the problem situation of western academics. Accordingly I have framed my book with regard chiefly to the intellectual issues involved, and have drawn on the interviews wherever relevant, without exhausting the material they contain. In particular I have neglected certain areas which they cover, such as politics, which are separable from my main concerns and the inclusion of which would make this book unduly long; I hope to publish some of it elsewhere in the near future. I must also stress that although my book is based on fieldwork in Sinhalese villages it is intended as a study of traditional Buddhism, *not* as a monograph on 'religion in a Sinhalese village'.

A work so ambitious cannot but have serious shortcomings, but to conclude this introduction I must mention what I consider to be its major deficiency. Close acquaintance with other ancient schools of Buddhism would certainly elucidate the origin of many Ceylonese Theravādin beliefs and practices, especially those branded as 'popular': veneration of the Buddha, attitudes towards the dead, and 'prayers' (*prārthanā*) are obvious examples. I hope that future research by myself and others will throw light on these problems.

1

Sinhalese Buddhism—Orthodox or Syncretistic?

LET me at the outset state a general conclusion. I found the Buddhism which I observed in Kandyan villages surprisingly orthodox. Religious doctrines and practices seem to have changed very little over the last 1,500 years. But Buddhism is 2,500 years old so why do I say 1,500 years, and what do I mean by orthodoxy?

I mentioned in the introduction that Buddhism came to Ceylon in the days of the Indian emperor Aśoka, about 243 B.C.[1] This was Theravāda Buddhism. The contents of Theravāda Buddhist oral traditions go back uninterrupted to the time of the Buddha himself, but we only have histories written nearly a thousand years after the Buddha's death,[2] so the accuracy of these traditions for the early period, especially before Buddhism came to Ceylon, is controversial. To enter this controversy lies outside my present scope, and so does the adjudication of Theravādin claims that they alone represent true Buddhist orthodoxy, and that other sects are heretics. But whatever we make of the Theravādin accounts which tell how three Buddhist councils within a couple of centuries of the Buddha's death established the scriptural canon and expelled heretics, it is certain that in Asoka's day schisms had occurred, that there were different sects and different (though perhaps only very slightly different) scriptures, and that from some of these sects was to grow Mahāyāna Buddhism, which became so influential in India, Tibet, and the Far East.

Theravādin orthodoxy rests on the Pali Canon; it is

[1]Malalasekera's arguments (op. cit., pp. 17–18) for the existence of Buddhism in Ceylon before this time repose much trust in the earliest part of the chronicles and rest on dubious inferences.

[2]Excepting the *Cullavagga* passage mentioned below; tradition may be right in claiming that this was written down in the first century B.C.

so defined by Theravāda Buddhists themselves, in so far as they are sophisticated enough to pose the question. More precisely, we may add, it rests on the Pali Canon as interpreted by the ancient commentaries, an interpretation which is accepted without question in Ceylon and with only very minor disagreement by most western scholars. At first glance scriptural authority thus seems to be two-tier; but this picture is rather over-simplified, because the Canon itself contains ancient commentaries, and its chronology is largely problematic. The Canon is called in Pali the *Tipiṭaka,* because it consists of three *Piṭakas* ('baskets'): the *Vinaya Piṭaka* (monastic rules), *Sutta Piṭaka* (sermons consisting in turn of five *Nikāyas,*[3] of which the first four contain the sermons and the last miscellaneous texts, many of them in verse), and *Abhidhamma Piṭaka* (systematic philosophy). Buddhists believe a passage at the end of the *Vinaya Piṭaka* (*Cullavagga* 11 and 12) which says that two councils of monks were held, one just after the Buddha's death and one a hundred years later, and that at the first council were composed the *Vinaya* and *Sutta Piṭakas,* in their final form.[4] The passage, being a part of the *Vinaya Piṭaka,* contradicts its own literal accuracy by mentioning the second council. Most other texts in these two *Piṭakas* claim to be, and therefore according to

[3]This use of the word 'Nikāya' has nothing to do with the one mentioned in the Introduction.

[4]The body of modern scholarship concerning these first two councils has been summarized and probably consummated by André Bareau, *Les Premiers Conciles Bouddhiques* (Presses Universitaires de France, Paris, 1955). On the general history of early Buddhist literature E. Frauwallner, *The Earliest Vinaya and the Beginnings of Buddhist Literature* (ISMEO, Rome, 1956), is now indispensable. Bareau decides that the first council was probably not a historical event, though the second was, and the independent conclusions of Frauwallner are in harmony. The most comprehensive and up-to-date work on early Buddhist history is Étienne Lamotte, *Histoire du Bouddhisme Indien* (Bibliothèque du *Muséon*, vol. 43, Louvain, 1958). On the third council (by the Theravādin reckoning) see H. Bechert, 'Aśokas "Schismenedikt" und der Begriff Sanghabheda', *Wiener Zeitschrift zur Kunde Süd- und Ostasiens* V, 1961, pp. 18–52.

Buddhist tradition are, the very words of the Buddha; but even in the four *Nikāyas,* the collection of sermons setting out the Buddha's teachings, there are some sermons attributed not to Buddha but to disciples. Some of these are said to have been delivered in the Buddha's lifetime; but a few explicitly state that the Buddha is dead, or refer to events after his death.[5] Part of the *Abhidhamma Piṭaka* is said by Theravādin tradition to have been compiled at the third council, held *c.* 247 B.C. under the auspices of Asoka, and whether or not such a council took place scholars agree with this relative chronology, and go further by assigning to the whole *Abhidhamma* a date when Buddhism was already organized and scholastic. Without discussing the dates of the miscellaneous texts (*Khuddaka Nikāya*) of the *Sutta Piṭaka*, of which scholars consider some as likely to be the Buddha's words as anything, some to be certainly much later, and some to be based perhaps even on pre-Buddhist material, we have found a measure of agreement between religious and scholarly opinion: the Pali Canon as we have it was not all compiled at one time. Therefore, we may add, it cannot reflect the state of the Buddhist religion at one given moment; nor indeed is it likely that so large and heterogeneous a body of material should be entirely free from contradictions.

Whatever its origins,[6] the Pali Canon must have ex-

[5]The contents of the thirty-four sermons (or, better, discourses) of the *Dīgha Nikāya* and the 152 sermons of the *Majjhima Nikāya* are listed in E. J. Thomas, *The Life of the Buddha as Legend and History* (Routledge, London, 1927), pp. 257–71, where an asterisk denotes a sermon attributed to a disciple. Examples of sermons delivered after the Buddha's death are the *Subha Sutta* (*D.N., Sutta* 10) and the *Madhura Sutta (M.N., Sutta* 84). In the *Anguttara Nikāya* (III, 57) is a story about King Muṇḍa of Magadha, who according to the *Mahāvaṃsa* (IV, 2) was fifth in line after the Buddha's contemporary, King Bimbisāra.

[6]Frauwallner has shown (op. cit.) that a large part of the *Vinaya Piṭaka*, including a biography of the Buddha on which all subsequent biographies are based, was composed about 110 years after the Buddha's death, and presupposes a good deal of earlier material. The precision of his deductions, which place some Buddhist scriptures nearer

isted more or less as we have it now in the time of Aśoka, when Mahinda brought it over to Ceylon. An Aśokan inscription lists seven texts, five of which we can identify in the Canon we know, though mostly under different titles, which suggests that the other two also may be in our Canon. Among the sculptures at Bharhut and Sanchi (second century B.C.) are pictures of stories in the Canon. These are by far the oldest records of the Canon physically to survive: the Pali Canon was not even written down till the first century B.C., and of course no manuscript from that era exists.

It may be a slight over-simplification that Mahinda and his colleagues brought the Pali Canon (in their heads) to Ceylon, but it cannot be far from the truth. We owe the story to the great commentator Buddhaghosa, who wrote in the early fifth century A.D. Buddhaghosa adds that they brought commentaries in Pali, which Mahinda translated or recomposed in Sinhalese. If Pali originals of the Sinhalese commentaries ever existed, they had been lost before Buddhaghosa's time. Adikaram[7] has shown that the Sinhalese commentaries on which Buddhaghosa's work is based were principally compiled in the first century A.D. The *Mahāvaṃsa* (XXXVII) says that Buddhaghosa came from North India to the Mahāvihāra in Anurādhapura because in India the commentaries (*aṭṭhakathā*) had been lost; his teacher told him that the Sinhalese commentaries were the genuine work of Mahinda, and he should translate them into Pali. His first work in Ceylon was the *Visuddhimagga*[8] (*The Path of Purity*), an exhaustive summary in Pali of Buddhist doctrine, still the best work of its kind.[9] He then wrote commentaries in Pali on most

to the events they purport to describe than can securely be done for the Christian gospels, is unlikely soon to be improved upon.

[7]E.W. Adikaram, *Early History of Buddhism in Ceylon* (2nd ed., Gunasena, Colombo, 1953). See especially p. 87.

[8]The best edition is that in the Harvard Oriental Series, edited by H.C. Warren and D. Kosambi (Harvard University Press, Cambridge, Mass., 1950).

[9]"There is no other compendium of Buddhism known at all like it,

works in the Canon.[10] The Sinhalese books on which these commentaries are based have perished, because he superseded them. Though he may at first have intended only to translate them he in fact edited and systematized them. He quotes nearly every earlier work of Pali literature known to have existed. His interpretations are mutually consistent. To this day Buddhaghosa's Buddhism is in effect the unitary standard of doctrinal orthodoxy for all Theravāda Buddhists, whether or not they are educated enough to be aware of the problem.

The authors of the Pali commentaries on the parts of the Canon which Buddhaghosa did not treat do not conflict with him, so the commentatorial stand-point is unified and homogeneous. We know very little about these other authors, but they probably were contemporaries of Buddhaghosa or lived slightly later. The two more important ones are Buddhadatta[11] and Dhammapāla.[12] Tradition has it that Buddhadatta was born in the Coḷa kingdom but became a monk at the Mahāvihāra; there is an unlikely story that he was on a ship going back to India when he met Buddhaghosa on his way out. Dhammapāla wrote in South India and was probably a Tamil too; 'he states. . . that he follows the traditional interpretation of texts as handed down in the Mahāvihara'; and 'it is quite

in consistency and completeness; and in the absence of any other such, it is just to assume that it was first in Buddhaghosa's mind that the Buddha system obtained its final shape. He identified himself with the Anurādhapura school of Buddhism, became its chief light, and gave to its traditions the form which they have ever since retained.' Copleston, op. cit., pp. 352–3.

[10]On the *Vinaya Piṭaka* as a whole and also on the *Pātimokkha*, which is part of it; on the four *Nikāyas (Dīgha, Majjhima, Anguttara, Saṃyutta)*, the *Suttanipāta*, *Khuddaka-pāṭha* and *Dhammapada* (though the authorship of these last three commentaries is disputed) of the *Sutta Piṭaka*; on the whole of the *Abhidhamma Piṭaka*.

[11]Author of a commentary on the *Buddhavaṃsa* and works on the *Vinaya* and *Abhidhamma*.

[12]Author of a commentary on the *Thera-* and *Therī-gāthā*, *Udāna*, *Vimānavatthu*, *Peta-vatthu*, *Itivuttaka*, and *Cariyā-piṭaka*; also of sub-commentaries on Buddhaghosa.

likely that he had the advantage of studying the Tamil commentaries (of which we know that at least two existed) as well'.[13] A further anonymous author wrote the Pali version of the *Jātaka* commentary which has come down to us; the *Jātakas* are stories of the 550 previous births of the Buddha; their Pali verses are canonical, but the prose parts, which carry the story forward so that without them the verses are mostly unintelligible, rank as commentary and for a while existed only in Sinhalese, like the other commentaries.[14] The author says that he follows the traditions of the Mahāvihāra at Anurādhapura. The commentary on the *Dhammapada,* which is not so much a true commentary as a collection of stories much in the style of the *Jātaka* commentary, is like the latter traditionally but probably wrongly attributed to Buddhaghosa. The other two authors[15] of commentaries whose names are known also lived at Anurādhapura and wrote in the same tradition.[16]

Though the Pali Canon is strictly the only sacred work and the supreme authority, there is another book which though neither Canon nor commentary has in Ceylon received the kind of fame and respect usually reserved for sacred books. This is the *Mahāvaṃsa*, the Pali verse chronicle of Ceylon, mentioned in the Introduction. The first part of it was written in the late fifth century by a monk called Mahānāma who lived in a monastery at Anurādhapura belonging to the Mahāvihāra. Like the commentaries, it was based on much Sinhalese written material, which has long since disappeared. It was based also on another similar

[13]Malalasekera, op. cit., p. 113.

[14]The retranslation of the *Jātaka* stories into Sinhalese in the early fourteenth century, a landmark in Sinhalese literary history, is mentioned in the Introduction, p. 33.

[15]Mahānāma, who commented on the *Paṭisambhidāmagga*, and Upasena or Upatissa, who commented on the *Niddesa*.

[16]The commentaries and their authors are most conveniently listed by Adikaram on pp. 1–2 of his *Early History of Buddhism in Ceylon*. This learned work is entirely based on the commentaries, and contains much information not elsewhere available in a European language.

Pali chronicle, the *Dīpavaṃsa,* which was written also in Anurādhapura, perhaps by nuns,[17] about a century earlier, which makes it the oldest work written in Ceylon to have survived. But the *Mahāvaṃsa* follows it so closely, quoting long passages verbatim, and at the same time is so superior, that the *Dīpavaṃsa* is comparatively neglected. Both chronicles are—luckily for us—predominantly histories of the Buddha's teaching (*sāsana*), and focus throughout on episodes of religious interest, beginning with mythical accounts of the Buddha's visits to Ceylon. The earliest date for which the *Mahāvaṃsa* is authoritative may thus be fixed by the most sceptical at the fourth century A.D., by the sanguine at the third century B.C. (Mahinda's mission to Ceylon), and by the pious during the lifetime of the Buddha himself. The chronicles are not primarily expositions of doctrine (albeit each chapter ends with a pious verse reflecting on the vanity of worldly pomp or some such orthodox sentiment); and though they afford fascinating material for the history of Buddhist ideas, they plainly do not form a touchstone of doctrinal orthodoxy as I have defined it; but they give accounts of religious practices and especially festivals which are rather outside the scope of the canonical literature. So though we may not be able to call a practice canonically orthodox, because the Canon does not mention it, we may often say that it stands in an orthodox tradition if it occurs in the *Mahāvaṃsa.* And it cannot fail to strike a modern observer that many festivals described in the ancient *Mahāvaṃsa,* as well as in its continuations, differ little, except in scale, from festivals in Kandyan villages today.

This then is what I meant when I said at the beginning of the chapter that I found the Buddhism which I observed orthodox: that the doctrines of the villagers would have been approved by Buddhaghosa and that most of their religious practices would have been familiar to him and his

[17]This interesting conjecture is that of Hugh Nevill, made in the introduction to his catalogue of his Manuscript collection, now in the British Museum. It is reported by Malalasekera, op. cit., pp. 136–7.

contemporaries. But I also said that I found this orthodoxy surprising. Why so? I suppose it is unusual for the religion of a society to change so little over 1,500 years; certainly it is unusual for societies of which we have the records. But my surprise was caused rather by the frequency with which I had been told, by books and by people, that Sinhalese village Buddhism was corrupt. 'Corrupt' was the word generally used by laymen; in academic circles this word sounds too pejorative to be respectable, and is replaced by 'syncretistic', or some periphrasis. One example, from a noted authority: Sir Charles Eliot wrote, 'At present there may be said to be three religions in Ceylon; local animism, Hinduism, and Buddhism are all inextricably mixed together.'[18] Let me examine this belief that village Buddhism is corrupt, and explain why I think it is mistaken.

Sinhalese villagers have been judged corrupt Buddhists because they say and do things which the judges think are incompatible with what is said in the Pali Canon. In particular, most Sinhalese believe gods and demons to exist and make offerings to them under various circumstances. (The relevant beliefs are described in Chapter 4.) The judgement that this is corrupt Buddhism is based on a misunderstanding which has arisen because the original people to make it were westerners, raised in a Christian culture, whose background made them think of religion as god-centred. The problem of God is central to

[18] *Hinduism and Buddhism*, vol. III (Edward Arnold, London, 1921), p. 42. To multiply instances is unnecessary, but it is noteworthy that this view was held even by the foremost scholar of Sinhalese culture. Geiger, in *Culture of Ceylon in Mediaeval Times*, following the arrangement of the indices at the end of the second volume of his translation of the *Cūlavaṃsa*, divided his section on religion into three: I Popular Religion; II Hinduism; III Buddhism. (All refer to the religion of Buddhists.) It would of course be possible to set up criteria, probably of a historical nature, for such a division; but Geiger offered no clear criteria, and his assignment of a belief to one or the other category seems largely arbitrary, except that beliefs about supernaturals are virtually confined to the first two categories. Even 'particularly Buddhist deities' (p. 178, para. 165) appear under Hinduism!

the Semitic, the monotheistic religions: it is essential that there is only one God, and all other gods are false gods, which means that they do not exist. It is true, though almost ludicrously inadequate, to say that Christians, Jews and Muslims consider God the most important thing in the universe. Buddhists with whom I talked, however, will admit the existence of the Christian God with perfect indifference,[19] just as they would no doubt admit the existence of any other god proposed to them; gods are not a problem in Buddhism. Some Buddhists recognize this explicitly: one old monk said to me, 'Gods are nothing to do with religion.'[20] Gods are powerful beings to be supplicated for worldly goods; Buddhism, as we shall see in the next chapter, is concerned with ethics, future lives, and release from worldly existence. An ordinary Buddhist layman is no more concerned to accept or deny the existence of some new supernatural being than a western layman is concerned to accept or deny the existence of some newly discovered type of nuclear particle or natural force. Both are just facts of life.

A Buddhist who acknowledges gods can thus be cleared of the charge of doctrinal incorrectitude. But of course some gods are much more important to him than others. These gods figure in what any casual western observer would call his religion; they come under any western academic definition of religion, including Spiro's '...interaction with culturally postulated superhuman beings', which I discussed in the Introduction. I explained there that I prefer the conventionalist use of terminology, to call something a religion if it is so called by its own practitioners. But I would also like to deny that the Sinhalese Buddhist religion, in any sense of the term, is syncretistic. I take it that we talk of cultural syncretism when elements from different cultures combine or fuse to produce a compos-

[19]They will not of course accept all the claims made on his behalf.

[20]Sir Charles Eliot, quoted above, might have retracted his opinion of Sinhalese syncretism had he heard this, for he himself wrote, '...when the Buddha preached in Kosala and Magadha...religion had little to do with the gods.' Eliot, I, 330.

ite which is not normal or not acceptable in either culture. There is of course no dividing line between what is syncretism and what is not, because syncretism has no 'essence'; but it seems to make sense to say that the culture of an Englishman who goes to dinner in an Indian restaurant is not thereby syncretistic, whereas the culture of an Englishman who preserves some English habits, but refuses cutlery and eats all his food with his right hand is: he has broken the unwritten rules of his original culture, without entirely adopting a new one (a feat which is rarely possible). Syncretism is a concept easier to apply with clarity to a system of ideas like Buddhist doctrine, both because there the rules are mostly written and explicit, and because strict logical incompatibility can occur between ideas but not between behaviour patterns.

It is claimed that Sinhalese religion is syncretistic when Buddhists acknowledge 'Hindu gods', by which is meant gods of whom they have learnt from Hindus. (This theory is implicit in the title of an article by E.R. Leach: 'Pulleyar and the Lord Buddha: an aspect of religious syncretism in Ceylon'.)[21] Let us leave aside the question of whether these gods are part of Sinhalese Buddhist religion, for we can at least agree that they are part of Sinhalese Buddhist culture. I still deny that the presence of Hindu gods in Sinhalese Buddhist culture is a sign of cultural syncretism. Buddhism has always acknowledged Hindu gods. This is not surprising because the Buddha, as Indians like to point out, was a Hindu, just as Christ was a Jew. (This does not mean that it makes much sense to think of Buddhism as a kind of Hinduism; the analogy with Christianity holds.) However much speculation may be devoted to dividing the Pali Canon into layers of authenticity, no rationalist western scholar has ever reached a bedrock stratum of 'primitive Buddhism' in which no gods and demons play a part. This statement will be amplified in Chapter 4; suffice it here to say that supernatural beings were as much a part

[21] *Psychoanalysis and the Psychoanalytic Review*, vol. 49, no. 2, pp. 80–102.

of the Buddha's universe as they are of a Buddhist villager's universe today.[22]

As Sinhalese Buddhism (like Buddhism in ancient India) has throughout its existence been geographically adjacent or even intertwined with Hinduism it is natural that theological (in the strict sense) developments accepted by the Hindus, and in particular by Tamil Hindus, have been accepted by Buddhists also. Over the ages the personnel of the Sinhalese pantheon has somewhat changed; contact with Tamils has brought the relative newcomers Kataragama and Pattinī into prominence, but some old-timers like Vishnu, whom the Buddha is believed to have made the guardian of Buddhism in Ceylon,[23] are still powerful. What applies to these 'Hindu' gods applies equally to the lesser beings, the demons, etc., of Eliot's 'animism'. In contrast the structure of the pantheon, which is brilliantly described in Obeyesekere's articles, has changed little; the kinds of change which have occurred are suggested in the Introduction. But the status of the whole pantheon in its relation to the Buddhist religion has changed not at all. The traditional Sinhalese Buddhist framework for interpreting reality has remained unaltered. It will be seen that my argument against the alleged syncretism of Sinhalese Buddhism has two levels. On the lower level I am claiming that the presence of 'Hindu' or 'animist' supernaturals in the Buddhist's universe is not a novel or syncretistic feature, but has always been the case. This is a historical and textual argument. Argument on this level should be sufficient to refute the charge; but the argument on the higher level is theoretically more interesting. I mentioned that

[22] "It is an unpardonable mistake for a historian to assume that only later tradition has incorporated them [i.e. gods] into the teaching in order to pander to the masses." H. von Glasenapp, op. cit., p. 30.

[23] *Mhv.*, VII, 5. The text refers to Uppalavaṇṇa ('he whose colour is like a blue lotus'). Whether this god has always been the same as Vishnu is not relevant here. The text actually says that the Buddha prophesied that his teaching would take root in Ceylon and asked Sakka to guard the country, whereupon Sakka entrusted it to Uppalavaṇṇa.

Buddhist villagers will acknowledge the existence of the Christian God. I have never known a Buddhist actually to pray to this God for health, wealth, or other benefits in their life; but if one did so I should still not consider his religion syncretistic; because such a prayer would still be consonant with Buddhist doctrine. This higher-level argument, the point I especially wish to make, is doctrinal and logical. So long as Buddhists continue to treat gods as a kind of supermen, able to grant favours to suppliants, but still ultimately of limited life and powers and subject to moral law, their beliefs are not syncretistic. Belief in gods like this is not logically (or otherwise) incompatible with Buddhist doctrine. Who the gods are is irrelevant to this point. That Sinhalese Buddhists have adopted gods from Hindus rather than from Christians is an accident of historical contiguity. Despite invasions and wars, relations with Tamil Hindus have been more intimate than with the European Christians. The period of friendliest contact with Europeans was probably the late nineteenth century, and under these circumstances Christianity began to influence Buddhism to the point of genuine religious syncretism. Copleston reports that during Buddhist festivals in Colombo walls would exhibit the slogan, 'God bless our Lord Buddha'.[24] This is syncretism, because it shatters the Buddhist framework. But I saw no such slogans; they are now only part of history.

The Buddha's teaching was limited to what he thought conducive to enlightenment. Most people have broader interests, so Buddhists are almost bound to have other beliefs besides those of Buddhist doctrine. To sum this up in a word, Buddhism in real life is *accretive*. This conclusion harmonizes with that of Professor Dumont when he writes of the currents in early India which produced Buddhism (and other religious movements): 'An individual religion based upon choice is *added on* to the religion of the group.'[25] (My italics.) I am not at all averse to de-

[24]Op. cit., p. 478.

[25]L. Dumont, 'World Renunciation in Indian Religions', in *Contri-*

scribing the original part of the Buddha's message as an 'individual' as against a 'group' religion; we must only remember that this 'individual' religion has never existed *in vacuo*. Evidently I could not be further from agreeing with an observer like Paul Wirz, who has written of Ceylon,[26] 'In reality, it is the same here as in other Buddhist countries; only very few comprehend the true Buddhist dogma in its real profoundness; the rest are Buddhists in name only, among them also a great part of those who wear the yellow gown... They are too deeply rooted in their old conceptions and customs... ' In another recent book which deals with the subject of contemporary Sinhalese religion, the American sociologist Professor Bryce Ryan says that, 'Pure Buddhism is a philosopher's abstraction.'[27] While I have tried to show in my Introduction that the concept of pure Buddhism can be meaningful, and in this chapter what I mean by it, it is doubtless to passages such as the above that Professor Ryan is referring.[28] The reader may

butions to Indian Sociology, IV, 1960, p. 46.

[26]*Exorcism and the Art of Healing in Ceylon* (Brill, Leyden, 1954), p. 236.

[27]*Sinhalese Village* (Univ. of Miami Press, Coral Gables, Florida), 1958, p. 90.

[28]I am sympathetic to the tenor of Ryan's remarks on Buddhism, and often agree with their substance, but elsewhere I feel that he over-simplifies rather drastically. He writes (op. cit., p. 90), '...non-Buddhist supernaturalism in the form of planetary influences, wood sprites, sorcery and ghosts is ubiquitous. To some extent Lord Buddha has been integrated with these complex bodies of supernaturalism. To a greater extent the supernaturalism stands as distinct systems of thought superficially rationalized to the agnostic, rational, and metaphysical concepts of pure Theravāda.' Reference to Obeyesekere's articles may suggest that some of the superficiality belongs to the author, not to the villagers and their ideology. Lower on the same page Ryan writes: 'Folk supernaturalism does not have its roots in Buddhism, nor is it considered "Buddhism". It is a world of power, elements of which may well antedate the Buddha Himself but have not been incorporated in His teachings.' The reader of my foregoing argument will see that I heartily agree with all this, provided that the first half of the first sentence is to be taken on the doctrinal, not on the historical level. I fear, however, that the 'roots' do refer to history, in which case the

be wondering what 'the true Buddhist dogma' is which Dr. Wirz comprehends 'in its real profoundness' while it eludes so many Buddhist monks. Clearly I cannot give a definitive answer to this, but I think I can indicate what Dr. Wirz has in mind, and the matter is worth a digression because Dr. Wirz's remarks are typical of a view of traditional Buddhism by no means confined to scholars and Europeans, but common also to English-educated Sinhalese.

The discovery of Buddhism by the West was mainly by British missionaries and civil servants in Ceylon in the nineteenth century. George Turnour, a civil servant, pioneered the study of Ceylon history when he discovered, edited and translated the *Mahāvaṃsa*, the first important Pali text to be published.[29] But it was the missionaries who took more interest in Buddhism, in order to know their enemy better. In particular the works of a Methodist minister, the Rev. Robert Spence Hardy,[30] were important sources for western knowledge of Buddhism, and were excerpted by encyclopaedias of religion.[31] The missionaries decided, with some justice given their own frame of reference, that Buddhism was an 'atheist creed',[32] since they

statement is false, because the 'folk supernaturalism' has always been associated with Buddhism, i.e. believed in by Buddhists. This failure to distinguish sharply between the historical (what has been the case) and the doctrinal (what the books say) levels of religion lends a certain imprecision to even such apparently simple remarks as the one quoted in the text. That is perhaps inevitable when religions are studied with no historical perspective.

[29]Turnour entered the Ceylon Civil Service in 1818, and was in it till his early death in 1843. He published his edition of the *Mahāvaṃsa* in 1836 and identified the King Piyadasi of the Asokan inscriptions, which had just been deciphered by James Prinsep, as Asoka.

[30]His two most important books were *Eastern Monachism* (1850), and *A Manual of Buddhism* (1853), both published in London by Partridge and Oakey. The latter consists mainly of translated Buddhist texts.

[31]e.g. James Gardner, *The Faiths of the World* (Fullerton, Edinburgh, 1858), who says (p. 42), 'The Buddhist system is essentially atheistical'.

[32]The words used for instance by Hardy in his introduction to *The Legends and Theories of the Buddhists* (Williams and Norgate, Lon-

were told that the Buddha was not a god. This information was seized on by western rationalists, atheists and agnostics, who were delighted to hear of a religion which was atheistic, and even claimed to be rational; Buddhism as they understood it seemed an ideal ally in the fight against Christianity. Indeed, Bishop Copleston, Bishop of Colombo, writing in 1892, saw in Buddhism's 'alliance with Western scepticism' one of its few hopes for survival![33]

In the meanwhile two Ceylon civil servants moved into the forefront of Buddhist and Pali studies. R.C. Childers began to publish Pali texts in 1869, and from 1872–5 compiled the first western Pali dictionary. T. W. Rhys Davids, probably the most influential Pali scholar of modern times, founded the Pali Text Society for the publication of Pali books in 1881; his book *Buddhism*, first published in 1877[34] and many times reprinted, may be said to mark the close of the pioneer period of Buddhist studies. Rhys Davids was an excellent scholar, but he naturally stressed the rationalist elements in Buddhism, because they formed the most striking contrast both to Christian, and, in Buddhist eyes, to other Indian traditions. I suspect that he also found them the most sympathetic. Buddhism became familiar to the educated public when in 1879 Sir Edwin Arnold published *The Light of Asia*;[35] this long poem on the Buddha, while presenting Buddhism in the way usual at the time, suggested an analogy between the Buddha and Christ which doubtless contributed to its popularity.

In their campaign against Christianity English secularists and free-thinkers soon found some curious allies, less sympathetic but more militant than the Buddhists of Ceylon. The president of the National Secular Society, Charles Bradlaugh, sponsored and gave lectures on comparative religion to disprove Christianity's claims to uniqueness. In 1874 Mrs. Annie Besant heard him lecture on similarities

don, 1866).

[33]Op. cit., p. 426.

[34]By the Society for Promoting Christian Knowledge, London.

[35]Published by Trübner, London.

between the stories about Krishna and about Christ. She joined the N.S.S., and soon became Bradlaugh's chief assistant and companion, and co-editor of the *National Reformer,* the N.S.S. newspaper. In 1882 Mrs. Besant devoted considerable space in the *National Reformer* to first criticizing and later attacking the Theosophical Society, which had been founded in New York in 1875 by Madame Blavatsky, a Russian, and Col. H. S. Olcott, an American, and in 1879 had moved to India. One of the earliest theosophist classics was entitled *Esoteric Buddhism,*[36] and the movement was sometimes referred to as Buddhist Theosophy, though it had in it no more of Buddhism than of divine wisdom. Early in 1889 a leading member of the N.S.S. contributed a series of articles also entitled 'Esoteric Buddhism' to the *National Reformer,* and Mrs. Besant, who had studied the book of that name, lectured on 'Buddha: His Life and Teachings'.[37] In the same year, to the infinite distress of Bradlaugh and her other rational friends, she was converted to theosophy; when Madame Blavatsky died in 1891 she became the leader of the movement,[38] and held this position till her death in 1933. In 1891 theosophy was described by her friend William T. Stead as 'the natural child of the marriage of Christianity and Buddhism'.[39] Mrs. Besant visited Ceylon for a week in November 1893 (when she was on her way to India for the first time), and received spectacular welcomes in Colombo, Kandy, and Galle. The arrangements had been made by Col. Olcott.

Col. Olcott himself first landed in Ceylon on 17 February 1880, a day which is still locally celebrated as 'Olcott Day'. (There are so far as I am aware no longer any special festivities, but articles on Olcott appear in the news-

[36]A.P. Sinnett, *Esoteric Buddhism* (Trübner, London, 1883).

[37]Arthur H. Nethercot, *The First Five Lives of Annie Besant* (Hart-Davis, London, 1961), p. 302. From this book comes all my information on Mrs. Besant.

[38]Nominally Olcott was still President of the Theosophical Society.

[39]Quoted in Nethercot, p. 384. On the next page is recorded a public debate between Mrs. Besant and a clergyman on 'Theosophical Symbols', with Professor Rhys Davids in the chair.

papers.) On this occasion he stayed for five months. His influence on Buddhism was in the first instance organizational. He founded the Buddhist Theosophical Societies, which ran schools which emulated and competed with the schools of Christian missionaries. (These schools remained under the B.T.S. until the government's takeover of schools in 1961.) Olcott drew up a 'Buddhist catechism', and encouraged Buddhists to celebrate Wesak (the anniversary of the Buddha's birth, enlightenment and death) with songs modelled on Christmas carols. It was Olcott who gave the impetus which before long resulted in the founding of further Buddhist institutions to parallel Christian ones: the Young Men's and Young Women's Buddhist Associations, and the Buddhist Sunday Schools (*daham pāsal*) at which monks teach the village children religion from books provided by the Y.M.B.A. The latest example of Buddhist imitation of Christian institutions occurred in 1966 with the introduction of the *poya* weekend: the weekly holiday of Sunday with Saturday afternoon has been replaced by the *poya* day (full moon, half moon or no moon) with the preceding half-day. This alone will suggest how much modern political Buddhism owes to Col. Olcott. Perhaps it also owes something more directly to the Christian missionaries.[40] In 1929 Sir Hugh Clifford, Governor of Ceylon 1925–7, wrote in the *Encyclopaedia Britannica*,[41] A great revival of Buddhism in the last 20 years is political rather than religious. Christian practice has prompted Young Men's and Young Women's Buddhist Associations, and Islam the doffing of shoes on entering Buddhist Temples. Simultaneously the broad toleration of other faiths, which from the earliest times has been so marked and so notable a feature of pure Buddhism, has shown a tendency to be replaced by vulgar abuse of tenets of other creeds of a kind with which the more ignorant types of Christian Missionaries 'to the heathen' have unhappily made the

[40]The other influences on political Buddhism, such as western political ideologies, lie quite outside my present scope.

[41]Article 'Ceylon', in *Encyclopaedia Britannica* (14th ed., London and New York, 1929), vol. 5, p. 179.

world familiar. Is it entirely a coincidence that of Ceylon's Prime Ministers since independence the least demonstratively Buddhist, Sir John Kotelawela, was the only one not educated at a Christian mission school?

From his first visit to Ceylon Olcott took back a young disciple to Madame Blavatsky in India, Don David Hēvāvitarana, later known as Anagārika[42] Dharmapāla. Though he spent most of his adult life in India, running the Mahā Bodhi Society, which he founded, Dharmapāla exerted crucial influence on the formation of modern Buddhist ideology in Ceylon. In 1893, under the auspices of Mrs. Besant, he represented Buddhism at the World Parliament on Religions in Chicago. At that time Professor Max Müller wrote to him in a letter,

> You should endeavour to do for Buddhism what the more enlightened students of Christianity have long been doing in different countries of Europe: you should free your religion from its later excrescences, and bring it back to its earliest, simplest, and purest form as taught by Buddha and his immediate disciples. If that is done, you will be surprised to see how little difference there is in essentials between the great religions of the world. And this must be done with perfect honesty. Nothing not quite sincere or truthful should be tolerated. Nothing has injured Buddhism so much in the eyes of scholars and philosophers in Europe as what goes by the name of Esoteric Buddhism. Madame Blavatsky may have been a dear friend to you, but Truth is a dearer friend.

Here then meet the two streams of western thought which have deeply influenced English-educated Buddhists in Ceylon: theosophy, and 'the scholars and philosophers of Europe' seeking Buddhism's 'purest form as taught by Buddha and his disciples'. Modern Buddhist fundamentalist movements and institutions, such as the Vajirārāma

[42]Anagārika is a title meaning 'homeless'; it applies to a layman who dedicates his life to Buddhism. This institution is an invention of Dharmapāla; the term 'anagārika' used to be reserved for monks.

in Colombo, plainly owe much to the preconceptions, as well as the researches, of scholars like Max Müller and Rhys Davids. The editions and translations of the Pali Text Society are more used than any indigenous materials by Sinhalese scholars. Several Europeans, especially Englishmen and Germans, have gone to Ceylon to become monks, and passed their lives there with great reputations for holiness. They probably owe their first acquaintance with Buddhist texts to the late nineteenth-century translations of Rhys Davids or Karl Eugen Neumann, and have contributed the results of their own western education to the current of Buddhist ideas. One community of these monks, headed till his death by a learned German, the Rev. Ñāṇatiloka, is very near to the place where Dr. Wirz stayed. Most recently a German disciple of the Rev. Ñāṇatiloka, the Rev. Ñāṇaponika, has from his Forest Hermitage in Kandy helped to found the Buddhist Publication Society, which distributes Buddhist pamphlets throughout the world; since 1958 they have published more than a hundred *Wheel* booklets and *Bodhi Leaves*. At first these were all in English, but some are now appearing in Sinhalese. The scholarship of the Rev. Ñāṇaponika is unimpeachable and his piety renowned; my purpose is merely to indicate the direction of his influence. At least half of these missionary publications are the works of Englishmen or Germans, many of them reprints of old works, going as far back as *Light of Asia*, which Mrs. Besant read in 1879.

The aim of this excursus has been to suggest that there are in Ceylon today broadly two types of Buddhism, the traditional and the modern. It is not surprising if those Sinhalese Buddhists who have been educated in English are themselves uncertain under these circumstances about the validity of indigenous traditions, and tend to cull their own Buddhism at least as much from western sources as from local clergy and customs; and this may be said with equal force of the Buddhist nationalist movements and organizations which have arisen within the last ten years, always under educated urban inspiration and leadership.

I disagree with those Europeans, like Copleston and Clifford, who consider the last hundred years to have produced a Buddhist revival: it was the previous hundred years, the period in which the three modern Nikāyas were founded (see Introduction, p. 41, and Chapter 8, pp. 360–362), in which Sinhalese Buddhism revived; this other Buddhism is something new. When I say that Sinhalese Buddhism is orthodox it is not to these recent movements that I refer; indeed, I wonder whether they are not heading towards the first genuine syncretism in Ceylonese Buddhist history.[43]

It may seem disappointing that a work professedly on religious change should devote its first chapter to saying that there has been little change. Little, but not none: we shall see, especially in Chapters 7 and 8, that there has been enough change to merit an examination. But this relative changelessness has its compensations. For if the Buddhism we can observe today is like the Buddhism of the Pali Canon, it follows, obviously, that the Buddhism of the Pali Canon was like what we can observe today. The Buddhism of the Pali Canon is at least 1,500 years, probably 1,900 years, old; how much older it may be we can only surmise. The Sinhalese Buddhist villager today may have a religion quite like the Buddhist villager nearly 2,500 years ago. With this exciting thought let us examine that religion.

[43]This chapter was written before the appearance of Heinz Bechert, *Buddhismus, Staat und Gesellschaft in den Ländern des Theravāda-Buddhismus: I. Allgemeines und Ceylon* (Band XVII/1 der Schriften des Instituts für Asienkunde in Hamburg) (Frankfurt am Main/Berlin, 1966). Bechert's large and excellent book deals extensively with the new Buddhism referred to above. The second half of the volume is devoted to the organization of Buddhism and its political role in modern Ceylon, mainly since Independence; the first half includes a lengthy description (pp. 37–108), more general in character, of 'Buddhist modernism' (as he aptly calls it), including the movement's intellectual and organizational origins. Although this section refers to all Theravāda countries, it is Ceylon which plays by far the most important part in it. I am in very substantial agreement with Bechert's presentation, and warmly recommend his pioneer work to the interested reader; in particular the footnotes are a mine of invaluable source material.

2

The Basic Vocabulary of Buddhism

In this chapter I shall try to assemble the elementary facts about Sinhalese Buddhism and to introduce those technical terms which are indispensable. To give some understanding of how a Sinhalese Buddhist sees his own religion I shall preface my exposition with remarks on the Sinhalese words used to denote the main religious attitudes, thus revealing certain contrasts with, for example, the vocabulary of English Christianity.

The beliefs, behaviour, institutions, and language which I shall describe in the rest of this work, and which for convenience I refer to as Buddhist, are those of the Kandyan Sinhalese inhabitants of Mīgala and surrounding villages as they explained them to me; in particular the beliefs are those of the local monks (see Introduction, section 4). Detailed and systematic introductions to Sinhalese Buddhist doctrine have been published in both English and Sinhalese, notably in books which are used as textbooks in Ceylonese schools. These books are authoritative, in the sense that they are written by learned and distinguished Ceylonese monks; they will doubtless mould the thinking of this and future generations. They are essentially summaries of the doctrine of the Pali Canon as understood by Buddhaghosa. Among such works I cannot too highly recommend the Rev. Narada's *The Buddha and his Teachings*.[1] My interest, however, was to find out what a group of people actually believe, so I shall not refer to the Ven. Narada's book, but use the information given me by the monks and villagers themselves. Though I am mainly in-

[1] No publisher, Saigon, 1964.

terested in Buddhist beliefs and ethics, these cannot be described or understood without some reference to Buddhist institutions, physical and social, so I shall insert such descriptions at places where they may not too much disrupt the argument.

I am concerned with religious beliefs. But does our very concept of religious belief correspond to a concept of the Sinhalese?

The Sinhalese word for 'religion' is *āgama*. *Āgama* is a Sanskrit word which in Sanskrit usually means 'tradition', 'sacred tradition', or 'sacred text'. It is not surprising that a people whose religion depends on writings should use for religion a word which used to connote texts. In Sinhalese, however, the word is fully naturalized and no longer has this connotation except by etymology; it translates 'religion' very well. Buddhism is *Buddhāgama,* Hinduism *Hindu āgama,* Islam *Muslim āgama,* etc.[2]

The adjective derived from *āgama* is *āgamika,* meaning 'religious', but it is not very idiomatic, nor is there an idiomatic word for 'secular'. These meanings are expressed by a periphrasis such as *āgama vaśayen,* 'by way of religion', 'to do with religion', and *melova vaśayen,* 'to do with this world'. Ames has written an interesting paper[3] in which he discusses Sinhalese religion in terms of Durkheim's categories of the profane and the sacred. He claims that these categories exist in the Sinhalese terms *laukika* and *lokottara.* It is perfectly true that these two words would be fair translations of 'profane' and 'sacred' respectively: *laukika* literally means 'of the world', *lokottara* 'above the world'. But these terms are pure Sanskrit, and purely learned; I have never heard them used in con-

[2]The word *samaya*, which is sometimes said to translate 'religion', is totally alien to the spoken language; anyway it implies heterodoxy, and is better translated as 'sect'.

[3]M.M. Ames, 'Magical-animism and Buddhism: A Structural Analysis of the Sinhalese Religious System', pp. 21–52 in E.B. Harper (ed.). *Religion in South Asia* (University of Washington Press, Seattle, 1964).

versation, and to most villagers they are not even intelligible. The sacred-profane dichotomy is not conceptualized by ordinary Sinhalese—which is far from saying that he does not know what is religion and what is not.

'Religion' is easy to translate into Sinhalese: 'belief' is a little harder. The verb 'to believe' or 'to believe in' is most often translatable by *adahanavā*. But *adahanavā* has a wider meaning. Geiger's *Etymological Glossary of the Sinhalese Language*[4] gives as translations 'believe in', 'trust in', 'worship'. This covers what seems like a whole range of religious attitudes. In the right context *adahanavā* does adequately translate 'to believe': *Buddhāgama adahanavā*—'(to) believe (in) the Buddhist religion'; *Buddhāgamaya ättamayi kiyalā adahanavā*—'(to) believe that the Buddhist religion is the very truth'. But unfortunately there is no noun which corresponds to *adahanavā* as 'belief' corresponds to 'to believe'. *Ädahīma* will sometimes do, but it is basically a verbal noun, 'believing'; it is awkward and unidiomatic in the plural. *Ädahilla* is a more literary word, and is specialized to denote not beliefs but acts of worship and devotion. Thus if one needs a noun to express 'beliefs' one will be forced to fall back on a more general word. *Adahasa* (which is etymologically unrelated to *adahanavā*) most usually means 'intention', but it can lose the volitional element and mean 'idea' or 'opinion'; *mataya,* slightly less colloquial, means 'opinion'. So in asking a Sinhalese his 'religious beliefs' a noun phrase would be *āgama gäna adahas,* or *āgama gäna mata,* 'opinions about religion'. But we can improve on this by turning to verbs. *Adahanavā* comes from Sanskrit *śraddhā*; the Pali noun *saddhā* derived from this appears frequently in the Pali Canon as a commendable quality; Sinhalese *śraddhāva,* locally pronounced *sardhāva,* is used in the same context. *Śraddhā/saddhā* has usually been translated 'faith'. But in her regrettably unpublished thesis for the University of Ceylon, 'The Role of the Miracle in Early Pali Literature', Dr. E. Ludowyk Gyömröi shows

[4]R.A.S., Ceylon Branch, Colombo, 1941.

that this translation is a bad one. Faith is a Christian concept; faith should lead to the acceptance of doctrines which have not been accepted by reason. Christianity admits that it contains doctrines which man will have to take on trust. But Buddhism makes no such admission: not only are all the truths it teaches intelligible to human beings, but doctrines should even be rejected if reason finds them wanting. *Saddhā* written in religious context might therefore be better translated 'confidence'; it is the confidence that Buddhist doctrine is correct, the confidence indeed that permits the issuing of such a challenge. It is trust, but not irrational or uncritical trust. Of course this is on the cognitive level; that the trust is in fact sometimes irrational or uncritical is not relevant here.

The point that emerges from this etymologizing is that Buddhism and Sinhalese do not make a distinction between faith, i.e. taking something on trust, on the one hand, and any other kind of belief on the other. The word semantically corresponding in Sinhalese to Pali *saddhā* is *viśvāsa,* which means 'trust' or 'confidence' in any context. It transforms into a verb by adding *karanavā*: *mā viśvāsa karanavā* '(to) trust me'. *Viśvāsa karanavā* can always function as a synonym of *adahanavā* in the sense of 'believe': *Buddhāgamaya viśvāsa karanavā*, '(to) believe in Buddhism'.[5] But unlike *adahanavā* it is not confined to religion: *Engelantē hima väṭenavā kiyā mama viśvāsa karanavā*—'I believe it snows in England.' Faith or 'fiduciary' belief is not distinguished from any other belief, however obviously rational. A better way, then, of asking a Sinhalese Buddhist about his religious beliefs will be, 'Āgama gäna monavāda adahanne?' or 'Āgama gäna mokadda viśvāsa karanne?'—'What do you believe about religion?'

Even these sentences, however, though linguistically

[5]The most idiomatic word for 'believe in' in such a context is *piḷigannavā*, which literally means 'accept': *mama Buddhāgamē piḷigannavā,* 'I believe in, accept Buddhism'. The verbal noun from this root, *piḷigänīma*, 'acceptance', will likewise be the best translation for 'belief' in such a context.

unexceptionable, still sound a trifle unusual. This is because culturally the only religious beliefs which matter are the true ones: Buddhist doctrine—*Dharma*. (This is the Sanskritic form; Pali *dhamma* and old Sinhalese *daham* or *dam* are confined to special contexts.)[6] *Dharma* can be and has been translated in a thousand ways: 'righteousness', 'truth', 'the Way', etc. It is best not translated at all. The scope of *dharma* will be explained in the next section; it does not cover all a Buddhist's beliefs, but if asked about his religious beliefs he will take the question to refer to *dharma*.

Let me interpose here that the above remarks are written from the point of view of one seeking to translate English concepts into Sinhalese; if we look at Sinhalese itself we must add an important item to our vocabulary. *Dharma* covers Buddhism's doctrinal side, its belief system. The normal Sinhalese word for Buddhism's institutional aspect, Buddhism as a spatio-temporal phenomenon, is *śāsanaya*. Thus *Buddhāgamaya, dharmaya*, and *śāsanaya* may all be translated into English as 'Buddhism'; and of these three words *Buddhāgamaya* is certainly the least frequent.

For an investigation of the belief system of a religion I have selected the term 'belief' as crucial in English, and the words *adahanavā, viśvāsaya*, and *dharmaya* (which is more limited in scope) as covering this semantic area in Sinhalese. Is it possible to decide on a similarly central concept for a religion's action system? I think English 'worship' and Sinhalese *vaňdinavā* will serve our purpose well: one is regularly used to translate the other, but their differences are again instructive.

Christianity is theocentric, Buddhism is not. Christianity is based on a concept of personality, that of Jesus Christ; for Buddhists the Buddha and his personality are extremely important, but their religion is based on a doctrine. There is a corresponding contrast between

[6]The actual village pronunciation of *dharma* is *daruma*; it is so spelt by uneducated people. Similarly, *karma* is pronounced *karuma*.

the attitude of Buddhists and Christians to the founders of their respective religions. Of course I am talking here of their cognitive attitudes, the attitudes they express in words; whether their affective attitudes, their true feelings, are similarly contrasted is a question which cannot be approached through language, but which I shall return to at the end of the next chapter. If a Christian were to be asked some such curiously vague question as, 'How do you stand to Jesus?', typical answers would be, 'I worship him', 'I adore him', 'I love him', 'I trust him'. The answers all speak as of someone still existent, which according to Christian doctrine Jesus is, in that he is God, who is eternal. That Jesus is God also makes it possible to say 'I believe in him'. No one will say 'I believe in Julius Caesar': he lived, is dead, and that is that. The Buddha is in the same case as Julius Caesar. We shall see that affectively he may be something more; but cognitively he is a dead man. The most we normally do for a dead man is to revere his memory, and that is just how Buddhists, if asked, claim that they view the Buddha. Perhaps they do love him in the way that Christians love Jesus Christ; but they never say so. The nearest they get to it is taking joy (*prīti*) in contemplation of the Buddha or in making offerings before his relics; but these are still the joys of pleasant thoughts, or even, as I was told, the pleasure of looking at the beautiful flowers which are being offered.

The typical verb for a Buddhist's attitude to the Buddha is *vaňdinavā*. In Ceylon this is taken as an exact translation of 'worship', which can be most misleading.[7]

[7]To illustrate in lighter vein the confusion about 'worship' explained below I reproduce in its entirety a news item from the *Weekly Times* of Ceylon dated 26 August 1966, which reached me as I was writing this chapter.

MMC WON'T 'WORSHIP' MAYOR

Kurunegala, Aug. 21.

At the monthly general meeting of the Kurunegala Municipal Council, presided over by the Deputy Mayor, Mr. Noel de S. Seneviratne, Mr. A.H. Weerasinghe said that he was not prepared to address the Mayor as 'Your Worship' as he had not worshipped any mortal.

He said he would address the Mayor as 'Your Lordship' or 'Your

The verb has two meanings, a physical gesture and a mental attitude. In the first place it denotes *any* respectful gesture of salutation. The least such gesture is merely to place the palms together in the Indian gesture called in Sanskrit *añjali*, which is like the Christian gesture of prayer. There are even gradations in the position of the hands—the higher the hands the greater the respect. Before a superior this is accompanied by bowing the head or the body, squatting or kneeling. When kneeling one may unclasp the hands for a moment and bend one's forehead to touch the ground, or the foot of the person saluted. Complete prostration I never saw practised by a Sinhalese, but it is used by Tamils before their gods, and gets the same name in Sinhalese. *Vaňdinavā* is the name of such a gesture in any context. Applied to the mental attitude which is obviously supposed to correspond to this physical gesture, namely reverence, the word is strictly religious: to use it of an attitude towards a layman is extreme, and clearly metaphorical. Accordingly the least misleading interpretation of the Buddhist's claim that he *vaňdinavā* is to say that he 'reveres' the Lord Buddha, and that when he is in a temple or in front of an image in his own home he behaves accordingly.

I wrote towards the end of the previous chapter of the influence of the West on Buddhism. Those remarks supplied the historical, the above lines the conceptual background to the curious judgements on Buddhism which were made to me by some of those people, even in the village, whose education had brought them in touch with western thought. I mention these judgements here to contrast them with the traditional attitudes. The western misunderstanding of Buddhism as atheistic explains the statement (in English) of a Sinhalese estate clerk that Buddhism is 'not a religion but a practice'. Later in my stay the news

Honour' but not as 'Your Worship'.

The Deputy Mayor: 'You may address the Mayor in any form in keeping with the dignity of the house. 'Your Worship' means a form of respect to the office and also does not mean that one is expected to worship the Mayor.'

that Buddhism is not a religion reached almost every villager, many for the first time. The Ministry of Education published a new primer for teaching Buddhism in schools,[8] intended for study by six-year-olds, no doubt the first book in a projected series. In the first paragraph of the introduction occurs the sentence, 'The Buddhist religion is not a religion' ('Buddhāgamaya āgamayek no vē'). This is immediately amplified: 'In the Buddhist religion there is no religion limited to offerings and devotions. The Buddhist religion[9] is a way of life.' ('Puda pūjā, ädahilivalaṭa sīmā vū āgamayek Buddhāgamayē näta. Buddhāgamaya jīvana kramayeki.') Didactically this may be admirable, but the amplification was not enough to avert attention and wrath from the simple statement that Buddhism is not a religion, a statement which through the very exigencies of the Sinhalese language stands in a self-contradictory form! There was a political storm: the Marxists who were in the coalition government had obviously infiltrated the Ministry of Education; this was part of their campaign to abolish Buddhism. Some of those who started these charges may have been disingenuous, but the Sinhalese villagers who heard them may be forgiven if not only the six-year-olds were unable to grasp the sophisticated claim that their religion was no religion.

The youngest monk in Mīgala temple was in much the same current of opinion as the writers of the textbook. (The fact that the monk considered himself a Marxist, however little he knew about Marxism, suggests that the political charges against the textbook may not have been quite groundless.) This monk had spent the last ten years of his life being educated in the Low Country, and had just got his B.A. from one of the two monastic universities near Colombo. During these ten years he had never returned to the village for more than a few days. Intel-

[8] *Buddhadharmaya. Mul pota* (Education Dept., Colombo, 1965).

[9] The word which I translate three times as 'The Buddhist religion' is more neatly rendered 'Buddhism'. My translation is literal to serve the point I am making.

lectually he no longer had anything in common with the villagers or with his two elder colleagues; when I appeared he seized me like a vulture swooping on a lump of carrion. It was not so much that I was a link with the outside world: his intercourse with me was his chance to demonstrate his superiority, while to me he could air his contempt for his surroundings. One day I appeared with a small book, *Bauddha Ädahilla* ('Buddhist Devotion'), a religious pocket book so popular that in its various editions it must have reached the majority of the literate Buddhist public, at least among the middle classes. It contains all the Pali verses which a layman is supposed to know or need, with Sinhalese translations and explanations.[10] I asked him if he had read it. He told me with great emphasis that he had never even looked at it. That was all just *viśvāsaya*; true Buddhism was the *darśanē*—philosophy. The young monk later told me that all the worshipping, etc.—what might be summed up as 'popular Buddhism'—was a Mahāyāna accretion. After six months he had made himself so unpopular—not through his views on religion, which he prudently kept to himself, but by his arrogant and insolent behaviour—that he was more or less forced to leave the village and return to Colombo.

Warned by his fate, let us approach the subject through the categories of the villagers themselves. To give a succinct account of an interlocking system is difficult. I shall try to summarize very briefly what classes of Buddhists there are and what they believe. I shall conclude the chapter with a general description of the physical context of village Buddhism, namely the temple. In subsequent chapters I shall expand on details of this summary.

The most frequent religious act of Buddhists is the recitation of a few lines in Pali. Many Buddhists recite them daily in private; their recitation begins, and often punctuates, every public religious occasion. Here they are,

[10]The table of contents of my copy of *Bauddha Ädahilla* is reproduced in the Appendix. It is edited by K. Ñāṇavimala Thero (Gunasena, Colombo, 1955).

with approximate translation.

Namo tassa Bhagavato arahato sammā sambuddhassa.
Worship to the Blessed *arhat*[11] truly fully enlightened.
(Three times.)

Buddhaṃ saraṇaṃ gacchāmi.
I go to the Buddha for refuge.

Dhammaṃ saraṇaṃ gacchāmi.
I go to the Doctrine for refuge.

Sanghaṃ saraṇaṃ gacchāmi.
I go to the Order for refuge.

Dutiyaṃ pi Buddhaṃ saraṇaṃ gacchāmi.
And a second time I go to the Buddha for refuge.

Dutiyaṃ pi Dhammaṃ saraṇaṃ gacchāmi.
And a second time I go to the Doctrine for refuge.

Dutiyaṃ pi Sanghaṃ saraṇaṃ gacchāmi.
And a second time I go to the Order for refuge.

Tatiyaṃ pi Buddhaṃ saraṇaṃ gacchāmi.
And a third time I go to the Buddha for refuge.

Tatiyaṃ pi Dhammaṃ saraṇaṃ gacchāmi.
And a third time I go to the Doctrine for refuge.

Tatiyaṃ pi Sanghaṃ saraṇaṃ gacchāmi.
And a third time I go to the Order for refuge.

Pānātipātā veramaṇī sikkhāpadaṃ samādiyāmi.
I undertake the precept to abstain from taking life.

Adinnādānā veramaṇī sikkhāpadaṃ samādiyāmi.
I undertake the precept to abstain from taking what is not given.

Kāmesu micchācārā veramaṇī sikkhāpadaṃ samādiyāmi.
I undertake the precept to abstain from wrong conduct in sexual desires.

[11] *Arhat* is a Buddhist technical term meaning any enlightened person.

Musāvādā veramaṇī sikkhāpadaṃ samādiyāmi.
I undertake the precept to abstain from telling lies.

Surāmeraya-majja-ppamāda-ṭṭhānā veramaṇī sikkhāpadaṃ samādiyāmi.
I undertake the precept to abstain from intoxicating liquors which occasion heedlessness.

The first line is a salutation to the Buddha. The next nine lines are the Three Refuges (*tisaraṇa*) thrice repeated. The last five lines are the Five Precepts (*pan sil*).

A person who takes the Three Refuges and Five Precepts is thereby a Buddhist layman. There is no ceremony for conversion to Buddhism beyond the recital of these lines, so anyone who says these words and means them can rightly call himself a Buddhist. To go so far and then to keep the precepts is considered sufficient for great religious progress. A Buddhist layman is called an *upāsaka* (feminine: *upāsikā*)—at least in religious discourse; in lay idiom the term is generally reserved for people of notable piety. The Five Precepts should be recited daily (at least), and kept always.

The status of *upāsaka* denotes a religious attitude, a certain relationship to the Dhamma. An *upāsaka* is also supposed to support those of higher religious status than himself (principally monks), and by virtue of this relationship to the Sangha he is called a *dāyaka* ('giver'). This sounds like a function. It is possible for a *dāyaka* not to be an *upāsaka* (i.e. for a non-Buddhist to make gifts to monks, etc.), though of course this is not normally envisaged. However, *dāyaka* is also a status. When an English parson would refer to his 'parishioners', a monk calls the laymen in his village not *upāsakayō* but *dāyakayō*.

Buddhists have the custom (doubtless pre-Buddhistic) that certain days are holier than the rest. These days, called *poya* days, are the quarter days of the lunar month: full moon, no moon, half moon. They are holy in that order; all the crucial events in the Buddha's life are believed to have happened on full moon days. Theoretically on any day, but by custom only on *poya* days, a layman may take the Eight Precepts (*aṭa sil*). These are the Five Precepts with the third changed and three added. The third becomes:

Abrahmacariyā veramaṇī sikkhāpadaṃ samādiyāmi.
I undertake the precept to abstain from unchastity.

This means giving up all sexual activity. The remaining three are:

Vikāla-bhojanā veramaṇī sikkhāpadaṃ samādiyāmi.
I undertake the precept to abstain from eating at the wrong time.

Nacca-gīta-vādita-visūka-dassana-mālā-gandha-vilepana-dhāraṇa-maṇḍana-vibhūsana-ṭṭhānā veramaṇī sikkhāpadaṃ samādiyāmi.
I undertake the precept to abstain from seeing dancing, music vocal and instrumental, and shows; from wearing garlands, perfumes and unguents, from finery and adornment.

Uccāsayana-mahāsayanā veramaṇī sikkhāpadaṃ samādiyāmi.
I undertake the precept to abstain from high beds and big beds.

The sixth precept means no solid food after midday. The seventh means dressing in plain white, with no more ornament than maybe a rosary of 108 brown beads as a necklace. The eighth means sitting or lying only on mats on the ground. Traditionally it has been customary only for elderly people to take the Eight Precepts, except perhaps once a year at Wesak, the full moon in May, the anniversary of the Buddha's birth, Enlightenment, and death. Hence those laymen taking the Eight Precepts are commonly known as 'laywoman mummy' and 'layman daddy'—*upāsikammā* and *upāsakappucci* were the local terms.

There is a further stage possible for laymen: the Ten Precepts (*dasa sil*). These ten are formed by splitting the seventh into two, and adding

Jātarūpa-rajata-paṭiggahanā veramaṇī sikkhāpadaṃ samādiyāmi.

I undertake the precept to abstain from accepting gold or silver.

In fact, although to do so is theoretically possible, no one takes the Ten Precepts for a limited period of time. They involve the same abstentions as those practised by the clergy, so men of such piety are likely to enter the Order, unless they are too old to make the break. Laymen (male) who take the Ten Precepts (*dasa sil upāsakayō*) wear white. They may be 'home-dwelling' (*gedara inna* or *gṛhastha*) or 'homeless' (*anagārika*). Anagārika Dharmapāla (see p. 64) was a 'homeless' layman, but I have never heard of a villager's becoming one. Nor did I meet even a *gṛhastha dasa sil upāsaka*, but I heard of two in my area, probably elderly widowers. On the other hand, the Order of nuns (*bhikṣuṇī sangha*) being extinct, to take the Ten Precepts is the highest religious status a woman can attain. Such women shave their heads and wear yellow, sometimes (informally) white. There are a few urban communities of them, but in villages they are infrequent and usually solitary. On the edge of Mīgala were two, who lived in adjacent caves. Though one of them was not old, they were known as *upāsaka māṇiyō*, *māṇiyō* being an extremely honorific word for 'mother'. Such ladies, like monks and Dharmapāla, renounce their lay names and take Pali names, to which they add the title *sil māṇiyō*.

On entering the Order (*mahaṇa vīma*) one becomes a novice. Novices are usually boys, and known as 'little monks' (*poḍi hāmuduruvō* or *puñci hāmuduruvō*).[12] A novice has to take and keep the same Ten Precepts. Even a monk has to do no more: he has to submit to 227 rules, but these rules are an elaboration, not an extension, of the precepts, and their detailed application to the life of a monk. Monastic life has its duties and even its rites, but most of these can be avoided by becoming a hermit; in the way of morality the Ten Precepts sum up all that is asked of a Buddhist. Monks and novices wear robes of some yellow

[12]The Pali word for novice, *sāmaṇera*, is occasionally used in a formal context. *Poḍi hāmuduruvō*, which is of course informal, can also refer to a junior monk.

or orange (no significance attaches to the shade). There are various words for monk, most of which have the honorific ending *vahansē*—literally 'sandal-shadow', but the meaning has been forgotten. Related to the Pali *bhikkhu* is *bhikṣunvahansē*. A rather surprising word for 'monk' is *sanghayā* (± *vahansē*), which in form is merely Sinhalese for *sangha*, the Order, which indeed is its usual meaning in the literary language. But the common words in the village, for both reference and address,[13] are *svāminvahansē* and *hāmuduruvō*, both meaning 'lord', but no longer used to denote temporal power.

The objects of the Three Refuges are the Three Jewels (*triratna, teruvan*): most people asked to explain Buddhism (*Buddhāgama*) would begin here. The Buddha is the founder of the religion, the Dharma is the truth he discovered, the Sangha is the vehicle for preserving and propagating that truth.

For the moment the Buddha and the Sangha require no further explanation than to say that doctrine views the Buddha as a human being who is now dead, but whose relics may be venerated, and the Sangha as other human beings who are supposed to emulate him and are venerated for this reason. But the Dharma must be further discussed. I have said that if you ask a Buddhist his religious beliefs he will assume you are talking of Dharma. But these beliefs operate in a context of other beliefs, of more basic assumptions. This is true both logically and historically: the Buddha grew up in a society dominated (ideologically) by brahmins and accepted many of their assumptions. A few words about these assumptions are necessary.

The universe is full of living beings, in hierarchically ordered strata. Men are somewhere in the middle (with their own hierarchically ordered strata—castes). Above them are various classes of gods and spirits, below them are animals, ghosts, and demons. Above this world are heavens,

[13] These are really the same, as polite address is in the third person. I disregard the vocative forms which are sometimes used.

below this world are hells. By and large, power, well-being and length of life increase as one goes up the scale. So do the power and inclination to do good. But at all levels there is death, the ineluctable reminder of the unsatisfactoriness of life. Death supplies the mobility between the different levels. Everywhere, constantly, are death and rebirth. One's station at birth is determined by *karma*. *Karma* is a Sanskrit word simply meaning 'action', but it has acquired this technical sense. It is the principle of 'Be done by as you did'; a good action will improve your station, a bad action depress it. One's *karma* may affect one's fortunes in other ways besides one's station at birth, but this is its most important effect. All this is accepted by all kinds of Hindus and by Jains—by all the major Indian religious systems. However, Buddhism was the first system completely to ethicize the concept. For Buddhists *karma* consists solely of actions morally good or bad, not of other actions such as ritual.

Karma is the most powerful, large-scale system of causation. (Buddhists do not believe that any creature, however exalted, has the power to override *karma*.) Operating within this system are others, which affect the details of specifically human affairs. Such systems are astrology and the (free-will) activities of supernaturals. These or similar systems are again accepted, with or without inconsistency, by the other major Indian systems. In Sinhalese Buddhist ideology these systems fit into each other without inconsistency, as will be explained in Chapter 4.

The belief system described so far is not *Dharma*; it is just the outline of a cognitive map of the universe, a map which the Buddha and his followers have not called in question. Taking all this for granted, the Buddha saw the truth—the Dharma.

In one formulation there are Four Noble Truths. They are

(1) Unhappiness.
(2) The arising of unhappiness.
(3) The destruction of unhappiness.

(4) The path leading to the destruction of unhappiness.

(1) The word I have translated as unhappiness is Pali *dukkha*, Sanskrit *duḥkha*, Sinhalese *duka*. *Dukkha* notoriously lacks an English equivalent, though the concept is not obscure. It is simply the opposite of *sukha* (in Sinhalese of *säpa*), which means 'well-being'. Unfortunately 'ill-being' is not an English locution. Translators have used 'suffering', 'unsatisfactoriness', etc. 'Frustration' would be philosophically accurate, but sounds too petty. 'Unhappiness' is also inadequate because it is only mental, not physical. Armed with this apology, I shall use *dukkha*.

In the Buddha story *dukkha* is symbolized by an aged man, a sick man, and a corpse. But it is far wider than the positive ills of disease and death. It is anything that crosses us, it is not getting what we want. It even exists for the normally content, because he wants to go on living, but must face the prospect of death. Death shows that all goods are impermanent (*anicca*). In this sense *dukkha* exists even in the highest heaven and for the greatest god. The Sinhalese often say 'jīvitē dukayi'—'life is suffering' or just 'life is sad'.

(2) *Dukkha* exists because of desire: it is desire's corollary. If we have no wants we shall suffer no disappointments. There are many words in Pali for this desire: a common one is *taṇhā*—thirst. The usual one in Sinhalese is *āsāva*. This derives from Sanskrit *āśā*, which is often translated 'hope'. It is desire, notably the desire for life, which gives the impetus for rebirth.

(3) The destruction of unhappiness is consequently the destruction of desire. Those who cease to desire life will not be reborn, and experience no more *dukkha*. They, and they alone, experience liberation (*mokṣa*) from the wheel of rebirth, i.e. phenomenal existence (*saṃsāra*), and attain *nirvāṇa*. Etymologically *nirvāṇa* means 'blowing out'. It is indescribable, being beyond the realm of words, which describe the world we know; it is defined negatively. The Sinhalese usually talk of 'seeing' or 'gaining' *nirvāṇa* (*ni-*

van dakinavā or *labanavā*); it is an intuition, a sudden awareness, a mystical state. Enlightenment comes during the course of a lifetime; one who has it is an *arhat* (Sinhalese *rahat*, respectfully *rahatanvahansē*). An *arhat* lives out the fated span of his physical life; its end is called *parinirvāṇa* (Sinhalese *pirinivan*).[14]

(4) The path leading to the destruction of unhappiness is the Noble Eight-fold Path. Rough translations of its eight constituents are 1. Right views. 2. Right resolve. 3. Right speech. 4. Right action. 5. Right livelihood. 6. Right effort. 7. Right mindfulness. 8. Right meditation. These eight are often summarized as *sīla, samādhi, paññā*. *Sīla* (morality) covers nos. 3–5; *samādhi* (meditation) nos. 6-8; *paññā* (wisdom) nos. 1 and 2.[15] Each of these three is to some extent a prerequisite for the next. Nos. 1 and 2 come both at the beginning and at the end: intelligence and motivation are needed to make a start; at the end they ripen to the true wisdom of Enlightenment.

The Four Noble Truths and the Noble Eight-fold Path are described in the Buddha's first sermon.[16] This short text makes one other point, with which indeed it begins. Because to see the Truth one must steer between indulgence and mortification of the senses, Buddhism is the Middle Path.

The path described by Buddhist doctrine is ethical, intellectual, and mystical. The innovations of the Dharma are very simple, and consist mainly of a recipe for action. This is easy to grasp. None of the doctrines I have written of so far would be unfamiliar to a villager. He could probably not list the Four Noble Truths or the constituents of the Noble Eight-fold Path; he might not even know the titles of the doctrines. But the substance of the argument he would know; indeed he could probably express most of

[14]In Pali literature *parinibbāna* is sometimes a synonym of *nibbāna* (technically called *sa-upādi-sesa*); but modern Sinhalese usage, to which I have conformed, confines it to the death of an *arhat* (technically *an-upādi-sesa*).

[15]*M.N.*, I, 301.

[16]*Dhammacakkappavattana Sutta, S.N.*, V, 420.

it himself if occasion arose. If asked to describe his religion he will mention most of what I have mentioned, from the Three Jewels on, probably with some more detail on the Buddha and on good and bad deeds. The Buddha I shall deal with in the next chapter. Before I say more on good and bad deeds there is one metaphysical question to be disposed of. It is too difficult for many villagers to hold views on it, but it is a necessary logical link for a basic understanding of Theravāda doctrine, so I had better dispose of it here.

What is it that transmigrates? Buddhist philosophy (*abhidhamma*) revolves round *anicca, dukkha*, and *anatta*, which are said to be three facets of the one truth. *Dukkha* and *anicca* I mentioned above under the first Noble Truth. *Anatta* is Pali for 'non-self'. In philosophy it came to be applied to everything, as a denial of essence, but originally it was merely a denial of the existence of a soul, an immortal part in living beings. Theravāda Buddhism is *anātmavāda*—the doctrine of no soul; this much is known to innumerable people who could not explain it. Most monks, however, can explain that *ātman*, self, is merely the name of an aggregate of mind and body which dissolves at death; it has no independent existence. What survives is *karma*, the effect of actions. If I may supply my own illustration, every act for good or ill is like a boomerang, which comes back at you. Whether you throw the boomerang is a matter of free will, but once it is thrown consequences must follow. Buddhist doctrine holds that if I die before the boomerang gets back someone else will have been born in my place and reap those consequences; moreover the nature of that someone is conditioned by what I was.

Plainly this is a rather subtle and difficult doctrine. The Buddha himself is supposed to have realized that his teaching was 'against the current'.[17] Even so, this doctrine understood only by the few has permeated the language. Sinhalese has no word for soul, in the sense of an immortal

[17] For references see W. Rahula, *What the Buddha Taught* (Gordon Fraser, Bedford, 2nd ed., 1967), p. 52.

part or adjunct of a human being. The Sanskritic word *ātma* is still in use, but it has acquired the meaning of 'life-span'. '[I shall not do it] in this life'—'mē ātmē dī'. '[We met] in a previous life'—'issara ātme dī'.

I asked the incumbent of Mīgala temple about *ātma* and rebirth. We have no *ātma*, he said, because *ātma* implies something changeless, and we change all the time. Even if we become gods we shall still be constituted of the five components (*skandhas*); we shall have lost only the name of man (*mānuṣyanāma*). We use the word *ātmē*, and talk as if it existed, for convenience (*pahasu piṇisa*). This is the realm of conventional truth (*sammuti satya*); ultimate truth is different ('paramārtha satya venayi'). The being who is born is neither the same as, nor different from, the one who died: he quoted the Pali 'Na ca so, na ca anyo' ('Both not he and not another'). The relation is like that between caterpillar and butterfly.

The doctrine of no-soul, *anātmavāda*, is canonical according to the interpretation of Buddhaghosa.[18]

But does not death nevertheless mark a decisive break? The doctrinal answer is no: our thought and even our bodies are changing at every moment. The element of continuity is precisely *karma*, the force of past actions; *karma* not merely binds one life to the next, but one collection

[18]In the Canon the *locus classicus* is the *Anattalakkhaṇa Sutta*, *S.N.*, III, 66. It is believed that it was Buddha's second sermon and that on hearing it his first five disciples attained enlightenment. On *anātmavāda* and the question of what transmigrates see Thomas, *Buddhist Thought*, pp. 98–106. In an attempt to avoid technicalities and give a clear picture I have slightly over-simplified the evidence there collected. In doing so I am following a monk who told me that it is not I who am reborn, but someone else (*vena kenek*) with my *karma*. For a full and beautifully lucid exposition of *anatta* see Chapter VI (pp. 51–66) in Rahula's *What the Buddha Taught*. Rahula, a Sinhalese monk, combines the authenticity of indigenous tradition with scholarship matured at universities both East and West. He deals specifically with the arguments of modern scholars who claim that Theravādin tradition has perverted the Buddha's meaning. I myself find this claim that on so essential a point the Buddha has been misunderstood by all his followers somewhat 'against the current'.

of the *skandhas* to the collection existing in the next moment. Just as a man can remember what he did yesterday, he can, with training, remember what he did in a former life; the difference is merely one of degree.

Although there were probably not more than half a dozen monks in my area who could have expounded the argument stated in the previous paragraph, I am sure all would have assented to it. It is the doctrinal position which everyone claims to accept, however little they are able to articulate it. On the other hand, people certainly talk as if they conceived a series of lives in terms of survival of the personality; terms such as 'My next life', sentiments such as 'We must have met in a former life', are freely expressed. In other words, a Buddhist seems to think of rebirth in very much the way that the concept first appears to a westerner brought up with the idea of a soul which survives death. Is the Buddhist then not being logically inconsistent? I think not. If it is merely conventional truth (*sammuti satya*) to talk of 'I' when in reality (*paramārtha vaśayen*) I am nothing but a series of groups (*skandhas*) strung together on the string of *karma*, why should it not be equally permissible to use convention to talk of 'my next life'? Logical inconsistency can only arise between cognitive positions; on the cognitive level the Buddhist is being consistent.

Where the clash may, and I think does, come is between the cognitive and the affective level. Despite the doctrine that we are but a series of groups connected by actions, people do in fact think of themselves as having a more or less stable and concrete existence. From this it is a short step to conceiving this existence as extending beyond death. That people affectively believe that *they* will survive death and be reborn cannot, by the nature of what I called affective beliefs, be demonstrated directly; but I think it can be inferred from other statements and actions, especially those discussed in Chapter 5. Moreover, I think that this affective belief in personal survival, clashing with the cognitive belief in merely karmic survival, is the basis for a whole system of affective religion which diverges from official doctrine. I shall return to this in my last chapter.

It would have been misleading to leave the impression, even in a summary, that villagers grasp all the subtleties of orthodox doctrine on *karma* and rebirth. It would be equally misleading to leave the impression that *nirvāṇa* is their immediate religious goal. I doubt whether this would be true of anyone I met, cleric or lay. Whether interested in *nirvāṇa* as an ultimate goal or not, people set their sights on whatever they consider the most desirable rebirth. What makes for a good rebirth is merit (*pin*), and what makes for a bad rebirth is demerit (*pav*). *Pav* is usually translated 'sin', but 'demerit' brings out its neat opposition to *pin*. *Pin* and *pav* are conceptualized as quantifiable and (in a sense—see Chapter 5) transferable. If you ask a villager how he acquires *pin* or *pav* the commonest answer will be, by keeping or breaking the Five Precepts. The Five Precepts are, however, negative: there is a list of Ten Good Deeds, which is not canonical, but widely influential. In an unmethodical way this list subsumes the precepts and includes all possible ways of earning *pin*. The Ten Good Deeds (*dasa kusala karma*) are listed in a Pali stanza:

Dānaṃ sīlañ ca bhāvanā
Patti pattānumodanā
Veyyāvacca apacāyañ ca
Desanā suti diṭṭhiju.[19]

These were paraphrased for me by a monk as:

Giving (material), keeping morality (i.e. the precepts), meditating, rejoicing in (another's) merit, giving (transferring) merit, giving service, showing respect, preaching, listening to preaching, right beliefs (*samyak dṛṣṭiya—viśvās-*

[19] A less common version of the second half of this stanza runs

Desanā savaṇaṃ pūjā
Veyyavaccaṃ pasaṃsanā.

Savaṇaṃ = *suti*; *pūjā* means acts of (ritual) worship; *pasaṃsanā* means praising.

aya). In an admirable article[20] J. F. Dickson gives a succinct explanation (pp. 203–7) of each of these terms; I could not improve on his account, and refer to it the reader who would like a fuller preliminary description before I deal in Chapters 5 and 6 with specific problems arising from the list. The term *pinkama* literally means 'act of merit', and so could apply to any item in this list; however, as Dickson remarks (p. 207), idiomatically the term is only applied to the outward manifestation of merit-earning—the public, not the private event. Canonical Buddhism is a religion for the individual: excepting only a few simple ceremonies for monks it neither prescribes nor contains any ritual. From the beginning there were inevitably religious occasions of a public nature, i.e. involving more than one person: the two typical occasions are feeding monks and preaching, which very often go together. No ritual was laid down for these occasions, but already in the Canon, which after all consists mainly of sermons and is full of invitations to meals, they are described in uniform language and the procedure is plainly standardized. In modern Ceylon any public Buddhist occasion is called a *pinkama*. The typical *pinkam* are still feeding monks (*dānē*—the word literally means 'giving' but has become a technical term) and preaching (*baṇa*), plus one related to *baṇa*, a particular kind of recitation of sacred texts called *pirit*. The morning meal is called *hīl dānē*, the (main) midday meal *daval dānē*, the evening snack *gilampasa dānē*. *Hīl dānē* should be given at about 7 a.m., *daval dānē* at about 11.30 (to be

[20]'Notes Illustrative of Buddhism as the Daily Religion of the Buddhists of Ceylon, and Some Account of their Ceremonies before and after Death' *J.R.A.S.* (Ceylon Branch), vol. VIII, no. 29, 1884, pp. 203–36. (The pagination is corrected by an erratum slip to pp. 297–330, which is how it appears in the table of contents, but to minimize confusion I cite the page references as printed.) Though there are a few points at which Dickson seems to me to be describing ideal rather than actual ceremonies, I find his article so good that I have hardly touched upon the things he has already described, and hope that his work can be read as a complement to mine. He is unique among ethnographers of Sinhalese Buddhism in reproducing in full (with English translations) the Pali texts used in the ceremonies he describes.

over by noon), and *gilampasa* normally between 5 and 6, but *gilampasa* may also be served just before the beginning of a *pinkama* in the early part of the night. For a *dānē* or *baṇa* the ritual is usually scarcely more elaborate than in canonical times. There are, however, other *pinkam*, of various degrees of canonical authenticity, and indeed villagers apply the term to any public activity in which monks take part: when just before the national election sixty monks gathered at Mīgala temple and walked in procession to the town council grounds to hold a political meeting, this was a *pinkama* too.

Most big *pinkam* take place at the temple, and in order to give a general picture of what a *pinkama* involves I shall conclude this outline with a brief description of the physical setting of Sinhalese Buddhism. Most villages—and the proportion is increasing—contain what, following Ceylonese practice, I call a temple. The language of Christian culture is again misleading. The essential of a Buddhist temple, the fact by virtue of which it is in use, is that one or more monks live there. The building in which the monks live, which is normally an ordinary bungalow like a layman's, is called a *pansala*. Typically a temple consists of a group of features, but any or all of these features may be absent except the *pansala*. When there is nothing but a *pansala*, which in practice means that the temple is new or inhabited only part-time, the temple as a whole is called an *āvāsaya;* otherwise, i.e. normally, it is called a *vihāraya*. The properly equipped temple of a certain village, e.g. Mīgala, is in conversation always referred to as, e.g. *Mīgala vihāraya*. Formally, however, the *vihāraya* usually has some given Sanskrit name, and this almost invariably ends in *ārāmaya:* e.g. 'Śrī Saddharmārāmaya'—'The Blessed Temple of the True Doctrine'. The average number of monks in a temple in the Mīgala area is two, though single monks are very frequent. There are usually anything up to four novices, but they spend most of their time away at school. (An educational establishment for monks is called a *piriveṇa*.) A temple servant (*äbittayā*) also often lives in the *pansala*.

The principal common features of a *vihāraya*, besides the *pansala*, are: a building containing religious art, including at least one sculpture of the Buddha; a peepal or sacred fig tree, locally known as a Bo tree; a relic mound, in English usually called a stupa; a preaching hall; and a building for monks to perform their communal rites (*vinayakam*). Of these only the first two were virtually constant features in the area where I worked, though the third, the stupa, an almost invariable feature of Low Country temples, was also very common. The first contains, the second and third are themselves objects of veneration. The building containing religious art (for which I can find no better English than the awkward locution 'image-house', a literal translation of *paṭimāghara*, its Pali name) is, confusingly, also called a *vihāraya*, or *vihāragedara* or *vihāragē* (*gedara* and *gē* are usually interchangeable synonyms meaning 'house'). It is of varying size, ornamentation and complexity. A Buddha image, often over lifesize and invariably seated or lying, is opposite the entrance door of the innermost shrine, and before it is always some kind of ledge or table on which offerings, principally flowers, can be laid. In theory, and usually in practice, the image contains a relic. Anyone who comes to the temple for religious purposes comes to pay his respects before this image. There are other statues, usually including Buddhas and gods, and the walls are painted with similar figures and with decorations. Almost invariably the entrance to the *vihāragedara* or to the shrine room (sometimes to both), and often the main Buddha image too, is framed by a *makara toraṇa* ('sea-monster arch'), a traditional arrangement of highly stylized motifs surmounted by a monster's head, *en face*, with mouth agape.[21] The

[21]On the form of the *makara* see A.K. Coomaraswamy, *Mediaeval Sinhalese Art* (no publisher, Broad Campden, 1908), p. 84. A *makara toraṇa* is illustrated in plate VIIIA (not VIIA, as stated in the text) of the same work. For a discussion in a pan-Indian context hypothesizing the origins and symbolism of the main motifs involved, see F.D.K. Bosch, *The Golden Germ* (Mouton, The Hague, 1960). Bosch gives

Bo tree (*Bō gaha, Bōdhinvahansē*), is the kind of tree under which the Buddha attained Enlightenment (*bōdhi*, old Sinh. *bō*); moreover, many trees are claimed to be grown from cuttings of the Bo tree at Anurādhapura, which is itself grown, according to the *Mahāvaṃsa*, from a cutting of the original tree. It is usually surrounded by a parapet (*bämma*), which includes a ledge or altar (*mal āsana*) for offerings of flowers. Many of these trees are old and magnificent, and I suspect that often they have determined the situation of the temple.

The stupa has many names. *Stūpa* is itself Sanskrit. Old Sinhalese is *dāgaba* or *dāgäba*, which indicates precisely what it is, a 'relic-container'. Another old Sinhalese word, now confined to proper names, is *sǟya* (derived from *caitya)*. The words I found mostly used were *caitya*[22] and *vehera*. (*Vehera* is merely the old Sinhalese form of *vihāraya*, which is another specialization of this versatile word!) The stupa probably existed in India in pre-Buddhist times as a burial mound. When the Buddha died his relics were distributed and buried in such mounds, and it soon became the custom to build them for other holy monks (*arhats*) too.[23] In Ceylon they are invariably built of solid masonry (with a small sealed chamber in the centre for the relics), and their shape is standardized. On a base, usually circular or octagonal, rises a dome, topped by a cube (*haraskoṭuva*) from which rises a thin spire which is usually of bronze. Modern stupas do not approach the scale of the ruins of Anurādhapura and Poḷonnaruva; in villages they range from perhaps fifteen to forty feet in total height. By a stupa again it is usual to build at least

further bibliography on the *makara* in art in his footnote to p. 21.

[22] *Caitya* is a pre-Buddhist Sanskrit word. It derives from a Sanskrit root meaning 'to pile up', and its basic meaning is 'burial mound'. However, in old literature *caitya* (and its Pali equivalent *cetiya*) can refer to any sacred spot, such as a sacred tree. In Sinhalese the meaning of the word has again contracted, and it refers only to the stupa.

[23] This practice is obsolete, in that it is generally believed that there are no more *arhats*, but the tombs of monks, which contain their ashes, have the form of a small stupa.

one flower-altar.

The preaching hall (*baṇa maḍuva* or *baṇa gedara*) is a simple building, usually square with walls only to half height so that people outside can see and hear what is going on inside. The central part of the floor is slightly raised; here monks sit (though laymen may do so too), and the monk who is preaching has a special chair, or one covered with the richest cloth available.

The building for monastic ceremonies, called a *poya gedara*, may be of any sort, and often one of the other buildings is used for this purpose. Normally, a *poya gedara* is enclosed, as acts of the clergy are private.

Most buildings are washed white or blue, and red-tiled roofs are common. In the hill country most temple premises are on a series of terraces, surrounded by foliage, and during a *pinkama* people stream up and down the steps. Ideally at the temple they wear white, but many wear their ordinary clothes of any colour, the women usually bright. The monks wear their robes, which range from yellow through orange to red. The flower offerings and five-coloured Buddhist flags add to the gaiety. *Pinkam* are noisy; specialists provide a lot of drumming (on drums called *hēvisi* and *bera*) and playing on a piercing wind-instrument not unlike an oboe (called *horaṇāva*). Proceedings are punctuated by cries from the crowd of 'Sādhu', which means 'good' or 'holy', and is used rather like the Christian 'Amen' to express participation and assent, but it tends to come in a triple burst of 'Sādhu sādhu sāāā', which feels more cheerful, like 'Hip-hip-hooray'.

Both monks and the *vihāra* fixtures are treated with decorum, which is not the same as solemnity. The decorum extends to the treatment of certain other Buddhist objects. The preaching chair (*dharmāsana*) has just been mentioned. When preaching a monk has a special kind of fan (*vaṭāpata*) with a decorated handle, which he sometimes holds to conceal his face. When I was given such a fan and had it in my house the villagers insisted that it be placed high up, and did not like my wife to handle it. But an even more sacred object is a manuscript of a sacred text (*baṇa pota*). (By mass production printed books—and pictures—have been largely desacralized, though a village neighbour did put a tattered book of religious verse (*kavi*) which he lent us on the flower ledge just below the picture of the Buddha.) The times are past when, probably under Mahāyānist influence,[24] sacred texts inscribed on metal would be buried in stupas; but the palm leaf manuscripts are kept wrapped in rich cloths, and when they are taken out for *baṇa* or *pirit* they are borne, like relics, on a man's head.

The rest of this book will have little to say about communal worship, which is neither doctrinally nor behaviourally nearly as important in Buddhism as for instance in Christianity. Pilgrimages apart (see pp. 128–132), there is very little concerted action involved in Buddhist worship. Monks may organize committees to promote temple welfare, but even fund-raising tends to be *ad hoc*, and to most temples meals are supplied according to a roster of households only in the four months of the 'rainy season' of the liturgical calendar. The biggest effort of co-operation probably goes into supplying the food for a major *pinkama* at the temple; on such occasions huge pots of rice, innumerable curries, cakes, sweetmeats, and fruits are carried up to the temple, and there is vast waste, from which beggars profit. Then the temple is thronged with people, many of them eager to help serve the food, and several hundred people may take the Five Precepts, invite the gods to share their merit, and assent to the monk's wish that they should all be reborn in the time of the next Buddha, Maitrī, and under him realize *nirvāṇa*. On arrival most of these people went up to the *vihāra* with a few flowers and worshipped the main Buddha image, and maybe the Bo tree and *caitya* too, perhaps muttering a few Pali verses, or merely remaining squatting with hands folded to forehead and head bowed; after the *dānē* many of them evaporate before the sermon, and the congregation becomes even more predominantly feminine, though to be

[24] S. Paranavitana, 'Mahāyānism in Ceylon', pp. 44–5.

sure a few elderly men in white are always conspicuously zealous. Even on a major full-moon day I have not known more than a hundred people, or more than twenty adult males, to take the Eight Precepts and spend most of the day at the temple, repeating Pali verses after a monk early in the morning, hearing a sermon at midday and maybe again in the evening, and in between chatting or meditating by droning Pali verses over a rosary. In towns of course the pious bourgeoisie are more assiduous.

3

The Buddha

I. The Buddha's Biography

GOTAMA BUDDHA, under whose teaching (*śāsanē*) we live, was the twenty-fifth in the line of Buddhas.[1] The twenty-sixth will be Maitrī Buddha and we do not know who or how many will come after him. The first Buddha was called Dīpaṃkara, and it was on seeing him that our Buddha, who in that life was a young brahmin ascetic called Sumedha, made the vow that he too would become a Buddha. A being who makes such a vow is called a Bodhisattva (Sinh.: *Bōsat*). The 550 lives which our Buddha lived as a *Bōsat* before he was born as Gotama are the subject of the book of *Jātaka* stories. The introduction to this book is called the *Nidānakathā*. It begins with the story of Sumedha, and then gives the life of Gotama (his family name), both before enlightenment, when he was a prince called Siddhārtha (Sinh.: Siduhat), and the first two years after it, when he can properly be called the Buddha. The relationship of the *Nidānakathā* to other biographies of the Buddha, which are in Sanskrit or based on Sanskrit originals, was long in doubt. Recently Frauwallner has shown that all the biographies probably derive from a lost one composed little more than a century after the Buddha's death. Therefore, although nearly all current Sinhalese beliefs about the Buddha's biography are based on the *Nidānakathā* and closely related texts (see below, p. 118), the main points of the story are of extremely ancient origin.

Sinhalese Buddhists today say the same as the Canon. The Buddha was a man; his status was human, not divine. He was of course the best possible man in every respect,

[1]In theory the line of Buddhas has no known beginning or end. But in practice, as will appear, the Buddha Dīpaṃkara is traditionally reckoned as the first. Three Buddhas before Dīpaṃkara are named at *Buddhavaṃsa*, XXVII, 1 (p. 66), and *Nidānakathā*, v, 247 (*J.* I. 44) = *Madhuratthavilāsinī*, p. 131.

a man of superlatives: born in the best caste, living the most comfortable life, capable by destiny and talent of ruling the world as a temporal monarch. He had a wife and son. By leaving all this he therefore made the greatest possible renunciation. In his search for the truth he then underwent the most extreme austerities. Even after his Enlightenment he was just a man. It is true that he performed some miracles, or rather wonders (for miracles imply the humanly impossible), and had marvellous powers; but these wonders are effected by the power of truth, the truth which it is open to any man to realize, and the powers likewise are those of any *arhat*—indeed some of the more trivial ones, such as levitation, may be attained by meditation even before the final goal of *nirvāṇa* has been reached.

Siddhārtha was 29 when he renounced the world. He spent six years as an ascetic, seeking the truth, and found it at the age of 35. After seeing *nirvāṇa* he spent forty-five years helping others to the same realization, and entered *parinirvāṇa* when he was 80. Since then he is dead. Being dead he is of course powerless for good or ill. He cannot hear prayers or aid supplicants. Moreover, even if he could it would not help very much. The Buddha was concerned only with spiritual goods, salvation; worldly goods he renounced. Each man has to work out his own salvation by his own effort. Man is a free agent, and makes his own *karma*, which determines where he will be reborn. The important things are not in the gift of any power in the world—except the free will of the individual himself. In the Canon's account of the Buddha's last days[2] we read the Buddha saying that one should rely only on oneself, only on the Dhamma;[3] his last words were, 'Compounded things by their nature decay; be attentive in your efforts.'[4]

This is the cognitive position, which is not affected by a slight over-simplification which I have made. Bud-

[2] *Mahāparinibbāna Sutta* (*Sutta* 16). *D.N.*, II.
[3] *D.N.*, II, 100.
[4] *D.N.*, II, 156.

dha means 'enlightened' in Sanskrit and Pali, so strictly speaking anyone who has seen *nirvāṇa* is a Buddha. A monk explained to me that strictly there are three kinds of Buddhas. Those usually referred to as Buddhas, the twenty-five plus, are *samyak sambuddha*, 'truly fully enlightened'. (Recall the formula: *Namo tassa Bhagavato arahato sammā sambuddhassa.*) They are *lokottara*, supramundane. Of course strictly speaking all Buddhas are *ipso facto lokottara*, having risen above the world of transmigration ('saṃsāra lōken uttara velā'), but by usage (*vyavahāra*) only the *samyak sambuddha* get this title. Such Buddhas found a *śāsanē*, they teach. Then there is the *pratyekabuddha* (Sinh.: *pasēbudu*), 'enlightened by himself'. He realizes *nirvāṇa* for and of himself alone ('tamangē nivan avabōdha pamaṇayi'). Like the *samyak sambuddha* they reach *nirvāṇa* without the help of a doctrine ready at hand, for they are born in periods when there is no *śāsanē* ('Budu śāsanē lōkē pavatina n̈ati kālaka äti vennē'); but they do not found one themselves, so they help no one. They mostly occur in the Himalayas and such remote regions. By definition none exist now. Finally, there are those who become enlightened (*buddha*) as disciples (*śrāvakayā vaśayen*) under the *samyak sambuddha*—the ordinary *arhats*, if we may so speak. All these three types of Buddhas are still normal human beings, and do not further affect the argument; we will revert to reserving the title Buddha for the *samyak sambuddha* like Gotama. The *pratyekabuddha* will hardly occur again, and the *śrāvaka buddha* will be simply called an *arhat*.

The cognitive position is logically coherent and canonically correct. Very little occurs which cannot be rationalized in terms of these beliefs. However, the Buddha has long since become the victim of a personality cult; and throughout recorded history behaviour towards him has been such that we may well question whether affectively he is viewed as no more than a historical personage long dead. Even the cognitive position expressed in words is not quite consistent.

The question whether Buddhists really view the Buddha as the mortal founder of their religion or as a being with at least some of the attributes of the Christian God (such as eternal life, omnipotence, and responsiveness to prayer) is the one that has most interested western observers, and I shall return to it at length in the second half of this chapter. The subject is a large one, but to arrive at a tentative answer it will be sufficient to focus attention on behaviour towards Buddhist images. This behaviour will turn out at times to be discordant with the cognitive position just stated. However, before we go on to examine these divergencies, and then to establish the Buddha's position in affective religion, more can and should be said about the cognitive position. For it would do violence to my chosen method of taking full account of the villagers' own views were I to restrict my statement of their beliefs about the Buddha to the one fact, most elementary from their point of view, that the Buddha was mortal. So the rest of the first half of this chapter will be devoted to what villagers know (or believe they know) about the Buddha. (I use the word 'know' because they do; I do not wish to imply by it any agreement or disagreement on my part.)

To indicate the state of knowledge about the Buddha I offer two kinds of evidence. Every image-house (*vihāra-gedara*) is adorned with paintings and sculpture which depict incidents from the Buddha's life, and in some cases his former lives, and the lives of previous Buddhas. Most of the image-houses I saw were the works of local craftsmen; some, especially the more recent, were the work of craftsmen from the Low Country (usually around Mātara in the extreme south). Villagers do not customarily pay a great deal of attention to the art in their temples—certainly details of artistic finesse or even of iconography have no meaning for them—but they naturally have some idea of the incidents represented.

My other evidence is two thin paper-back books which together form the primer for the bottom class, children about 5 years old, of a Buddhist Sunday School (*daham pāsala*). These equivalents to Sunday Schools were started about the turn of the century by the Young Men's Buddhist Association (Taruṇa Bauddha Maṇḍalaya), which publishes the books used. (It still owns the rights to most of them, but those for the first five classes are owned by the Government's Department of Culture.) Books are supplied free to all registered schools. These can be run by anyone, but in practice they are normally run by a monk at the village temple with or without the assistance of other monks and local schoolmasters. They are free and the books are loaned to the children. The children sit for annual exams set by the Y.M.B.A., and receive appropriate certificates. There were *daham pāsal* attached to about half the temples I visited; they meet on Sundays, but since I left the Government has substituted for the western weekend the *poya* day and the half-day preceding it, so they now meet on *poya* days. In Mīgala the *daham pāsala* was the concern of the chief monk, who took great pride in it. Children came from four villages, and most of the younger children in Mīgala attended. The chief monk claimed that when I enrolled (in the bottom class) I was the 518th pupil, but I think attendance rarely exceeded 300. The senior class was mostly taken by the monk, all the other classes by senior children. The lower classes, which were larger, were subdivided by sex. The classes spread across a grassy space at the foot of the stone steps leading up to the temple which served as a kind of village meeting-ground for the rare organized game or visit of the Government film unit; they occupied a permanent school-type building also used for meetings of the village council, etc., and a shed which will no doubt be replaced in due course by something permanent; but the roof space was inadequate for the masses of children. Proceedings were supposed to last from 9 to 11, timed by an alarm clock the monk had carried down from the monastery. He would administer the Three Refuges and Five Precepts; the children then divided into their classes and took turns in reading out the lesson. In our class we read through the lesson twice and then answered in writing the questions on it given in the book; the teacher corrected our answers. There then was recitation of Pali or old Sinhalese verses, also from the books, which had to be learned by heart, and the class usually managed to get away before the two hours were up.

The pattern of the textbooks for the lower classes was that for each class there were two volumes which we used on alternate weeks. The arrangement of my books was typical: the first volume contained the chapters on the life of the Buddha, in fact on his life till he became Buddha (i.e. saw *nirvāṇa*), and some Pali stanzas which everyone has to know, with their explanations in Sinhalese; the second book had five *Jātaka* stories and a selection of moral stanzas in old Sinhalese by a fourteenth-century poet. In the Appendix I give a translation of the first two chapters of the Buddha's early life, to give some idea of their flavour, the full table of contents of the primers of the two bottom classes, and a list of the other *daham pāsala* books in use at our temple. The wide circulation of these books, which pass from hand to hand, can be judged from the fact that of the first grade primer which we were using the first volume was the third edition, of 27,500 copies, printed in 1960, and the second volume was the fifth edition, of 20,000 copies, printed in 1961.

It will make for clarity if I begin by summarizing without comment the best known incidents concerning Gotama Buddha. If any reader finds that I have omitted a detail, or even a whole story, which he considers crucial, or introduced something unimportant, I can only apologize. That my selection should to some extent be arbitrary is inevitable, and I have tried to justify my choice by the documentation which immediately follows the summary. Finally I give some brief indication of the ancient sources on which this documentation rests. Well over half my summary is concerned with the life of Gotama before he became Buddha; this disparity reflects the ancient sources which the Sinhalese artists and authors have used.

(1) *Sumedha*. He became a Bodhisattva in the time of the (first?) Buddha, Dīpaṃkara, when he was a young brahmin ascetic called Sumedha. Dīpaṃkara was visiting a city with his monks, and the inhabitants were preparing the way. Sumedha offered to prepare a muddy stretch. He

had not finished making it dry when Dīpaṃkara Buddha appeared, so he threw himself prone in the mud so that Dīpaṃkara Buddha and his monks could walk over him and thus avoid the puddles. On seeing Dīpaṃkara Buddha he made a resolve that he too would become a Buddha. Dīpaṃkara Buddha stopped before him and prophesied that after countless ages he would become a Buddha called Gotama.

(2) *The other Buddhas.* He performed great services for twenty-three more Buddhas after Dīpaṃkara Buddha, and all prophesied that he too would become a Buddha. These Buddhas before our Buddha are collectively known as the twenty-four (*sūvisi*) Buddhas. The next Buddha will be Maitrī (Pali: Metteyya). All the Buddhas have similar biographies; e.g. they have two chief male disciples and attain Enlightenment under a particular tree which becomes sacred to them.

(3) *Jātakas.* The future Gotama Buddha lived through many lives as a Bodhisattva, accumulating the Perfections (*dasa pāramī* or *pāramitā*) which are essential to a Buddha. These lives are the material of the *Jātaka* stories. Many *Jātakas* are well known, but none better than the story of his last human birth before Buddhahood, as King Vessantara. King Vessantara practised the perfection of giving (*dāna pāramitā*) by bestowing on suppliants not only his wealth but even his wife and children. However, all was restored to him within his lifetime.

(4) *The gods' invitation.* Like every Buddha, Gotama was born in one of the lower heavens called Tusita, and when in due course the gods there requested him to be born on earth to become a Buddha he had to consider the right time, place, continent, family, and mother. Our Buddha decided to be born then, while the term of human life was 100 years, at Kapilavastu (Sinh. Kim̆bulvat) in India in the family of Suddhodana, king of the Śākyas, from his chief queen Mahāmāyā.

(5) *Conception.* At the Äsaḷa full moon *poya* (in July), ten lunar months before Wesak, Mahāmāyā was observing

aṭa sil and sleeping alone. She dreamt that a white elephant carrying a white lotus in his trunk entered her right side.

(6) *Birth*. Exactly ten lunar months later Queen Mahāmāyā was on her way to the city of Devadaha where her parents lived, planning to give birth there. On the way she turned aside at a grove of *sal* trees called the Lumbinī grove. There the birth-pangs came upon her, and she gave birth standing, holding on to a branch. The future Buddha descended spotless from the womb, and was caught by gods. He took seven steps and exclaimed, 'I am supreme in the world. This is my last birth.'

(7) *Asita*. A wise old man called Asita or Kāḷa Devala (both mean 'black') heard of the prince's birth and asked to see him. When he saw him he smiled and then wept. Asked the reason, he said he smiled because this child would become a Buddha, but wept because he realized that he would not be alive to see it (he was going to be reborn in a formless heaven). Having left the palace Asita told his nephew to renounce the world in expectation of the time when he could become a monk under the Buddha.

(8) *Koṇḍañña's prophesy and the name-giving*. For the name-giving ceremony King Suddhodana invited 108 brahmins. The eight wisest brahmins examined the prince's body, and seven prophesied that he would become a universal monarch or a Buddha, but the youngest, Koṇḍañña, said that he would surely become a Buddha after seeing an old man, a sick man, a corpse, and an ascetic. Koṇḍañña later became one of his first disciples. The name given was Siddhārtha, meaning 'He whose purpose is fulfilled'. (Siddhārtha is the correct Sanskrit form, Siddhattha the Pali, Siduhat the Sinhalese.)

(9) *Ploughing festival*. Once at a ploughing festival, while his father was ploughing, Prince Siddhārtha sat under the shade of a rose-apple tree and meditated. He attained the first trance (a technical term of Buddhist meditation) and the tree's shadow did not move away, whereupon his father worshipped him.

(10) *Education*. At his studies Prince Siddhārtha was outstanding, but he took no lessons in the use of arms, and the rumour spread among his warrior kinsmen that he would be useless in war. Accordingly he arranged a demonstration at which he strung and shot the most difficult bow.

(11) *Marriage*. Prince Siddhārtha at the age of sixteen was married to Princess Yasodharā, the daughter of King Suppabuddha of Devadaha, his mother's brother. He was then officially installed as heir apparent (*yuvarāja*).

(12) *The three palaces*. King Suddhodana did not want his son to renounce the world, so he kept him in the royal park, into which he allowed no old or sick men, no corpses and no ascetics. He built his son three palaces, one for each season, and here the prince lived surrounded by every luxury.

(13) *The four omens*. When he was 29 years old the future Buddha asked to go out to a park with his charioteer Channa. On the way he met an old man. Channa explained the sight to him, and told him that he too was subject to ageing. At this Prince Siddhārtha lost his inclination for amusements and returned home. In the same way he saw a sick man and then a corpse. On their fourth excursion they saw a man who had renounced the world and looked serene. This sight filled Prince Siddhārtha with joy and he resolved to renounce the world himself. He proceeded to the park, where he received a message that Yasodharā had borne him a son. At this he remarked, 'Rāhula is born' (Rāhula is supposed to mean a bond, though this popular etymology is incorrect), so his son was called Rāhula.

(14) *The great renunciation*. That evening Prince Siddhārtha sat thinking in his palace while slave girls danced and sang before him. He fell asleep, whereupon they too lay down just as they were and slept. During the night, the prince awoke and saw them lying around; he was disgusted, and resolved to renounce the world instantly. He summoned Channa and had him prepare the royal steed Kanthaka. He went to Yasodharā's bedchamber and from

the threshold gave her a last look as she lay sleeping, holding Rāhula to her. Then he rode out of the city on Kanthaka, while Channa clung to the horse's tail. Māra, a wicked god, tempted him to stay and become a universal monarch, but he paid no attention.

(15) *Hair-cutting*. The Bodhisattva had travelled thirty leagues by morning. He reached the broad River Anomā and spurred Kanthaka across in one bound. On the sands of the opposite shore the Bodhisattva dismounted and cut off his hair with his sword. The great god Śakra took the hair to heaven where it is kept in a stupa called the Siḷumiṇi sāya. He also took off his royal garments and replaced them with mendicant's robes, supplied by the great god Brahmā. He sent back Channa and Kanthaka, and went on alone. Channa later became a monk, but Kanthaka died of a broken heart and was reborn in heaven.

(16) *Self-mortification*. The ascetic Siddhārtha began to beg for his food. He visited the city of Rājagṛha, capital of Magadha, where King Bimbisāra offered him the kingdom; he refused, but promised to come back to that kingdom first when he had found Enlightenment. He meditated under the direction of two teachers, but finally left them dissatisfied. With five other ascetics, headed by Koṇḍañña, he undertook the most rigorous asceticism, starving himself until he nearly died. But he decided that this too was useless, and started taking proper food again. At this his five disciples left him in disgust.

(17) *Sujātā's milk-rice*. After taking a proper meal he went and sat at the foot of a banyan tree called Ajapāla ('goatherd'). A merchant's daughter called Sujātā had prepared an offering of milk-rice for the guardian deity of that tree. When her maid saw Siddhārtha she thought he must be the tree-deity making himself visible. She fetched Sujātā who came and offered the rice in a golden bowl. The Bodhisattva went and bathed in the Nerañjarā River. Then he divided the milk-rice into forty-nine parts, and having eaten it all he launched the bowl in the water, wishing that if he was that night to attain Buddhahood the bowl should be carried against the current. It swam

upstream.

(18) *Battle with Māra.* That night, the full moon night of Wesak, his thirty-fifth birthday, the Bodhisattva sat comfortably cross-legged at the foot of a peepal tree, vowing not to get up till he had attained Enlightenment. Now Māra brought up all his hosts of demons to scare the Bodhisattva, but though all the gods fled in terror to the corners of the earth the Bodhisattva meditated unmoved on his ten perfections, so nothing was able to touch him. As he was alone Māra then sought to confound him by boasting of his own past charity. All the demons gave witness that Māra had given alms, and he challenged the Bodhisattva to produce a witness himself. The Bodhisattva said he had given alms in his birth as Vessantara and called the earth to witness. The earth spoke in witness, and Māra fled with his hosts, leaving the Bodhisattva victorious.

(19) *Enlightenment.* The Bodhisattva then meditated through the three watches of the night. In the first watch he acquired omniscience about the past, in the second omniscience about the present, and in the third he understood the chain of dependent origination which reveals the origin of suffering. At dawn he attained *nirvāṇa*, at which the earth quaked and many marvels were seen.

(20) *The seven weeks.* The Buddha remained for seven weeks deep in meditation. Each week was signalized by a different event. In the fifth week the three daughters of Māra tried to seduce him by appearing to him as beautiful women, but he did not look at them. At the end of the seventh week two merchants, Tapassu and Bhalluka, passed and gave him alms. They took refuge in the Buddha and the Dharma, thus becoming the first *upāsakas*.

(21) *Invitation to teach.* The Buddha doubted that people would be able to understand what he had realized, but the great god Brahmā begged him to teach. On consenting he wondered to whom he should preach first. He thought of his five disciples, who were now in the Deer Park at Benares. On his way there he met an ascetic called Upaka, whom he told of his enlightenment. Upaka said 'It may be so', and went on. The Buddha reached Benares on

the full moon day of Äsaḷa.

(22) *First sermon.* When his five former disciples saw him coming they did not intend to rise for him, but he concentrated his benevolence on them till they were affected, so they paid him the usual respects. He preached to them the first sermon, 'The Turning of the Wheel of the Doctrine' (Pali: *Dhammacakkappavattana Sutta*; Sinh.: *Damsakpävatum Sūtraya*).[5] On hearing it Koṇḍañña entered the path to *nirvāṇa*, as the other four did in the next three days. On the fifth day he preached the sermon 'On the Non-Existence of the Soul' (*Anattalakkhaṇa Sutta*),[6] and all five attained *nirvāṇa*.

(23) *Rainy seasons.* The Buddha preached for forty-five years. Most of the time he was travelling with some of his monks, but each year the rainy season, which lasts three lunar months starting on Äsaḷa full-moon day, was spent at one place. There is a list of where they were spent. Two were in heavens, one of them preaching to his mother who had died seven days after his birth and been reborn in the Tusita heaven, the other, the seventh, expounding the *Abhidharma* to the gods of the Heaven of the Thirty-Three (Pali: Tāvatiṃsa; Sinh.: Tavatisā Devlova).

(24) *Visit to Śākyas.* During the first year of his ministry the Buddha paid a visit to the Śākyas at Kapilavastu. As many of them doubted his abilities he caused rain to fall on only those who wished to get wet, and made marvellous phenomena appear in pairs. He ordained his half-brother Nanda by a trick, and when Yasodharā told Rāhula to go and ask his father for his inheritance he ordained him too. King Suddhodana was distressed, so the Buddha promised that in future no one should be ordained without the parents' permission.

(25) *Devadatta.* The Buddha was subject to various hostile attacks, but he always quelled them as he had quelled Māra. His great enemy was Devadatta, a son of King Suppabuddha, who became a monk but created

[5] See Chapter 2, p. 83.

[6] See Chapter 2, p. 85.

schisms, and even plotted against the Buddha's life; he sent a rutting elephant against him, but the elephant fell worshipping at the Buddha's feet. The Buddha explained that Devadatta had been his enemy in many previous births.

(26) *Disciples.* The Buddha's two principal disciples were Sāriputta and Moggallāna (Sinh.: Säriyut and Mugalan). His personal attendant was Ānanda. Other famous monks included Upāli, who had been a barber and became the greatest authority on the rules of monastic discipline, and Mahā Kassapa ('Kassapa the Great'; Sinh. (= Skt.): Mahā Kaśyapa). A monk called Sīvali sometimes attended the Buddha on journeys because he was always able to find food. There is a list of eighty famous monks. The greatest *dāyaka* was Anāthapiṇḍika (Sinh.: Anēpiḍu) who bought for the Order the Jetavanārāma at Śrāvastī by covering the ground with gold coins; in this grove the Buddha then spent many rainy seasons. The greatest *dāyikā* (female *dāyaka*) was Visākhā.

(27) *Visits to Ceylon.* During his life Buddha paid three visits to Ceylon (see p. 128).

(28) *Death.* The Buddha entered *parinirvāṇa* at Wesak at the age of 80. He became ill after eating pork at a *dānē* offered by a smith called Cunda. In a grove at Kusinārā he lay on his right side between two *sal* trees and died while meditating, surrounded by hosts of men and gods. After his cremation his relics were distributed by a wise brahmin called Droṇa (Pali: Doṇa).

The traditional themes of Kandyan temple art are a bit restricted. Sculpture is generally confined to images of the Buddha (often with *makara toraṇa*), Maitrī, and a few gods. Paintings, leaving aside donors' portraits, *arhats* (including Säriyut and Mugalan), gods, and decorative motifs, mainly show the twenty-four (*sūvisi*) previous Buddhas and the seven weeks (*sat satiya*) passed by the Buddha immediately after his Enlightenment. Other traditional subjects, slightly less frequent, are the sixteen (or eight) sacred places in Ceylon (see p. 128), the battle against Māra, Śakra's heaven (both the last two tend to be painted on ceilings), and the *Vessantara Jātaka*. Before about 1900 other subjects are exceptional, and these subjects are still the main stock-in-trade of local Kandyan artists. Round 1900, however, temple artists from the Low Country, especially from the area round Mātara in the extreme south of Ceylon, began to invade the hill country. Today at a guess more than half the temple art extant even in the Kandy District itself is Low Country work, though in my area the proportion is a bit lower. Influenced by European painting, the Low Country craftsmen attempted perspective, used a far wider range of colours (which they tended to buy commercially rather than concoct them according to the traditional recipes), and—most relevantly for our purposes—introduced a far wider range of subjects both in painting and in sculpture. The most important of these subjects were scenes (often shown in a cycle) from the *Buddhacarita*, the life (especially the early life) of the Buddha, a subject not unknown but rare in earlier Kandyan painting. The Kandyan painters have gradually assimilated the subject matter and some of the methods (notably the use of mass-produced glossy paints) of their more prestigious Low Country colleagues, so that today there is not so much difference between the two styles. Regional differences in subject matter, in so far as they exist, can probably be ascribed to the taste of the patrons, that is the monks, who at least in theory decide on the themes with which their *vihāras* are to be decorated. Typical subjects gaining in popularity through Low Country influence are sets such as ten *Jātakas* illustrating the Ten Perfections, or the eight 'victories' hymned in successive verses of a mediaeval Pali poem, the *Jayamangala Gāthā*. Some differences in manner are still discernible: Kandyan artists still sometimes eschew perspective, and the brightly coloured sculpted tableaux depicting scenes from the *Buddhacarita*, the *Mahāvaṃsa*, or *Jātaka* stories are not yet, to my knowledge, in their repertory—they keep to painting for narrative and confine sculpture to isolated figures.

I visited thirty-two temples in my electorate with finished examples of religious painting and sculpture. (In seven temples the image-house was not yet begun or was under reconstruction.) Usually, but not necessarily, the art is confined to one image-house; my remarks apply to whole temple complexes. Of these thirty-two art complexes, nineteen were, I think, by Kandyan artists only, eight, I think, only by Low Country artists, three by both and two not ascertained. I ascribe the comparative paucity of Low Country art to the relative poverty, remoteness, and conservatism of much of the area.

The subjects of every paragraph except 27 in my summary above are depicted in local temples. I shall confine myself to mentioning those shown more than five times. The paragraph numbers below refer back to the summary.

(1, 2) There are fourteen representations (two in one temple!) of the twenty-four previous Buddhas; of these all but three are paintings, and all but one of the sculpted sets are by Kandyans. (The exception is doubtless an imitation of the sculpted *sūvisi* in an older temple in the same village belonging to the rival Nikāya.) When painted they are shown seated; when sculpted, standing. The twenty-four figures are identical; they are differentiated by the worshippers kneeling, very small, to their left (our right—but the side sometimes changes). These worshippers represent the future Gotama Buddha renewing his vows as a Bodhisattva before each Buddha. In most of these lives the Bodhisattva was human, but for instance in the time of Paduma, the eighth Buddha, he was a lion. Sumedha is not depicted separately but appears at the beginning of the *sūvisi* lying prone at Dīpaṃkara's feet.

There are ten statues, all standing, of Maitrī Buddha; he is identified by his tall headgear in which sits a small meditating Buddha. This iconographic detail shows the representation of Maitrī to be descended from representations of Avalokiteśvara, a Bodhisattva of Mahāyānist provenance, statues of whom, similarly identifiable by a small Buddha seated in the headgear, have survived from the late Anurādhapura period. When represented by a statue Maitrī Buddha is painted white or pink and holds a lotus. Most of the statues of Maitrī are Low Country work. The traditional Kandyan way of representing Maitrī is to paint him seated cross-legged in the Tusita heaven awaiting the gods' invitation to be reborn on earth; in this style he has neither lotus in his hand nor Buddha in his hat. In three temples he is so painted over entrance doors, and in seven on the ceiling, though about this last figure there is some doubt because some informants said that the person shown in heaven was Śakra. However, in eighteenth-century temples (e.g. Daṁbulla) we know that similar scenes are intended to portray Maitrī. In one temple is a cycle of eighteen paintings depicting Maitrī's life. The incidents are all repetitions, with new proper names, of the listed incidents in Gotama's life.

(3) I have counted altogether forty-two depictions of twenty-one different *Jātaka* stories, disregarding the fact that some are shown in cycles and some in single scenes. There is a general tendency for those *Jātakas* which are canonically associated (see p. 119) with the Bodhisattva's acquisition of a particular perfection (*pāramitā*)[7] to be more widely known. Other popular stories are the *Telapatta J.* (96),[8] *Culladhammapāla J.* (358), *Sāma J.* (540) and *Dahaṃsoňḍa J.*, a post-canonical Sinhalese story. The *Vessantara J.* (547) (eight times) and the *Dahaṃsoňḍa J.* are most shown locally (six times).

(4) The scene showing the gods requesting the Bodhisattva, seated at ease in their midst, to be born on earth is depicted six times.

(6) There are ten representations of the birth. The sky is full of gods. The scene is depicted at the moment when the Bodhisattva has taken the seven steps; to mark each step there is a lotus, and he is standing on the last. One cycle precedes the birth with the queen and her party setting

[7]The Sanskrit names of the Ten Perfections are: *dāna* (liberality), *śīla* (morality), *naiṣkramya* (renunciation), *prajñā* (wisdom), *vīrya* (energy), *kṣānti* (patience), *satya* (truthfulness), *adhiṣṭhāna* (perseverance), *maitrī* (kindness), and *upekṣā* (equanimity).

[8]The numbers in brackets refer to the numeration in Fausbøll's standard edition.

out for Devadaha. Two show the return to Kapilavastu.

(14) The Great Renunciation lends itself to portrayal in three separate scenes:

(i) Siddhārtha awakes to find the dancing girls asleep and repulsive. Shown once.

(ii) Siddhārtha gazes on his wife and child. Shown five times. Usually the Bodhisattva is shown standing at the door with a calm expression, but in one picture he is walking away with what can only be described as a sneer. Maybe this is due to a maladroit executant.

(iii) The Bodhisattva leaves the city on his horse. This is shown six times. In the sky in front of him invariably appears Vasavatti Māra, tempting him to return. In this episode Māra is coloured green.

(15) This episode is especially popular with artists, and divides into two scenes:

(i) The leap across the Anomā River, shown five times.

(ii) The Bodhisattva cutting short his hair, shown nine times.

Most representations include Śakra catching the hair and turban in mid-air, and some have a picture of the Siḷumiṇi sǟya in heaven. Some add the god Brahmā on the other side of the picture, bringing robes. According to one version the Siḷumiṇi sǟya is likewise balanced by the Saḷumiṇi sǟya, a heavenly stupa in which are kept the clothes the Bodhisattva discarded on this occasion. There are also two separate depictions of the Siḷumiṇi sǟya and the Saḷumiṇi sǟya, which might be considered the heavenly prototypes of our man-made stupas, and one of the Siḷumiṇi sǟya alone.

(17) Sujātā offering the milk-rice is depicted six times. The Bodhisattva is shown twice launching the bowl upstream on the Nerañjarā River.

(18) The battle against Māra is shown in six versions; the scene gives the artist ample scope for the exercise of the imagination in creating hideous monsters. In two of the representations the Bodhisattva is shown calling the earth to witness; a small female figure, shown from the

waist up, rises up from the ground in front of him; this is Mahī Kāntāva, the earth personified.

(19) The actual moment when Gotama became the Buddha is not represented as an episode in his life, though it could be said to constitute the first part of the *sat satiya* (see below). On the other hand this moment furnishes the paradigm for the *samādhi piḷimaya* ('meditation image'), in which the Buddha is shown in a symmetrical pose, legs crossed, hands folded in lap, eyes closed or half-closed. Successful *samādhi piḷim* convey a great tranquillity. This seated *samādhi* posture is the commonest one for a Buddha statue, the one opposite the entrance to the shrine, which contains or is supposed to contain the relic. The Buddha was perhaps first shown seated, and the possibly most ancient Buddha image to survive, the famous stone seated Buddha on the Outer Circular Road at Anurādhapura, is in the *samādhi* position. A *samādhi piḷimaya* is not normally thought of as representing the Buddha at a particular moment in his life, but it seems to me possible that it originated as a representation of the Enlightenment.

In an image-house a *samādhi piḷimaya* usually has its back against a wall, in which case the wall is painted with a large halo (*budu räs*) in white, yellow, orange, red, and blue. Such a halo may also be attached to a Buddha image in some other position.

The usual representation of the enlightened Buddha is as a statue rather than a painting. This reminds us both that it is his Enlightenment which made the Buddha worshipful (in contrast to Jesus, who is sacred from birth), and that the Buddha image, at least as an object of devotion, originated as a relic container (p. 132 below), a function which a two-dimensional painting cannot fulfil.

(20) There are nine representations of the *sat satiya*. The locations of those seven weeks are listed in a Pali stanza:

Paṭhamaṃ bodhipallaṃkaṃ Dutiyaṃ ca animmisaṃ
Tatiyaṃ caṃkamanaṃ seṭṭhaṃ Catutthaṃ ratanāgharaṃ
Pañcamaṃ ajapālanaṃ Mucalindena chaṭṭhamam

Sattamaṃ rājāyatanaṃ Vande taṃ bodhipādapaṃ.[9]

First the seat of Enlightenment; second unwinking; third the most excellent ambulatory; fourth the house of jewels; fifth Ajapāla(na); sixth with Mucalinda; seventh the royal area; I worship that Bodhi tree.

(i) The Buddha remains in *saṃādhi* without moving for a whole week.

(ii) Without blinking he contemplates the *bodhi* tree.

(iii) He makes a jewelled ambulatory in the sky up and down which he walks in meditation.

(iv) Similarly, he makes a jewelled house.

(v) On return to earth he goes back to sit, for the next three weeks, under the banyan tree where Sujātā saw him. The three daughters of Māra try to tempt him. They are depicted as seductive women playing musical instruments.

(vi) During a storm the Buddha is sheltered by the supernatural serpent king (*nāgarāja*) Mucalinda, who puts his great hood over him. The Buddha is shown sitting on the snake's coils, half enveloped in the five-headed hood.

(vii) The visit of Tapassu and Bhalluka, which occurred at the end of the seventh week, is not always included in it. In such cases the Buddha may again just be shown in meditation, or the cycle may be limited to six weeks, the main *samādhi piḷimaya* in the shrine perhaps standing for the seventh.

(22) There are eleven representations of the first sermon. It is a favourite subject for a tableau, in which the five disciples sit in front of the Buddha, facing him, and gods protrude from the walls all round, arriving on clouds to listen.

(23) There are several preaching scenes depicted, often

[9]This stanza must be based on *Dīpavaṃsa*, I, 29:

Pallaṅkaṃ animisañ ca caṅkamaṃ ratanāgharaṃ
ajapālamucalindo khīrapālena sattamaṃ.

Seat and unwinking, walk, jewelled house, Ajapāla <banyan tree>, Mucalinda <serpent>, seventh with Khīrapāla <grove>.

as companion pieces to the first sermon. The favourite (six times) is the Buddha expounding the *abhidharma* in the Heaven of the Thirty-three.

(26) (i) The Buddha's two chief disciples, Sāriputta and Moggallāna, are shown in almost every temple, invariably as a pair (I counted twenty-six pairs, one per temple). They are known as the Buddha's right-hand disciple (*dakuṇat sav*) and left-hand disciple (*vamat sav*) respectively, and flank the Buddha's image accordingly. Sāriputta always has a pink, Moggallāna a blue face; otherwise they are represented like any other monks, and always mirror each other in every other respect. Generally they flank the main Buddha image in the shrine, especially so if it is a seated image, and they usually are shown facing or inclined towards this image in a reverent posture.

(ii) The other two disciples who fairly often have statues to themselves are Ānanda and Mahā Kassapa. Neither of them seem to have any iconographic peculiarities, so it is hard to tell them apart. A monk told me that Mahā Kassapa could be distinguished by his size, but I found this unreliable. To make matters worse, both are especially likely to be portrayed standing near the feet of a Buddha who is entering *parinirvāṇa* (see para. 28 below), and the monk in this scene was identified for me now as one, now as the other. In the canonical account of the Buddha's death Ānanda figures prominently; Mahā Kassapa arrives after the Buddha has died, and worships his feet as the body lies on the pyre. Either the iconographic tradition has intentionally conflated the two events, which is unlikely, or one of the two disciples was originally meant and it has been forgotten which. It seems more likely that the person represented is Ānanda, as there is no sign of a pyre; in that case the position near the Buddha's feet would be a mere coincidence. If I count under Ānanda those statues accompanying the *parinirvāṇa* which were identified for me as Ānanda, and the others as dubious, leaving to Kassapa only his isolated representations, the totals are six statues of Ānanda, three of Mahā Kassapa, and three dubious.

(iii) The only other disciple to rank a statue is Sīvali (one). In an *āvāsaya* with no image-house but a shrine at one end of the room, I noticed a framed picture of Sīvali as the only wall-decoration. Because he is connected with a constant food supply Sīvali is usually considered a patron more appropriate for laymen than for monks.

(iv) There are two pairs of portraits of Anāthapiṇḍika and Visākhā.

(28) When the principal Buddha image in a shrine was not seated, it was invariably lying in a pose called the 'lion-lying' (*siṃha seyyāva*); the Buddha lies on his right side, his head on a pillow on which his right hand also lies, his left arm straight down by his side and his feet one on top of the other. According to my informants this pose can represent the Buddha meditating in a lying position; usually, however, it is clear that the *parinirvāṇa* is intended. (I have heard that if the toes are all in line he is alive, but if the big toe of the left foot is raised he is dead; however, it is rare for the toes not to be aligned, so I am not sure that this interpretation is to be credited.) The lying Buddha is called a *sätapena piḷimaya*. I counted thirteen such images.

The evidence from *daham pāsala* textbooks can be summarized more rapidly, there are two textbooks, of which the first is principally concerned with the life of Gotama, the incidents being arranged in ten chapters. Naturally each book is rather more detailed than its predecessor, and written rather less simply, but there is a good deal of repetition from year to year; for instance, the Bodhisattva's birth is described in each of the first three years. In comparison to visual representations there is far less emphasis on the spectacular; for instance the accounts of the birth omit the seven steps and subsequent pronouncement, and the accounts of the Enlightenment omit the battle with Māra, and describe the event rather in terms of my paragraph 19 than of my paragraph 18. This probably reflects western influence. On the other hand, the early books maintain the concentration on Gotama's life before Enlightenment: the first year ends with the barest mention of that event; the second year has six chapters on his life as Siddhārtha, the seventh chapter takes us to the first sermon, then there are two chapters on the years of teaching, and the last is on the *parinirvāṇa*. The events in the first book, which I would assume to be the best known, are covered at not much greater length than I have given them, in the very simple and rather repetitious style suitable for small children. There is a fair amount of descriptive detail, especially about the three palaces (my para. 12), which I have omitted, but not much which I would judge substantive. On the other hand some important details are missing. Each chapter is two small pages long in the original. This said, a fair notion of the primer's coverage and emphasis can be gathered from the following tabulation of its contents.

Chapter of primer	*Paragraphs in my account*
1	1
2	4, 5, 6 (no details on birth)
3	7
4	8
5	10
6	11
7	12
8	13
9	14 (no Māra), 15 (no gods, no dismissal of Channa and Kanthaka)
10	16 (no Bimbisāra or teachers), 17 (no bowl), 19 (no details)

The primers also include a number of *Jātaka* stories. These hardly coincide with those represented in temples, nor am I able to discern a pattern, such as illustration of the Ten Perfections, underlying their selection, so I shall merely refer the interested reader to their listing in the Appendix.

The two sources cited, temple art and the *daham pāsala* primer, account for all paragraphs in my account except paragraph 27, the Buddha's visits to Ceylon. On what are these contemporary sources based? Almost entirely on ancient commentatorial literature. Almost everything mentioned under my paragraphs 1 to 22 and 24 is based on the *Nidānakathā*. Paragraphs 23, 25 and 26 are gleaned from various canonical sources; more relevantly, perhaps, those events and persons are frequently mentioned in the introductions (*paccuppanna-vatthu*) to individual *Jātaka* stories which were presumably composed at the same time as the *Nidānakathā*, the introduction to the whole book. Paragraph 27 is based on the first chapter of the *Mahāvaṃsa*. Paragraph 28 is based on the canonical *Mahāparinibbāna Sutta*.

Someone who reads the *Nidānakathā* will find in it almost everything now known about the Buddha by a Sinhalese villager. It is not my concern here to trace the origins of the contents of the *Nidānakathā* in any detail—that has already been well done by Dr. E. J. Thomas in his learned work, *The Life of the Buddha as Legend and History*,[10] which covers the main stories found in all ancient Sanskrit and Pali sources. However, a few more words about the *Nidānakathā* in its relation to other literature will be appropriate.

The introduction to the Pali prose commentary on the *Jātakas* is formed by the *Nidānakathā*. As explained in Chapter 1, the Jātaka stories are themselves technically a commentary, i.e. the prose stories are a commentary on the verses which form their nucleus; but the work of which the *Nidānakathā* is a part is a commentary on the *Jātaka* stories taken as a whole. It is not the first such commentary, because it mentions an earlier one with which it disagrees; this is probably the Sinhalese version on which it is based. Its introductory verses indicate[11] that it was composed in the Mahāvihāra in Anurādhapura, but it is anonymous. It cannot be securely dated, but as will appear from the analysis of its contents, it is likely to be roughly contemporary with Buddhaghosa, and as Buddhaghosa was the first to translate Sinhalese commentaries into Pali this work can-

[10]Routledge and Kegan Paul, London, 1927 (3rd ed., 1949).

[11]*Jātaka*, p. 1, verse 11.

not precede him.[12]

After brief (but involuted) introductory verses the *Nidānakathā* is in three parts: I *Dūre-nidāna* ('Distant Origin') II *Avidūre-nidāna* ('Not so Distant Origin') and III *Santike-nidāna* ('Proximate Origin'). I is half the length of the whole, II and III a quarter each. I contains the story of Sumedha, including his decision to attain each of the Ten Perfections; matter on Dīpaṃkara and the rest of the twenty-four Buddhas; and a bare mention of various births in which he attained the Ten Perfections. II contains the life of Gotama from his decision to be born to his Enlightenment. III tells of the first year of his preaching, ending with Anāthapiṇḍika's gift of the Jetavanārāma.

Three other texts between them cover almost everything that is in the *Nidānakathā*. Two are canonical, though generally considered late: these are the *Buddhavaṃsa* and the *Cariyāpiṭaka*. The third is the commentary on the *Buddhavaṃsa*, the *Madhuratthavilāsinī* by Buddhadatta. The *Nidānakathā* uses the first two, but seems itself to be used by the third.

The *Buddhavaṃsa*, in verse, has twenty-eight chapters, all but one of them short. The first sets the scene: the Buddha tells how he came to attain Buddhahood. The second chapter is by far the longest, and tells the story of Dīpaṃkara and Sumedha; all of it but the last verse is quoted, with acknowledgement, by the *Nidānakathā* (as vv. 12–222). Chapters 3 to 25 inclusive tell of the other twenty-three Buddhas before Gotama. Just the first verse of each chapter is quoted (with some variant readings) the *Nidānakathā* (as vv. 223 and 225–46). The 26th chapter

[12]The stratification of the *Jātaka* book which has come down to us has not been finally settled. In his edition Fausbøll differentiates typographically between (1) the prose of the stories; (2) the general commentary, which consists of the *Nidānakathā* and the introductions to the individual stories and their conclusions in which the characters are identified by the Buddha as former incarnations of himself, his relations and followers; and (3) the explanations of difficult words in the verses. Though in origin (1) must be far older than (2), it seems to me quite possible that in the form in which we have them they (and (3)?) were composed by the same person.

gives a biography of Gotama, as brief as the preceding chapters, and is not itself quoted. Chapter 27 is a list of Buddhas, ending with Metteyya, who is not mentioned elsewhere in the work; chapter 28 gives a list of relics and their distribution. Neither of these last two chapters has a commentary, so they are probably late additions. So much for the *Buddhavaṃsa*.

So far (up to page 44) the *Nidānakathā* consists entirely of these verses from the *Buddhavaṃsa* and of prose passages which enlarge on them or (in the case of Buddhas after Dīpaṃkara) paraphrase the verses not quoted. The *Nidānakathā* then lists the Buddhas before Gotama, a list which is also found in the *Buddhavaṃsa* commentary (pp. 131–2). Next there are a few lines summarizing the story so far and listing the qualifications (such as male sex) for becoming a Buddha. The last three pages of the *Dūre-nidāna* then list births (all of them *Jātaka* stories) in which the Bodhisattva attained one of the Ten Perfections, and for each perfection a verse is quoted. At the end the author says that the stories mentioned can be found in full in the *Cariyāpiṭaka*. Interestingly enough this is not true of the *Cariyāpiṭaka* as we know it. The *Cariyāpiṭaka* is a canonical book which similarly selects *Jātaka* stories to illustrate the attainment of the Ten Perfections, and retells them briefly in verse. But the selections made by the *Nidānakathā* (by title only) and the *Cariyāpiṭaka* differ in about half the cases, and of the eleven verses quoted, despite the contrary impression given by the author and the contrary statement by Rhys Davids,[13] only six[14] are in fact taken from our *Cariyāpiṭaka*. This strongly suggests that the version of the *Cariyāpiṭaka* then known was not the one which has reached us.[15] So much for the *Cariyāpiṭaka*.

[13]*Buddhist Birth Stories* (Trübner, London, 1880), p. 54, note 2.

[14]Even of these six, only 259, 260, 268, and 269 occur in the *Cariyāpiṭaka* in the same form with the same referents. 267 occurs in a different story, and 266 occurs in three different stories in slightly varied forms from which it is conflated (cf. *Cariyāpiṭaka*, III, I, 6 (p. 92) = III, III, 10 (p. 94), and III, VI, 18 (p. 97)).

[15]This is the conclusion of Jarl Charpentier, 'Zur Geschichte des

This disposes of the *Dūre-nidāna* of the *Nidānakathā*: it depends entirely on the *Buddhavaṃsa* and *Cariyāpiṭaka*; all of it not duplicated elsewhere is of a purely commentatorial nature. The rest of the *Nidānakathā* is largely duplicated by the commentary on the *Buddhavaṃsa*. This was noted by Rhys Davids,[16] and Miss Horner cites the parallel passages in the footnotes to her edition of the commentary. The commentary on the story of Dīpaṃkara and Sumedha is largely the same as the first part of the *Nidānakathā*. The first part of the commentary on the 26th chapter of the *Buddhavaṃsa*, the one about Gotama Buddha, is an abbreviated version of most of the rest of the *Nidānakathā*, adding only a few short bridge passages and a few verses. This section of the commentary (p. 272, line 6–p. 291, line 31) takes the story as far as the first sermon, covering *Nidānakathā*, p. 47 (beginning of the *Avidūre-nidāna*) to p. 82, line 12. The remaining twelve pages of the *Nidānakathā* are not to my knowledge duplicated or closely paralleled in another Pali text, except that parts of it recur in the introductions to individual *Jātaka* stories, which are usually presumed to be by the same hand.

The relevance of this analysis to our subject is that the traditions I encountered derive not only from the *Nidānakathā*. For example, the Sunday School primer gives the names of Siddhārtha's three palaces as Ramma, Suramma, and Subha. In the *Nidānakathā* they are not named. But these names occur in the *Buddhavaṃsa* (27, 14)[17] and hence in its commentary (p. 278). The commentary goes on to give the story about the feat of arms, more or less as given in the Sunday School primer. In the *Nidānakathā* this incident is mentioned only briefly, but the author refers one for it to the *Sārabhanga Jātaka* (522), in which a sim-

Cariyāpiṭaka', *Wiener Zeitschrift zur Kunde des Morgenlandes*, vol. XXIV, no. 4, 1910, pp. 351–415.

[16] *Buddhism*, p. 13.

[17] Only as quoted in the commentary, p. 293. The P.T.S. edition of the text reports only variant readings, as it does in the next line for the name of Siddhārtha's wife (also not mentioned in the *Nidānakathā*). Miss Horner draws attention to the two names of the wife.

ilar, but even more elaborate story is told of the Bodhisattva in a *former* life. The version before us therefore seems to come from the *Madhuratthavilāsinī*.

Sometimes one has to look even further. When a monk was telling me about the birth of the Buddha (see Chapter 7, p. 337) he recited a pair of Pali verses. The first is not in the *Nidānakathā*, but is in the *Buddhavaṃsa* and in its commentary. Its original appearance in the *Buddhavaṃsa* is in a very short reference to the Buddha's birth, but it is quoted again in the commentary in the context of the full story. The second verse, however, is in none of these texts, but in an even shorter version of the whole early biography, perhaps potted from the *Madhuratthavilāsinī*. This very short version is in the commentary to the *Dhammapada* (vol. 1, pp. 83 et seq.). This text, like my informant, closely follows the first verse with another;[18] so this is presumably his source.

Of course the traditions under discussion do not necessarily or even probably derive *directly* from the Pali texts. In most cases the Pali texts have been mediated through the great Sinhalese classics, prose accounts of the Buddha's life such as the *Butsaraṇa*, the *Pūjāvaliya*, the *Saddharmālaṃkāraya* and the *Saddharmaratnāvaliya*, as well as through the folk literature deriving from them. But these Sinhalese works closely follow the Pali texts discussed above.

II. The Buddha as Worshipped: Man or God?

Now that I have reviewed the Buddha's life and works (*caritaya*), the primary interest of the Buddhists themselves, it is time to return to his ontological status, if I may so call it, which has been the primary interest of academic observers, and to discuss the cult of the Buddha and his image. The bridge to this cult of the Buddha is the relic (*dhātu, dhātunvahansē*). We already hear of relics in the

[18] *Dh. A.*, I, 84, note 14. Norman, the editor, seems to consider the verse an interpolation.

Canon. Shortly after the Buddha's last words (quoted on p. 96 of this chapter), in the same text, is recounted how after the Buddha's body had been cremated all the peoples of that area sent asking for his remains. They were divided into eight parts by Doṇa; a tribe who applied late got the embers of the pyre, and Doṇa kept the vessel in which the remains had been collected. The original text ends by telling us that there were then ten portions, and for each a stupa was built and a festival celebrated. To this is appended a verse, which Buddhaghosa says was added in Ceylon, which adds to the earlier eight portions of bodily remains four teeth, one of which was allegedly in heaven, and another in Kalinga in South India. This latter became of great importance to the Sinhalese, for it was brought to Ceylon in the fourth century, and from that time on accompanied the king of Ceylon, and had a temple in its honour in his capital. Its history is chronicled in Pali verse in the *Dāṭhāvaṃsa*[19] ('The Chronicle of the Tooth'), composed by Dhammakitti in the twelfth century. The Portuguese claimed to have taken it to Goa and destroyed it in the sixteenth century, but the Sinhalese claim that by miraculous intervention they failed to do so. The Sinhalese kings built a temple for it in Kandy which has the title, unique for a religious edifice, of 'palace'—the Daḷadā Māligāva (literally 'Palace of the Tooth Relic'). The temple is controlled by a lay administrator, the Diyavadana Nilamē, and is likewise unique in not belonging to a monastery, though monks of the two great monasteries of Kandy, Malvatta and Asgiriya, alternately officiate there, preaching on *poya* days, etc. It is nowadays—as has perhaps always been the case—exhibited only to people of the greatest importance, such as heads of state and prime ministers. But once a year it is on view to the public for several days, during which period it is taken in procession (*perahära*) inside its casket (*karaňḍuva*) on the back of the largest available elephant; though it is said that these days an empty substitute casket

[19] Ed. R. Morris and T.W. Rhys Davids, *Journal of the Pali Text Society*, 1884, pp. 109–50.

is taken, in case of accidents. This is the Äsaḷa Perahära, Ceylon's most famous tourist attraction;[20] it takes place on the ten nights leading us to the full moon of the Sinhalese month of Äsaḷa (in August) and on the day itself. The tooth is preceded by the *perahäras* of the four gods whose temples are near by; the five processions coalesce into one great spectacle of elephants and men, officials in pompous Kandyan costumes of white, purple and gold, drummers bare-bodied leaping and turning, a din of their drumming and chanting, the whole illuminated by the flames of resin torches. Probably no other occasion attracts so many Sinhalese visitors from all over the island and specially the Kandyan provinces; the procession is certainly a *pinkama* and attendance is meritorious; but the Tooth Temple is not one of the sixteen great places of pilgrimage, because the Buddha never visited Kandy. We shall return to this question.

To trace the progress of other individual relics is beyond the scope of this work. Relics have always followed close upon the spread of the doctrine; the arrival in Ceylon of the Buddha's begging bowl and right collar-bone and a branch of the sacred Bo tree were mentioned in the Introduction. Most recently the Ceylonese Buddhist Mission to England has been supplied with relics from Ceylon; the first relic was judged perhaps too obscure when Mrs. Bandaranaike, then Prime Minister, arrived in London with a second, taken from Mihintalē (the site of Mahinda's arrival and conversion of King Devānaṃpiya Tissa), and astonished the inhabitants of Chiswick with a *perahära* including an elephant from a circus.[21]

Relics may be of the Buddha or of any *arhat*, male or female. By the excavation of a stupa in Kashmir in which was found an inscribed reliquary containing the bones of Majjhantika, striking confirmation was given to the historical accuracy of the *Mahāvaṃsa*, which records this *arhat*'s mission to Kashmir in chapter XII. However, in practice

[20]For the tooth relic festival in ancient Ceylon and the impressions of a fifth-century tourist, see Rahula, *History*, pp. 280–1.

[21]*Times of Ceylon*, 13 October 1964.

only relics of the Buddha are important.[22] They have been divided by doctrine[23] into three classes: *sārīrika* (pieces of the body), *pāribhogika* (things he used) and *uddesika* (reminders, i.e. representations). It is these three classes of relics, or their most typical examples, which are listed in this Pali verse, known by heart by most villagers and recited by the pious laymen who take the Eight Precepts at the temple on *poya* days:

> *Vandāmi cetiyaṃ sabbaṃ sabbaṭṭhānesu patiṭṭhitaṃ*
> *Sārīrika dhātu mahā bodhiṃ Buddharūpaṃ sakalaṃ sadā.*

> I worship always every shrine, standing in every place,
> the bodily relics, the great Bodhi tree, and every image of the Buddha.

The worship of relics, as Obeyesekere put it in his lectures, resolves the clash of the cognitive fact of the Buddha's absence with the psychological (I would say affective) fact of his presence. In a recently published article[24] he suggests the linguistic and doctrinal origins of the belief that an enlightened person is immanent in his relics. Linguistically, *dhātu* in Sanskrit and Pali, and hence in learned Sinhalese, means an 'element'; for instance, it can refer to the essences of man and woman embodied respectively in semen and a posited equivalent female fluid. This does not mean (*pace* Yalman)[25] that an ordinary Sinhalese villager knows that the word can mean 'semen' and hence

[22] All relics are included in beliefs about their spectacular disappearance at the end of our *sāsanē*, for which see Chapter 7, section on eschatology.

[23] *J*. IV. 228, where the adjectives are attached to *cetiya*. Cf. *Milindapañho*, 341. For the theory and practice of relic worship in ancient Ceylon see Adikaram, pp. 135–42.

[24] G. Obeyesekere, 'The Buddhist Pantheon in Ceylon and its Extensions', in M. Nash (ed.), *Anthropological Studies in Theravada Buddhism* (Yale University Southeast Asia Series, 1966), pp. 1–26. This argument is on p. 8.

[25] Nur Yalman, *Under the Bo Tree* (University of California Press, Berkeley and Los Angeles, 1967), p. 137, note 8. Bones are not dirt, nor does *dhātugarbhaya* mean '*dhatu* in the womb'.

that relics have connotations of pollution or sexuality.[26] It does, however, mean that unlike the word 'relic', which suggests something merely left behind, the word *dhātu* suggests a basic constituent, perhaps even a sort of essence. This of course applies in the first instance to the ancient Sanskrit and Pali, and is not a Sinhalese innovation. Far more interesting, to my mind, is Obeyesekere's hypothesis that this conception of relics derives from one of the 'undecided questions' mentioned in the Introduction (p. 8). The Buddha would not say, when asked, whether an *arhat* after death exists or does not exist or both or neither. Though that can hardly have been his intention, his silence leaves room to conjecture some sort of after-life for the enlightened. Moreover, the doctrine that Enlightenment, the *summum bonum*, is a 'blowing out' of the personality is counter-intuitive. 'Thus the dhātu is the visible representation of the immortal nirvāna state.' From the orthodox doctrinal point of view this is a misunderstanding, but it could date from the earliest times. As Obeyesekere shows, it fits in well with the popular ascription to relics of the same abnormal powers of locomotion as *arhats* are supposed to possess, typically the ability to levitate and fly.

Such holy powers should, by the logic of this argument, inhere only in bodily relics. Indeed, certain functions are reserved for the bodily relics. With a few celebrated exceptions, such as the Buddha's begging bowl (*pātra*), they are the only ones to be enshrined. Enshrinement can be in stupas, in relic caskets (which usually have the form of miniature stupas), or in images—which will be explained below. Relics are of course usually to be found in temples, though exceptionally one is owned by a layman. In theory it is not a relic which makes a temple holy—it is monks who sanctify it by their presence—but in my researches I came

[26]On p. 9 Obeyesekere refers to the myth that the Buddha will be reassembled from his relics at the end of the *sāsanē*, and says, 'This is strikingly similar to the notion that male *dhātu* and female *dhātu* unite in orgasm to form a new being.' For once I must disagree with him: I do not find the similarity striking or the analogy plausible.

across only one temple which did not claim to possess a relic. Though they are of course handled with the greatest veneration, in a wider sense these relics are casually dealt with: I invariably asked after the origin of a relic, but never got any reply more interesting than that it was inherited from the monk's teacher (*paramparāven*). This is not the uncritical attitude of fanatical regard, which would retail some elaborate myth, but an indifference entirely proper to monks. However, I think the indifference is shared by laymen: I was sometimes told quite casually that some relic had been lost ('näti vunā'). These village relics are indeed not very impressive objects: as a special favour I was shown those in Mīgala, precious casket removed to reveal precious casket, until the last tiny stupa contained a couple of minute white balls of what I presume was bone.

When monks formally visit a layman's house, typically to receive a meal or to recite *pirit*, they probably take with them the small temple *karaṅḍuva* containing relics, and there is a *perahära*. (A *perahära* need not be religious at all, but usually it is. The sort of *perahära* I am discussing involves monks or relics, probably both. There are also *perahäras* for gods, in which their images are carried.) On the way to or from a *pirit* the sacred books (*pirit pot*), palm-leaf manuscripts, are carried and treated in the same way as the relic. The relic casket, covered with a rich cloth, is carried on a cushion on a man's head, and a canopy is held over it. It is preceded by drumming and, on grander occasions, dancing; small boys run ahead throwing fire crackers, other children carry white pennants tied to sticks, and maybe Buddhist flags, and all the laymen frequently shout 'Sādhu sādhu sā'. The monks walk behind the relics, carrying their umbrellas. When the procession reaches its destination it halts for a final climactic salvo of drumming and then dissolves. Before monks enter the building they take off their sandals, if any, and as they reach the threshold their feet are washed by one layman and dried by another. (The reader who recalls biblical parallels should be reminded that in Ceylon such personal services to monks are always performed by men.) In a well-conducted ceremony the monks from this point walk on white cloths, the provision and spreading of which is a special function of the washer caste. At a really big *perahära* like the Kandy Äsaḷa Perahära these cloths are used throughout the procession, but this is too extravagant for villagers. Inside the house the relic casket (with manuscripts, if brought) is put on a table; the essential is that it should be higher than the seats of those present. When monks are fed, a portion is usually set aside—traditionally by one of the monks—in front of the relics. This is a substitute for the normal *Buddha pūjā* (offering to the Buddha) which is made at every temple before every meal. Such offerings are discussed below. In the village, however, the *Buddha pūjā* is usually sent straight up to the temple to be offered in the normal way, so no food need be reserved at the scene of the *dānē*. When the monks have been satisfied the remainder of the food is served to the guests, but the *Buddha pūjā* may be given only to animals or beggars; in cities it is often just thrown away. The return procession is similar to the arrival but much less ceremonious.

The commonest *pāribhogika dhātu*, object used by the Buddha, is a Bo tree. Under its shade he attained Enlightenment. There is one in almost every temple, and some grow elsewhere besides. Wherever a Bo tree grows it is sacred: it may not be cut down, and it may receive offerings. The nature and rationale of offerings (*pūjā*) made before relics will be extensively discussed below. Here I shall only remark that one type of offering seems to have entered Buddhism from earlier tree worship via the Bo tree: a piece of cloth, nowadays formalized as a flag (*koḍiya*), may be tied on to a branch.

It is the *pāribhogika dhātu* which provide occasion for pilgrimage. In the canonical text already quoted which describes the Buddha's death is a passage in which the Buddha, on the last day of his life, recommends pilgrimage to four places: where he was born, attained enlightenment, preached the first sermon, and died. These places should be seen and admired, and if anyone dies with a contented mind while on a pilgrimage (*cetiya-cārikā*) they will be reborn in heaven.[27] These four points, or the places believed to be them, are the supreme goals of pilgrims; every year tours are arranged from Ceylon, and several of my monastic informants had been on them. However, more places of pilgrimage have been found nearer home, on the above model: anywhere visited by the Buddha provides occasion for religious awe, so he visited Ceylon.

According to the first chapter of the *Mahāvaṃsa* the Buddha paid three visits to Ceylon, arriving by air. His first visit was to Mahiyangana, at the eastern foot of the central massif; his second to Nāgadīpa (Tamil: Nainativu), an island near Jaffna in the extreme north. On the third visit he went to Kälaṇiya, on the west coast near Colombo, and on his way back planted his footprint on Siripāda, known in English as Adam's Peak, in the south-west part of the hill country, the second highest mountain in Ceylon and by far the most spectacular; he further tarried and meditated in a cave at the foot of Siripāda, at Dīghavāpī on the east coast, and four or five spots in Anurādhapura. According to another ancient version (*Samanta-pāsādikā*, I, 89) the third visit included Mutiyangaṇa in the south-eastern highlands. What these places have in common is that, like the Bo tree, they were used by the Buddha. At Mahiyangana the Buddha also left some hairs of his head and that temple later miraculously acquired a bone of his neck;[28] at Nāgadīpa he left the seat from which he had preached and the tree which had served as his parasol, themselves *pāribhogika dhātu*; but at the other places he originally left nothing, and Siripāda, the place of pilgrimage *par excellence*, has nothing material to offer the worshipper except the Buddha's footprint, recently covered in concrete.

There are altogether 'sixteen great places' (*soḷos mahāsthāna*) which are said to have been visited by the Buddha and are therefore sites of pilgrimage. Such a group of six-

[27] *D.N.*, II, 140–1 (*Sutta* 16. 5. 8).

[28] Not a collar-bone, which is in the Thūpārāma. See Geiger, *Culture of Ceylon*, p. 213 note.

teen is alluded to in the last chapter of the *Cūlavaṃsa* (C. 128 and 253) but for reasons given below I suspect that the group is far older. The list is not stable, and I think I have discovered the basic reason for its instability: in the passage in the *Mahāvaṃsa* describing the Buddha's third visit to Anurādhapura, and in the passage in the *Dīpavaṃsa* on which it is at least partially based, there is an ambiguity,[29] so that they can be interpreted to mean that the Buddha stopped at the future site of the Bo tree *at* the future site of the Mahāvihāra, or to make these into two separate stops. The other points visited in Anurādhapura, as listed in the *Mahāvaṃsa*, are the Ruvanväli sāya, the Thūpārāma and the Laṅkārāma. There are thus eleven[30] *or* twelve[31] sites which according to fifth-century sources (the *Mahāvaṃsa* and the *Samanta-pāsādikā*) were visited by the Buddha, and the number sixteen has to be completed by the addition of four or five names. Candidates for the other places are Tissamahārāma near the south-east coast (always included); Kataragama, near Tissa; Mihintalē, very near Anurādhapura; and at Anurādhapura the Mirisaväṭi sāya, Abhayagiri, and Jetavana. When the Buddha is supposed to have visited these places is obscure to me, but their other sacred associations are all recorded in the first part of the *Mahāvaṃsa*.

What can we deduce from the size and shape of the list about its history? Though I know of no ancient evidence for a list of sixteen places of pilgrimage, the number sixteen has ancient connections with stupa worship in Ceylon:

> On the lowest terrace of a stupa there were sixteen marks of footsteps known as *pādapīthikā* fixed at regular points round the cetiya. They indicated the places where the pilgrim should stop and kneel

[29] *Mhv*, I, 80–1, *Dīpavaṃsa*, II, 61–5.

[30] Thus Geiger in his note to his translation of *Mhv*., C. 109, attributing his list to Wijesinha, a previous editor; and Obeyesekere, 'Buddhist Pantheon', p. 23.

[31] Thus Professor Jayawickrama, *The Inception of Discipline and the Vinaya Nidāna* (Luzac, London, 1962), p. 116, and depictions in the local temples I visited.

> down and worship in the course of his circumambulation, after offering flowers at the upper terraces ...'[32] 'Guruḷugomi...(12th c.) says that there were sixteen *pādapīthikās* fixed at the Ruvanvälisāya indicating the points at which sixteen golden Buddha-images were enshrined inside the cetiya...[33]

As for the list's composition, it is notable that none of the superb sites of Poḷonnaruva are included, but that all the places named have sacred associations going back at least to the fifth century A.D. Moreover, it can hardly be a coincidence that half the places listed are so well distributed round the country, while the other half are in the ancient capital. It certainly looks as if the list antedates the Poḷonnaruva period, and symbolically brings the whole of Ceylon under the religious suzerainty of Anurādhapura.

These then are the sixteen places of pilgrimage, fifteen of which the devout Buddhist hopes to visit at least once in a lifetime. (Fifteen, because the site of Divyaguhā ('Day-time Cave'), in which the Buddha took a siesta at the foot of Siripāda, has not been determined.) A pilgrimage is simply called a *vandanāva* ('worshipping') or a *pin gamana*—a 'merit journey'. It may well be the longest journey in a villager's life. It is normally undertaken in large groups, without differentiation by age or sex. A monk may go too, in which case he is of course provided for by the others, but I do not think monks travel on more pilgrimages than do devout laymen. Pilgrimages may take place at any time, but there are recognized seasons for the most famous spots, and nowadays the Government makes appropriate arrangements. The season starts[34] with Siripāda, which is usually climbed in the four months ending at Wesak (in May), because that is the part of the year when it is least

[32] Rahula, *History*, pp. 117–18, with references to Buddhaghosa's commentaries.

[33] Rahula, *History*, p. 118, note 1.

[34] Kälaṇiya used to hold a *perahära* in February; this has been suspended during that monastery's difficulties since the then incumbent was jailed for his part in Mr. Bandaranaike's assassination.

likely to rain there and the sunrise may be seen in its full glory. Siripāda is the only pilgrimage necessarily to involve physical exertion, but the 3,000-foot climb up steep stone steps, up by night and down in the morning, deters neither the aged nor the pregnant woman with another baby on the hip; I went along with such a cross-section of Mīgala, and all of us made the ascent in three hours and the descent in one and a half. Poson, in June, is the time to visit Anurādhapura, because it is the anniversary of Mahinda's arrival in Ceylon. The fortnight before the full moon in August (Äsaḷa) is the time of Ceylon's two most famous religious festivals, though neither of them is on our list of pilgrimages: the procession for the tooth relic in Kandy and the festival of the god Kataragama at his eponymous centre in the south-eastern jungle. A Buddhist's visit to Kataragama, whether it is considered one of the sixteen places or not, is inevitably combined with a pilgrimage to nearby Tissamahārāma; witnessing the procession of the Tooth is anyway meritorious. Finally, September is the month of the *perahära* at Mahiyangana.

In the old days, of course, people walked on most pilgrimages, but nowadays they hire a bus from one of the companies which cater principally for this demand. Some enterprising people decide to organize a trip, calculate that they can fit fifty or sixty bodies into a bus, and divide the cost equally among the lay travellers. Some buses take pilgrims to all the sixteen places, and several besides, in a tour lasting a week or more. These buses have materially altered the character of pilgrimages. The sentimental outsider may deplore the rapid disappearance of the religious picnic party adventuring through the forest towards some scene of ruined grandeur. The safer bus journey to a repaired and whitewashed antiquity, electrically illuminated by night, may seem less romantic, and may exclude the very poor, but few Kandyan villagers in the old days can ever have reached Nāgadīpa, and the wider travel may even have marginal political advantages in increasing national sentiment. The ritual character of the pilgrimage has been equally altered: all improvements in communications work to the detriment of purely local deities. Less mobile villagers used to worship the local god before leaving his territory; then the god's overlord, the bigger god who controlled a wider area; and so on till at their destination they reached the Buddha, lord of all and god above the gods (*devātideva*). The remains of these customs, if any, are hard to recognize. On leaving Mīgala for Siripāda no one ever dreamt of bothering with our local god, Piṭiya Deyyō; but on our way we stopped in Kandy to pay our respects to the Buddha at the Temple of the Tooth, and as we climbed the mountain we chanted.

Apē Budun api vaṅdinna
Saman deyyō pihiṭa venṭa.

We praise our Buddha; god Saman, help us.

That Saman is the god of Siripāda everyone knows, but few know how far his territory extends. Much less obvious is the vestigial nature of our stop in Kandy: to go from the Buddha's tooth to the Buddha's footprint is a geographical, but not a religious ascent; however, we were worshipping the local and familiar relic before venturing into the unknown.

The two classes of relics already discussed have probably been venerated since the Buddha's death, worshipped by pilgrimage and prostration, like an old and respected teacher. The third class, the *uddesika dhātu* which 'indicate' the Buddha to remind one of him, are an innovation, though an ancient one. Though the very shape of a stupa, through its association with physical relics, has itself acquired the status of an *uddesika dhātu*, the most important example is the image of the Buddha, his representation in painting or sculpture. The Sanskrit word for any image, *pratimā*, has become specialized: in Ceylon it and its derivatives, such as Sinhalese *piḷimaya*, refer only to sacred sculpture, for the sculptured image is culturally the important one.[35]

[35]The ordinary word for sculpture in Sinhalese is *rūpaya*. Painting is *citrakarmaya* or *pintūraya*; the latter word more naturally applies

In the earliest Buddhist art, which is of course Indian, the Buddha was represented only symbolically by an empty seat under a Bo tree, a footprint, an umbrella, or the *dhammacakka*, the wheel of the law which he discovered. Or probably it would be more accurate to say that the Buddha was not shown at all, to symbolize the fact that he was *nibbuta* ('extinguished'), and certain emblems served to indicate the scene portrayed. Where and when his body was first depicted is still disputed: art historians say that it was either in Gandhāra on India's north-west border, where art was influenced by contact with the Roman Empire, or well within North India in the Mathurā school of art, and that it probably happened some time in the last two centuries before Christ. They thus reject or ignore the evidence of the *Mahāvaṃsa*, which says[36] that a stone image of the Buddha was set up by Devānampiya Tissa, i.e. in the third century B.C. This image was the most famous one in ancient Ceylon; it is frequently referred to in the chronicles, and was probably the one which so impressed the Chinese pilgrim Fa Hsien in the early fifth century A.D. (He says the image he saw was made of green jade, but that is most improbable.) It is possible that it is the same as the famous *samādhi piḷimaya* (seated Buddha image) still visible (though disfigured by restoration) on the Outer Ring Road at Anurādhapura; though this statue is far less tall than the two *chang* (about 22 feet) vaguely claimed by Fa Hsien. This *Mahāvaṃsa* testimony occurs in an account of events in the third century A.D., and was written still later; the author may have been mistaken about the statue's origin.[37] Error is, however, even less likely in the

to a framed picture, so that the wall-paintings typical of temples are generally called *citrakarma*, or *situvam*, the Eḷu form of the same word.

[36] XXXVI, 128.

[37] For more detail on this interesting question of the origin of the Buddha image see Rahula, *History*, pp. 121–5. It is sad that the facts he adduces are still so unfamiliar to art historians. I would also recommend the curious reader to his subsequent investigation of the origins of the image-house in Ceylon.

long account (chapter XXX) of Duṭugämuṇu's decoration of the relic chamber in the early first century B.C.; he had a golden Buddha image made, and many other sculptures and paintings which are enumerated. The similarity of the subjects then chosen to what I saw in the village temples I visited is quite remarkable.

Buddha images are sacred objects. They are made by special people: their manufacture is—or was before the days of mass production—the prerogative of *sittaru* (literally: 'painters'). *Sittaru* do all the art-work, both painting and sculpture, in a temple. They form a sub-caste of the *navandannō*, the caste which includes all types of craftsmen, from carpenters to goldsmiths. Another person, an artist, may in these modern times make a Buddha image, but if he has any trace of traditional sentiment left he will refrain from giving it the finishing touch, which consists in putting in the eyes, and leave this to a *sittarā*, who will perform the appropriate ceremony, a *nētra pinkama* ('eye festival'). Only then is the image sacred. As Knox put it: 'Before the Eyes are made, it is not accounted a God, but a lump of ordinary Metal, and thrown about the Shop with no more regard than anything else... The Eyes being formed, it is thenceforward a God.'[38] Though in this passage Knox calls the image a god, he elsewhere shows that in the seventeenth century the cognitive position was just as I have explained it: 'As for these Images they say they do not own them to be Gods themselves but only Figures, representing their Gods to their memories; and as such they give to them honour and worship.'[39] The *piḷimaya* is an *uddesika dhātu*. But it is also usually the repository of a *sārīrika dhātu*. For Buddhaghosa, it seems, an image was not itself a relic (*dhātu*), and was of importance only if it contained one: he only mentions regard being paid to an image (*pratimā*) which has a relic (*sadhātuka*). I have mentioned above that to this day portable relics are always in a container shaped like a stupa, or else in

[38]Knox, op. cit., p. 130 (original folio p. 82).
[39]Knox, op. cit., p. 116 (folio p. 73).

a small Buddha statue; this must have been how Buddha images acquired their sacred character; and the doctrine of the *uddesika dhātu* is still very close to the viewpoint, which seems to have been Buddhaghosa's, that an image is worshipped only for the relics it contains.

A relic is not worshipped merely by contemplation or physical gesture. Offerings are made, and such an offering is called a *pūjā*: the word does not differentiate between the act and the thing offered. Typical offerings which may be made before a *Budupiḷimaya*, a Bo tree or a stupa are flowers, incense and lights, flowers being much the commonest. Villagers visit the temple on *poya* days and other religious occasions to make these offerings but more often they are made at home. Some homes have a picture or small image of the Buddha,[40] before which these offerings are laid on a small altar. The word which here and throughout I translate 'altar', *mal āsana*, literally means 'flower seat'. In addition the main *Budupiḷimaya* in a temple is offered the same meals as the monks.

Most of the offerings I am about to describe are accompanied by Pali verses. With one unimportant exception (*Pūjemi Buddhaṃ...*, the second verse cited below) all these verses, as well as several more, are reproduced by Hocart in his account of the ritual at the Temple of the Tooth in Kandy.[41] It seems a fair guess that the verses are the same age as the rituals they accompany, but unfortunately their origin is unknown. The best that we can do at the moment is to surmise that these and the other popular devotional verses printed in the *Bauddha Ädahilla* and elsewhere, including the *Jayamangala Gāthā*, were composed in mediaeval Ceylon between say 1200 and 1500. In my opinion a later date is most unlikely, as the sixteenth century saw a great decline in Pali learning. This does

[40]Professor Obeyesekere has pointed out to me that domestic shrines to the Buddha have certain modernist implications. In any case they are unlikely to antedate the mass production of Buddha images.

[41]A. M. Hocart, *The Temple of the Tooth in Kandy, Memoirs of the Archaeological Survey of Ceylon*, vol. IV, London, 1931. The verses are on pp. 20–7 and pp. 30–1.

at least suggest that Christian influence can have played no part in their formulation. Rules for the worship of the Tooth, quoted in Hocart (pp. 34–7) from the *Daḷadā Sirita* give no details of the rituals but show that they were already elaborate. They date from soon after 1300.

The reader interested in ritual procedures should study Hocart. (I am told by Mr. H. L. Seneviratne that what Hocart describes still takes place.) I describe only the rituals I witnessed in the village, which are simpler forms of the same; moreover, my main interest in the rituals is in their ideological implications, and I arrange them accordingly. The rituals in the Temple of the Tooth form an ordered sequence not perceptible in village temples.

I shall begin with those offerings which are both the commonest and doctrinally the least problematic. In towns flowers can be bought outside every temple; in villages they are readily available. A flower should be offered without leaf or stalk, and each bloom is laid down to face the image (or Bo tree, etc.). This is merely the kind of good manners one shows to any superior, to whom one does not present one's feet or one's back. According to a sermon on the subject delivered in Mīgala at Wesak, the custom of offering flowers was started (and is still practised) by the gods. When offering a flower it is usual, but not essential, to recite these two Pali stanzas.

Vaṇṇa-gandha-guṇopetam etaṃ kusuma-santatiṃ
Pūjayāmi munindassa siripāda-saroruhe.

This heap of flowers, which has colour and scent,
I offer at the blessed lotus feet of the lord of sages.

Pūjemi Buddhaṃ kusumen' anena puññena-m-etena ca hotu mokkhaṃ.
Pupphaṃ milāyati yathā idaṃ me kāyo tathā yāti vināsabhāvaṃ.

I make offering to the Buddha with this flower, and by this merit may there be release (*mokṣa*). Just as this flower fades, so my body goes towards destruction.

Not every kind of incense is appropriate to the Buddha;

those with grosser fragrance are reserved for lower beings. The Buddha receives joss sticks, which are lit and left to smoke before him. They are generally confined to the worship of an image, maybe because the sweet smell would be lost in the open air. These are the verses which accompany respectively an offering of incense (*suvan̆da*) and of 'fragrant smoke' (*suvan̆da dum*), i.e. burning incense.

Sugandhi-kāya-vadanaṃ ananta-guṇa-gandhinaṃ
Sugandhinâhaṃ gandhena pūjayāmi Tathāgataṃ.

To him of fragrant body and face, fragrant with infinite virtues, to the Tathāgata <i.e. the Buddha> I make offering with fragrant perfume.

Gandha-sambhāra-yuttena dhūpenâhaṃ sugandhinā
Pūjaye pūjaneyyaṃ taṃ pūjā-bhājanam uttamaṃ.

With this fragrant smoke full of perfume I make offering to the supreme recipient of offerings, worthy to receive them.

The lights offered nowadays by individuals are sometimes candles, the influence of western technology and the Roman Catholic church, aided maybe by Col. Olcott. In villages the usual light offered is still an oil lamp, a little clay dish containing a strip of cloth lying in coco-nut oil. On special occasions after dark the entire premises of a temple may be outlined with such small lamps; in Mīgala this was done to commemorate the anniversary of the death of D. S. Senanayake, independent Ceylon's first prime minister. A few temples in the area have provision for a perpetual lamp to burn, a *doḷos maha pahana* (literally 'twelve-month-lamp'). This is still a coco-nut oil lamp as described, but a big one on a separate structure, e.g. a short pillar, standing in the courtyard, with some protection from the wind and rain. Here is the Pali verse for offering lights (*pahan*).

Ghana-sāra-ppadittena dīpena tama-dhaṃsinā
Tiloka-dīpaṃ sambuddhaṃ pūjayāmi tamo-nudaṃ.

With this lamp which blazes with firm strength, destroying darkness, I make offering to the truly Enlightened lamp of the three worlds, the dispeller of darkness.

The order in which I have presented these verses corresponds to how well they are known: the flower verses are in the first book of the Sunday School primer, and known to every normal person, whereas I think only the very devout layman would know the last two.

Flowers, incense and lights are the only offerings commonly made within the home. It is the remaining types of *pūjā*, those more peculiar to public places, which raise the more complicated problems. Before considering these, however, let me deal with the question raised by any offerings before relics and images: can such worship be reconciled with the cognitive position that the Buddha is dead and powerless to help? Yes certainly—it can and it is. Such offerings raise not only the question of the ontological status of the Buddha, with which we are here concerned, but also connected problems concerning 'prayer' (which will be discussed in Chapter 5) and concerning ethics (see Chapter 6) of which I can here do little more than take cognizance. However, it is essential for an understanding of the Theravādin position that I here give a brief explanation of the rationale for all such offerings.

Ask any monk, and the cognitive position is quite clear: no offering, no flowers, no recital of verses has any intrinsic merit; it is the thought that counts. The Buddhist ethic is an ethic of intention; and doctrine is consistent on this point. We may accept this, but question whether the intention in offering flowers or food is not to receive some favour in return. The answer is no. What then is the intention? There are two ways of answering this. The first is to say that there is no further intention: the thought itself, the emotion on the mind of the worshipper, if it is pure (*śuddha*), makes for what we might translate as spiritual development (*hita diyuṇuva*)[42] which is furthered by the earnest aspiration to achieve *nirvāṇa* which should ac-

[42]The literal meaning is 'mental development' or 'development of thought'.

company the offering. This answer is doctrinally orthodox and clear. The other answer might be to say that there is an intention to acquire merit (*pin*). This perhaps begs some further questions, as it seems to be coming close to granting to an act the intrinsic merit which has just been denied; but the answers of an adept informant will take us back to the same position as that disclosed by the first answer. The relation between these two answers, which cognitively can be harmonized, but affectively seem to differ, will be examined in Chapter 6. For my present purpose it suffices to note that all answers come down to talk of pure thoughts, and emphatically deny that the Buddha is seen or considered as a god, still alive or powerful.

The nature of the emotion which the worshipper is supposed to feel might be conjectured from some of the verses. The stanza on lights contains a play on words which gives it a philosophical twist: the darkness which the Buddha dispelled was the darkness of ignorance. The second stanza in the flower offering contemplates the transience of the body. Are such philosophic moods the ones that are experienced or supposed to be experienced? Very many people, though they do not know Pali, have had the meanings of the stanzas explained to them, and monks certainly understand them precisely. However, when I asked the head monk at Mīgala about *mal pūjā* he said that they are not for the Buddha, who is dead, but for us to derive joy (*prīti*) from looking at them. Buddhaghosa says[43] that one gets *Buddhālambanapīti*, joy derived from contemplation of the Buddha, by looking at a Bo tree or *caitya*. The head monk's reply was therefore in this tradition in describing the emotion of a worshipper as *prīti*, joy, though he gave it an interesting and perhaps idiosyncratic twist by making the flowers themselves the immediate reason for joy. What occasions a pure emotion is, however, irrelevant, so the discrepancy is unimportant. It is more interesting that

[43] *Sammohavinodanī (Vibhanga Aṭṭhakathā)*, p. 243; see also *Atthasālinī (Dhammasanganī Aṭṭhakathā)*, p. 91. Cited by Rahula, *History*, p. 126.

despite the clear contrary implication of some of the verses recited for particular offerings, the general emotion felt to be appropriate to *pūjā* is joy.

We now come to consider the offerings and ceremonies which are commonly said to be borrowed from Hindu practices, and thus incur the suspicion of Hindu ideological backing. Most Ceylon Tamils (the Hindus in question) worship at temples containing images which are believed to incorporate a god and thus to be in some sense alive and divine. It is, however, possible, *prima facie*, that the Buddhists should have adopted ceremonial forms and changed their meaning; this becomes all the more plausible if the forms turn out on closer inspection to have been modified.

Here is the first example. Before every meal in the monastery the principal Buddha image has a portion of the food, etc., laid before it. The shrine is emptied for a couple of minutes; then the food is taken out again, and thrown away or handed to dogs or beggars. No self-respecting Buddhist would touch it, or anything which has been offered to the Sangha, which is in the same category. In Mīgala I think it was usually eaten by dogs, as a normal *Buddha pūjā* is too small to be worth the trip for a beggar. But when lots of monks were fed and so plenty of food was left over Tamil beggars assembled behind the temple and had a feast. In their eyes such food is not even degrading, for after a Hindu *pūjā* the worshippers share the food which has been offered; but to the villagers this was a vivid illustration of the beggars' degradation, and among themselves they made some quite nasty comments to this effect. The food is offered before the Buddha image by whoever is giving the meal to the monks, or by a monk if it comes from their provisions. (Food is supplied by laymen in some monasteries always, in others almost never, in the rest somewhere in between.) Monks have two meals, breakfast and the midday meal, and in the evenings they drink tea, maybe suck sweets, and are offered also the materials for chewing betel and other things they may like to chew. A portion of all these is first offered to the Buddha image; e.g. the midday meal, which the monks eat at

11.30, is offered to the statue at 11 or soon after. The Pali stanza which may accompany this runs:

Adhivāsetu no bhante bhojanaṃ parikappitaṃ
Anukampam upādāya paṭigaṇhātu-m-uttamaṃ.

May the Lord accept the food we have prepared; taking compassion (on us) may he receive the best.

The Pali is somewhat ungrammatical. The vocative *bhante* is a normal way of addressing a senior monk in the Canon. It crops up here because *adhivāsetu no bhante* is a common phrase which (like *anukampam upādāya*) may be used when asking a monk to administer the precepts (*pan sil* or *aṭa sil*). According to the *Nidānakathā*, the two merchants who give the Buddha his first food after Enlightenment say:

Paṭigaṇhātu no bhante Bhagavā imam āhāraṃ anukampam upādāya.

May the Blessed Lord accept this food from us, taking compassion (on us).

The above verse is merely a versification of this prose formula. There are minor variants for this verse, most of which are to modify its application: instead of *bhojanaṃ*: 'food' one may offer *vyañjanaṃ*: 'curry', *taralaṃ*: 'rice gruel', *khajjakaṃ*: 'sweets', *pānīyaṃ*: 'water', *pānakaṃ*: 'drink', *bhesajjaṃ*: 'medicine', or *gilānapaccaya*, which also means 'medicine' (literally 'requisites for disease'), but in its Sinhalese form *gilampasa* is the generic term for the evening *dānē*.

At this point it may be objected that the production of sentiments of joy or philosophic contemplation may be an adequate explanation for the comparatively insubstantial offerings of flowers, incense, and lights, but that when food is offered surely something else must be involved. The *idée reçue* runs something like this: flowers, etc., are the true Buddhist offerings; food is offered to their gods by Hindus (who make no careful distinction between the image and the presence of a divinity); food is laid before the

Buddha image just as it is laid before statues of Vishnu or Kataragama (which may even be found in the same shrine); therefore the offering of food to the Buddha is a practice borrowed from the Hindus. The fact that the food thus offered is rendered sacred, in that no Buddhist will afterwards eat it, is sometimes adduced in support of this theory. To take the supporting argument first: the sacredness of the offering is of a very different character, for in a Hindu *pūjā* food which has been offered to the god is then distributed among the worshippers in a kind of communion. The practice implies that one derives benefit from the close contact of one's food with a divinity. The Buddhist attitude we saw to be just the opposite: food offered before an image is treated as if it were *sānghika*, i.e. like something given to the Order, and for this reason no longer allowed for lay use.[44] This distinction is perfectly clear, though maybe not so theoretically expressed, to the Buddhist inhabitants of Mīgala. Some of them occasionally visit a Hindu temple to Kataragama about 5 miles away which is run by and mainly patronized by Tamils. Like the Hindus they take food, offer it to the god, and then eat their share of what has been offered. They accept the Hindu theory that Kataragama has enjoyed the food, and have no theory about why they then eat it themselves. But all this has no effect on their behaviour in a Buddhist temple. An interesting question is what happens to food which is offered to, say Kataragama, in a Buddhist temple. On this I cannot speak from experience. In Mīgala temple there were no statues of gods at all, which is rather unusual. In most temples in the area there are statues of gods, but most of them are purely decorative. Even

[44]Ancient inscriptions recording gifts to the Sangha mention the unpleasant rebirth awaiting anyone who should feed on Sangha property, and a dog and crow are sometimes illustrated. The Rev. Rahula has suggested to me a contributory cause for the tradition. In the *Dhammadāyāda Sutta* (*M.N.*, *Sutta* 3) two monks arrive hungry when the Buddha has dined, and he offers them the rest of his meal. One accepts and one refuses. He praises the latter, saying that to be an heir (*dāyāda*) to material goods is nothing: one should inherit the *dhamma*.

those which are worshipped are never, to my knowledge, given offerings of food. But in some Buddhist temples in other districts a god is offered e.g. the *daval dānē* after another portion has been offered to the Buddha. Some of this can be returned to the worshipper according to the Hindu custom. Every god who is worshipped and receives offerings has his own priest (see next chapter), who in fact of course receives the offerings for him; this would apply also to offerings of food, which are not *sānghika* and are therefore fit for human consumption. Moreover gods, like Buddhist temples, have their parishes (*godurugama*) from which they receive offerings by customary right and into which no outsider intrudes without the incumbent's permission.

But the offering of food to the Buddha need not be explained by a diffusion of Hindu practices in Ceylon. Buddhaghosa says[45] that wise men before a meal offer food and drink to an image or casket (*cetiya*) containing a relic which they place before them. This is exactly the practice we saw to be followed today at a *dānē* when the *Budu piḷimaya* in the temple is too far away for convenience. The offering before the portable relic is the older custom: to make it before the large, stationary image which contains a relic is but a logical extension. This is not to deny that Hindu influence may have been helpful in formulating modern procedure: the *Buddha pūjā* at mealtimes is no doubt sociologically overdetermined. This conclusion is reinforced by the tenor of other offerings and ceremonies.

The crucial respect in which modern practice seems to have changed from that commended by Buddhaghosa is the recitation of the verse quoted above, in which the Buddha, being asked to accept the food, is addressed as if he were alive. This looks like a break-through of what I shall show to be the affective attitude to the cognitive level: feelings that the Buddha is a living presence here seem to find expression in words. The case is not clear-cut: the

[45] *Samanta-pāsādikā* (*Vinaya Aṭṭhakathā*), III, 264–5. Cited by Rahula, *History*, p. 125.

man reciting the Pali formula *Adhivāsetu no bhante*, to which he is also accustomed in other contexts, may not fully understand its meaning, let alone its implications, nor is he likely to understand the exact meaning of the rest of the verse; after all, it is one thing to compose such a verse oneself, quite another to mouth a half-understood conventional phrase in a dead language. Still, when all is said and done, I think the words do amount to a cognitive inconsistency, which is not removed by saying outside the immediate context of the *Buddha pūjā* that of course the Buddha is not there to hear the words or accept the food.

One very particular *dānē* had best be mentioned here, the *kiripiḍu pātraya* ('bowl of milk-rice'). This is—or was– an annual harvest festival, an offering to the Buddha of first fruits in the form of a huge bowl of milk-rice. The festival is obsolete in my area, and my information is unfortunately scanty. I was told that the rice was prepared in the presence of only male villagers, some of whom danced as it was cooking. In these respects the festival sounds similar to the *aḍukku*, offerings of first fruits to the local village gods, which I mention in the next chapter. On the other hand I was told that originally the rice was buried after being offered, though in more recent times it had been given to beggars which is to say that it got the normal treatment of a *Buddha pūjā*, whereas *aḍukku*, like other offerings to gods made off *vihāra* premises, are eaten by the participants. Moreover, the dish of milk-rice was offered in commemoration of the dish of milk-rice which Sujātā offered to Gotama the day before his Enlightenment. The rice was cooked on temple premises (in Mīgala on the porch of the *vihāra gedara*), and if the ceremony was correctly performed the relic in the stupa emitted rays (*Budu räs*) in the five colours of the Buddha's halo. This happened in the days of my informants' grandfathers. (No doubt the event was always ascribed to the past.) The ability to emit such rays is a property of *sārīrika dhātu* and does not appear as anomalous or miraculous to those who do not share western ideas concerning the laws of nature. A schoolmaster was, however, worried by the idea and suggested that the rays were an illusion arising from the 'fumes' of the cooking rice.

We have now enumerated all the types of offerings accompanied by Pali verses recorded in *Bauddha Ädahilla*, which may suggest that those still to be described are doctrinally less orthodox. Though most of the standard objects which can be offered have been listed, any offering for the embellishment of a sacred object or improvement of the shrine can count as *pūjāva*, and such miscellanea as a vase for flowers or a table to serve as a *mal āsana* need not detain us. However, the offerings of cloth (*redi*) deserve special mention. Before the main *Budupiḷimaya* there is always a curtain rail on which hangs a curtain, which is often of fine material, and may have the name of the donor embroidered on it. The custom is an imitation of the curtains which hang before Hindu images, and hence also before many Buddhist statues of gods. However, the contrast with Hindu usage is again instructive.

In a Hindu temple (*kovil*) the image, which is conceived of as incorporating a living presence, is kept veiled behind its curtain or curtains and can never be seen by a casual observer. The statues of gods in Buddhist buildings devoted to them (*dēvālē*) are also kept behind curtains, but the curtain will always be drawn by the attendant priest (*kapurāḷa*), or indeed by other people, on request. Those statues of gods which are inside a *vihāra gedara* may not even have curtains, and be treated with no respect at all, their importance diminishing with their proximity to a Buddha image.[46] All this is as much as for the Buddhists to say, 'We know that as Hindu gods you are entitled to such prerogatives as curtains, but here you are quite secondary to the Buddha.' The living Hindu images, then, are entitled to privacy, or even secrecy; but there should be no

[46]Analogously: in more than a hundred visits to photograph *vihāra* I have only twice been refused permission to photograph a Buddha image; statues of gods in the *vihāraya* may always be photographed, even those behind curtains, but one sometimes feels that the laity do not like it; images in separate *dēvālēs* may usually *not* be photographed; images in shrines of *kovils*, in my experience, never.

restrictions on access to a Buddha image, in the first place because it is not alive, and in the second place because, even if it were, Buddhism is exoteric and anyone should have access to the Buddha. I shall have occasion to return to this point.

The influence of Hindu practice is also suggested by the various cloths which sometimes cover the Buddha's hands or feet and legs. A standing Buddha has the right hand raised in blessing, and in some temples this hand is covered by a cloth. A seated Buddha may have a cloth covering the entire lap. Apart from a cloth, a particular kind of ornament, which I might call a cloth rosette but is doubtless intended as a lotus, is often placed on the folded hands, and maybe elsewhere. This 'cloth lotus' is a round cloth disc, made in patchwork and multi-coloured, with many tiny 'petals' radiating from the centre. The idea of covering the hands and feet (both of which are painted with auspicious marks) may be an analogue with Hindu practice; the form of the cloth lotus I can only surmise to show the influence of flower offerings.

A final specific offering of cloth is the offering of flags (*koḍi*), or rather pennants. These pennants may be strung up in rows in an image-house; but the usual practice is to tie them to the Bo tree. Here the influence is not specifically Hindu; ancient evidence shows the custom to be a survival of tree worship which has occasionally gravitated into the shrine. To place *koḍi* in the *vihāragē* was not customary in my area, and in Mīgala and its immediate surroundings they were not even tied on to trees, so I am no authority on the practice. It seems clear, however, that originally any strips of coloured cloth were used, as they still are in some parts of Ceylon, and the pennant shape is a mere formalization, perhaps under western influence. Such pennants, made of paper, are carried on sticks in village *perahäras* by children, and their shape is that of some church flags, of which they could be a miniature version.

Claims made by the worshippers that they are merely commemorating a dead man, who lived as a simple monk, become increasingly difficult to justify in the context of the ceremonies still to be discussed. For clarity of analysis I have now stated the cognitive claims as two: that the Buddha was a man, and that he was a monk on the same level as any monk who attains *nirvāṇa*. The doctrinal position is unequivocal on both points; but in our context the former seems the more crucial: it is less jarring to treat an image of a dead monk as if it were a dead king than as if it were alive. It is over the question of the Buddha's earthly status that the first discrepancies seem to arise; and I shall show that they date from ancient times.

The only common offering which I have not so far discussed is the 'offering of sound' (*śabda pūjāva*), which consists essentially of drumming. This drumming is the prerogative and duty of a certain caste, the *beravāyō*. In Mīgala these drummers are attached to the temple as feudal villeins; they have a hereditary right to tenure of lands owned by the temple in return for which they must perform hereditary services. If the temple agrees the service may be commuted for a cash rent, but the tenure is always revocable by the temple. This system of social organization will be mentioned at greater length in Chapter 8; for present purposes only a passing remark on it need be made. Originally there was a wide variety of such service tenures; indeed it is arguable that the great majority of Sinhalese castes originated in this way. Normally, of course, the services are due to people, and in the case of *vihāragam*, villages owned by monasteries, they are due to monks.

In the 150 years since the end of the Kandyan kingdom the feudal organization has gradually declined, and though most people still work on land owned by others, service tenures in the strict sense have become a rarity. Drummers, however, perform a service which is principally required for the Buddha, and is therefore in continued demand. Any temple of some age—say fifty years—is almost certain to own land, and some of this land is probably leased to drummers in return for their professional services. Although drumming is not the only caste-bound profession—laundering is another—it is the only one, at least in the area where I worked, which is regularly associated with service tenures, and this to such an extent that the term *rājakāriyō* literally 'workers for the king', which used to designate all feudal villeins, is now widely taken to refer only to drummers living off temple lands.

There are various types of Sinhalese drums, and their use shows some regional variation. In the Mīgala area the basic and essential drum on religious occasions is the *bera*, the long drum, tapering at both ends, which gives the caste its name. The drum is worn slung round the neck, and struck with the hands at both ends. In Mīgala it was invariably accompanied by the *horaṇāva*, a shrill wind instrument looking like a large and simplified oboe, with a limited range of notes. The players of the *horaṇāva* are hereditary specialists, also of the drummer caste; the playing does not seem to require much skill, as the notes produced follow no discernible pattern. In Mīgala drumming usually consists of one or two *bera* and a *horaṇāva*, sometimes accompanied by a *hēvisi*, a squat cylindrical drum. The other instruments, a couple of which are mentioned in my article on the *nētra pinkama*, are not used in Mīgala.

The paradigm case of a *śabda pūjāva* is that which occurs at the temple itself on *poya* days and any other special occasions, such as a big *pirit*. The drums are beaten for a few minutes at three times on those days, to coincide with the three offerings of food. Ideally the drumming begins when the food is taken in to the shrine, continues for a few minutes while it is left there, and stops when the food is taken out again. Drumming may also occur at other times of the day, but this is said to be 'for no particular reason' (*nikam*) not 'as worship' (*pūjāvaṭa*). However, a formal *śabda pūjāva* can be offered at other times, as an item by itself. I observed this after a *tun māsa dānē*, at which a householder feeds monks three months after the death of a relation: drummers stood outside a shrine and played for a few minutes without any other ritual. The giver of the *dānē* acquired merit by this (merit which he was to pass on to the dead man), in that he paid the drummers for their services. In Mīgala and most other old temples, drummers are attached to the temple by feudal ties, and so do not get paid. Temples which do not command the services of drummers almost invariably hire them on *poyas*, though a poor temple may miss out the quarter (*aṭavaka*) *poya* and even the *māsa poya* (when there is no moon). The going rate for such drumming is two rupees a day. In Mīgala there was a drummer living near the temple who usually performed, but for full moon days and other big occasions drummers came from the temple's *vihāragama* a few miles away, bedding down in a corner of the *pansala*. Even in such cases, when the drummers perform unpaid, as a duty, the mere making of the offering is meritorious, and all who participate in thought earn merit. To the end that more might hear the drumming and hence have the opportunity to participate in the offering, the head monk had built while I was there a *hēvisi maṇḍapa*, a small roofed enclosure on a rocky prominence near the temple, from which it was estimated that the sound could carry to the furthest parts of the village.

Drumming also accompanies any *perahära* or *pinkama* worth the name, attending the relics whenever they leave the temple; but this is not strictly a *pūjāva*, for such processions with drumming—and sometimes with dancing too—are by no means necessarily religious, but may take place for any secular festivity, from occasions of state to the homecoming of some newly-wed rich villager. This identity of religious and secular ceremonial is the point to which I wish to draw attention.

The *śabda pūjāva* is last on my list of regular offerings, and the only common one for which no Pali verses exist. It is not hard to imagine why this should be so. In the first place, anyone who has experienced such drumming inside a *vihāraya* will realize that during it one cannot hear oneself think, let alone recite. More important, perhaps, is the non-religious nature of the offering, on which I shall expatiate after describing the *sūvisi pinkama*. Finally, there is a subtle difference in the form of the *pūjā*, in that other offerings are presented by the worshipper himself, whereas in this case he is merely paying others—professionals—to make the offering.

The three remaining ceremonies which I shall describe deviate increasingly from doctrinal expectations, and are all rather major affairs reserved for special occasions. The first can be viewed as an elaborate extension of the drumming offerings described above. This is the *sūvisi pinkama. Sūvisi* is the old Sinhalese for 'twenty-four', and the reference is to the twenty-four previous Buddhas. The ceremony, if that is the correct word for an occasion which does not seem to be highly formalized, consists in Kandyan dancing by a troupe of dancers and drummers, who meanwhile chant religious poems, in particular about the lives of the previous Buddhas. The show goes on for three (or six) nights, theoretically with eight (or four) dances a night; in my experience the dances invariably start so late that there is not time for eight before dawn at 6 a.m., when the meeting breaks up; but nevertheless the second and third nights always start with the ninth and seventeenth Buddhas respectively. Sometimes the three-night *sūvisi* is supplemented by a fourth night on which the *sat satiya* is danced, one dance for each of the seven weeks Gotama Buddha spent immediately after Enlightenment.

The *sūvisi* and similar dances are called *pantēru näṭum*, 'tambourine dances', because the dancers carry tambourines. These dances were devised by Mr. H. M. Kiri Baṇḍā of Halāgiriya in Kāgalla District (which is between Kandy and Colombo); they were inspired by certain rituals at the Temple of the Tooth, and first performed in 1912. Initially confined to that part of the Kāgalla District known as the Four Kōralēs, they have in the last twenty years become very popular in the Up Country. Despite their modern date their inspiration is wholly traditional.

A troupe is led by a 'teacher' (*gurunnānsē*), who in the performance faces the dancers, keeping time with a tiny pair of cymbals called *tālampaṭa* and leading the recitation. The poetry recited may be his own composition, or his teacher's, or derive from a published source like the *Arahata Vandanāva*, a long and rather miscellaneous religious poem, dating from the Kandyan period, which Mr. Kiri

Baṇḍā used before writing his own poems. In the *sūvisi* the dance for each Buddha begins and ends with verses about him, but the major part in the middle is danced to religious verses on any subject. The actual drummers always belong to the drummer caste (*beravāyō*), but the *gurunnansē* and his dancers may belong to any caste. Formerly only males could dance, but recently—'by popular demand'—girls have been included: this appearance of dancing girls in a Buddhist temple is flagrantly untraditional.

I attended three different *sūvisi pinkam* for a total of five nights, and though detailed accounts would here be out of place, it will be convenient to describe them in outline. They were not arranged for a date of any religious significance. They were major features in fund-raising drives for new temple buildings, and from the point of view of their organizers, the temple incumbents, were purely commercial undertakings. This is certainly the standard, perhaps the invariable pattern. The performing troupe was hired for so many rupees a night (R.150 in one case), but the organizers could be sure of collecting enough money from lay spectators to make a considerable profit. Although this commercial motive was obvious to all, for the spectators the occasion offered both entertainment and religious merit. In this it resembled all *baṇa* (preaching); indeed, a *sūvisi pinkama* has much in common with *baṇa*, and will have to be mentioned again under that head; here I am concerned only with its relevance to worship of the Buddha. The entertainment element is more obvious than is usual with *baṇa*, as spectators could watch singing and dancing; religious merit could be acquired both by listening to the words about previous Buddhas and by contributing financially—and of course, as always, by rejoicing in the acquisition of merit by others.

The night's events began with two pure fund-raising activities. First came an auction (*salpiḷa*) of sundry objects donated by laymen. There followed a *malvatti vendēsiya*, the sale of a tray of flowers to the last bidder, a universal feature of temple fundraising occasions. An arrangement of opulent flower blossoms on a tray is shown to the assembled laity, and young men who act as ushers then move among them collecting donations. In my experience this takes the form of a competition between villages, but this competitive element seems quite artificial. Each donation is announced by an usher standing in a commanding position and using a microphone at maximum volume; he announces the amount, and the village of the donor. Each large amount is greeted by 'Sādhu sādhu sā'. The event continues for two or three hours, and the ushers make frenetic efforts to maintain enthusiasm. The money is not added up, but the flower-tray is 'won' for his village by the last person to make a donation—in other words, when no more money can be elicited. What is really won is the right to offer the flowers to the Buddha—not that this confers any religious distinction, as the flowers are first carried round for everyone to touch with folded hands and thus share in the merit of the offering.

It is only at this point—usually after midnight—that monks appear on the scene. They take no particular notice of the images of the twenty-four Buddhas; they participate throughout the proceedings *de haut en bas, not* as worshippers. They are first offered requisites (*pirikara*).[47] At one of the *sūvisi pinkam* I attended, twenty-four sets of monks' robes (*sivuru*) had been bought beforehand by donors who subscribed at least ten rupees (their names were read out), and the idea was to offer one of these before each dance. Before a robe was offered it was carried round among the audience for people to put coins (*pan̆duru*) on it as an additional contribution. Each set of robes was offered before the pictures of the twenty-four Buddhas; moreover, there were twenty-four Buddhas but not twenty-four monks present; so in some sense the robes were being of-

[47]The eight requisites are three robes: the two-fold robe (*depaṭa sivura*), the single robe worn at home (*tanipaṭa sivura*) and the lower robe (*an̆danā sivura*); a belt (*sivuru paṭiya*); razor (*dāḷipihiyē*); filtering cloth (*perahankaḍaya*); needle and thread (*idikaṭuva* and *nūl bōlē*); and alms bowl (*pātrē*). This list, which I reproduce exactly as it was told me, is canonical; it was (and is) supposed to comprise an exhaustive list of a monk's personal possessions.

fered to the Buddhas though they were to become the property of the monks. The offering of robes will be discussed below in connection with a ceremony which affords a more clear-cut case. Towels (also reckoned as *pirikara*) were also there, to be offered by any person or group who put up two rupees, a feat only achieved after considerable exhortation from the incumbent monk. These were offered to the monks direct.

Before each dance a monk gives a 'sermon', consisting of a reading from the *Nidānakathā* or one of its Sinhalese versions in the *Pūjāvaliya* or the *Saddharmālaṃkāraya*. He reads out the story of each Buddha whose story is about to be danced. After the sermon the dancers appear and begin their performance. They dance before a screen on which have been put up pictures of the twenty-four previous Buddhas. On two occasions this took place in the *baṇa gedara* (preaching hall), on the other under a pavilion (*maṇḍapa*) erected *ad hoc*. On no occasion therefore were they dancing in the presence of a consecrated Buddha image, nor do I imagine that they ever do so, as there would be no room for the dancers, let alone the spectators, in a shrine room. Nevertheless I feel entitled to suggest that they dance primarily for the Buddhas, only secondarily for the spectators. No Sinhalese would put it like this; they consider the object of the *pinkama* to be to gain merit and to raise funds, and the question 'for whom' the dancing is intended does not arise explicitly. However, the dancers behave as if performing a religious ritual: they begin by taking the Three Refuges and Five Precepts. Moreover, they then dance as if the pictures were the principal audience, facing them most of the time; most of the human audience view the performance from *behind*, the monks and other privileged people usually getting a side view.

These notes on the *sūvisi pinkama* may be completed by an impression of the first troupe I saw (not the family troupe). There were six dancers, accompanied by three drummers on *bera*. The costume showed red, white, and gold against the dark bodies. Each dancer had a white headdress, a kind of turban with two long ends falling waist-length behind him. His only other garment was a white sarong, bunched in a frill at the waist in front. Over this he wore a red belt and a red kerchief tied round the waist, and he had coloured side-pockets on the sarong. Feet, like torso and arms, were bare, but he wore golden armbands, heavy golden anklets, and long golden earrings. He held a tambourine, which he frequently passed between his hands or tossed in the air. The dancing varied between slow and fast tempi, and during the slow passages verses were chanted in an unmelodious monotone. For an outsider the fast passages were much the more exciting; egged on by the drummers, they went faster and faster, till at the climax the pattern of group movement would be broken by individual displays of twirls, somersaults, etc., which reached great acrobatic virtuosity.

To explain the form of this ceremony, of which there is no published account, has involved some digression from my theme, the compatibility of such rituals with explicit doctrine. The seventh precept listed in Chapter 2, which is taken by all monks and all laymen undertaking any special religious observance, is 'to abstain from seeing dancing, music vocal and instrumental, and shows'. A *sūvisi pinkama* is sponsored, organized, and presided over by monks, and watched by laity, however pious, as an act of religious merit. No villagers (or village monks) seem to regard this as an infringement of the seventh precept, because the *sūvisi* and allied *pinkam* are classed as *baṇa*. One might add that many monks do not scruple to attend performances of Kandyan dancing even in a completely secular context, classifying it as 'culture' (*saṃskṛtiya*) rather than mere entertainment (*vinōdē*). Kandyan dancing is widely supported by the Government and officially considered educational.

However, my principal concern here is not the keeping of the precepts, but the behaviour towards the Buddha (and his predecessors). In considering the first set of offerings we saw that the Buddha is usually addressed in the accompanying verses by terms which refer to his monastic status, and behaviour is compatible with this conception.

To offer musical performance in the *śabda pūjāva*, let alone a night-long combination of music and dancing, is plainly not to treat him as a monk should in theory be treated. Rather it is to treat him like a king. This interpretation does not originate with me but with some of my informants. It is a doctrinal inconsistency of which they are aware, and which they tend to excuse by saying that these things were done for the kings of Kandy, who ordered that they should be done for the Buddha likewise.

In fact, however, both the dancing and singing before relics and the explicit attribution of kingship considerably antedate Kandyan times, for they occur in the first part of the *Mahāvaṃsa*. It is recorded (chapter XXXIV) of King Bhātikābhaya (A.D. 38–67) that he not only offered the Great Stupa (the modern Ruvanvälisāya) incredible masses of flowers, perfumed unguents, lamps, water (as an offering to stupas outside my experience, but perhaps a transference from watering the Bo tree), and jewellery including 'lotuses of gold, the size of wheels' (line 47), but also arranged in honour of the Great Stupa 'various dances and plays with various instrumental music' (line 60). His brother King Mahādāṭhikamahānāga, who succeeded him, seems to have been equally munificent; when he had built the Ambatthala stupa on Mihintalē he covered it with a red woollen blanket festooned with pearls and gold balls (line 74), put up flags, triumphal arches, etc., and had dancing, singing, and instrumental music (line 78). The entire description of this ceremony is very reminiscent of modern practices, though if the account is credible modern times have not witnessed anything comparably lavish. The fact that the focus of a *sūvisi pinkama* is likely to be a *Budupiḷima* loses most of its significance as possible image-worship if such festivals have traditionally been associated with all types of Buddha relics, and the claim of the worshippers that the image is quite secondary gains plausibility.

The ascription of temporal sovereignty to relics dates virtually from the introduction of Buddhism to Ceylon, and subsequently was to become almost a commonplace.

King Devānampiya Tissa worshipped (Pali: *pūjesi*) some young Bo trees by offering them a white umbrella, emblem of royalty, and performing the royal consecration (*abhiseka*) (*Mhv.* XIX, 59). Duṭugämuṇu did exactly the same (same Pali roots) for the relics he was enshrining in the great stupa (XXXI, 90), and gave them sovereignty over Ceylon for seven days (XXXI, 111). The purely symbolic nature of such gestures is surely indisputable; they do not ascribe life or the capacity to rule to the saplings or the bones. Though, as I must repeat, the ceremonies I have described are no doubt sociologically over-determined, it seems to me more relevant for their interpretation to recall Buddhist practice of 2,000 years' standing than to equate them with the usage of Hindus who treat their images as gods and their gods as kings, and provide them with music at mealtimes much as the drums are beaten during the *Buddha pūjā*.

Before passing to the next ceremony, let me finally note the linguistic evidence for what an outsider might call 'confusion of spiritual and temporal power' in the Sinhalese concept of the Buddha. I have already mentioned that the commonest Sinhalese word for monk is *hāmuduruvō*, meaning 'lord'. Like the English equivalent, the word can refer to spiritual or temporal authority, so when the Buddha is referred to as *Buduhāmuduruvō* this ambiguity is preserved. The only other common title of the Buddha is *Budu rajānanvahansē*, which may be translated 'His Majesty King Buddha'. In writing of the Buddha, or speaking of him with formal correctitude, certain honorifics are used; for instance the ending *-sēka* after a verb is reserved for him alone. I believe that all these honorifics were formerly used for kings of Kandy. Finally, the word *tēvāva*, which used to denote personal services (e.g. fanning) involved in waiting on the king, was used as a synonym of *pūjāva* in the context of the next ceremony to be described, in which several such operations are performed. Linguistically the Buddha is the last remaining, the permanent Sinhalese king.

The inconsistency with orthodox doctrine in treating

a Buddha relic or image like a king may be said to be interesting but not glaring. After all, it is natural that respectful behaviour should be modelled on situations in human society; moreover, it can even be objected that the Buddha *could* have become a universal monarch, but rejected temporal power for a career in which even kings bowed down to him. But, most important of all, the confusion perhaps began with the Buddha himself. In the canonical text already quoted for evidence of relics and pilgrimages, the Buddha tells his attendant Ānanda that he should be cremated like a great king, and a stupa (Pali: *thūpa*) should be erected for him at a crossroads. 'And whoever shall put there garland or perfume or paint, or worship there (*abhivādessanti*) or calm their minds, that will long conduce to their welfare and happiness.' He goes on to say that he, the Sammāsambuddha, a Paccekasambuddha, any other *arhat* (a *Tathāgata-sāvaka*),[48] or a righteous emperor of the world is worthy of a stupa, because on recollecting their excellence people will become tranquil and go to heaven after death.[49] This reason for relic worship is exactly that which I was given by villagers and have already recorded above. Whether these passages are interpolations I cannot here discuss; even if they are, they are extremely ancient (before Buddhism came to Ceylon); and for the Sinhalese the question does not arise.

So far it is only the Buddha's monastic status which has been compromised, and for this he himself sowed the seed. That he was mortal is still not in doubt: when I asked about this at the *sūvisi pinkama* a monk told me firmly that the whole performance was merely out of respect (*gauravayen*) for the Buddha's memory

There are, however, two further ceremonies involving a Buddha image which cannot be explained in the same way—at least, when I questioned the monks present at the ceremonies no one attempted a rationalization, but

[48]For these three types of Buddha see above, pp. 81–2, where they have been given the Sanskritic names used by my informant.

[49]*D.N.*, II, 141–3 (*Sutta* 16. 511–12).

explained them as traditions of no religious significance. These two ceremonies also appear to be less ancient. We have seen that chapter XXXIV of the *Mahāvaṃsa* mentions every *pūjā* with which I have so far dealt[50] (with the exception of the food offering mentioned by Buddhaghosa slightly later), and a few more besides. The next ceremony concerns the anointing of an image, and I know of no references to it in early literature. However, the *Cūlavaṃsa* (chapter XXXIX) tells how a general under King Kassapa I (478–496) was refused permission to perform an *abhiseka* festival for a Buddha image (1, 7), but held it under his successor. *Abhiseka* means anointing: though it is the same word as that used for royal inauguration, that meaning can hardly fit here. Rahula[51] and Geiger[52] say they do not know what ceremony is being referred to, and we shall never know for certain. But it does seem possible that it was related to the *nānumura mangalya* which I shall now describe, as that word means 'Festival of Anointing'. The *nānumura mangalya* is mentioned in the regulations of Parakkama Bāhu IV (early fourteenth century).[53]

The *nānumura mangalya* is performed only annually,[54] at the Sinhalese New Year. The Sinhalese New Year centres on 14 April, but various observances and celebrations stretch over about a week. Astrologers declare a day, shortly before or after 14 April, on which people are supposed to bathe for the New Year; and the ritual has been

[50] The *sūvisi pinkama* is not attested, but I am merely concerned with its character as dancing and singing, covered by the Pali term *naṭanacca*.

[51] Op. cit., p. 283.

[52] Note to his translation of *Cūlavaṃsa*, XXXIX, 7 (*Cūlavaṃsa*, vol. 1, p. 43). I agree with him in rejecting Wijesinha's interpretation that the *abhiseka* is a *nētra pinkama*. There is no evidence that a *nētra pinkama* can be referred to as an 'anointing'; moreover, this would be the earliest reference to a *nētra pinkama* by over a thousand years.

[53] Hocart, p. 35.

[54] In the Temple of the Tooth it takes place every Wednesday. See Hocart, pp. 30–1. It is also said to be performed every Wednesday at Lankātilaka and Mahiyangana.

extended to the Buddha image.[55] There is no special auspicious moment (*näkät vēlāva*) at which the ceremony has to be performed, but it must be over in time for the monks to go and bathe in the river themselves, in the stretch reserved for them, and return in time for the *dānē* at 11.

The ceremony I witnessed was at Mīgala at about 8.30 a.m. on 10 April 1965, and was performed by the two adult monks in residence at the time. At Mīgala there are two *vihāragedara*, one dating from the eighteenth century. The incumbent explained the ceremony as a relic of the days of the Sinhalese kings, now preserved in only a few old temples; the things done for the Buddha image, he said, used to be done for the kings, who then ordered that they be done for the Buddha likewise. The crucial difference in performance was that the Buddha was only anointed on his mirror image. Normally no laymen witnessed this ceremony, but I was allowed to do so as a favour. To this and the use of the mirror I shall return below.

In the *pansala* the unguents (*nānu*) are prepared on a tray: saffron bark (*kokum potta*), margosa leaves (*kohom̆ba koḷa*), turmeric (*amu kaha*), sesamum (*tala*), green gram (*mūn äṭa*), punac (*mīmura*), coco-nut (*pol*), red and white sandalwood (*rat* and *sudu han̆dun*), and 'all kinds of sour things' (*okkoma äm̆bul jāti*): limes (*dehi*), sour oranges (*äm̆bul doḍam*) and tangerines (*nas nāram*). The pieces of red and white sandal, from which a little has been shaved, are said to date from the Sinhalese kings. Each of the ingredients is mixed with oil and made into a paste; then a little of each paste is taken and mixed into one paste in the centre of the tray.

There is a small *perahära* up to the temple, with the usual drummers (*bera* and *horaṇāva*). Someone carries on his head under a canopy not only the unguents but also a mirror, a kettle of water, a fly whisk (*cāmara*), a small bell, and a set of the eight requisites in a package. At the

[55]The *nānumura mangalya* which I saw was on 10 April, but most of the villagers put special unguents on their heads and then bathed on 17 April. Probably the two events ideally take place on the same day; but life in Mīgala was never so tidy.

temple an oil lamp is lit on either side of the door, and the junior monk sweeps out the temple. Someone blows a conch shell many times, and the drums and fife play. The shrine room is shut, with only the two monks and me inside it, and for light a single candle is placed by the head of the main Buddha image, which is a recumbent one. All is now ready, and the chief monk shouts to the drummer through the door 'Strike up' ('Gahāpan'). The two monks then kneel before the Buddha image and worship, bending their heads to the floor three times. They are very serious. The chief monk then wedges the mirror on the pedestal by the Buddha's head, so that it reflects the head at an angle, and uses a flower head left there in offering to smear paste onto the mirror. The junior monk pours water over the mirror from the kettle, and the chief monk removes the paste with the same flower. The same is repeated for a smaller Buddha statue in the same shrine, a seated image. The chief monk then offers the robes to the lying Buddha, and in turn waves the fan and the yak's tail before him and rings the little bell. After each action he bows deeply with folded hands. Finally both monks kneel and mutter a few words beneath their breath. Exactly the same sequence of events, minus the initial worshipping, was repeated at the other *vihāragedara*. The chief monk, who had a skin complaint, preferred to bathe in hot water and did not proceed to the river, but the junior monk went with two novices and many male hangers-on to the river, where before bathing they all anointed their heads with a mixture of sour stuffs from a brass urn.

This simple ceremony combines elements which can be said to correspond to at least three different conceptions of the Buddha. The analogy with a secular king was sufficiently explained by the chief monk and I need only add a reminder that a yak's tail is a traditional Indian accoutrement of royalty, and the waving of a fan and ringing of a small musical bell (in addition to the usual drumming) likewise were the actions of royal attendants performing *tēvāva*.

A different conception is reflected in the action of offering the eight requisites. It may at first seem implausible to argue that food laid before a statue argues a different attitude from clothing similarly offered, and certainly the two can be seen as a continuum; nevertheless there are certain contrasts which I wish to stress. First, I must repeat that the former (offering food) was justified by the monks themselves in canonical terms, whereas the latter (offering robes) was not, so that there is a clear distinction for the participants themselves. Secondly, the offering of food has been shown to stem from an ancient tradition, whereas I know of no ancient authority for offering robes to a relic of any kind. Finally, food may be offered to anyone, but the requisites can only be offered to monks and novices (*pävidi*). At first sight this looks orthodox: did we not say that the Buddha was a monk? But there is something odd about a monk's offering the requisites, because while occasions can and do arise (as when a junior monk waits upon the others at meals) when a monk offers food (and the monk who offers food before the Buddha can be said to act on this analogy), on no occasion does a monk offer requisites—they are always offered by laymen. The requisites, in short, are always offered to someone of distinctly higher religious status. Therefore when the chief monk offered the requisites before the Buddha image he was behaving not merely as if the Buddha were a monk, but as if he were a person on another religious plane. While the respect shown in making the offerings first discussed (from flowers to food) was shown to be modelled on that shown by laymen to monks, here it is monks who are treating the Buddha as a super-monk.

The Buddha has been treated as if he were a king and/or a super-monk. Whether he has been treated as alive in the statue[56] is on the evidence so far still ambigu-

[56]Discussion in this chapter centres on treatment of the Buddha image. It would be possible to draw a distinction between treatment of the image and treatment of the Buddha himself; logically it could be argued that the image might be conceived of as alive while the Buddha was still conceived of as dead. This would imply that the image had a life which was not the Buddha's. That this distinction

ous; but it is this question to which we must now turn. One detail which seems incongruous with the claim that the Buddha was a mere mortal is the case of the mirror. Kings have yaks' tails waved before them, and monks are offered robes, but no human, dead or alive, has his face anointed in its reflection only. A possible interpretation of this use might be that it arose merely from a veneration so great that the monk considered himself unworthy to touch even a representation of the Buddha's face. This, however, becomes implausible when we find that a monk has no general reluctance to touch representations of the Buddha. A far stronger interpretation emerges when we take into account another ceremony in which a mirror is used, my final example.

However, before leaving the *nānumura mangalya* I must mention a less tangible point: the atmosphere of secrecy surrounding the main part of the ceremony. Esotericism and secrecy are wholly untypical of Theravāda Buddhism. Access to the sacred is free for all. A Hindu deity is tucked away in his shrine, usually visible only to the attendant priest, and in many Hindu temples permitted proximity is graded by the caste and ritual purity of the worshipper. The contrast between Buddhist and Hindu practices in Ceylon is neatly exemplified by the use of the curtain before the image, to which I have already referred. The shut doors of the shrine—which we shall also find again in the next ceremony—suggest not merely Hindu forms but also Hindu ideology: the image has become a god—only affectively, of course.

My final example of a ceremony involving a Buddha image is the *nētra pinkama*, or 'eye festival'; the final touch, which completes an image, is to paint in its eyes. I have described this ceremony at length elsewhere,[57] so I shall

would be over-complex and unnecessary is shown by such phenomena as the recitation of the qualities of the Buddha as a spell, which will be discussed in Chapter 4 in the context of the use of sacred texts. All these actions imply a living presence, and whose if not the Buddha's?

[57] 'The Consecration of a Buddhist Image', *Journal of Asian Studies*, vol. XXVI, no. 1, 1966, pp. 23–36.

restrict myself to the barest recapitulation of my conclusions. Certain elements of the ceremony made me agree with Knox's interpretation (quoted above on p. 134) that, 'The Eyes being formed, it is thenceforward a God.' That adding the eyes should be the action which consecrates the image is itself significant; the features of a mere image could presumably be finished in any order. The ceremony is undertaken by the specialist craftsmen who made the image as the culmination of long and elaborate ritual. It seems very dangerous, for it can only be undertaken at an extremely auspicious moment. The craftsman and his assistant shut themselves into the shrine and everyone is warned to keep clear even of the outer door. A mirror is again used; the craftsman does not paint the mirror which would be ineffective, but he looks only at the mirror while painting the statue's eyes sideways or over his shoulder. Afterwards he is led out blindfold, and the covering is removed when his eyes will first fall on something, such as water, which he can then destroy symbolically with a sword-stroke.

What the craftsman fears is obviously the gaze of the image, which is conceived as being so powerful that it cannot be borne direct; everyone else must put closed doors and as much space as possible between themselves and the gaze, while he who has seen it come into being, even reflected in a mirror, has dangerous potential in his own gaze till the evil has been transferred and killed. The concept of the dangerous look or gaze (*bälma*) is common currency among the Sinhalese, and of course in many other cultures: for instance illnesses (notably psychological troubles) for which medical diagnosis is not accepted are usually ascribed to the gaze of some evil spirit (*yakā*). Indeed, the *nētra pinkama* contains elements common to most Sinhalese exorcism. That the circumstances of a *nētra pinkama* imply the attribution of life to the image cannot be and was not denied; the monks pooh-poohed the whole thing as a meaningless (but harmless) tradition. In the terms of my analysis, the ceremony treats the Buddha as a god. But what is especially striking is that his gaze is treated as dangerous, potentially maleficent. It is not an excess of holiness which the craftsman fears from the new-born gaze. None of the other ceremonies contained this element of fear and danger. With knowledge of the *nētra pinkama* it is possible to attribute the use of the mirror in the *nānumuru mangalya* to a similar fear, though the emotion may no longer be felt. (I mentioned that in fact the whole ceremony is almost obsolete.) Certainly the monk did not conspicuously avoid the gaze of the image's eyes, and he was only grave where the craftsman seemed positively scared. But the totally undoctrinal danger of the *nētra pinkama* is clear and unambiguous. Moreover, the introduction of the *bälma* makes it impossible to claim that the image is only being venerated for the relic it contains. After stating the doctrinal position that the Buddha was a monk who is now dead, I have shown that certain ceremonies performed before his images imply otherwise. Though nearly all the ceremonies can be explained, as they are, as gestures of respect for his memory, certain others can not, and in turn imply minimally that he was a king, that he was (or is) a monk above other monks, that he is alive in the image, and that his living presence is potentially maleficent. The hierarchic order of these assumptions could be slightly varied, for instance by claiming that it is implied that he is a living rather than a dead king and that this is further from doctrine than the implication that he is a live super-monk. This is not important if all the implications listed are granted; the most interesting result, which seems to me incontestably proven by the last two examples quoted, is that certain ceremonies only make sense on the assumption that the statue is alive, which I take to amount to calling the statue a god.

It is, of course, open to the outside interpreter of these rituals to work in the opposite direction, and to claim from the evidence of the *nētra pinkama*, etc., that the Buddha always appears to his worshippers as a god. This is in effect what has usually been done, though interpreters usually stop short at extrapolating from the *nētra pinkama* the danger of the Buddha's gaze (of which they may not be aware) when they declare the Buddha's image to be considered a living idol but admittedly benevolent. I have suggested that this is too simple a view. I prefer to see in each ceremony the minimal supernaturalism, and hence the minimal deviation from the canonical doctrine, that the facts will bear, because this approach pays due attention to the views of the participants themselves. Moreover, it allows me to preserve the distinction between what people say they believe and what they behave as if they believe—what I called cognitive and affective beliefs. In this context I must stress that it does not follow at all that because an image is treated as alive in one ritual it is generally so viewed: many villagers are not even aware of the proceedings at a *nānumura mangalya* or *nētra pinkama*, and those who are may, like the monks, explicitly repudiate their implications and declare their ceremonies meaningless.

The importance of context clearly emerges when we investigate a final piece of evidence. In all the complex evidence adduced from *Buddha pūjā* there is only one statement in words to imply that the Buddha is still a living presence. There is, however, a widely known Pali couplet which runs as follows:

> *Kāyena vācā cittena pamādena mayā kataṃ*
> *Accayaṃ khama me bhante bhūripañña Tathāgata.*
>
> Forgive me my transgression committed through carelessness by body, word or thought, O Tathāgata of great wisdom.

This verse is quite unlike that used in the *Buddha pūjā* in that it is no mere formula; in particular, the Buddha is here addressed not only as *bhante*, which can apply to any monk, but as *Tathāgata*, which applies only to him. Apparently he is being asked to forgive sins, just like the Christian God. This would contradict two cardinal points of doctrine: that the Buddha is dead, and that sins can never be cancelled by forgiveness.[58]

[58]At several points in the Canon, people ask the Buddha to accept a

At first sight one suspects Christian influence. But it turns out that this is of a piece with the other Pali verses cited earlier; like them, it originated in the context of the daily ritual at the Temple of the Tooth, of which indeed it is the final verse. The monk performing the ritual addresses the Buddha image, and asks to be forgiven if he has made any mistake in the ritual. The mistake need not be mechanical: impure thoughts too require forgiveness.

There can be no doubt that in its original context this verse involves addressing the Buddha image as if it contained or embodied the living presence of the Buddha. The question is rather how it is generally used and understood. Inquiries among the village laity suggest that there the verse is indeed confined to the ritual context: it is recited at the end of *Buddha pūjā*, either in the temple or at home, and taken to refer to the period of the preceding *pūjā* only. But in the middle classes—and possibly elsewhere—the verse seems to be of more general application: it acts as a request for pardon for wrong-doing, as an attempt to elude the laws of moral causality. Middle-class people are no doubt aware, if the matter is brought into discussion, that this is contrary to doctrine, and hence attempt the sort of rationalization I was given by the monks I questioned: that of course the Buddha is dead and can *not* forgive sins, but this is just a way of saying one is sorry, a device to purify one's own thoughts. This is the same as the explanation, quoted earlier, which monks gave me for the verses that accompany offerings; in this case I have ventured to call it a rationalization because to me it carries no conviction.

Village laity, however, are generally simply inconsistent. If pressed they reveal that although the Buddha is

confession: *Bhagavā accayaṃ accayato paṭiganhātu*, literally "May the Lord accept the fault as a fault." (*D.N.*, I, 85; *M.N.*, I, 438; *M.N.*, III, 246–7.) This will help them not to repeat the offense, which is also the rationale for monks' confessing to each other. But nothing can undo what is done. (That one should forgive offenses against oneself is another matter.) In the canonical passages cited, forgiveness is not mentioned though confession is commended.

dead there is a certain Buddha force (*Budubalaya*), which will exist till at the end of this dispensation, in another 2,500 years, the Buddha's relics (including images) will collect at the Ruvanväli säya at Anurādhapura and after a last sermon the Buddha will finally disappear. (For the details and origin of this belief see the last part of Chapter 7.) But the inconsistency is interestingly limited, because this *Budubalaya* does not seem to operate outside the ritual context as part of the world at large, but only in the presence of images; it is virtually a force inherent in the image. To say that this force is put in by the craftsman who completes an image by painting in the eyes would be a logical final step, but we cannot take it because the Sinhalese do not take it. Things are just not so tidy.

Our general conclusion must therefore be that cognitively the Buddha is dead and without further power, but that even this cognitive position is not consistently maintained in the ritual context; we may, however, suspect, especially after taking into account some of the material in the next two chapters, that affectively the Buddha is felt still to be potent, even when an image is not present.

After all, the very phrase *Buddhaṃ saraṇaṃ gacchāmi*– I go to the Buddha for refuge'—has a theistic tinge, however it may be interpreted by pundits, and any inspection of Sinhalese religious literature or behaviour suggests that few Sinhalese Buddhists would object—though they would probably not originate such words—to the sentiment of the great seventh-century Indian Mahāyānist poet, Śāntideva:

> *Atītya yuṣmadvacanaṃ sāmpratam bhayadarśanāt*
> *śaraṇaṃ yāmi vo bhīto bhayaṃ nāśayata drutam.*[59]
>
> I transgressed your command; now, on seeing my danger, in fright I go to you for refuge: quickly destroy my fear.

I hope in the above discussion to have illustrated some of the principles stated in the first part of my Introduc-

[59] *Bodhicaryāvatāra*, II, 54.

tion. I have been concerned with several logically distinct but contextually related problems raised by worship of the Buddha. The only ones which I have attempted to answer in full, are what the Sinhalese say about the Buddha, how they behave towards him (on which I shall have more to say), and how their behaviour compares with their professions. The answers to the first two are descriptive (although all description of course involves interpretation), to the last interpretative. I have also touched on the historical problem of the evolution of the ceremonies among Buddhists and the question, also primarily historical but doomed to remain largely matter for conjecture, of what has been borrowed from Hindu neighbours. The subject holds other problems, of course, including ones which I have not even noticed.[60] But if the Buddha is generally said to be dead, this raises in the western mind many questions about the Sinhalese universe and its laws, especially about places filled and functions performed by the Christian God, for the Sinhalese never see the Buddha as a creator god or attribute to him power to interfere with the moral law of *karma*. To answer some of these general questions, and to provide a background for others more strictly doctrinal (to a Buddhist mind), will be the purpose of the next chapter.

[60]Of these the most important is the relationship with the Mahāyāna. For instance, confession of sins (*pāpadeśanā*) before Buddhas/Bodhisattvas is so important in Mahāyāna that it is part of the standard *introduction* to a ritual. Future research should try to disentangle Mahāyānist influence on Ceylonese Theravāda from parallel development. Yet it remains the separateness of Theravāda from the developments on the Indian mainland which must strike us most.

4

A Sketch of the Universe as seen from Mīgala

I. Causation

THE Christian God is the First Cause and the Final Judge. The Buddha showed little interest in eschatological questions, which he pronounced irrelevant to man's problems, and the Sinhalese have inherited his attitude. The universe, according to general Indian belief, goes through cycles of evolution and devolution; though our physical environment is periodically destroyed it comes into being once more. The Buddhists see no beginning or end to this process, so have no need of a first cause, nor of any cause to bring the world to a halt. Nor can there be any question of an omnipotent judge; for while the universe lasts, so long results, pleasant and painful, follow from the inexorable law of *karma*.

The law of *karma* would fill a central position in any account of Buddhism (or any other religion) which attempted to treat their problems as counterparts of those of the great monotheistic religions, for it replaces the omnipotence and omnibenevolence attributed to the Christian God, and resolves that conflict between them technically known as the problem of theodicy. Problems and modifications in the operation of *karma*, which fall more properly in the sphere of Buddhist doctrine and my subject matter, will be discussed in the next chapter; but here it concerns us more generally, as the foundation of the Sinhalese view of causation and the way in which the universe functions.

The traditional Sinhalese view of the universe, what we might call their cognitive map of the world, does not have a concept corresponding to our 'laws of nature'.[1] Things

[1]It must be remembered that I am talking here of the world of the Sinhalese villager, not the schemata of learned literature. The Pali

operate according to the way they are, their 'own essence' (*svabhāvaya*); of course this usually leads to nothing unexpected; if a man walks into a wall he will stop with a bump. But if he practises meditation successfully he may be able to go through the wall. The regularities of the physical world are not 'laws', and may on occasion be evaded.

There is, however, one universal law of which everyone is aware, and that is the law of *karma*. This law applies to all living beings, always. *Karma* means 'deed' or 'act'. Strictly speaking your *karma* is what you do, not what is done to you—that is the maturation (*vipāka*) of your *karma*, the result of one of your previous acts in this or one of your former lives. *Karma* is a doctrine of free will. Indeed, will is paramount: the doctrine is that what counts is the intention, not the effect. 'It is intention (*cetanā*) that I call *karma*,' said the Buddha.[2]

For all the inconsistencies which will be probed in Chapters 5 and 6, everyone knows and broadly subscribes to this doctrine, even if perhaps they cannot formulate it. The doctrine is logically very far from fatalism; indeed it might be said to go to the other extreme. On one level the imprecision of linguistic usage is misleading. When a villager meets with misfortune he is liable to say, 'It's *karma*' ('Karumē'), by which he means—and will, I think, say so if questioned—that the misfortune is the *result* of his former bad actions. To this extent 'it can't be helped', but that does not mean that it is not his fault, or that he is not responsible. Determinism is a heresy (*mithyā dṛṣṭiya*).[3] Moreover, *karma* is not necessarily responsible even for

commentaries have the concept of *niyama*, which might be translated 'law'; it covers regularities as diverse as *utuniyama* (the regular succession of the seasons), *bījaniyama* (i.e. from acorns grow oaks), and *karmaniyama*, the law of *karma*.

[2] *A.N.*, III, 415 (*Sutta* VI. 63. 11). The full quotation reads: '*Cetanāhaṃ bhikkhave kammaṃ vadāmi; cetayitvā kammaṃ karoti kāyena vācāya manasā.*

[3] For this heresy, cited as point 167 in the *Kathāvatthu*, see Nyanatiloka, *Guide through the Abhidhamma-piṭaka* (Bauddha Sāhitya Sabhā, Colombo, 1957), p. 81.

everything that happens to you: it operates, if I may so put it, in a gross way. One monk said that *karma* determines the station in which you are born, and your luck (*vāsanāva*); after that, it is up to you—the present you. 'Luck is one's former habits' ('Vāsanāva kiyanne pera purudda'), said another monk. The idiom is as in English: 'luck' usually means 'good luck'. If he has good fortune, a villager will probably say, 'Vāsanāva'; if bad, 'Karumē', but he knows that his *vāsanāva* is due to his *karma*.

But the response to misfortune 'Karumē' does in fact have a fatalistic ring, which suggests that on the affective level the villager may not accept the total responsibility which he admits cognitively. In practice the distinction between these two logically so different positions may be a fine one: a thief is not allowed by doctrine to claim that he is stealing because of his *karma*, but he may—and probably does—claim that it is his *karma* which has caused his rebirth as a man who has to steal to keep alive. In fact villagers do often say 'We are sinners' (*api pavkārayō*), not in any mood of contrition or of defiance but simply meaning, 'Look, we are so poor that we have to sin to keep alive', and probably further, 'and we are born poor because we sinned before'. Moreover animals too—to say nothing of lowly spirits—are as they are because of former misdeeds; now they have little chance to do good, but must live by killing others, etc.; this bad *karma* can set up a vicious circle, only to be broken by the greatest willpower. In this light the world of the poor villager seems a pathetic spectacle.

Theodicy (popularly known as 'the problem of evil') is in the first place a logical problem: if God is Love, and can do anything, how is it logically possible that he allows suffering? In Buddhism the *karma* theory disposes of this problem on the cognitive level: suffering is a punishment for sin committed either in this or in a former life. There exists, however, no general consolation for undeserved suffering, so that psychologically *karma* does not solve the problem; in fact, by making a man responsible for even his 'luck' it may be said to aggravate it. In other words, *karma* resolves the problem of theodicy on the cognitive, but not on the affective level.

One of the affective legacies of the *karma* theory is an uncertainty very similar to that felt by Calvinists anxious to know whether they were predestined to salvation or damnation. The Calvinists interpreted worldly success as a sign of divine favour and so worked hard to achieve it; the Buddhists—rather more logically, if I may say so—tend to consult astrologers. You cannot avoid the results of bad *karma*, but you can at least be prepared for it. A man's luck, which is really his current stock of *karma*, is largely reified in his horoscope (*kēndraya*): if his *karma* is good he will be born at a moment when the stars are favourable. According to a Mīgala astrologer, everyone has three *kēndra*, based on his sign of the zodiac (*lagna*), the sun (*ravi*), and the moon (*candra*), but the first of these is the most important. The planets (*grahayō*) are pan-Indian: *ravi* (sun), *candra* (moon), *kuja*[4] (Mars), *budha* (Mercury), *guru* (Jupiter), *śukra* (Venus), *śani* (Saturn), *rāhu* and *kētu*. (The last two are the head and tail of a mythical demon who is supposed to cause eclipses.) They may be in any of the twelve lunar mansions (*näkät*—the word is also used to denote the stars in astrology generally), and the horoscope is drawn up like this.

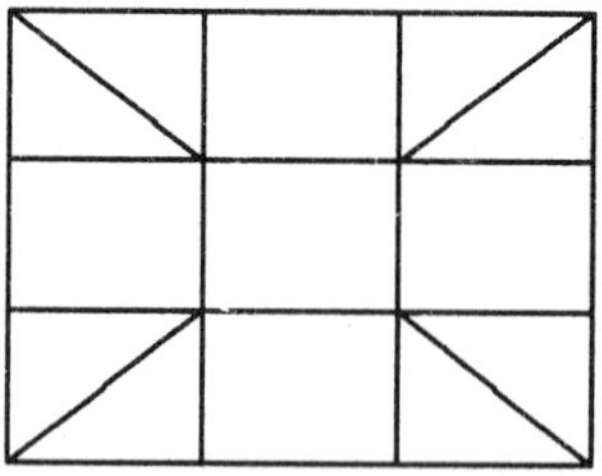

Lunar mansion number one is top centre and they are numbered consecutively anti-clockwise. I believe that mansions 1, 4, 7, and 10 are the most important, and if they are all empty the outlook is very bad. The horoscope indicates

[4]I have listed the planets' astrological names. In other contexts, e.g. the names of the days of the week, *kuja, budha, guru, śukra* and *śani* are respectively Aṅgaharu, Badā, Bṛhaspati, Sikurā and Senasurā.

the outlook for material prosperity, and if it is very poor a solution for males is to make them monks, in which condition they are supposed to have no stake in good fortune. So at least I was told by laymen, though monks usually denied it. Of course I was not so impolite as to ask a monk outright whether he had a bad horoscope; their denial came by implication because they would say that a monk needed a 'suitable horoscope' (*sudusu kēndrayak*); many said they did not know in what this consisted, but one specified that it should have Saturn in the ascendant (*senasuruyōge*), while another added to this that in a monk's horoscope (*pävidi yōga*) five planets should converge in mansions 1, 4, 7, and 10. Altogether nineteen monks out of twenty-one asked stated that a suitable horoscope was needed to become a monk, although a couple added that exceptions could be made; and the general implication was that the suitable horoscope was a favourable one. However, a contrary case gives some confirmation to lay gossip: one monk told me, with disarming frankness, that when he was 22 years old his horoscope was inspected as he was about to marry, and it was found to be such that instead of marrying he hastily entered the Order.

Horoscopes are always matched in arranging weddings to make sure that the couple are suitable; but otherwise villagers rarely consult them, as the above story illustrates, and often they even lose them. Another branch of astrological practice, besides casting horoscopes, is determining auspicious (*subha*) days and moments; almanacs listing these are widely diffused, but auspiciousness may be general (for everybody) or particular (for oneself) and the latter can only be determined by consulting an astrologer. Although Mrs. Bandaranaike was plausibly rumoured in December 1964 to be awaiting an auspicious moment for the dissolution of Parliament, villagers have little interest in these moments and observe them, if at all, with very little precision. Altogether villagers tend to pay less attention to astrology than do members of the middle and upper classes. Partly no doubt this is because astrology—like magic—caters for the emotional insecurity of those who have left behind the ascribed status of traditional village life for the competitive strains of a more 'open' society. Dr. Obeyesekere, however, suggests a more specific explanation: that here again we encounter the anxiety caused by the doctrine of *karma*. The more conscious a man is of the doctrine, the more anxious he becomes to know what the future holds in store for him; the more Buddhism, the more astrology. I think this an interesting and plausible hypothesis.[5] Traditionally astrology would predict only the events of this life; yet I came across the case of an elderly professional man who, while he was turning to religion, had astrologers predict for him his next rebirth. His doctrinally induced anxiety must have been unusually great. Dr. Obeyesekere further substantiates his hypothesis by a comparison of villages he knows; one in remote parts, with little knowledge of Buddhist doctrine, has correspondingly little interest in astrology, and many of the villagers never even had horoscopes. I made the same observation: middle-class people in and around Mīgala were punctilious in observing auspicious practices at the New Year to which villagers paid little or no attention.[6] But on the personal level among the villagers I may have detected a contrary tendency: those who put most trust in Buddhism were least inclined to astrology. This I would explain by canonical tradition: the Buddha himself condemned astrology, palmistry, and all similar practices, though his condemnation was specifically directed against their practice by monks: he did not deny their possible validity, but declared them a distraction from the road to salva-

[5]My friend David Pingree, whose knowledge of Indian astrology is unrivalled in the West, remarks with his usual good sense that astrology is less used by poor people because they cannot afford the fees. I do not find this economic argument strong enough to stand alone, especially as village astrologers, including monks, are sometimes part-time amateurs who give advice cheaply or possibly even *gratis*; but financial considerations must at least reinforce those adduced in the text. Furthermore, Dr. Bryan Wilson has pointed out to me that astrology holds for the semi-educated the appeal of a pseudo-science.

[6]It must of course be admitted that all these cases could be covered by the 'open society' hypothesis; it is so hard to isolate the variables.

tion. This attitude was exemplified by the monk, devout and well versed in the scriptures, who told me that astrology is not lies (*näkät śāstrē boru nä*), but to become a monk no horoscope is necessary, only faith (*kēndara ōnänä, sraddhāva*). But another monk who struck me as being unusually devout took the opposite view: one needs a suitable horoscope to become a monk, and a novice who is found to have an unsuitable one must leave, because his religious conduct would turn out poorly; moreover one should be ordained at an auspicious time. This I would judge a flagrantly uncanonical position in its implied assimilation of spiritual to temporal success. The behaviour of the monk who took a correspondence course in astrology and has a government certificate to prove that he passed the final examination also strikes me as uncanonical, even though he told me that the study of astrology is traditional in his line of pupillary succession. A few other monks said they knew some astrology but only one said he practised; several said it was wrong for a monk to do so. However, astrology was till recently taught at the primarily monastic university (*pirivena*) of Vidyodaya.

A sceptical western reader will not be surprised to learn that even the predictions of astrology are usually imprecise; a villager who wants a specific piece of information will probably consult another specialist who employs other means (see below). What astrology generally predicts is an *apalē*,[7] an unlucky period, which may be either general or individual, just as a day may be lucky either for everyone or for an individual in accordance with his horoscope. There was an *apalē* all over the Indian cultural area in February 1962 when there was a conjunction of planets so dire that Indian predictions of the end of the world reached western newspapers. In Ceylon there was widespread ritual chanting of Buddhist texts (*pirit*, discussed below), and in Mīgala temple thirty monks chanted (in rotation) for a week, ending with a colourful ritual (the *dorakaḍasnē*). One of the monks described it to me with

[7]The word is connected with Skt. *aphala*, 'fruitless'.

great enthuaiasm and said the final ritual was very fine (*hari lassanayi*); there was a photo of the participants hanging in the *pansala*, and everyone seems to have had a lot of fun. Equally cheerful was a young villager who told me his horoscope showed he had an *apalē* of fifteen years, of which he had about eight years to go. In the end, he said, things would turn out OK. If he did *pin* he would be reborn in a better state. On the other hand a middle-class villager for whom an *apalē* was diagnosed immediately had a specialist come and perform white magic, and stayed home from his job when the astrologer so advised.

Bad *karma* means that one is due for misfortune. An *apalē* is not a specific misfortune, but a period of being prone to misfortune. Specific misfortunes are caused by other beings—gods, men, or devils—who operate as freewill agents, or they may result from natural causes such as eating the wrong food. These causes interlock and cannot be rigidly schematized. A man who falls ill will probably first try western medicine at the local hospital, and if that fails try Ayurvedic ('Sinhalese') medicine administered by a village specialist. If that fails his next resort will be determined by his sub-culture and individual temperament. He may ascribe it to human agency (black magic), and employ suitable countermeasures (white magic). He may ascribe it to demons of disease or to malign planetary influences (i.e. simply the influence of the *apalē*) personified as planetary divinities, and banish or appease them by more or less elaborate exorcistic ceremonies. He may ascribe it to the actions of a god, or rather the failure of that god's protection, and make the god a vow, promising him some present or service if he recovers. If the remedy does not work this may be due to a wrong diagnosis, or, much more likely, it may be because the man's *karma* is too bad, and he is due to suffer longer.

The theories and remedies listed are not mutually exclusive: for instance, a man may make a vow to a god at the time when he enters hospital, or think that the failure of a god to offer protection has let a malign demon do his work. What they have in common is that none of them have anything to do with religion as the Sinhalese understands the term. The western observer who makes cross-cultural classifications could find in the above list first science, then magic[8] and finally religion; but to the Sinhalese this has no relevance: all are means of combating worldly misfortune and therefore are worldly and *ipso facto* not religion. Nor are the beliefs on which these practices are founded considered religious beliefs: they form no part of the Buddha's message, but are just facts of life. From this point of view there is no difference between gods and demons, between the higher and the lower supernaturals, although Dr. Obeyesekere has made the interesting point that it is easier for a Buddhist to deny the existence of gods than of demons, as the activities of demons—principally inflicting disease—are the more obvious. In fact the only person I found positively to deny the existence of gods was a lay villager, though some monks were sceptical about their powers. However, the Sinhalese are aware that other religions set store by gods, so that when I asked monks about gods a couple of them made a point of stressing that their gods have nothing to do with Buddhism. Belief in gods is not contrary to Buddhism, but has no connection with it; belief in gods is not a matter of religion (*āgama vaśayen adahanne nä*); Buddhists as such have no devotion (*bhaktiya*) to gods and make no demands (*illīma*) on them; to worship just gods (*deviyanma ädahīma*) is heretical (*mithyā dṛṣṭiya*). It is crucial to the Buddhist theory of monasticism (*mahaṇakama*) that a monk should not be concerned with worldly goods and ills; but it is only worldly goods and ills that gods and devils (whom for convenience I shall call supernaturals, though the concept is un-Sinhalese) have it in their power to bestow or remedy. Accordingly, while theory has nothing to say against the existence of these supernaturals, it does not become

[8]As stated in the Introduction, I take magic to mean a process by which the practitioner is believed to compel the result, and not to depend on the free-will acquiescence of another being.

a monk worthy of the name to make any use of them or their institutions; to seek worldly gain is improper, and so it is improper to require the favour of a divine or a human potentate. Both are sometimes solicited, from an ignorance which does not know of this impropriety or a greed which chooses to ignore it; but supernaturals are far less often solicited than men, whether because such intercession with a god or demon, requiring as it does a lower-class human intermediary, is a more conspicuous lapse, or because efforts at propitiating human favour are regarded as the more fruitfully expended, we can only conjecture. I do not know how many of the monks I interviewed had at some time or other been involved in civil litigation over temple property, but the number was at least double the two who said that monks do occasionally make vows (*bāra venavā*) to gods, of whom only one admitted doing so himself; and a monk in a law-court is a far commoner sight than a monk in a god's shrine (*dēvālē*). To this ideological reason why a monk may not placate gods or demons the sociologist may conjecturally add another: that it is the very function of the Buddhist clergy to preserve Buddhism, not merely in the sense that they preserve the texts and are themselves coterminous in time with Buddhism, as they themselves admit, but also in their keeping the doctrine distinct from the theocentric religious tendencies of the laity. To preserve the Theravāda tradition the Order need not deny the existence of gods, but it must keep sufficiently aloof from theocentric practices to allow laymen a vision of a life lived independent of supernatural favour.

The distinction between propitiation of super-humans and religious actions is clear-cut, for, however ambiguous the ontological status of the Buddha, he cannot be dealt with like the gods on a *quid pro quo* basis, nor of course can he be compelled by spells like a demon. In Buddhist theory, however, the distinction is only incidentally one of means, namely that gods and demons (being alive) can be reached and affected while the Buddha (being dead) can not; essentially it is one of ends: gods and demons can be asked for any worldly benefit, from the destruction of an enemy to recovery from diseases; the Buddha is in fact asked to forgive sins. But it is also possible to use religious instruments to further certain limited worldly ends. (This raises no more problems of definition than getting a priest to post a letter.) Buddhist texts are used (and have perhaps always been used) for what at least to an outsider looks like white magic, and it might even be argued, although I would hesitate to agree, that in certain contexts the Buddha himself is invoked for similar worldly ends, namely protection from sickness and danger.

The use of Buddhist texts to gain protection and relief from misfortune is generally formalized in a ceremony called *pirit*; the text used in informal contexts which could be taken as an invocation to the Buddha is the '*Iti pi so*' *gāthā*. Both will be discussed in detail at the end of this chapter, where they have been placed at the end of the section on white magic. I have included them in this chapter rather than in the next one, which is on some problems of doctrine, and deals with some other Buddhist practices which might be described as magical, both because they seem behaviourally more on a par with other practices for counteracting misfortune and because they are doctrinally unproblematic, which the *prārthanā* discussed in Chapter 5, being concerned with future lives and religious goals, are not. On the other hand I juxtapose *pirit* and *prārthanā* to draw attention to their similarity, exemplified in the words of the *Mahā Jayamangala Gāthā*. To elaborate would be premature; I mention this rather complex argument here merely to point out, in accordance with my principle of paying attention to the sentiments of the Sinhalese themselves, that their explanation of *pirit*, etc., does not exactly parallel their explanation of the cases listed above, in which gods and devils were propitiated directly and remedy was clearly matched with cause. *Prima facie* it might seem that the obvious explanation for the recitation of sacred texts at a sick-bed would be to say that as the situation is due to bad *karma* the direct remedy is to acquire better *karma* by the performance of meritorious actions. But this explanation is rarely if ever used, because it does not really work: the doctrine of *karma* requires that bad acts bear fruit, so that the *pin* of the sacred text will be rewarded in the future, but can have no effect on the current punishment of *pav*. On the other hand *pirit*, etc., can by more than one argument be made to harmonize with the rationalist position of canonical orthodoxy. I shall return to these interpretative problems at the end of the chapter.

II. The Contents of the Universe

The bulk of the remainder of this chapter must be devoted to a descriptive account of the non-human inhabitants of the Sinhalese Buddhist universe and the institutions directly connected with them. Although this subject matter mainly[9] falls outside the local definition of Buddhism, much of it is necessary for a wider understanding of the way in which the Buddhist sees the world, and in particular for an appreciation of the ambiguous position of the use of Buddhist texts just alluded to, to which I shall return at the end of the chapter. For the most part I confine myself to the minimum information necessary for this purpose, but at times I shall supply some further data. I hope that these descriptive digressions may not be felt to impede the flow of the argument, but I think it right to attempt to complement the ethnographic data collected by my predecessors in the field. There is plenty of detailed literature on the Sinhalese pantheon, ritual and magic,[10] but most of

[9]As will become plain, some of the beliefs described, though few of practical importance, are derived from Buddhist scriptures. Whether a villager considered them part of *Buddhāgamaya* (or *dharmaya*) would probably depend on whether he was aware of their provenance. The line between religious and secular beliefs is not more stable than, say, in our own culture.

[10]Notably M. M. Ames, 'Magical-animism and Buddhism: A structural Analysis of the Sinhalese Religious System', pp. 21–52 in E.B. Harper (ed.), *Religion in South Asia* (University of Washington Press, Seattle, 1964); ibid., 'Ritual Prestations and the Structure of the Sinhalese Pantheon', pp. 27–50 in M. Nash (ed.), *Anthropological Studies in Theravada Buddhism*, (Yale University, South-east Asia Studies, Cultural Report Series No.13, 1966); D. de S. Gooneratne, 'On

this literature depends[11] on material collected in the Low Country, and in these matters there is much variety between the Low Country and Kandyan sub-cultures, and even between smaller areas.

In treating this kind of material much use—and misuse—has been made of Redfield's distinction between great and little traditions. The great tradition in a community consists of the common inheritance of the whole civilization to which it belongs, and is transmitted principally by the learned (usually in books); the little tradition consists of the other, local elements of a culture, varying between communities, for the most part transmitted orally and ignored in the works of litterati. Dr. Obeyesekere in his article 'The Great and Little Traditions in the Perspective of Sinhalese Buddhism' has brilliantly demonstrated the utility and the limitations of these concepts in the interpretation of field-work material, using as his example the subject matter of this chapter. He himself has drawn[12] a useful distinction between the ideal and the actual pantheon, between supernaturals whom people merely believe to exist and those with whom they interact. I think it is possible usefully to relate this latter distinction to that of Redfield and thus clearly to schematize the whole situation. The graph paper on which this schema will be drawn is the Sinhalese map of the physical universe.

According to canonical Buddhist doctrine the world

Demonology and Witchcraft in Ceylon', *J.R.A.S.* (Ceylon Branch) vol. 4, no. 13, 1865–6, pp. 1–117; E.R. Sarathchandra, *The Sinhalese Folk Play* (Ceylon University Press Board, Colombo, 1953); W.A. de Silva, 'Note on the Bali Ceremonies of the Sinhalese', *J.R.A.S.* (Ceylon Branch), vol. 22, no. 64, 1911, pp. 140–60; E. Upham, *History and Doctrine of Buddhism*, (Ackermann, London, 1829); P. Wirz, *Exorcism and the Art of Healing in Ceylon* (Brill, Leyden, 1954); N. Yalman, 'On some Binary Categories in Sinhalese Religious Thought', *Transactions of the New York Academy of Sciences*, series 2, 24, 1962; ibid., 'The Structure of Sinhalese Healing Rituals', pp. 115–50 in E.B. Harper (ed.), op. cit. I am unable to profit by the publications of Professor Pertold. Obeyesekere's articles are mentioned separately.

[11] Yalman's work is the main exception.

[12] In lectures at the University of Ceylon in 1965.

consists of three spheres or areas (*dhātu*), each with many named subdivisions. The lowest sphere is that of desire (*kāmadhātu*), the next up is the sphere of form (*rūpadhātu*), and the highest the sphere of non-form (*arūpadhātu*); they are inhabited respectively by creatures with sensual desires, with no desires but formed bodies ('made of mind'), and with no bodies. This categorization is scholastic, so we need not further pursue such questions as whether the spheres are literally on top of each other. The sphere of non-form is so far out that no one knows anything about its formless inhabitants except that they are very near attaining *nirvāṇa*. At the top of the sphere of form are five heavens called 'pure abodes' (*suddhāvāsa*); as their inhabitants are immaterial they cannot be illustrated or usefully described beyond saying that they are minds sunk in meditation. The lower heavens sometimes are depicted on temple ceilings; there are at the lower end of the sphere of form seven Brahmā heavens (*brahmaloka* or *baṁbalova*), and below them are six divine heavens (*divyaloka* or *devlova*) which constitute the top segment of the sphere of desire. The inhabitants of these *divyaloka* enjoy divine bliss (*dev säpa viňdinavā*). These heavens have a drawback: they are so pleasant that no one bothers to meditate and make spiritual progress. Most of my informants agreed that an inhabitant of one of these heavens, i.e. a god, cannot attain *nirvāṇa*; that can only be done by a human being or an inhabitant of one of the higher spheres. Nevertheless, these *divyaloka* are the heaven (*svargaya*) in which most people aspire to be reborn.

The heavens are a place up in the sky; *nirvāṇa* of course is not a place but a state. A schoolgirl, 12 years old, said that *nivan* is in the sky above the heavens, and the stars are lamps which they light in heaven, but adult villagers are more sophisticated, if less poetic. But her statement that in *nirvāṇa* one has no body, only thoughts, is interesting in that it answers the canonical account of the higher spheres and illustrates how these have resulted from attempts to imagine rarefied worlds to correspond to the most sublime mystical experiences. In fact one canonical formulation has it that there are four stages or stories (*bhūmikā*): sphere of desire, sphere of form, sphere of non-form, and supra-mundane (*kāmadhātu, rūpadhātu, arūpadhātu* and *lokottara*). 'Supra-mundane' is of course *nirvāṇa*. It is this highly specialized word, *lokottara*, that M. M. Ames takes as a translation for 'sacred' as opposed to 'profane', which illustrates the pitfalls in matching Buddhist with Durkheimian concepts.

The bottom stratum of the sphere of desire, and thus of the universe, consists of various hells under the ground, hells hot and cold in which demons torment those who must pay for past sins. Black monsters are shown in temples inflicting on their naked victims the most sadistic tortures. Often the punishment fits the crime: in a special hell depicted in one temple those who have killed hair-lice are crushed between huge boulders which appear to them as human finger-tips must appear to a hapless louse.

In between the heavens and the hells, roughly in the middle of the sphere of desire, is the human world (*manuṣyaloka*) we know, which includes the sun and moon and other planets in the sky, as already mentioned, and a great variety of other non-human beings, including gods [*sic*], animals, demons, and goblins.[13]

This map of the universe taken from the Pali Canon has

[13]Canonical geography need not detain us. Ancient Indian geography divided the earth into four or more continents, the southern one being the Indian continent (Skt: Jambudvīpa, Sinh: Daṁbadiva), which includes Ceylon. One monk said that England is the northern continent (Uturuguru). This traditional geography is far less widely known than the modern geography we all share in the great tradition of science. I came across a monk who held to both geographies, apparently without feeling an inconsistency. Though I did not normally discuss geography in my interviews, knowledge of the subject among the clergy seemed to be very poor, probably poorer than among laymen; doubtless this was because geography has only recently been taught in monastic schools. One monk thought England was very hot, and asked how it got water; another, who ran a small *piriveṇa* which did teach geography, told me proudly that London was a country divided into four parts: England, Scotland, Ireland, and New Zealand; moreover he confused it with the United States (*Eksat Janapada*), which he did not know to be in America.

not, and probably never had, any clear effect on religious behaviour, but it illustrates a pattern which I see repeating itself. In the scheme of the three spheres man's world is rather near the bottom of the pile. However, when we focus on the world in which we as men have any immediate or practical interest we ignore the top two spheres and concern ourselves only with the sphere of desire, a world of which man is the centre, with gods in heavens above him, demons in hells below him, and other men, animals, goblins and ghosts around him; a world moreover in which man is unique in his ability to attain *nirvāṇa*. Even for the Buddhist in ancient times there was a difference between what Obeyesekere calls the ideal and the actual universe: some parts he just knew about from teaching, while some were psychologically real because he felt he might easily visit them himself. I suggest that this narrowing of focus has repeated itself: the heavens and hells of the canonical sphere of form are now psychologically more distant, and the supernaturals with whom man has any contact, who constitute the ideal pattern, are only those of the human world (*manuṣyaloka*) in its centre.

As with areas of the world, so with their inhabitants: no one has ever met one of the disembodied denizens of the Pure Abodes, but some gods and many ghosts are regular village visitors. This was as true in ancient times as it is today. The non-human inhabitants of the canonical universe have been catalogued by Father Joseph Masson; a glance at his survey of what he calls (counter to the tenor of this thesis) 'popular religion' in the Pali Canon[14] reveals even within the Canon a difference between an ideal and an actual pantheon, between supernaturals who appear in formal catalogues and those who figure in stories. For anyone who wishes to 'get the feel' of a religion this distinction is surely most important. It is a distinction which cuts right across the question of origins with which Redfield's dichotomy between great and little traditions is properly concerned. When the relevant part of the Canon

[14] *La Religion Populaire dans le Canon Bouddhique Pâli.*

was compiled[15] the great tradition was that of Vedic Brahmanism, and fragments of the Vedic pantheon survive in the Buddhist texts, though the only parts of it to occur in the actual Buddhist pantheon have been transformed and 'Buddhicized'. The Vedas were, however, composed at least 500 years before the Buddhist scriptures, much further west, by high-caste Aryans (i.e. speakers of Vedic Sanskrit). Buddhism therefore incorporated material from the little tradition of a different time, a different place, and people with a different ethnic, social and linguistic background. Some of this too was obsolete or obsolescent. To all this were added the innovations of the Buddhist *litterati*, a new great tradition which made a rather successful attempt to systematize the jumbled heritage.

This situation finds its parallel today; if anything, the historical constitution of the modern Sinhalese pantheon is the less complicated. It is less complicated because there has been no structural innovation; the custodians of the Buddhist great tradition are still the monks, and the systematized schema they offer is the very one invented by their predecessors more than 2,000 years ago. It is the schema which I have just introduced. It is ideal, not actual, but so it always has been. The most important gods of the actual canonical pantheon, Sakka and Mahā Brahmā, were borrowed from the Hindu great tradition, but changed in character and station so as to appear suitably Buddhist; the most important gods in the modern Sinhalese pantheon, notably Vishnu and Kataragama, have likewise come in through contact with Hindus, and Vishnu at least has been Buddhicized by being made a Bodhisattva. (Kataragama is rather a special case, as we shall see below). Sakka and Mahā Brahmā were assigned their heavens in which to live; the universe now being partitioned there are no new worlds for the new gods to inhabit, so they live in the human environment with us. (For gods

[15] For simplicity and economy I am concerned here only with the first four *Nikāyas* of the *Suttapiṭaka* (see p. 43), the sermons which were collected in NE. India roughly between 500 and 300 B.C.

living in the human world there are canonical precedents). As for the demons and goblins, both then and now they are mostly local individuals fitted into traditional categories.

Although the modern Sinhalese have preserved memories of several other categories of canonical supernaturals (most of which were probably ideal, not actual, even when the Canon was composed), there are only three categories of supernaturals in the actual pantheon: god (*deyyō* or *deviyō*[16]—this plural form is used also to denote the singular), devil (singular *yakṣayā* or *yakā*, plural *yakṣayō* or *yakku*), and ghost (singular *prētayā* or *perētayā*, plural *pretayō* or *perētayō*). Of these three classes the first two are much the more important. 'Devil' and 'ghost' are extremely inaccurate translations, as I shall soon explain, so I shall refer to these two categories by the Sanskrit terms *yakṣa* and *preta*. Added to men and animals this makes five classes of beings, and so corresponds to the standard canonical list of five *gati* (states in which one can be reborn); in ascending order these are hell, animals, *preta*,

[16]Derived from Sanskrit and Pali *deva*. I am here disregarding the term *devatā*, 'deity'. E.R. Leach ('Pulleyar and the Lord Buddha') has completely muddled this issue and probably misled subsequent researchers. *Deviyō* he says is the Sinhalese word for a 'Hindu deity' (p. 84, note); he assigns opposed meanings to *deva* and *devatā*. His distinction has no correlate in Sanskrit, Pali or Sinhalese. If we translate *deviyō* as 'god' and *devatā* as 'deity' we will have given a fair idea of their interrelation: the two terms are virtually synonymous. The term *devatā* in Pali, as can be seen from the entry *sub voce* in the P.T.S. dictionary, had a very wide meaning, covering objects as disparate as Brahmā, stone, ascetics, and domestic animals. It was, however, particularly often applied to nature deities, the morally neutral *yakṣa* group which I discuss below. Modern Sinhalese usage is similar: *devatā* generally connotes a rather low deity, one in the actual pantheon and not too powerful at that, though usage is imprecise. (Gooneratne gets tied up in his attempts to explain the word precisely; he attempts it five times, on pp. 11, 14, 17, 26, and 62. The version on p. 17 is the one which seems to me best.) Ames ('Ritual Prestations', p. 43) has listed *devatā* as a separate 'type of spirit' 'interstitial between deviyās and yakās'. In fact, as I show below, in certain cases even the terms *deviyō* and *yakṣa* are interchangeable; in similar cases *devatā* is merely a less common (more literary) synonym of either.

men, and gods.[17]

The category of god, as conceived both now and in the Canon, is well-defined and fairly straightforward: a meritorious person is liable to be reborn in heaven, and the inhabitants of heaven are all gods. The only problem arises in connection with the gods of this world. In the canonical account of the Buddha's first sermon it says that the gods of the earth (*bhummadevatā*) were delighted with it and their applause attracted the attention of the gods in the various heavens;[18] in the account of the Buddha's death the Buddha tells Ānanda that there are gods of the earth with perceptions of the earth (*santi devatā paṭhaviyā paṭhavisaññiniyo*), who weep and mourn at his passing.[19] These gods of the earth may be the minor spirits who proliferate in the Canon rather than gods of the power and importance of Vishnu in Ceylon, but they do provide a precedent for locating gods in our world rather than in heaven: one monk told me that Vishnu, Kataragama, etc., live mainly in this world; whether or not they go up to the heavens (*divyaloka*) we do not know. The general opinion concerning Kataragama, the most important god in modern Ceylon, was that he was powerful but a sinner, and definitely an inhabitant of our world. The opinions of one monk deserve to be reproduced in detail. Concerning Vishnu he held the unusual theory (which he told me was his special private theory) that he is a personification of nature ('Viṣṇu kiyanne svabhāvaya'); this does not mean that it is futile to pray to him—on the contrary, he is very powerful. The other gods he divided into 'big gods' (*loku deyyō*) and 'little gods' (*poḍi deyyō*). (Compare the canonical distinction quoted by another monk between gods of little and of great power (*alpēsakya mahēsakya*).) The 'big

[17]e.g. *M.N.*, I, 73, *D.N.*, III, 234. In other passages, e.g. *D.N.*, III, 264, six *gati* are listed, with *asura* inserted between *preta* and men. The *asura* were a Vedic class of fallen gods, already ossified in the Canon; the discrepancy is trivial.

[18]*S.N.*, V, 423.

[19]*D.N.*, II, 140 (*Sutta* 16. 5. 6) repeated *D.N.*, II, 158 (*Sutta* 16. 6. 11).

gods' he mentioned were the canónical gods who survive in the Sinhalese ideal pantheon, namely Śakra and the Four Guardian Deities, who live in their heavens; the little gods, he explained, are merely humans who had developed minds (*hita diyuṇuva*) in life and have been deified. He applied this to all the non-canonical gods except Vishnu. We can see the process with Mr. S. W. R. D. Bandaranaike, who will soon be *Riḍavē Ḍayas Baṇḍāra*.[20] Similar cults await other men who have little passion, hatred, and delusion (*rāga dvēsa mōha aḍu minissu*). It would be invidious to reproduce the rest of our discussion.

The above exposition suggests a rather mixed intellectual background. According to Buddhist doctrine all gods were men in a former life, so it should not be necessary to specify this for any particular gods. On the other hand the same Buddhist tradition makes euhemerism a favourite explanation of gods among sceptical Buddhists. The difference between the Buddhist and the euhemeristic position is that the former allows the gods to exist in their own right, the latter claims that they exist only in the popular imagination. My informant was probably implying that the 'big gods' of the Canon really exist but the 'little gods' do not, a position not illogical but incongruous.

The categories of *yakṣa* and *preta* are far less clear, and the muddle goes back to the Canon itself. Both then and now the category *yakṣa* overlaps with that of god on the one hand and that of *preta* on the other. The former overlapping is a mere semantic unclarity, the preservation (or repetition?) of which is a historical curiosity; the latter reflects the more fundamental difficulty, met with also among Christians, of reconciling doctrine on the fate of men—especially bad men—after death with a half articulated belief in their return as ghosts.

The range of meanings of *yakkha*, the Pali equivalent of *yakṣa* in the Canon, can best be studied in the Pali Text Society dictionary entry for that word. The term

[20] Ridgeway Dias were two of the prime minister's names. *Baṇḍāra* is a Kandyan type of minor god discussed below.

covers a great variety of supernatural beings, usually of a religious and moral status somewhere near that of man. Two kinds of beings seem principally to be covered by the term: morally neutral or ambivalent nature deities who live in trees or on mountains; and extremely malevolent and hideous demons who frequent cemeteries and lure lonely travellers to sudden death. The female of the former class is frequently portrayed, according to the general interpretation, in the lush female figures at Bharhut and Sanchi; the female of the latter class is apt to beguile the wayfarer or shipwrecked sailor by appearing as a lovely woman, only to turn into a cannibal ogress. This latter, demoniacal, class widely supplants in Buddhism the similar *rākṣasa* (Sinh.: *rakusa*) of Sanskrit literature. However, the word *yakṣa* has a wider meaning of 'supernatural being', for it is even applied to the Buddha. I think the importance of this passage can be over-stressed,[21] for it is in a long verse eulogy during which the Buddha is also called *Sakka purindada* ('Śakra sacker of citadels'); but the great god Śakra is himself called a *yakkha*.[22] At the other extreme one kind of *preta*, those with great power (*mahiddhika*), are all *yakṣas*. For the middle ground let me adduce the passage[23] in which *yakṣas* are cited as a distinct group parallel with three other kinds of demigods: *gandhabba*, *kumbhaṇḍa* and *nāga*.[24] Their king is the guardian of the

[21] *M.N.*, I, 386. The other place where the Buddha is allegedly called a *yakkha*, *S.N.*, I, 234, is even more dubious.

[22] e.g. at *J.* IV. 4.

[23] *D.N.*, II, 257 (*Sutta* 20. 9). On the basis of this passage J. Przyluski and M. Lalou in 'Notes de Mythologie Bouddhique. I Yakṣa et Gandharva dans le Mahāsamaya Suttanta', *Harvard Journal of Asiatic Studies*, 1938, vol. 3, no. 1, pp. 40–6, claim that *yakṣa* was at first a general term which then narrowed in meaning; but I find their argument unconvincing, especially in view of the imprecision of usage current to this day.

[24] *Gandharvas*, celestial musicians associated with fertility, and *nāgas*, five-headed cobras, are Vedic. The word *kumbhaṇḍa* literally means "pot-testicle", and indeed the ancients apparently attributed to them elephantiasis of the scrotum (commentary on *Jātaka*, III, 147). Ancient literature tells us nothing else about them, and the reference

north, Vaiśravaṇa (Pali: Vessavaṇa *alias* Vessamuni *alias* Kubera, Sinh.: Vesamuni), who is elsewhere said to be the god of wealth and live in the Himalayas. He has survived till modern times. He lives in the lowest of the *divyaloka*, but to judge from what I was told can properly be called a *yakṣa* himself.

The semantic spread of the term *yakṣa* in modern Ceylon is almost the same, except that it is never used of the Buddha or a 'big' god; it implies at least potential sinfulness and generally residence in the human world.[25] There are native divinities who live in big trees, especially *Bō* (sacred fig) or *nā* (ironwood) trees;[26] these are vaguely conceptualized and poorly integrated with the rest of the pantheon, but the day before cutting down a big tree the woodmen will inform the resident divinity by mentioning the fact as they pass by, and maybe decorate another tree with lights and strips of cloth to indicate it is a suitable al-

to them in Wirz (op. cit., p. 186) suggests that in the Sinhalese Low Country too there is no agreement as to what they are.

[25]The same seems to be true of systematized Hinduism. 'The Yakṣas and Yakṣinīs make up the great class of local divinities into which the Hindus finally incorporated all minor religious forms, most of them aboriginal. The term *yakṣa* appears for the first time in the *Jaiminīya Brāhmaṇa* (III, 203, 272) where it means "a wondrous thing", but the ordinary meaning of "spirit", "genius" becomes prevalent only with the *Gṛhya-sūtras*. In the *Mahābhārata*, the Yakṣas are already fairly well known, and a late passage in the same epic says that men of a 'sāttvic' temperament worship the gods (*devas*), those of the 'rājasic' temperament venerate the *yakṣas* and *rākṣasas* [*sic*], and those of the 'tāmasic' temperament the *pretas* (phantoms) and *bhūtas* (spirits of the dead, generally evil spirits). This represents the first attempt at assimilation and classification by a Hinduism confronted with this crowd of geniuses and demons from the aboriginal religions. Comparatively few Yakṣas have names...' (Eliade, *Yoga*, p. 345.) This precisely parallels the Buddhist data in my text.

[26]As mentioned in Chapter 3, the day before his Enlightenment Gotama was meditating under a sacred fig tree. Sujātā had made a vow to the deity of that tree, in fulfilment of which her maid brought the milk-rice. On seeing Gotama she thought him to be the tree-deity (*J.* I. 69). Similarly Maitrī, the next Buddha, will obtain Enlightenment under a *nā* tree.

ternative residence. (*Bō* and *nā* trees are not cut down at all.) The more important and better-known sort of *yakṣa*, however, is distinctly malevolent, and in the Low Country is exorcized by devil-dancing. These *yakṣas* generally bring disease, and certain diseases are even associated with particular *yakṣas;* but in my area these individually named *yakṣas* have little currency, and misfortune may be ascribed to any *yakṣa* fairly indiscriminately. There is a clear tendency for the named *yakṣas*, those with individual personalities, to be assimilated to the important class of minor deities called 'the Twelve Gods' and known to scholarly literature as 'the *Baṇḍāra* cult'. The Twelve Gods will be discussed in detail below; here suffice it to say that they are known collectively as gods (*deyyō*) and most of them include 'god' or 'deity' (*dēvatā*) as part of their name, and yet most of them are freely described as *yakku*. The expression may be pejorative, but this depends on the speaker's expression and tone of voice; the term is not itself loaded, but retains its canonical ambiguity. At the other extreme are the devils who torment sinners in hell: for these too there is no word but *yakā*. But whereas all the other *yakku* are part of the actual pantheon the devils in hell are only part of the ideal universe.

Already in the Canon the *pretas* (Pali: *peta*) are an adaptation of an older idea to the Buddhist conceptions of rebirth and punishment, and seem to be poised on the borderline between the actual and the ideal; they are still in exactly the same position. In the Vedas there is no cycle of rebirth; the dead go down to some kind of Homeric underworld, where they exist as ancestor spirits or 'fathers' (*pitaras*). These *pitaras* were to receive offerings (*bali*) from their male descendants, and this obligation persisted, illogically, despite the new doctrine of rebirth first met in Upanishads. Buddhism resolved the illogicality but retained some incongruity. A class of *pretas* was invented, hungry ghosts who roamed the dark corners of the earth just slightly better off than if they were in hell, and liable to reform just like all other classes of beings. *Preta* and *peta* mean 'departed', the term being used to mean 'dead' as in English; but the term is linguistically confused with the *pitaras*'[27] thus revealing the ambiguity of the concept. In fact, as B. C. Law writes,[28] 'with the Buddhists the *Petas* are dead kinsmen'. Another compromise with the older ideas was achieved when in non-canonical Pali literature the *pretas* were divided into four[29] (or three)[30] categories of which one was designated as 'living on what others give' (*paradattûpajīvino*); but in this case what they receive is not a physical offering, but merit given them by human beings, notably by relatives at the funeral feast. These feasts and their underlying ideas will be discussed in the context of merit transference at the end of Chapter 5. Here it must suffice to say that the semantic overlap between *pitaras* and *pretas* is still a living reality, in this sense: although cognitively —and logically—*pretas* can be anyone's relations, the only *pretas* of whom people usually think and with whom they interact are their own dead relations.

I mentioned above that the *pretas* 'of great power' are said in the Canon to be *yakṣas*. In modern Ceylon the categories *yakṣa* and *preta* are never formally stated to overlap; but they seem somewhat confused in matters concerning their manifestations and treatment—in a word, when they are ghosts. Sinhalese has a word appropriately translatable as 'ghost'—*holman*. It is important to note that a *holman* is not a separate class of being; it is a mere apparition, a manifestation (*avatāraya*) of a being.[31] (The word *avatāraya*, which has a distinguished history in Hinduism,

[27] *D.N.*, II, 234 and II, 264 have *petti visayo, M.N.*, I, 73 has *pitti visayo*. Both show connection with Sanskrit *paitrya*, an adjective formed from *pitṛ*.

[28] B.C. Law, *The Buddhist Conception of Spirits* (2nd ed., Luzac, London, 1936), p. 5.

[29] *Milindapañha*, 294.

[30] *Vibhanga Aṭṭhakathā*, 455.

[31] Gooneratne defines *holman* rather more widely (p. 48) as 'ominous signs' which betoken the presence of *yakku*. Of *avatāra* he says (pp. 46–7): 'Although demons are said to shew themselves in these ways to men, yet the opinion of those, who may be called the more orthodox of the demon-worshippers, is that these apparitions are not the demons

has in Mīgala so far come down in the world as to be used as a *synonym* for *holman*.) These *holman* are much associated with scenes of death, which leads the westerner to expect that they might be manifestations of *perētayō*, but in fact they are generally said to be *yakku*. *Perētayō* are said to have huge bellies and very small mouths (their uncouth appearance and insatiable appetite perhaps justify their being called 'goblins');[32] *holman* on the other hand never have this form, but appear typically as a naked white figure or as a dog. They are, however, not necessarily seen; they may be heard (as pursuing footsteps), or even felt (as a hand on the back). They appear at night, and the hours of 6 p.m., 6 a.m. (twilight) and midnight are said to be especially dangerous. The most dangerous place is a cemetery—and here we are reminded not only of ghosts but, perhaps more pertinently, of the necrophagous *yakṣa* of the Canon. The worst such ghoul is Mahasōnā,[33] who may lay his great hand on the back of a lonely wanderer near a cemetery at midnight. People dead of shock have been found to bear his livid imprint on their backs,[34] a phenomenon comparable to the bleeding stigmata of Padre

themselves but certain puppet-like spectres, which they create and present to the eyes of men, in order to frighten them;. . . This opinion, however, is one, which is confined to the more learned of the demon worshippers; the more ignorant believe that the demons themselves are bodily present at these scenes, although they assume some sort of disguise, whenever they choose to make themselves visible to men.'

[32]e.g. by M.M. Ames, 'Buddha and the Dancing Goblins: A Theory of Magic and Religion', *American Anthropologist*, vol. 66, no. 1, 1964, pp. 75–82.

[33]Sinhalese *sohona*, 'cemetery', is generally pronounced *sōna*, so that the name means, or at least suggests, 'great cemetery'. At the same time it is homonymous with the name of one of the ten great warriors of Duṭugämuṇu (see especially *Mhv.*, XXIII, 45-48), who is Mahāsoṇa in the Pali. The demon's origin myth connects him with Duṭugämuṇu and in particular with another of the ten warriors, Goṭhaimbara (Wirz, op. cit., pp. 28–9). I am not suggesting that the hero is the original of the demon, merely that the present demon represents the sort of conflation of maleficent spirit with dead leader which I show below to be frequent in the aetiology of *yakku*.

[34]I owe this information to Gananath Obeyesekere.

Pio and other Christians. Though I heard of no such extreme case in Mīgala, the villagers do not allow their womenfolk near the cemetery at night, and I heard of one lady who had come across Mahasōnā and been frightened into a fever. However, *holman* do not necessarily do you any harm; they can be kept at bay by reciting a Buddhist text (the '*Iti pi so*' *gāthā*—see end of chapter) or a consciousness of rectitude, and some seem to view them with more curiosity than alarm, though such people, as one might expect, have usually not met one—and some do not even believe that they are anything but figments of the imagination.

I am not an authority on *perētayō*, because so far as I could discover the inhabitants of Mīgala do not interact with them; outside the context of the funeral feast I think they are part of the ideal rather than the actual pantheon. It is in the Low Country that they are actual: Obeyesekere writes,[35] '*Pretas*... are given inferior foods like *pulula* or marijuana and sometimes fecal matter'; but I came across no such offering, and an informant wise in local lore even refused to draw the Low Country distinction between offerings to *yakṣas (pidēni)* and offerings to *pretas (dola)*, but said that as both were *amanuṣya* (a Sanskrit word literally meaning 'non-human') both received *dola*. Obeyesekere tells me that in the Low Country *pretas* are quite frequently perceived as troublesome ghosts, poltergeists, etc., and pacified or exorcized in a spirit of loathing and contempt; psychologically this is very interesting, for *pretas* are one's own relations—typically parents. Thus one may offer one's own father blood and pus to eat, or confine one's own mother in a small box and dispose of it in a latrine.

Another term for creatures in this murky area is *bhūta* (Sinh.: *bhūtayā*, pl. *bhūtayō*), which literally means 'has-been'. In the Canon the word is common only in the compound *bhūtavijjā*, literally 'science of *bhūtas*', which is the normal word for exorcism. The word is not commonly

[35] 'Great Tradition', p. 144.

used in Mīgala—though again I believe it to be common in the Low Country—but I have had to explain it in order to render intelligible the opinions on this subject of the euhemeristic monk quoted above; his opinion on the lower spirits will illustrate how the line between *yakṣa* and *preta* is blurred. At first he said that *yakku* are wicked men, such as the black cannibals in Africa; the *yakku* who were in Ceylon when the Buddha[36] visited it were of this sort. This statement is ambiguous: it could mean that wicked men are reborn as *yakku*, which would be traditionally orthodox, or that they tend to be mistaken for *yakku*, a rationalization on the euhemeristic lines of his remarks about gods. Then, however, he added that some *yakku* are also *bhūta; bhūta, perēta* and *holman* are the same, though *perēta* is really the general name for a dead man. He then spoke of *yakku* possessing people: when the possessed person is exorcized the *yakā* shouts 'Hū' and leaves by the mouth. *Yakku* are very fond of drumming: he told a story of a woman who while possessed could drum marvellously, but lost the art when exorcized. There are many *yakku* in Colombo, but some everywhere—even in Buckingham Palace there are ghosts.

The above is the only note I have of someone specifically connecting *holman* with *perēta* (rather than with *yakṣa*); but equally significant is the remark of a schoolgirl that there are *holman* only when bad men, not when good men, die. Moreover, to add to the confusion there is a category of *yakṣa* called *maḷa yakā* ('dead *yakṣa*'). I only came across the term once in my field-work (description of Kaḍavara—see below, p. 220), but Gooneratne gives this account of them (p. 19): 'If a man, who lives at enmity with another, remember, on his deathbed, just before he dies, and at the very moment of his expiring, any thing relating to that enmity and if, instead of a feeling of forgiveness, resentment and hatred take possession of his mind, he is supposed to become, after death, a demon of this kind. These demons are not so powerful, as [big demons

[36] *Mhv.*, I. See Chapter 3, p. 128.

like Mahasōnā], nevertheless they too cause sickness.'

The indeterminate position of the wicked dead seems established. It is aggravated by the ideas about hell. In the doctrinal picture hells have two classes of inhabitants, the wicked and the devils who torment them, but this is incongruous with the picture of heavens in which the good are reborn *as* the gods. Moreover, people are supposed to identify with the tormented, not with the tormentors; but it is dubious which should be considered the worse fate, for the tormented are expiating their sins and so will be reborn elsewhere, whereas the tormentors by their cruelty are sinning more. My objections are a purely academic quibble, for the hells are part of the ideal rather than the actual universe; they are certainly believed in, but as men cannot interact with their inhabitants the only effect they can have on behaviour is to deter from sin, an effect not measurable by the social scientist. However, these slight inconsistencies even on the cognitive level do suggest that affectively the doctrine of unpleasant rebirth for bad *karma* matching pleasant rebirth for good *karma*, all rebirths being transient states, does not carry full conviction. The ambiguous nature of the *preta* and their imperfect demarcation from *yakṣa* I have shown to be canonical; the dilemma about hell is canonical also. In the canonical list of five rebirths (*gati*) the others are all as types of creature; but the worst is just 'hell', whether as tormentor or tormented being unspecified. There is in fact no rebirth as devil mentioned in this list: it was no doubt to remedy this deficiency that the otherwise obsolete Vedic *asura* were introduced to extend the list of *gati* to six. The Sinhalese *holman* are a local product of the very widespread human hopes and fears that the dead may revisit their former dwellings and acquaintances; but in so far as such an event would be inconsistent with the doctrinal Buddhist scheme of things, the inconsistency is nothing new.

Working up from the bottom of the universe in the same way as the list of *gati*, we have now dealt with hell, *preta*, and indeed *asura*. Animals require only a few words. They too are vaguely considered to form some kind of hierarchy, with the elephant, hero of Sinhalese folklore, at the top. As in western culture, animals traditionally symbolize certain vices: the pigeon stands for lust, the pig, dog, and crow for rapacious greed. A man subject to a particular vice is likely to be reborn as the appropriate animal. The cobra (*nayā*—Skt. *nāga*) has a peculiar position: though it is always a sin to kill, to kill a cobra is especially sinful and extremely unlucky—two different ways of saying that it is so bad that bad results are sure to ensue before long. If a cobra is known to be living somewhere he is not disturbed, but often offered saucers of milk. Cobras sometimes are said to guard sacred places. In the Canon *nāgas* are a separate class of beings, semi-divine five-headed cobras, and the cobra's special status is a survival of this belief.

The next on the list of *gati* is man. The human world is itself hierarchically structured in the caste system (see Chapter 8). To be reborn in a good human station is more desired by some than to be reborn in heaven (see Chapter 6), nor is this wish necessarily irreligious, as it must seem to a westerner, for men are held to have a better chance than the lower gods of attaining *nirvāṇa*. Any human being, irrespective of status, may attain *nirvāṇa*, but it is widely believed to be much harder for women. The relations of all human beings to the physical world are the same, except that enlightened people (*arhats*) have supernormal powers (*ṛddhi*) which enable them to pass through solids, fly through the air, etc. (In the Canon the acquisition of these powers comes several stages before Enlightenment, but in the popular imagination this gap has disappeared.) *Arhats* are finished when they die, and are not normally worshipped, though in ancient times (when there *were arhats*) their relics were venerated. However, an *arhat* called Sīvali occupies a somewhat anomalous position. He is little mentioned in the Pali texts, and then mainly in connection with his birth; but the Buddha called him 'preeminent among recipients of gifts',[37] and the merit he had gained by giving honey to a former Buddha was so great

[37] *A.N.*, I, 24.

that in this life he would never go hungry, so the Buddha took him along on journeys through difficult terrain.[38] He is portrayed as an ordinary monk, seated, holding an alms bowl, and his picture is in many homes (including some *pansal*), and even on buses over the driver's seat (when the driver is a Buddhist). He does not receive prayers or offerings; his picture merely seems to serve as a general 'lucky charm'.

We are now back with the gods and the problems they raise. I have already shown that all the main Sinhalese beliefs about the workings of the universe and the pantheon are part of the great tradition. Even Vishnu and Kataragama (both described in more detail below), who are most typically cited as innovations in Theravāda Buddhism, are certainly not ascribable to a 'little tradition'; they are pan-Sinhalese and not local gods; worshipped by members of the educated classes (probably more than by poor villagers); historically derived principally from the great tradition of Hinduism; long absorbed into Sinhalese literate culture as their presence in the *Mahāvaṃsa* will testify; and fitting comfortably into the Buddhist doctrinal scheme of things. Certain individual local godlings and demons have no such respectable histories to offer, and can certainly be ascribed to little traditions, but this is trivial—the point is that they all fit into the structure which the great tradition has provided. To my mind the principal interest of the little traditions (sub-cultures) in Ceylon lies in their *selectivity* from the great tradition. In Mīgala there is a proliferation of minor gods, but little stress on *yakku*, and *perētayō* are so little considered that they have by and large retreated from the actual to the ideal; a glance at the work of Ames or Wirz will show by contrast the enormous exuberance in the Low Country of belief and practice concerning all the lower and nastier spirits; and I believe that this is a general contrast between the Low Country and the Kandyan provinces. On the other hand I think that Obeyesekere's distinction between

[38] *Dh.A.*, II, 192–3. For Sīvali's full story see ibid., 197–200.

the ideal and the actual pantheon can be explained in terms of the system itself: it is the inhabitants of our world, the human world—'little' gods, men, animals, *yakṣa*, and ghosts—who are actual, and *preta* are on the borderline because of their unclear status and their confusion with *holman*.

The two most important gods in the Canon—so much so that they alone deserve to be called 'actual' canonical gods—are the two who have survived to head the ideal Sinhalese pantheon, and of these two Śakra (Sinh.: Śakrayā) is—as he was—more important than Mahā Brahmā. Śakra has remarkable staying power because under the name of Indra he was the most important god in the Ṛg Veda. However, after a vigorous youth as a rumbustious warrior god and a respectable middle age as a highly moral supporter of the Buddha, he has declined into a feeble and somewhat disgraceful senility; for he is now little considered, and his only appearance in ritual of which I am aware is as a lecherous old man![39] In the Canon Śakra rules a heaven (called in Pali the Tāvatiṃsa heaven) which is one away from the lowest; the lowest is ruled by the Four Great Kings or 'world guardians' (*lokapāla*), one for each point of the compass: Dhṛtarāṣṭra, Virūḍha, Virūpākṣa and Vaiśravaṇa rule E., S., W., and N. respectively. Except for Vaiśravaṇa, king of the *yakṣas*, these four are totally colourless. These six gods, Śakra, Mahā Brahmā, and the four world guardians, are frequently portrayed together at the entrance to image-houses, usually forming a standardized framework for the *makara toraṇa* on the outside entrance wall of the central shrine. Śakra and Mahā Brahmā may also appear in representations of scenes from the Buddha's life, even attending on him like divine correlates of the two chief disciples; but the four world guardians have no more than a decorative function. Vaiśravaṇa may be said to lead a double life: as king of the *yakṣas* he is

[39]In the Pattinī *gam maḍuva* scene of the birth of the goddess from a mango, described by Obeyesekere in his lectures.

imagined as a kind of super-*yakṣa* himself, but in temple iconography he is a good-looking young king not distinguishable from his colleagues.

Below the four world guardians we enter the human world and the actual pantheon, gods with whom the Sinhalese interact. At the top of the hierarchy are the four guardian deities (*hatara varam deyiyō*) of Ceylon, two of whom are always Vishnu and Kataragama. Traditionally these gods were associated with a particular area of Ceylon in which also stood their principal shrine: for instance, Kataragama is at home in Ruhuṇu, the south-eastern part of the country, which contains his eponymous shrine. However, the country was in ancient times divided into three parts (Pihiti, Māyā and Ruhuṇu) not four, and the list of guardian deities fluctuates. That their number was fixed at four only because of the influence of the four world guardians of the Canon is virtually proven by the evidence of those Sinhalese books retailing canonical material in which the four world guardians are confusedly called the *hatara varam deviyō*.

Now that we are getting down to the human world it is time to remark on the structure of the pantheon. Here I can do little better than recapitulate the conclusion of Dr. Obeyesekere's brilliant article. He has shown that the structure of the pantheon follows the structure of authority in the feudal system which was once so exactly represented in the Kandyan kingdom: all power derives ultimately from the Buddha, who has given the gods *varam* ('warrants'), and similarly the greater gods give warrants to the lesser gods, who form their retinue (*pirisa* or *pirivara*). I entirely concur with this interpretation: indeed I was given it spontaneously by an elderly monk who can never have heard of Dr. Obeyesekere's work, a startling tribute to Obeyesekere's acumen. There are various symbolic ways in which the gods are made to defer to the Buddha's superior authority, and a few of them will be pointed out in the remainder of this chapter; but none of them require that the Buddha be conceived as still living. Obeyesekere presents his feudal model with the Buddha as the king at its head, alive and active at least to the extent that he is still able to issue new warrants. He is fully justified in so doing, as he cites a Low Country drama as evidence for the active Buddha. However, it is not logically necessary that the Buddha be alive for the warrant mechanism to function if he has already delegated his power to some high god or gods; new warrants can be issued by further delegation.[40] In fact I never heard anyone suggest even in this context that the Buddha is still alive or active. On the contrary, my informant clearly stated that Śakra was king of the gods—a position which I may say has been attributed to him in very different times and circumstances. At the top of the pyramid of current divine authority I would accordingly substitute for Obeyesekere's Buddha my informant's Śakra. Śakra is the king; if the Buddha is anything in this model we will have to transfer to the feudalism of mediaeval Europe and call him God who has legitimated the occupant of the throne.

Theoretically the four guardian deities of Ceylon derive their power from Śakra, or his council of ministers or parliament or whatever device he governs by, and the local gods, each with his rigidly defined territory (*sīmāva*—'boundary'—the same term as is used for parishes) are retainers of the guardian deity in charge of their area; but in fact there are several gods of indeterminate, or rather varying, status, and the whole thing does not work out so neatly. Probably it never did, but I suspect that some of the confusion has arisen through the gradual dissolution and merging of local cultures which has followed political centralization, improved communications, and the population explosion. Especially in the last twenty years, since the eradication of malaria and general advance in public health, villages have spilled over till the old boundaries have only legal or historical existence, and the people are no longer quite sure where the jurisdiction of the lo-

[40]In his next article Dr. Obeyesekere makes precisely this point ('Buddhist Pantheon', p. 13), thus correcting a slightly misleading impression given by the former article.

cal god ends. Improved communications mean the spread of ideas: outsiders give the villagers new ideas about the gods, as about everything else; and a god who hits the headlines, as it were, is likely to displace his old colleague or rival. Political centralization has made the old model of regional autonomy obsolescent, and the replacement of feudalism by modern parliamentary and bureaucratic government has blurred the clarity of the traditional hierarchy. Some now compare the god's arrangements to Parliament. The main beneficiary of all these changes has been Kataragama, who seems to be on his way to ousting all the other guardian deities. Obeyesekere even suggests[41] that within a few years this stern and punitive father-figure, originally a war-god, will have made Ceylon monotheistic (my term) for the first time in history. I saw his power rising locally: while I was there the first Sinhalese shrine (*dēvālē*) to Kataragama in the area was opened. Moreover, he was said to be the god from whom the local village gods derived their warrants; but as the god of Ruhuṇu I would think that he can originally have had no business in the hill country, and I would guess that he has filched the retinue of Saman or one of his other declining colleagues. This last is, however, rather light-hearted conjecture; against it may be adduced Kataragama's long established position as one of the Four Gods in nearby Kandy, where Saman has no shrine of any importance.

Kataragama has long been the most important deity of the Tamil Hindus of Ceylon, who are all Śaivites and whose religiosity contrasts markedly with that of the Kandyan Sinhalese, so that Ruth Benedict, using Nietzschean concepts, would have called the former Dionysian, the latter Apollonian.[42] Coloured red, he has six heads and twelve arms, which hold weapons; his mount (*vāhana*) is a peacock. He is Śiva's second son, known to Sanskrit mythology as Skanda,[43] Kumāra, or Kārttikeya, and to his Tamil

[41]'Buddhist Pantheon', p. 25.

[42]See *Patterns of Culture* (Mentor Books, New York, 1959), p. 79.

[43]Obeyesekere writes (p. 146): 'Skanda is considered a manifestation

worshippers by these and several other names;[44] the name Kataragama, far the most commonly used by the Sinhalese, is no doubt originally the name of his shrine in the extreme south-east corner of Ceylon.[45] Here he has two wives, Tēvānī and Vallī Ammā. Both are in fact Tamil names for his wife, who in Sanskrit is called Devasenā. Sinhalese belief has it that Tēvānī is the Tamil wife he brought with him from India, with whom he lives most of the time; Vallī Ammā is the Sinhalese or Vädda wife he met in Kataragama, whom he visits in July/August during the annual festival there. Such annual festivals are celebrated in all his Hindu temples, and involve processions (*perahära*) and fire-walking; the festival at Kataragama itself is well on the way to becoming, if it has not already become, the most important event in the religious calendar, attracting even more pilgrims than the Äsaḷa Perahära for the Buddha's Tooth in Kandy. Though the Kataragama festival is primarily for Hindus, drawing Tamils from all parts of Ceylon and even from India,[46] it has since ancient times been a place of Buddhist pilgrimage also, and Sinhalese in increasing numbers are going there and making vows to the god. (There is now also a Muslim shrine there so that Muslims may have a religious excuse for joining the pilgrimage. Christians have no such excuse—but go.) The character of some of these vows inclines towards the gruesome: in their fulfilment men—and women—not only shave their heads (or half their heads) and walk on fire, but put skewers through their cheeks, or even hang in mid-air from strings passed through the tendons of their backs. The more arduous of these devotions are practised

of the god Śiva.' This must be a slip.

[44]e.g. Shanmugan ('six-faced'—because he has six heads), Murugan (the ancient Tamil god of war), Subrahmanian, Kandan. Some of these names are extremely common components of the personal names of Ceylon Tamils.

[45]In Mīgala the place was often referred to as *maha* ('great') Kataragama, to distinguish it from *poḍi* ('small') Kataragama, his local Hindu temple (*kovil*).

[46]Leonard Woolf, *Growing* (Hogarth Press, London, 1961), p. 226.

mainly by Tamils, but fire-walking is not entirely alien to the Sinhalese tradition, and more and more non-Hindus are undertaking such vows, and coming under the influence of Kataragama's dark and violent spirit.

Most of the monks I asked (twenty out of twenty-seven), had visited Kataragama, several more than once, though they usually hastened to add that they went just to look, not for worship (*bhaktiya*) or to make a vow (*bāra venṭa*). Several, however, mentioned that he should be given merit (like other gods), and some said he gave protection (*ārakṣā-va*) to Buddhism (*sāsane*) or Buddhists. Opinions and knowledgeability about him varied greatly, and seemed to constitute one of the best indices of traditionalism, the more traditional monks knowing and caring little about him and holding him in low esteem. A very old monk, who had never been to Kataragama, seemed to put him on a level with *yakku*, saying that he rules over cemeteries (*balapānnē sohonaṭa*). Several mentioned that he inspired fear, but one said there is no reason to be afraid; he came to Ceylon in flight from India after losing a war, and people just believe that he has supernormal power (*tējasa*). His harshness to Tamils was stressed, and is explained by a myth: he came to Ceylon from India, and assumed the form of a boy. When he landed it grew dark and he needed shelter for the night. He knocked at the hut of a Tamil, who refused him. He then went to the hut of a Sinhalese, who not merely asked him in but went out himself, to give the whole hut to the visitor. For this Kataragama is now making the Tamils pay (*vipāka denavā*) and the main priest (*kapurāḷa*) of his shrine has to be a Sinhalese. The hut in which he stayed is reconstructed in front of his *dēvālē*. The monk who told me this was just back from a trip to Kataragama, and far more positive about him than most: Kataragama, he said, was very good and truthful (*satyavādī*). It is widely known that Kataragama is supposed to have killed *asuras* in a great battle; the above monk who favoured Kataragama justified this conduct, explaining that the *asuras* were very wicked, committing the ten sins (*dasa akusal*), and therefore deserved to be punished. Another monk, less pleasantly, explained that the *asuras* were in fact Tamils. The sufferings which Tamils undertake in his worship are felt to require explanation, and this explanation coincides with Sinhalese nationalist prejudice. The monk who made it connected Kataragama with Duṭugämuṇu's victory over the Tamils—not unreasonably as Duṭugämuṇu grew up in and began his march from the immediate vicinity of the shrine, which indeed another monk said he built in fulfilment of a vow to the god. I asked some monks whether killing did not make Kataragama a sinner (*pavkārayek*), and they usually agreed. Moreover, said one, he has servants who are *yakṣas*, and he also sins through them. Only one monk held him to be a Bodhisattva, and he was a man of deviant opinions who nevertheless cannot have held him in high regard, as he had never been to Kataragama. As for his history, he was generally connected with the human world and with India. One monk said that most of the gods were just men (*minissu mayi*) who were born in India, and because of their merit were reborn as powerful gods. The statement of another monk that Kataragama is not a man but a god by birth (*utpattiyen deyyō*) does not contradict this; it is rather aimed against the euhemeristic type of explanation which I have already cited, and of which I came across several more examples in this context. To say clearly that he was a man *in a previous life* fits the traditional Buddhist scheme of things; but it is hard to know how to interpret the remarks of the monk, an intelligent and modern-minded person, who said that all these gods were originally men, and there is a popular feeling that they have been reborn as gods; this implied no scepticism, for he also said that Kataragama had the power to help people, and he knew of cases in the village where he had cured barrenness.

Kataragama's arrival in Buddhism as a Hindu alien was remarked on by several, not only in metaphorical terms. One monk by implication put the Hindu influence back to the time of Duṭugämuṇu (c. 100 B.C.) or earlier. A second told me that *vihāras* and *dēvālēs* have been built together since the Poḷonnaruva period. A third associated a more recent dating with an unusually outspoken condemnation: popular beliefs about Kataragama are heretical (*vaituli adahas*). The last kings of Kandy, he said, were of Śaivite origin and brought Śaivite queens from South India. These queens believed in Vishnu and Kataragama (who was once a man in India), and so they became popular. When the kings went to worship the Buddha, the queens wanted to go and worship Kataragama, so they put the shrines together for convenience, which is how shrines to gods came into temple compounds. Then according to Śaivism (*Śivāgamē häṭiyaṭa*) you must make a vow, and give a hand for a hand, etc. [a reference to *ex voto* offerings]; this is contrary to Buddhism (*Buddhāgamaṭa viruddhayi*). But Kataragama has no real power; his influence (*balapǟma*) depends on belief (*visvāsa*), and, like a magician, he works on credulity.

According to Professor Hans-Dieter Evers there are a lot of myths according to which a *vihāra* was built by the king, an accompanying *dēvālē* by the queen. Though this was the only case I came across, I can well believe that the assertion is frequent, for it is a natural way of expressing that the two systems represented by these buildings are conceptually distinct but complementary.

The above monk was the only one to say that making vows was 'contrary to Buddhism', though the maverick monk who said that Kataragama was a Bodhisattva came rather near it when he said that to worship gods is heretical (*mithyā dṛṣṭiya*), and it is wrong (*varada*) to believe in gods alone (*deviyanma ädahīma*), and it is wrong to ask for individual gain, as people do at Kataragama, rather than for liberation (*mokṣa*). I am, however, sure that these two monks did not mean to express any disagreement with the clearly-expressed opinion of several others, that the worship of Kataragama is simply irrelevant to Buddhism.[47]

[47]That the worship of gods is not relevant to Buddhism is one of my theses—see Chapter 1. This is of course not to say that it is irrelevant to Buddhists. In this context I am content to reify Buddhism; in so

Belief in gods is not contrary to Buddhism, but has no connection with it, said one. Buddhists *as such* have no devotional worship (*bhaktiya*) and make no requests (*illīma*) of gods, said another. Belief in gods is not a matter of religion (*āgama vaśayen adahanne nä*) said a third, who certainly believed in some of them. The same attitude was expressed by numerous monks who said that one should give the gods merit but nothing else. What the monk who associated Kataragama with Śaivite queens had in mind was that worship of Kataragama is specifically Śaivite and not found in the texts; he also was probably thinking of what the maverick monk went on to say: that vows to Kataragama are often of a dubious moral nature—victory in law suits, or worse—and people who ask the god for favours against others are reborn as *yakṣayō*.

So much space has been given to Kataragama because it was concerning him, as by far the most important god in modern Ceylon, that I mainly questioned the monks, and their attitudes to him exemplify their attitudes to 'popular beliefs' in general. The other guardian deities of Ceylon can be disposed of more briefly, especially as they are already the subject of much scholarly literature. There are in Kandy four *dēvālēs* which have for many centuries combined to hold the Äsaḷa Perahära[48] (see Chapter 3), and they belong (in order of ceremonial precedence) to Nātha, Vishnu, Kataragama, and Pattinī. This tetrad is not the same as that which appears as the protectors of Ceylon in inscriptions and literature of the fourteenth and fifteenth centuries: Upulvan (i.e. Vishnu—see below), Saman, Vibhīṣaṇa, and Skanda-Kumāra (Kataragama).[49]

doing I am merely reproducing the usage of my informants.

[48]Since the Buddhist revival of the mid-eighteenth century the Temple of the Tooth has joined with them to form the spectacle still visible today. At that time Buddhism reasserted its sovereignty, and the Buddha's tooth (its replica) leads the emblems of the gods in the procession. For a description and sociological analysis of the Äsaḷa Perahära see H.L. Seneviratne, 'The Äsaḷa Perahära in Kandy', *Ceylon Journal of Historical and Social Studies*, vol. 6, no. 2, 1963, pp. 169–80.

[49]S. Paranavitana (ed.), *History of Ceylon*, Vol. 1 (Ceylon Univer-

Only Kataragama and Vishnu are in both lists, so it is not surprising that when I asked people to name the Four Gods (*hatara deyyō*) they were the only two always named. Were the analogy of divine with human government consistently applied we would expect the Four Gods to have Ceylon, or perhaps Sinhalese Ceylon, divided between them into four non-overlapping territories (*sīmā*), but the reality is not so tidy. Of Vishnu I was often told, in accordance with the *Mahāvaṃsa* story, that his territory is the whole of Ceylon.[50] His chief shrine in Ceylon is at Devundara, on the south coast. Ancient and mediaeval references which are commonly assumed to be to Vishnu, including the *Mahāvaṃsa* passage and references to the Devundara shrine, in fact say Upulvan/Uppalavaṇṇa. The name means 'having the colour of a blue lotus', and Vishnu has. Professor Paranavitana questions whether Upulvan really was Vishnu,[51] but as the two have been popularly equated the question is purely academic. Vishnu's traditional character is benevolent and colourless; his character as *fidei defensor* is his only salient characteristic. As in India he is shown as blue, with four arms, and his mount is a kind of eagle (*garuḍa*).

Nātha (the name means 'lord' in Sanskrit and Pali) has almost been forgotten. His main shrine is at Toṭagamuva on the southwest coast, but to my knowledge he is never considered the guardian deity of that or any other particular region. His Kandy shrine is probably the oldest of the four *dēvālēs* there, being built in the second half of the fourteenth century, and was used for ceremonies at the

sity Press, Colombo, 1960), part II, p. 765.

[50]Cf. Paranavitana, *History*, Part II, 763: 'In the fifteenth century, Upulvan was looked upon as the national god of the Sinhalese.'

[51]Paranavitana, 'Mahāyānism in Ceylon', pp. 66–7. Here he suggests that '...Uppalavaṇṇa was a local form of one of the Mahāyāna Bodhisattvas.' In a later monograph he wishes to identify Upulvan with Varuṇa, a Vedic god. See *The Shrine of Upulvan at Devundara, Memoirs of the Archaeological Survey of Ceylon*, vol. VI (Colombo, 1953).

inauguration of kings of Kandy.[52] The disappearance of the court dealt him a severe blow. Nātha was once a mere epithet of Avalokiteśvara, an important Bodhisattva of the Māhāyāna Buddhism which came to Ceylon in late classical times, but this has been forgotten—Avalokiteśvara is a name not known to villagers. However, he was twice named to me when I asked which gods were Bodhisattvas, so a memory lingers. A middle-class lady in Kandy told me that people do not make vows to him as to the other gods, and explained this by saying that he is to be the next Buddha Maitrī, so presumably has lost interest in vows. Monks too said that Nātha is Maitrī. It is also notable that he does not share his shrine with other gods, but lives apart. Maitrī today shares an iconographic feature, the small seated Buddha figure in the headdress, with the classical Avalokiteśvara. Maitrī and Avalokiteśvara Nātha are several times mentioned together in inscriptions and literature from the fourteenth to the eighteenth century.[53] There has clearly been some conflation. However, I doubt the Kandyan lady's explanation of why people make no vows to Nātha, although it would support my thesis; I suspect that once they did, but that he has simply drifted out of the actual pantheon for reasons unconnected with his Bodhisattva nature, and so lost power and prestige.

Pattinī too is losing ground. She still has shrines all over the country, including two in my area of research, but few people name her as one of the guardian deities. She is a goddess from South India, with a highly distinctive cult which has been exhaustively studied by Obeyesekere. She is notable as the only lady in the pantheon, actual or ideal. Her rich background of ritual and mythology has been largely forgotten in my area: I was merely told that she was powerful (*satta*) and could cure pox; one monk identified her with Nāgammā, a mother goddess who has a temple in Nāgadīpa near Jaffna. Her headquarters are at Navagamuva near Colombo.

[52] Paranavitana, 'Mahāyānism', pp. 52–60.
[53] Ibid.

More commonly listed as one of the Four Gods (*hatara deyyō*) than either Nātha or Pattinī is Saman. His historical origins are the subject of another learned monograph by Dr. Paranavitana,[54] but again its contents are not in any sense known to the villagers. Saman is *par excellence* the god of Adam's Peak, which in Pali is perhaps named after him (Samantakūṭa)—or he after it—and so he is the god of the Kandyan hill country. In fact he has another major centre, even closer to Kandy, at Mahiyangana. It is interesting that in both places he is intimately associated with the Buddha, for these are the sites of the Buddha's footprint and his first visit to Ceylon respectively. There is thus something very Buddhist about Saman; his figure appears frequently in *vihāra* in my area and one monk went so far as to say that he is the very highest god, next to the Buddha in rank, with Vishnu, Kataragama, and Alutnuvara below him. He is represented as white, and his mount is a white elephant. I was told in Mīgala that the season for pilgrimages to Adam's Peak ends at Wesak; on the two nights of the Wesak full moon festival no pilgrims, not even monks, make the climb, but the way is left clear for Saman's white elephant, who lives secluded in the jungles on the mountain slopes, to ascend and pay solitary homage to the Buddha.

Vibhīṣaṇa, the last god with a historical claim to be one of the Four, rarely cropped up in my informants' lists. His main shrine is at Kälaṇiya near Colombo. Mr. Malalgoḍa tells me that it was razed by the Portuguese; this must be a cardinal reason for his decline. In the Sanskrit epic, the *Rāmāyaṇa*, he is a brother of Rāvaṇa, the wicked ruler of Lankā. He sides with the virtuous Rāma, and is rewarded with his brother's throne. But none of this seems to be remembered in Mīgala.

The gods mentioned so far are all, I believe, of nationally recognized status. Of more strictly local reputation is Däḍimunda alias Alutnuvara Deyyō *alias* Dēvatā

[54] S. Paranavitana, *The God of Adam's Peak* (Artibus Asiae, Ascona, 1958).

Baṇḍāra Deyyō. (Three such different names may suggest the conflation of three gods; if this is so the conflation is complete, as several informants told me that these names denoted the same person, nor were there any statements to the contrary.) Däḍimunda's status and function are very differently assessed. Some say he is in the retinue of Kataragama, some (more circumstantially and so more plausibly) of Vishnu; but some even counted him (under the name of Alutnuvara) as one of the Four Deities, and so he must be mentioned here. His main shrine (under the names of Däḍimunda and Alutnuvara) is some twenty miles west of Kandy, near Māvanälla in the province of Sabaragamuva.[55]. I was told at the shrine, which is large and extremely prosperous, that it is about 800 years old, and was originally to Vishnu, but since Vishnu's shrine was moved to Kandy in 1748 the chief god is Vishnu's minister (*amātyayā*), Däḍimunda Dēvatā Baṇḍāra. According to a Mīgala villager, Däḍimunda got this shrine built by *yakṣa* labour recruited from Bengal and South India. The image at the shrine is a gold figure of a prince, only about a foot high; I saw no mount there, nor did he have one in Mīgala—a most distinctive feature. I was given more news of him by various informants in Mīgala. He is the son of the *yakṣa* Pūrṇaka and a *nāgakanyā* ('cobra maiden'): Pūrṇaka figures in the *Vidhurapaṇḍita Jātaka*,[56] so this gives Däḍimunda canonical antecedents. The main story about him is this. When Gotama was seated under the Bo tree striving for Enlightenment, Däḍimunda was one

[55]According to Gooneratne (p. 39) this temple belongs to 'the chief of all Ceylon demons...Wahala Bandara Dewiyo, or as he is more commonly termed, Wahala dewiyo.' The myth he retails of how this 'Dewatawa' had the temple cut from a huge rock by his *yakṣa* slaves leaves no doubt that these are just more names of the same god. (Mr. H.L. Seneviratne has sent me a folk poem, *Galakäppu Sähälla* (N.J. Kūrē at the Anula Press, 1961), in which the same story is told of Alutnuvara Däḍimunda Devatā Baṇḍāra Dēviyō.) Gooneratne goes on to give a most interesting account of pilgrims to the temple, which he describes as the national headquarters for exorcizing women possessed by *yakku*

[56]*J.* VI, pp. 255–329.

of the godlings in attendance on him. At the approach of Māra all the godlings fled, but Däḍimuṇḍa, being rather slow, could not make his getaway, and hid in the Buddha's robe. When Māra and his host had been routed the Buddha looked round, and at that moment Däḍimunda appeared before him. 'You alone of all the gods did not desert me,' said the Buddha, and in gratitude put him in charge of Ceylon. So I was told that Däḍimunda is a guardian of Buddhism (*sāsanarakṣaka*) for all Ceylon, and this fits him to Vishnu, who received a similar trust. I shall have more to say of Däḍimunda below when he crops up in less exalted company.[57]

Before going on to describe those deities who are definitely lower in status, I should explain how the *Bodhisattva* (Sinh.: *Bōsat*) fits in. Bodhisattva is a religious, not (like god) an ontological status;[58] a Bodhisattva is simply one who has taken a vow to become a Buddha, or, in the phrase used by a monk of Vishnu, who fulfils the requirements for Enlightenment (*bōdhi sambhāra puraṇa aya*). Whether someone is a Bodhisattva may be known only to himself. (This does not imply that one would keep it a secret.) In the *Jātaka* stories Gotama Buddha's lives as a Bodhisattva are recounted, and he is always born as a god (usually quite a minor deity), a man, or one of the higher animals. A Bodhisattva would be virtuous, so that a lower rebirth would be most unlikely. We have seen that in tenth century Ceylon all kings were believed to be Bodhisattvas. Nowadays, however, only a few of the ancient kings (Duṭugämuṇu, Devānampiya Tissa, Mahāsena) and some of the higher gods are named as Bodhisattvas, and on asking for names of Bodhisattvas I found disagreement. Most claim that Vishnu is one, but one monk denied it. The claim was variously made for Saman, Alutnuvara, Nātha, Vaiśravaṇa,

[57]For further information on Däḍimunda see L. D. Barnett, 'Alphabetical Guide to Sinhalese Folklore from Ballad Sources', *Indian Antiquary*, Supplement 1916-17, *s.v.* 'Däḍimunda' and 'Devatār Baṇḍāra'.

[58]Ames ('Ritual Prestations', p. 43), in calling Bodhisattvas 'higher deviyās' [*sic*], has missed the point that Bodhisattvas and *deviyō* are not terms on the same continuum.

Kataragama, and perhaps Tārā;[59] most monks denied, either directly or by implication, that Kataragama was a Bosat. Saman seemed to have the best religious reputation; he was given me as an instance of a good Buddhist, and another monk told me that he is the only god free from sin (*keles*) and has entered on the path to enlightenment (*sovan*). One monk held deviant views which must reflect some reading: Tārā is supposed to be above the gods; Mahāyānists believe in her and think she is a Bosat; she is powerful in India. This was the monk who rejected Vishnu, but accepted Kataragama as a Bosat.

The rest of the pantheon in my area consists of gods who are permanent or floating members of a group called the Twelve Gods (*doḷos deyyō*), and the group is usually considered to form the retinue of Kataragama. Most of these twelve gods are village gods (*gambāra deyyō*)—that is, they are individually believed to be in charge of a village, or rather a group of villages. There is said to be an analogy between the human and the divine power structure; using the title of the administrative officers who superseded the feudal nobility, I was told that the Four Gods were like Government Agents (who were in charge of a district) and the Twelve Gods like District Revenue Officers (their immediate subordinates). The Twelve Gods thus hold power on warrants from one of the Four Gods—nowadays from Kataragama. An implied modification of this analogy was, however, supplied by the old Mīgala *kapurāḷa*; he said that though our local god, Piṭiya Deyyō, is a retainer of Kataragama, he is in absolute charge of his own territory, so that if Kataragama wishes to visit it he has to get Piṭiya Deyyō's warrant. This seems to take us back to the days before the bureaucratization of the feudal structure, when nobles had full local autonomy.

Local gods (like the Twelve) are of rather different character from regional gods (i.e. the Four). Local gods in some sense validate the social structure: their rituals emphasize

[59]'Nātha's consort, Tārā, was worshipped at a shrine at Doravaka in the fourteenth century.' Paranavitana, *History*, Part II, 762–3.

the traditional status differences of caste and sex, and they are supposed, through the *kapurāḷa*, to ensure good harvests and freedom from disease. Traditionally they are the only gods of whom the members of the village community make requests. But once a year the villagers are supposed to go to the shrine of the regional god, just as the sharecropper pays his annual visit of homage to the landlord, who may live in the city. Villagers used to be somewhat frightened of leaving the territory of their local god—as they walked through the forest on their way to the regional centre they would repeatedly say 'Karuṇāvayi' ('Mercy') and hang strips of cloth on trees to placate the spirits through whose territory they were passing. The ritual at the regional centre paid no attention to status distinctions—in the *dēvālē* of a major god all are equal; nor was this the place to ask for anything specific: one just worshipped and received edification. This pattern is rapidly disappearing. As it becomes easier for people to get to the bigger gods, by bus, they visit them more often and informally, and ask them favours; the visits for purely religious edification are those paid to the Buddha's relics. The regional centre for Mīgala should be Mahiyangana; a large group of villagers went there, but it was at Poson, a day associated with the Buddha, and it was to see the *vihāra* and worship the relics that they went. It is not only because villagers now go to the big gods that the little gods are in decline; the big gods are also coming to the village. What this amounts to is the supersession of specifically Kandyan tradition by the religiosity of the Low Country and the middle classes—which is the same thing. Low Countrymen outnumber Kandyans by about five to one; they have also enjoyed the dubious advantage of about 300 years more of European rule. Their traditional society was modified long ago under European laws along European-built roads. With greater mobility, and more education, they became economically dominant; the trade in a Kandyan town is almost entirely in the hands of Tamils, Muslims, and Low Country Sinhalese. Geographical (horizontal) mobility long ago disposed of local gods in the Low Country and introduced Low Countrymen with their emphasis on big gods and little devils into Kandyan towns and villages. Social (vertical) mobility produced among Low Countrymen a middle class, something which hardly yet exists among Kandyans, whose feudal aristocracy still own most of the land; the emancipation of the middle classes disinclines them towards village gods whose rituals remind them of their caste status and narrower social horizons, while the notorious strains of social mobility incline them to belief in astrology and even in black magic. Meanwhile they enter the professions and the bureaucracy, and become the models for ambitious villagers to emulate. A lady in the village took to visiting regularly the Hindu temple to Kataragama a few miles down the road, though she said she was afraid of him, and spoke ill of our local village *kapuvā* as a fake (though she still had her daughters stand well clear when he became possessed); the explanation lies I think not in her very pleasant personality, but in the fact that as a low-caste woman she would be at a double status disadvantage in the local cult, and visits to Kataragama made her feel a more progressive and socially superior person.

It is in the context of the worship of the Twelve Gods (though it would also apply to the worship of the major gods) that I came across the concept of ritual impurity (*killa*) in Mīgala. *Killa* is conferred by menstruation, by parturition, and by contact with death. Caste impurity is *not* covered by the term, and thus is not conceived of as having anything particularly to do with ritual; there is thus a disjunction between temporary and permanent impurity, which contrasts with the Hindu situation. This is just what Professor Dumont's theories would lead us to expect of a society subscribing to a 'world-renouncers'' religion. Moreover—and still in conformity with Dumont's theories—*killa* affects only the cult of the gods; there is no *killa* for monks, and it has no relevance to the worship of the Buddha or to anything else that the villagers themselves conceptualize as 'Buddhist'. For this reason I need say no more about it.

The worship of the Twelve Gods is sometimes known as the '*Baṇḍāra* cult'. *Baṇḍāra* was a Kandyan title, and the word figures in the names of many of these gods. The term '*Baṇḍāra* cult' would be a good one, were it taken merely to imply that these gods function in ways analogous to noblemen under the old order. However Rahula (*History*, p. 37) calls it 'the adoration of deceased chiefs and prominent ancestors', an explanation to which the term lends itself but which I believe to be only partially correct; so I refer to them simply as the Twelve Gods.

Ethnography on the Twelve Gods is rather scanty. Seligmann wrote a short article[60] on them which does not entirely agree with any other data I have come across. However, Barnett (op. cit.) retails lots of stories about them which he extracted from the manuscripts of folk poetry collected by Hugh Nevill in the late nineteenth century and deposited in the British Museum. Wirz (op. cit.) has data on the more maleficent spirits (see below). There is also much relevant information in Parker's *Ancient Ceylon*,[61] especially in Chapter IV. This is interesting, because Parker's book is ostensibly about the Väddas; it shows how hard it is to disentangle Vädda and Kandyan Sinhalese culture. The stories—and even some of the names—of the gods show too how strong is the Tamil element in this cultural area.

There were in or near Mīgala three shrines to Piṭiya Deyyō, the local patron, each with its own priest called *kapuvā*, *kapurāḷa*, or *kapumahattayā*. The title is used for a marriage broker, so it might be translated 'go-between'; it indicates that the priest in this cult acts as a medium, or shaman. The priests of these shrines were related, an uncle (whom I shall call K 1) and two nephews (K 2 and K 3). K 1 and K 2 (who were not on speaking terms) were my

[60]C.G. Seligmann, 'Note on the "Bandar" cult of the Kandyan Sinhalese', *Man*, vol. 9, 1909, no. 77, pp. 130–4. He says that the *baṇḍāra* gods can only get in touch with the living world by sending sickness or animals, usually the latter. I never came across any belief that they send animals.

[61]H. Parker, *Ancient Ceylon* (Luzac, London, 1909).

main informants on the Twelve Gods, and I asked them to list the gods. K 1 said that there are altogether sixty-seven gods, of whom he made offerings to twenty-four; of these, twelve are the main ones and twelve are their attendants. Asked to name the twelve he then listed fifteen, and when I pointed this out eliminated three, whom I have put at the end of his list. The second list is that of K 2, who initially listed twelve, but later in conversation referred also to Amusīri Deyyō. The third list was given to me by the ex-headman (*āracci*) of a village about eight miles from Mīgala. It is worth reproducing because he seemed a competent and spontaneous informant on this subject and his list seems the least repetitious. It does not include Piṭiya Deyyō, whom he confirmed to be in charge of the Mīgala area, but said his own area was under Kandē Deyyō, who protected the village and cured diseases. I reproduce the titles on p. 218 exactly as given. Allowing for some regional variation we seem to have a well standardized list. I agree with K 1's second thoughts, for his last three names do not really belong: Hūniyam is a pan-Ceylonese deity who will be discussed below; the other two were not named by anyone else. Similarly, I would eliminate Siddamulā Hūniyam from the second list—he looks like a makeshift variant on Hūniyam to complete the number. Kiriammā Deyyō is the only female.[62]

K 2 told me that some gods are *jīvamāna*. This is a Sanskrit word meaning 'alive'. I deduce, however, that he used it to mean 'perceptible' or 'perceived'; its opposite he expressed by the sentence 'when they are born they live without being visible' ('Ātmayak labāgena innavā pēnen nätuva'). He said that Alutnuvara Baṇḍāra Deyyo and Hūniyam Dēvatā Baṇḍāra were *jīvamāna*: Alutnuvara can go on flowers, over rocks, or in the water; Hūniyam can take any form, e.g. a black dog or a tall white figure. K 1 said

[62]In Mīgala there are usually said to be seven Kiriammās, and they are not among the Twelve Gods. I have devoted a separate article to them and their rituals: 'Food for Seven Grandmothers', *Man*, vol. 6, no. 1, March 1971, pp. 5–17.

K 1	*K 2*	*Āracci*
Piṭiya Deyyō	Piṭiya D.	
Gan̆gē Baṇḍāra Deyyō	Gan̆gē B.D.	Gan̆gē B.D.
Dēvatā Baṇḍāra Deyyō = Däḍimunda	Alutnuvara D.	Dēvatā B.D.
Kīrti Baṇḍāra Deyyō	Kīrti B.D.	Kīrti B.D.
Kaḷu Baṇḍāra Deyyō		Kaḷu B.D.
Vanniya Baṇḍāra Deyyō	Vanniya B.D.	Vanniya B.D.
Kaḷukumārayā	Kaḷukumāra D.	Kaḷukumārayā
Kohom̆ba Deyyō	Kohom̆ba D.	Kohom̆ba D.
Kaḍavara	Kaḍavara Deyyō	Kaḍavara D.
Kandakumāra	Kandē Deyyō	Kandē D.
Amusīri Yakā	Amusīri Deyyō	Amusīri D.
Mangara Deyyō		
Hūniyam	Hūniyam Dēvatā Baṇḍāra	
Valkōn Baṇḍāra Deyyō		
Abayakōn Baṇḍāra Deyyō		
	Siddamulā Hūniyam Dēvatā Baṇḍāra	
	Pallebädda Deyyō	Pallebädda D.
		Kiriammā D.

Translations:

Piṭiya:	a tract of flat ground
Gan̆gē:	in/on/at/of the river
Kīrti:	fame, glory
Kaḷu:	black
Vanniya:	of the Vanni, a desolate area in northern Ceylon
Kaḷukumārayā:	black prince
Kohom̆ba:	Margosa (a kind of tree)
Kandakumāra:	mountain prince
Kandē:	on/of the mountain
Amusīri:	raw blood
Hūniyam:	void
Kiriammā:	milk-mother (term for wet-nurse, also for grandmother)
Pallebädda:	a place name

that none of the Twelve Gods was married; ten were born of woman (*mäṇikē*) like us, but Gan̆gē Baṇḍāra Deyyō was born of a blue gem in a blue sea, and Kandakumāra was born from the mountain at Kataragama, so these two were born without pollution (*killa*) and no one polluted may approach them. Another kind of status difference was indicated by K 2: the only gods who can be served by a *kapuvā* who is not *goyigama* ('high-caste'—see Chapter 8) are Kaḍavara Deyyō and Amusīri Deyyō. This seems to match the fact that neither of these gods is ever called *baṇḍāra* or *kumāra*. The word which K 2 used for 'service' was *rājakāriya*, which historically means the service obligations attached to feudal land tenure—yet another analogy (if that is not too weak a word) between the religious and the secular.

As all the above deities except Valkōn and Siddamulā Hūniyam, on neither of whom do I have any more information, have their stories told by Barnett, I shall only report from my own notes enough detail to suggest their general character. Certain stories—of a prince or noble banished for a misdemeanour; of the miraculous removal of a rock impeding irrigation—are variously told of most of the Twelve; as is common with such groups, their individual characteristics are largely interchangeable.

I was given most information on Piṭiya Deyyō, our local patron. For 50 cents K 3 showed me his picture, or photograph (*chāyarūpaya*) as he called it, which he claimed to be ancient and could well be fifty years old. It is a picture of a man in the costume of a Kandyan nobleman (*radala*) with a horse (Piṭiya Deyyō's invariable mount) and four attendants, painted on a piece of wood shaped rather like a wine glass, with ornamentation round the borders. It is kept under a cloth and hence is well preserved. The picture of Piṭiya Deyyō produced by K 1 was a less venerable object, a cardboard cut-out of a bearded man with a white horse. K 2 at his shrine also showed me a Kandyan noble with a white horse: he also had pictures of Pallebädda Deyyō, over whose 'photograph' cockroaches were crawling, Vanniya Baṇḍāra Deyyō and Alutnuvara Baṇḍāra Deyyō. All look like Kandyan noblemen. Vanniya B.D.'s mount is an elephant; Alutnuvara has no mount.

Piṭiya Deyyō, says K 2, escaped from India after committing some misdemeanour there and came here in the days of Kīrti Śrī Rājasiṃha [i.e. about 200 years ago]. He visited sixty-seven places and from each acquired a follower; all of them are now gods and form his retinue (*pirisa*); Pallebädda Deyyō was his first and chief follower. According to K 1, he came from India five or six hundred years ago; his story went on to connect him with various local places: where he first stopped, ate, bathed, etc. He is in charge of everything locally, and (like all gods) knows the future, on which he can be consulted at his shrine via the *kapuvā*. Not all, however, agreed that Piṭiya Deyyō came from India; a monk identified him as the son of the righteous Tamil king of Ceylon, Eḷāra. While driving in his chariot that unfortunate prince accidentally ran over a calf, for which, on complaint from the calf's mother, he was executed by his father. (The story comes from the *Mahāvaṃsa*, XXI, 15–18.) Another informant told me the same story but located it in India. All agree that Piṭiya Deyyō is (the reincarnation of) a prince, that he is connected with a (perhaps unintentional) misdemeanour, and that he was Tamil.

Kaḷu Baṇḍāra Deyyō has a *dēvālē* on a large mountain nearby, but no-one knows where it is. Once an old farmer lost his two buffaloes and went searching for them with his son. They found them in a pond. They were so tired that they too bathed in the pond, and when they came out the father was young again, and so were the buffaloes. When they returned home the farmer's wife at first refused to have anything to do with him, and was convinced only with difficulty that it was he. The villagers then went out looking for the pond, but it had disappeared.

Kaḍavara Deyyō is a *yakṣa* who lives in trees in the jungle. He used to be a minister in India of a certain King of Malaya (i.e. South India), but having died as a man he became a *yakṣa* (*manuṣyek märilā yakṣek vunā*); he is a *maḷayakā* [literally 'dead *yakṣa*', i.e. the reincarnation of a man]. He cut a rock to make a watercourse at the Temple of the Tooth in Kandy. It is tempting to associate this with the fact that according to the dictionary *Kaḍavara* means a ditch or channel, but the meaning is given as lexical only, so the connection may be fortuitous or the dictionary mistaken. Parker (p. 157) shows that the name is Tamil and means 'the Celestial who escaped', which fits another myth.

Kaḷukumārayā, the black prince, is unambiguously maleficent. As his name indicates, he too is or was a prince, and he is said by K 2 to have 6,000 followers. According to K 1 he was the son of a Kandyan king. He and his father each reared a *koṇḍeya* bird. One day he let out the two birds and they fought, and his bird killed his father's. At this the king sentenced his son to death, but on the insistence of his ministers the sentence was commuted to banishment, and he came to a river called the Maha Oya and settled down there in the Maha Oya Dēvālē. [The Maha Oya is in south-western Ceylon.] But the main point about Kaḷukumāra is that he afflicts women, appearing to them in dreams or otherwise casting his gaze (*bälma*) upon them to disturbing effect—I gather he is a kind of incubus and may then have to be exorcised. Though he usually confines his attention to women, an elderly man in Mīgala told me that Kaḷukumāra was always in him and would possess him during ceremonies so that he was carried away (*vähenavā*); it might be significant that the man was a bachelor.

Hūniyam or Sūniyam has a most peculiar history, and it is doubtful whether he should properly appear here, up among the deities, or down among the *yakku* and *holman*. He is especially liable to appear at night as a black dog or naked white figure; according to K 2 he can bring good or evil, but another villager said he was definitely benevolent. This opinion contrasts violently with his character in the Low Country, where he is predominantly associated with black magic, which may even generically be called *hūniyam*. He certainly is fond of assuming different shapes: I was told that he has eighteen different forms or disguises (*vēsa*) and wears clothes of five colours with a garland of flowers, usually white. He is often associated with Däḍimunda. At Däḍimunda's big temple near Māvanälla he is the only other god represented, and is said to be Däḍimunda's minister. One monk even identified Hūniyam with Alutnuvara. I found him sharing one *dēvālē* in the grounds of a *vihāra* with Vishnu, Mahasēna Kataragama,[63] and Däḍimunda. On this occasion I was told that Vishnu is in charge of the whole world, Sūniyam of Ceylon, and Däḍimunda of the Kandyan provinces (*uḍa raṭa*). Of Sūniyam there was a small statue dressed in white as an ascetic (*tāpasa*) taking the precepts (*sil*), and a picture of him as a village deity (*gambāra deyyō*), which I was told to be his own usual form (*niyama svarūpaya*), with four arms. Whether his appearance as a virtuous Buddhist is more or less surprising than his nocturnal behaviour as a black dog depends on one's view of the etymology of his name. According to De Lanerolle in Geiger's *Etymological Glossary*, it has evolved (via Tamil) from Sanskrit *śūnya* 'the void', the dominant principle according to those Mahāyāna philosophers who declared the world to be 'empty' in that things have no essence. (In this they were developing the concepts, which they shared with Theravāda, of impermanence (*anityatā*) and non-self (*anātmatā*); though Sūniyam be a degenerate, I would not wish to call him a heretic!) But according to Geiger himself, in an article[64] which De Lanerolle refers to in his entry but apparently disagrees with, *hū-niyam* is Eḷu for 'thread-method', i.e. magic, so that Hūniyam is a personification of magical practice. Geiger's theory seems to me the more probable.

The above information on the Twelve Gods, although sketchy, sufficiently demonstrates that to describe their worship as an ancestor cult is a gross over-simplification. Even the title of *banḍāra* is no guarantee of a god's human origin (in the euhemeristic sense), for it is accorded to Hūniyam too; it is rather a Kandyan naturalization certifi-

[63]This god was explained by his *kapurāḷa* as not the Kataragama from India, but a local god. Mahāsena was an ancient king of Ceylon whom it would not be surprising to find deified, but his acquisition of the name Kataragama seems most anomalous.

[64]W. Geiger, 'Hūniyam, Ein Beitrag zur Volkskunde von Ceylon', in *Aufsätze zur Kultur- und Sprachgeschichte... Ernst Kuhn... gewidmet* (Breslau, 1916), pp. 185–92.

cate. The most conspicuous characteristic of the shrines of the Twelve Gods was that though themselves unimpressive they were always associated with a striking natural feature: a huge rock, a cave, above all a spot with a wonderful view. All the three local shrines to Piṭiya Deyyō were on or by huge rocks, one of them in a cave in the jungle just above a great sloping rock slab, another on a rock overlooking the river and covered with temple trees, a third on a great rock which, though not very high, commanded a magnificent view of the village territory. The shrine to Kandē Deyyō near the village of the headman quoted above was on a mountain, and so inaccessible that it was now visited only once a year. Gaňgē Deyyō's shrine was on an island in the middle of a big river. Moreover the names of at least four of the gods (Piṭiya, Gaňgē, Kandē, and Kohoṁba) associate them with natural phenomena. In this they recall the canonical divinities of trees and parks (*vanadevatā, ārāmadevatā*), and the *yakṣas* associated with trees and mountains: a group of morally neutral nature divinities.

A second current associates them with the more distinctly malevolent type of canonical *yakṣa*. The confusion of this group with the nature divinities is, we recall, a canonical feature. Here probably fit those gods who are most often called *yakku*: Kaḍavara, Amusīri, Kaḷukumārayā, and Hūniyam. It is notable that these are the very members of our list who figure in Wirz's account of the demonology of the Southern Province.

Thirdly there is indeed the ancestor element, represented in the titles *baṇḍāra* and *kumāra*, suggested also by such names as Kīrti ('Glory') and by Alutnuvara and Pallebädda, which are place names. Local people themselves incline to this type of explanation of the cult; we have already discussed the ambiguity involved in this interpretation among Buddhists, who are anyway committed to a belief in the rebirth of all beings and therefore to a type of euhemerism as an explanation of any god or demon. What is noteworthy is that the stories so often involve the banishment of a prince or minister for some misdemeanour. This has the ring of historical authenticity, as the mountains have long served as strongholds for disgraced potentates and rebel chieftains. The fact that they are usually said to be Indians, or at least Tamils, likewise sounds authentic. This true *baṇḍāra* element therefore provides a third strand in the constitution of the Twelve Gods. What must, however, be noted is that two or three of the elements—nature, maleficence, and ancestry—combine to form the individual divinity. Piṭiya Deyyō has a name associating him with nature, is supposed to have been a prince, and left India under a cloud; Kaḷukumārayā was also a prince who left under a cloud, brings a particular kind of disease, and has a shrine in a river.

Our catalogue of the inhabitants of the universe seen from Mīgala is now concluded.

III. Attempts to influence non-human beings

> Buddhism being considered to be the *sacred* religion, while Demonism is only a religion relating to one's temporal interests, it is natural that the influence of the former should to a certain extent be felt on the latter.
>
> Gooneratne, p. 15

The institutions and ceremonies appropriate to each class of being have been described at length by such authors as Wirz and expertly classified by Ames. Tambiah has contributed an account of the hierarchy of languages used in ritual.[65] In the following paragraph I wish to do little more than give a picture of the types of worship distinctive to Mīgala, and this will again involve a concentration on the Twelve Gods.

The higher and more powerful the divinity, the more imposing the edifices and personnel devoted to him; the lower and weaker the devil, the more the attitude of human beings, both laymen and specialists, changes from worship

[65] S.J. Tambiah, 'The Magical Power of Words', *Man*, new series, vol. 3, no. 2, June 1968; see pp. 176–8.

to control.

The Institutions

(1) Conceptually the Buddha lies outside this scheme, for in his case control is out of the question; but from the sociological (i.e. behavioural) point of view, as Ames has demonstrated, monks, *vihāras*, and *Buddha pūjā* fit in well. The *vihāra* is described in Chapter 2, *Buddha pūjā* in Chapter 3. The main ritual language is Pali.

(2) After *vihāras* the largest (and richest) religious institutions in the area are the Tamil temples (*kovil*) to Kataragama. In each there is a brahmin in permanent residence; the one I visited was specially brought down from Jaffna. The ritual is entirely Śaivite Hindu, and the great majority of the clientèle are Tamils from the plantations. The main ritual language is Sanskrit.

(3) The Buddhist god has a *dēvālē* served by a *kapuvā*, though the major gods are also usually represented in *vihāra*, in which case they generally have no *kapuvā* (and no organized worship). In accordance with the reformist principles of the Rāmañña Nikāya (see Chapter 8) their *vihāras* have no gods or *dēvālēs* on the premises; there were only three Rāmañña *vihāras* in my area. *Dēvālēs* to the Twelve Gods exploit natural sites and often lack buildings; there may be no more construction than a shelf to serve as altar. The *kapuvō* are always of *goyigama* caste, except, I was told, for the gods Kaḍavara and Amusīri, whom we have seen to be more properly called *yakku*; the *kapuvā* of one Kaḍavara *dēvālē* was said to be *padu*, a low caste. By tradition the office of *kapuvā* runs in families, but where new shrines are opened to regional gods new men are sometimes recruited. The main ritual language is Sinhalese.

(4) Minor spirits have no buildings, and the specialists devoted to them could appropriately be called exorcists. Material on this subject is more prolific and classification more precise in the Low Country. An exorcist of *yakku* is called a *yakädurā*, of evil planetary influences a *baliädurā*, but usually these are the same person, according to con-

text. A supplier of amulets (*yantra*) and charms (*mantra*) (who may in a specific context function as *yakädurā* or *baliädurā*) is a *kaṭṭaḍiyā*. These exorcists are usually (but not necessarily) of low caste. The drummer caste (*beravāyō*) are supposed to be skilled in these matters, and are especially associated with appeasing the planetary deities. A general term for a magician is *mantrakārayā*, 'charm-maker'. His spells are in a hotch-potch of languages, normally unintelligible.

There is a general tendency, exemplified by the last paragraph, for those who are specialists in one type of causation to pick up knowledge and practice connected with other types. We have already seen how monks, who may be said to have specialist knowledge of *karma*, and are involved in rituals to avert and cure misfortune through *pirit*, tend also to become experts in astrology and Ayurvedic medicine. The same goes for the other specialists: astrology and Ayurvedic medicine are very often found together also in laymen. As both are associated with learning they tend not to be practised by the low-caste drummers, who are often socially depressed; but these drummers, who participate in rituals for the Buddha, are knowledgeable in ritual at all levels and are generally reputed to be good at magic. *Kapurāḷas* also tend to be suppliers of *yantra mantra;* and the one man in Mīgala who knew astrology (which he had learned from a monk) practised Sinhalese medicine (part-time and for little or no money), and was the son and brother of *kapurāḷas*.

Before I describe the local rituals, it will give a fair idea of their relative importance if I list the religious institutions in my area. There were about forty *vihāra*, which do not concern us in this chapter, and two Hindu *kovil* to Kataragama, which will not be mentioned again. There are two old shrines to Pattinī (whose priests are called *pattinīrāḷas*). Otherwise the only *dēvālē* of any age to a god of national standing was a *dēvālē* to Kataragama, which was in a village entirely surrounded by tea estates, and had a Tamil as *kapuvā*; though it was within the grounds of a *vihāra* it therefore hardly qualifies as a Sinhalese institution. With this dubious exception twenty years ago there was not a single *dēvālē* to Vishnu or Kataragamạ in the entire area. However, this is changing fast. A Vishnu *dēvālē* recently opened next to one of the *kovils*, and during my stay a Kataragama *dēvālē* started in a cave in the woods, very much in the style of the homes of local gods. The habit of having a *dēvālē* in the *vihāra* grounds, extremely common in the Low Country and a feature of some of the principal old Kandyan temples, was gaining ground even faster: the first had been built in 1949—and was run by a *kapurāḷa* imported from Mātara in the south—and four more were being built or projected. I am excepting an old *dēvālē* to Piṭiya Deyyō which stood in one small *vihāra* (commanding, as ever, a superb view), and a tiny shrine to Vishnu in an uninhabited monastery. But I must not give the impression that Vishnu and Kataragama are strangers to the area. Most image-houses contain their statues, or at least that of Vishnu, standing behind a curtain in the Hindu fashion, and the worshipper can always worship them, drop a coin in the box provided, or even make a vow if he should be so inclined.

Accurate information on *dēvālēs* of the Twelve Gods is hard to get, as many of them are falling into disuse. I asked about them when interviewing monks and my list may contain duplications. I listed fifteen *dēvālēs*, all said to be to Piṭiya Deyyō, Kandē Deyyō, Kaḍavara Deyyō or Kīrti Baṇḍāra Deyyō. All of these except the one already mentioned had no physical connection with a *vihāra*. Though I could not investigate them, I think the two shrines to Pattinī properly belong in this category, not merely because of their age but also because they must have performed the functions of shrines to village gods.

The meaner spirits are only noticed when something goes wrong, and as far as most people except the *kapurāḷa* are concerned this is true also of the Twelve Gods, excepting perhaps the annual harvest festival. Statues of gods in *vihāra* are of course accessible to visitors at any time, as the *vihāra* is always open:[66] but any *dēvālē* which can be locked up is only opened by the *kapurāḷa*, who attends on certain days called *kemvara*.[67] The *kemvara* in my area are Sundays, Tuesdays, and Fridays. In other parts of the country they are Wednesdays and Saturdays.[68] But this does not seem to be purely a question of locality. A village lady told me that it varies from god to god; that Alutnuvara's days are Wednesday and Saturday. The days at the big Alutnuvara *dēvālē* at Māvanälla are in fact Wednesday, Saturday, and half-day Monday (*varu kemvara*—afternoon only), but whether this is determined by the identity of the god or by the shrine's location (in Sabaragamuva Province) I have not enough data to judge. The same lady considered that of the three *kemvara* the most auspicious day on which to visit Kataragama's *kovil* (possibly because it is generally an auspicious day) is Friday. On the other hand a little used *dēvālē* to Piṭiya Deyyō opened only, if at all, on Sundays. When a *dēvālē* to one of the Twelve Gods is in operation the *kapurāḷa* becomes possessed (*māyam venavā*), but interestingly enough he will not do this on a *poya* day. On the one hand the god gives precedence to the Buddha; on the other there is something not quite proper about becoming possessed, even if it is your role. I have never heard this something made explicit, but I judge that it violates the Buddhist ideal of self-control. To become possessed on a *poya* day would therefore be like getting drunk on a Sunday morning.

[66]It is usually kept locked to prevent theft, but the key is in the *pansala* and will be produced on request. A *dēvālē* in temple grounds will probably be similarly accessible.

[67]The word *kemvara* has another use, completely distinct, as a synonym for *gam maḍuva* (see below). In my area it is always pronounced *kembara*.

[68]Gooneratne, whose material comes principally from the Low Country, wrote (p. 14): 'Every Saturday and Wednesday, all the respectable demons attend a sort of pandemonium called *Yakṣa Sabawa*, where each chieftain gives an account of those under him to the principal chiefs,...' Knox, who lived west of Kandy, wrote (p. 121), 'Wednesdays and Saturdays are the days, when people who have any business with the Gods, come and address themselves;...'

Traditionally, as I have mentioned, people do not make vows (*bāra venavā*) to the higher gods, but only worship (*vaňdinavā*) them for their blessing, which is conceptualized as 'peace' (*śāntiya* or *set śāntiya; set* is merely the old Sinhalese form of *śānti*). There is some disagreement whether the gods do in fact do good, or merely give protection (*āraksāva*) from harm, especially the harm brought about by *yakku*; in any event it is sufficient to transfer merit to them and perhaps occasionally to give a coin towards their expenses.

To the village gods, however, people hardly ever go unless they have some specific request; they go to make contact with the god, the *kapurāḷa* acting as intermediary. Even if no one turns up he is supposed to perform some rudimentary ritual (*pūjāva*) for the god; what in fact happens no one can know, but I am sure the ritual is most perfunctorily performed, for I never met anyone who seemed to hold the local gods in awe. I saw *pūjā* to the Twelve Gods at all three local *dēvālēs* to Piṭiya Deyyō. The *kapurāḷa* is naked to the waist and wears a white sarong with a red cloth tucked in at the waist; he always wears his hair in the traditional style, long and done up in a bun (*koṇḍē*) at the back of the head. The basic *pūjā* consists merely of his blowing a conch shell and then reciting an invocation (*yātikā*) while shaking a timbrel, ringing a bell, and burning a little incense (*dummala*) before the god's image. He then smears ash or saffron paste on his throat and chest. Anyone who wishes to be associated with the offerings must give a coin (*paňḍuru*—the plural form is used proleptically) purified with lime juice and wrapped in a betel leaf. Usual additional offerings are candles, coco-nut oil (for lamps) or even flowers—much the same things as are commonly offered before the Buddha. An offering entitles the worshipper to be mentioned in the invocation—the *kapurāḷa* makes an entreaty (*kannalavva*) to the god for his welfare. All invocations to these gods begin with the words 'Ai bō' several times repeated; this is a clipped version of 'Ayu bo van', the normal greeting between human beings, meaning 'May you live long'. During the invocation the worshippers are supposed to squat with hands respectfully folded. At the end the *kapurāḷa* makes a mark (*tilaka*) with saffron paste on the forehead of each. Further services cost extra. At some *dēvālēs* I have seen tariffs posted, but the only tariff I saw in my area was at a *kovil*, and I doubt whether the institutions of the Twelve Gods will not disappear altogether before they become so formalized. What most people want is to be told either their future or the cause of a malady, and this usually costs a rupee for a villager, though maybe much more for a well-to-do visitor. To tell the future (or the unknown past) is generally called *śāstra kiyanavā*; I was told that there are four main methods: *pēna kiyanavā* (which is what the *kapuvā* does), palmistry, looking at a man's horoscope, and asking at what moment he left his house to come and ask his fortune (we might subsume the last two under astrology). To tell the future a *kapuvā* becomes possessed (*māyam venavā*), which he achieves by dancing on the spot, shaking the timbrels, and breathing very rapidly; he tosses his head till his long hair falls about his face. He then gasps out the answers. I saw another method employed. When a village lady wanted to know the cause of a disease the *kapuvā* had a small palm-leaf manuscript book with a long thread tied to one end like a bookmark; the lady plunged this thread into the book at random while he held it loosely shut, and he then opened it at that place and gave a diagnosis; the recommended remedies are to tie on a thread as an amulet (*nūl bañdinavā*), to perform a lime-cutting exorcism (*dehikäpima*), to make a vow (*bāra venṭa*) to one of the Twelve Gods, or simply to do a *pūjāva* as above—or a combination of these. (All involve a little expenditure from which the *kapuvā* will profit.) To make a vow (*bāra venṭa*) it is not necessary to visit a *dēvālē* beforehand; the vow can be made in thought, and a coin for the god is put aside. The offerings vowed are often little replicas of objects in the vow, like Christian *ex voto* offerings; a tin-foil leg for a leg made well, even a silver-foil elephant (the party symbol) for U.N.P. victory at the elections. For the Twelve Gods, however, the most usual offerings are weapons (*āvuda* (from Skt. *āyudha*)) for the god: the vower gives the smith the materials and the pattern, which is taken from a picture or another weapon. These weapons are about a foot long and not much like real weapons, but this is explained by saying that such weapons were current in the days of the god (i.e. when he was a man). They have wooden handles which are brightly painted and sometimes bear the name of the donor; but they tend to be left out on the stone altar, so that they soon fade and rust. To fulfil (*oppukaranavā*) the vow (*bāra*), the weapon is given to the *kapuvā* for the god, and tied on to it, wrapped in a piece of cloth, is the coin put aside when the vow was made.

A vow for a good harvest results in a ceremony of giving *aḍukku* (first fruits), which is still an annual[69] event in most villages some time in April, when the spring harvest (*maha*) has been gathered in. Most informants held that this vow and offering were made to Vanniya Baṇḍāra Deyyō, though he was not the village deity; but the headman whose list I cited above said it was to all Twelve Gods. Some middle-class friends gave theirs to Kataragama. The *aḍukku* themselves are a portion of rice which is set aside; if offered in the morning, I was told, the rice is then sent up to the temple for *Buddha pūjā* at midday, but if offered in the afternoon people just eat it themselves. People can give *aḍukku* individually for the success of their own crop, but the tradition is to hold a collective ceremony at which the *kapurāḷa* becomes possessed and dances to each of the gods in turn to the accompaniment of drumming and chanting.[70] After dancing he tells the future (*pēna kiyanavā*). This type of ceremony, which locally is to my knowledge held only for the Twelve Gods, is called

[69]Obeyesekere ('Buddhist Pantheon', p. 15) reports from a very remote village that *aḍukku* are offered twice a year, after each harvest. He gives interesting data on status distinctions during the ritual.

[70]I once observed some such drumming and chanting at a Mīgala *dēvālē*, and noted that it was done by high-caste (*goyigama*) men, not by the drummers (*beravāyō*) who perform in *Buddha pūjā*. In exorcisms, however, only *beravāyō* may drum.

'to dance *kemvara*' (*kemvara naṭanavā*), and *kemvara* in this sense is used as a synonym of *gam maḍuva*[71] (verbally: *gam maḍuva naṭanavā*). (This differs from Low Country usage, where a *gam maḍuva* is usually in honour of the goddess Pattinī and is a much more elaborate affair lasting several nights with a variety of dramas and other rituals.) It takes place on a Tuesday or Friday night. I was told that only men are present and that some of the spectators become possessed and dance too (my informant had done so himself), which is ascribed to the gaze of the god falling on them *via* the *kapuvā*. This is the ideal picture of the ceremony, but it is locally in decline and held only irregularly. Though occasionally it still approximates to the ideal, the only one I saw was on a small scale, half-way between a communal and a domestic rite: it was held by an individual fanner in front of his house, and though two *kapurāḷas* took turns to get possessed, dance, and tell the future, only about a score of male spectators came, while the organizer's female relatives and neighbours watched from the verandah. None of the spectators was inspired to join in. The object of an exorcism is to free the patient from the evil influence (*dos* or *vas*) which has fallen on him from the gaze (*bälma* or *dṛṣṭiya*, generally pronounced *bäluma* and *diṣṭiya*) of some evil spirit or person. (The person need not be malevolent: one can have the evil eye without knowing it.) All large-scale exorcisms are somewhat akin to the *kemvara* just described: a specialist dances all night to the drumming and chanting, becoming possessed by (or impersonating—the distinction is often unclear) the spirits to whom this is principally addressed. Explanations vary: the *yakṣa* is forced or persuaded by the exorcist to leave the patient, or banished by a more powerful *yakṣa* or god who is his master. Sometimes the patient becomes possessed too and joins in the dancing. The famous devil-dancing of the Southern and Western Provinces, in which men of the drummer caste exorcize demons of disease, are

[71] Literally 'village shed'. *Maḍuva* means any kind of temporary structure, especially if it is used to house ritual.

of this type. Another spectacular type of ceremony in the Low Country is *bali*, which is directed to appeasing the planetary deities. However, devil dancing is unknown in my part of the country, and *bali* (usually called *tovil* or *bali tovil*) are rare: I do not think there had been one in Mīgala for three years. I saw a *bali* ceremony in a nearby town, but it was far simpler than I understood the Low Country ceremonies to be. *Bali* ceremonies feature an image of the planetary deity, which may be huge, and is itself called a *bali*. A monk told me that these are of three types: *malbali* (made of flowers), *aňdinabali* (drawn or painted), and *aṁbanabali* (moulded, i.e. three-dimensional figures). A schoolmaster (not locally born) said that the dances for *yakku* and for *bali (yaknäṭuma* and *balinätuma*) were the same, being differently named according to context. Often I found my informants on this topic unwilling to make the distinctions which Ames has documented for the Low Country; they obviously had little experience of these matters.

In view of this it is perhaps not untypical that the only lime-cutting ceremony I attended in Mīgala was in the house of an immigrant from the Low Country, and performed by a *yakädurā* from another village. The man, whom I shall call Perera, had been in poor health and felt that he was resented as an outsider; he suspected that malicious neighbours had practised black magic and brought a *yakā* into his house. He got a *yakädurā* to come from some way away so that people—I suppose he meant his enemies—should not know about it. The lime-cutting (*dehi käpīma*) was to nullify the spell. Detailed descriptions of similar ceremonies have been published, so I shall only summarize. The exorcist prepares indoors the offering (*pidēniya*) for the *yakā*; the items in it, which are minutely specified, are called *puluṭu* (literally 'burnt': the word properly refers to the five kinds of parched grains which are included) and include meat. He then takes up in a leaf a little of each ingredient and leaves it, in great secrecy, at a place where three ways meet. The *yakā* is presumed to have gone out for the food, and then not to find his way back. Indoors a bowl containing five oils is then put over a fire; Perera covers his shoulders with a white cloth and sits on a mat; he is now 'the patient' (*āturayā*). The chair on which lies the rest of the *pidēniya* is put next to him with limes and an egg. The exorcist burns joss sticks before pictures of the Buddha and gods, which are hanging on the walls, and begins. Each lime in turn he holds against the patient's body at some crucial anatomical point, or moves it backwards and forwards between such points, and mutters very fast and low; at the end of each spell he cuts the lime with cutters and tosses the two halves into the sizzling oil. He uses twenty-one limes and covers the whole body, then puts the cutters too into the oil. Finally he takes the egg, passes it from Perera's forehead down to his feet, cracks it on the ground and throws it into the pot. The *dosa* has all been drained out and burnt.

The piece of meat included in the *pidēniya* was the only element in the rite which jarred with Buddhist principles, and after all, men as well as *yakku* eat meat. In the Low Country, exorcisms sometimes involve the sacrifice[72] of a living victim (*billa*)—in fact a chicken—to the *yakṣa*, and I did hear of one such case in Mīgala. My informant, a very poor and uneducated local man, unfortunately would not tell me whether the patient too was a local, as the matter was supposed to be somewhat secret. The exorcist was again procured from outside the village, and the rite took place in the cemetery. The patient had to give as *bili* a cock, a bottle of toddy and a bottle of arack. My informant was present and said it was all fake (*boruva*), for who but a man takes toddy and arack?

The only kind of magic which my informant believed in, he told me, was the tying on of thread, because this was accompanied by reciting the '*Iti pi so*' *gāthā* qualities of the Buddha. This thread is a simple amulet, and the

[72] Usually blood sacrifice is in token, i.e. a few drops of blood from the chicken's comb; but on occasion it is beheaded.

measure is a prophylaxis rather than a cure.[73] It was often performed by a *kapuvā*, but I found out that my informant, who was also high-caste, had tied on a thread himself for someone who had been frightened by a *holman*. Besides the thread some people supply amulets (*yantra*),[74] pieces of copper foil on which are engraved linear diagrams with letters of the alphabet and which are then rolled up and kept in a small cylinder round the neck. Children usually wear one. The *yantra*, as well as parts of the spells, are in Malayālām, and are the same as those used by the Tamils in the area. The spells (*mantra*) are used when making and applying these amulets; normally a *mantra* should be recited over a *yantra* 108 times, but further repetition will make it stronger. I was told that besides Sinhalese and Malayālām they use Tamil and Telugu.[75] The word *mantra* is generally used only to denote spells of white magic; they begin with at least a brief invocation of the Buddha (e.g. 'Ōṃ Buddhāya'), tantamount to an acknowledgement of his supremacy over all forces. White magic, however, usually implies the existence of black magic to be counteracted; but to believe that black magic is being used against you argues a certain degree of paranoia. The villagers of Mīgala were not much given to paranoia, and generally conceptualized the evil influences to be counteracted as *yakku*. I did not come across cases, common enough in the Low Country where people were believed to have an evil eye or evil tongue, nor did anyone ever tell me that he was the victim of black magic. I would not deny the possibility of these things going on in Mīgala, but they are certainly not obtrusive. The only story of black magic which came to my ear sounds a cheerful note. A group of women disliked a lady teacher in the village. They ap-

[73]On the general use of thread in magic cf. Gooneratne, pp. 57–60. He refers to prophylactic thread (*āraksā nūl*) on p. 60.

[74]Historically *yantra* should refer strictly to the diagram on the amulet, but it is used to denote the whole object.

[75]Tambiah, 'Magical Power of Words', p. 177, reports that *mantra* are 'compounded of Sinhalese, Tamil, Sanskrit, Malayalam, Telugu, Bengali and even Persian'. There may be some regional variation.

proached a *kapurāḷa* to put a spell on her, so that she would have some misfortune and wish to leave. He asked 150 rupees (nearly a month's salary for a junior teacher), 50 of it in advance. He then went to the husband of the unpopular lady, who had on occasion helped him out financially, and told all, saying that as they were good people no harm would come to them, but he would like the lady to feign illness and stay away from school. Accordingly while teaching at the school next day she complained of a violent headache, and immediately took three days' sick leave. The women were much delighted with their quick results, and handed over the outstanding 100 rupees. In their glee they went—as would be customary—to call on the sick lady, pretending to condole. But to their chagrin, after three days she reappeared at the school, hale and hearty. They went to complain to the *kapurāḷa*; at first he claimed to be nonplussed, and questioned them, only to be told they had visited the victim. No wonder she had got well! They had spoilt it all by going to see her. Now some of it might even have rubbed off on to them. Would they not like some protective amulets?...

Earlier in this chapter (p. 176) I listed the ways in which the Sinhalese feels he can cope with misfortune, and control his environment; I have now placed these ways in their setting of belief and ritual. Most of them have nothing to do with Buddhism (*Buddhāgamaya*). But Buddhism does have some contact with secular welfare, not through any attempt to propitiate the Buddha himself, but through the use of sacred texts, the Buddha's word (*Buddhavacanē*). Behaviourally viewed, certain canonical texts are used as spells. However, for the Buddhists there is no incongruity in most of these uses; they are still quite explicable in their own terms; moreover they are of great antiquity. The principal such use of texts is institutionalized in a ceremony called *pirit*.

Pirit is derived from the Pali word *paritta* meaning 'protection'. The word now denotes a prescribed text or set of texts (which may, however, be abridged) recited in a particular ritual. This ritual has certain features, shared with other Sinhalese rituals, to which no reference is made in the texts recited and for which no rationale is given. A reel of thread or string (*pirit nūl*) is held by all the monks reciting and passed round to enclose the spectators, any of whom may also clasp it. At least one bottle of water (*pirit pän*) is kept on or under the table on which the manuscripts of the texts (*pirit pot*) lie during the recitation, and at the end of the ceremony a monk sprinkles this water over everyone present. These features, not rationally explicable in doctrinal terms, allow us to mention *pirit* here in the context of magic as well as in Chapter 5 in the context of soteriology.

There is to my knowledge only one text which has a specialized application: the *Angulimāla Paritta*, for use in childbirth (on which see Chapter 5, p. 263). All the other applications of *pirit*, which are listed below, make use of a collection of Pali texts, mostly *suttas* from the Canon, made in Ceylon by the tenth century[76] called the *Catubhāṇavāra* ('Four sections of sermons'). The texts which make up this collection are listed, not in strict order, by Rahula;[77] the list dictated to me from memory by a local monk coincides with Rahula's in all but one particular which is plainly a slip. The *Catubhāṇavāra* begins with three texts, the *Mangala* (*alias Mahāmangala*) *Sutta*, the *Ratana Sutta*, and the *Metta* (*alias Karaṇīyametta*) *Sutta*, all of which are from the canonical book called the *Sutta-nipāta* and also from part of the canonical chrestomathy, the *Khuddaka-pāṭha*. Two *sil māṇiyō* who lived together near my village told me that whenever possi-

[76] Geiger, *Culture of Ceylon*, p. 173, para. 161, refers to a tenth-century inscription containing the name of the book. According to Wells (*Thai Buddhism*, p. 268) there is a Thai tradition that the book was compiled in A.D. 357 by Sinhalese monks headed by Revata.

[77] *History of Buddhism*, p. 278, see especially note 6. Rahula says that the book contains these texts 'among others', but so far as I know his list is complete, plus the *Angulimāla Paritta*, which I believe is not in the *Catubhāṇavāra*. (I have not seen a copy of the work.) For further details of the texts used, notably their references in the Canon, see the notes in E. Waldschmidt's article 'Das Paritta', *Baessler-Archiv*, XVII, 1934, pp. 139–50.

ble they recite these three texts twice a day, at 5 a.m. and 7 p.m. These texts, followed by verses called the *Mahā Jayamangala Gāthā*, constitute the *Maha Pirita* ('Great *Pirit*') which begins and ends long *pirit* ceremonies, and is always recited by all monks present. The other text which must be singled out for mention is the *Āṭānāṭiya Sutta* (from the *Dīgha Nikāya*); this is always recited twice and comes last, immediately before the final recitation of the *Maha Pirita*, which means that its recitation falls at about 4 in the morning.

Pirit may be 'said' by anyone (even a layman, if no monk is available), and there is no limit to the number of participants. During long ceremonies however the full complement usually is present only for the *maha pirita*; most of the time the recitation is carried on by two monks (*yuga pirita*) or four monks, who work in two-hour shifts. Continuity must be preserved, not necessarily by an uninterrupted flow of sound, but by the continuous presence of at least one monk in a preaching seat holding the thread.

A *pirit* ceremony using the full range of texts (i.e. the *Catubhāṇavāra*) may last all night (*sarvarātrika pirit*), which in practice means roughly from 9 p.m. to 6 a.m.; for thirty-six hours (*tun tis päya pirit*), roughly from 9 p.m. to 6 a.m. a day later; or for a week (*sati pirit*),[78] as happened when the whole world seemed in danger from the fearsome conjunction of the planets. (At the end of a week's *pirit* there is a ceremony called the *dorakaḍasnē*.)[79] A standard form of shorter *pirit* is *varu pirit*, which is said for an hour in the evening before the monks' *gilampasa pūjā*, an hour before breakfast (*hīl dānē*) the next morning, and an hour the next evening, i.e. roughly at 5 p.m., 5 a.m. and 5 p.m. However, *pirit* can come in much shorter chunks: Radio Ceylon began every day with about fifteen minutes of it,

[78] Dickson, op. cit., pp. 227–31, has some interesting details for which I cannot vouch: he says that for a week's *pirit* at least twenty-four monks are needed, and that on the eve of the ceremony they all chant the *paṭicca-samuppāda*.

[79] For descriptions see E.R. Sarathchandra, op. cit., pp. 19–21, and Waldschmidt, 'Das Paritta', pp. 147–9.

immediately after the Three Refuges and Five Precepts, broadcast at 6.30 a.m. However, *pirit* by radio obviously becomes a totally different affair, as the thread and water are missing. It is, probably consciously, a reversion to canonical practice, in that the texts are used, theoretically at least, for the meaning they convey; for *pirit* originated as a kind of preaching—to a supernatural audience. The use of water in this connection is, however, very old. In the reign of Upatissa I (end of the fourth century A.D.) Ceylon:

> ...was afflicted by famine and disease. The king inquired from the Sangha if anything was done by the Buddha in such a situation to alleviate the suffering of the people, and the monks described to him how the *Ratana-sutta* was recited by the Buddha when Vesāli was visited by such a calamity. Thereupon the king had a golden image of the Buddha made, and placing in its hands the Buddha's stone alms-bowl filled with water, mounted it on a chariot. Then he organized a great almsgiving and ordered the citizens to observe the moral precepts (*sīla*), himself observing them.
>
> The city was beautifully decorated, and a large crowd of monks following the chariot with the golden Buddha image walked the whole night round the streets reciting the *Ratana-sutta* and sprinkling water. The king himself took part in the ceremony, walking with the monks. Rains came and famine and pestilence disappeared. Upatissa decreed that this ceremony should be performed whenever there was a similar calamity in the Island.[80]

The Ratana Sutta is still one of the texts comprising the *maha pirit*. In a footnote to this passage Rahula gives the story of the Buddha's alleged use of *pirit*.

> When Vesāli was afflicted by famine and pestilence, the Buddha visited the city on the invitation of Licchavis, and recited the *Ratanasutta*. (It is included

[80]Rahula, *History*, pp. 276–7.

> in the *Khuddakapāṭha* as well as in the *Suttanipāta*.) The Buddha first taught this sutta to Ananda and requested him to go round the city accompanied by Licchavi princes, reciting the sutta and sprinkling water from the Buddha's almsbowl. The city was saved from the calamity. A great festival was held in honour of the Buddha's visit. Two boats on the river were joined together and a pavilion was built thereon. After this successful mission to Vesāli, the Buddha returned to Rājagṛha along the Ganges. This journey is called Gangārohaṇa, and the name was given to the festival itself. (SnA. pp. 204–5; CBhA. pp. 97 ff.)[81]

This story comes from Buddhaghosa's commentaries; the use of water has no canonical authority. Rahula also quotes (p. 279) a description from the commentary on the *Dīgha Nikāya* of how *pirit* should be recited for a sick man. He then says that '... the *pirit* ceremony as we know it today can be seen only after the Poḷonnaruva period'.[82] I am not sure what he is referring to. The description in the *Dīgha Commentary* does not mention water or thread, but adds other minor non-canonical features, now obsolete, such as that the monk reciting the *Āṭānāṭiya Sutta* should not have eaten meat or flour. *Pirit* water, however, we have just seen to be ancient; for *pirit* thread I know of no reference unambiguously connected with a ceremony, but in a famous *Jātaka* story Prince Telapatta 'had a *pirit* done by *paccekabuddhas*, and took the *pirit* sand and *pirit* thread' (*paccekabuddhehi parittaṃ kārāpetvā parittavālikaṃ c'eva parittasuttakaṃ ca ādāya*),[83] and later in danger sprinkles the sand on his head and ties on the thread.[84] For me this is evidence enough that no important feature of a modern *pirit* ceremony post-dates commentatorial times. There is frequent reference in the Canon to monks being disturbed in their meditations in forest solitude by trouble-

[81] Rahula, *History*, p. 277, note 2.
[82] Ibid., p. 280, note 1.
[83] *J.*, I. 396.
[84] *J.*, I. 399.

some *yakṣas*. The beginning of the *Āṭānāṭiya Sutta* (D.N. xxxii) refers to this circumstance; Vessavaṇa, king of the *yakṣas*, comes to the Buddha saying that *yakṣas* trouble monks in the forest and recites to him a long poem consisting largely of the names of various spirits, to keep them at bay; the Buddha then repeats it to his monks. There are several other verse texts which, though they lack a similar introduction, can be deduced to have been intended from the first to serve a similar purpose. The commentary says as much of the *Karaṇīya-metta Sutta*[85] which preaches universal love and good-will; and it is probably significant that the *Ratana Sutta*, which has a similar purport, begins by addressing 'Whatever beings of the earth or sky are here assembled'. In Buddhist terms, the *yakṣas* are being preached to, converted to Buddhist benevolence so that they will no longer want to harm anyone. (The Rev. Rahula contrasts the Christian expulsion of devils with the Buddhist way of winning them over by the exercise of loving kindness.)

I was present at several *pirit* ceremonies, but as descriptions of *pirit* have been published[86] I shall refrain from reproducing my own. It will suffice to remark on the ex-

[85]The commentatorial accounts of the origin of the *Karaṇīya-metta Sutta* and of the *Mangala Sutta* were told me (of course as fact) by a young layman.

[86](1) Nur Yalman, 'The Structures of Sinhalese Healing Rituals', pp. 120–1. Yalman's statement that the *pirit* book 'tells of the struggle between Buddha and his rival Maraya' is incorrect, and his spelling of Sinhalese words, as in all his publications, extremely erratic, not to say slapdash.

(2) André Bareau, *La Vie et L'Organisation des Communautés Bouddhiques Modernes de Ceylan* (Institut Français d'Indologie, Pondicherry, 1957), pp. 55–7. Bareau says that the *Patthana Sutta* is part of the *maha pirit*; there is no text of this name, so this must be a mistake for *Ratana Sutta*. What he calls an 'orchestra, playing in the interval' is the usual drumming, etc., which accompanies every public *pinkama*.

(3) J. F. Dickson, 'Notes Illustrative of Buddhism'. Though brief and generalized, I find this account the best in English.

(4) E. Waldschmidt, 'Das Paritta', *Baessler-Archiv*, XVII, 1934, pp. 139–50, is the most exhaustive.

tremely unspecific nature of the ceremony, which we can see from Rahula's work to have been the case in ancient times also. *Pirit* is used at a sick bed, to commemorate a death, to consecrate a new building, to avert a public misfortune, to celebrate the opening of Parliament, or simply to acquire merit.

The canonical explanation of *pirit* is that it converts, or at least mollifies, the *yakku*. As a variant, when the Buddha said *pirit* on behalf of the boy Dīghāyu there was such a press of gods that the *yakṣa* who was due to eat the boy could not get in.[87] Another explanation, also with some canonical authority, is the general one that it is meritorious to recite canonical texts or have them recited. The recitation of texts is always considered equivalent to preaching (*baṇa*), and is listed (as *desanā*) among the Ten Good Deeds (*dasa kusala karma*) (see Chapter 2, p. 87). Moreover, listening to preaching (*suti*) is similarly listed, being considered the equivalent of 'causing to preach'. This rather formalistic attitude to the sacred texts clashes with the Buddhist doctrine of intention (*cetanāva*) (see Chapter 6). What is here more to the point is that this explanation does not fit the case of *pirit* recited (as so often) to allay an already present misfortune. To earn merit in any way, including this, will improve one's *karma*, but *karma* is a long-range affair, and there is no reason why the merit just gained should take immediate effect, so as to make a sick man well. To say that *pin* can cancel out *pav* is in fact a heresy, discussed at the beginning of Chapter 5. Indeed, if one is thinking in terms of *karma* the presumption must be rather the other way: if a man is ill because of a past sin he will go on being ill till the sin is expiated, despite any *ad hoc* remedial action. In the case of misfortune, to explain *pirit* as 'merit in a hurry' will therefore not wash. This line of explanation *is*, however, applicable when *pirit* is used at a celebration—indeed it sometimes fits the case far better than the explanation involving *yakku*. On the occasion of his fiftieth birthday the chief monk of Mīgala

[87] *Dh.A.*, II, 237–8.

temple had *pirit* chanted for thirty-six hours and gave alms to fifty monks, including the Mahānāyaka of Malvatta. He was of course not trying to dispel any *yakku*, but simply making himself a birthday present of a vast quantity of merit.[88] To be sure, there is no reason why the texts used should have been *pirit*—any *baṇa* would have served the same purpose—but he used the institution which was at hand. (The celebration of his own birthday—with great advance publicity—strikes me as flagrantly untraditional conduct in a monk, but was well thought of by the villagers, who gained both the sight of a festivity and the chance to acquire merit by sympathy.)

What *pirit* is in public, the '*Iti pi so*' *gāthā* is in private. The '*Iti pi so*' *gāthā* is a short prose[89] formula, beginning with the words 'Iti pi so', which eulogizes the Buddha. There are similar formulae eulogizing the Dhamma and the Sangha, which are often recited in succession; the three together form a statement of faith somewhat analogous to the Christian Creed. These Pali sentences occur frequently in the Canon.[90] The '*Iti pi so*' *gāthā* is also known colloquially as *Buduguṇa* (or *Buddhaguṇē*), 'the qualities of the Buddha'. The *Buduguṇa* are the most frequently employed spell in white magic. Someone frightened by a ghost will recite the *Buduguṇa* and thus keep the ghost at bay, even if he has to repeat them all the way home. The *Buduguṇa* are highly recommended in Mīgala. The ex-headman said that in an *apalē* (astrologically dangerous period) one should just recite the *Buduguṇa*, and not bother about *bali-tovil* and such ceremonies. The old *kapurāḷa* (K 1), who did quite a bit of business with amulets, etc., himself said that the *Buduguṇa* were the best guard against *yakku*, while the most effective cure for any ill is

[88]At the cost of nearly 5,000 rupees. He told me afterwards that the total expenses were about R.6,000, of which R.1,300 were contributed by laymen. However, he explicitly denied that the quantity of merit depended on the size of his expenditure (see Chap. 5, p. 265).

[89]The term *gāthā* usually denotes verse; that these prose passages are so called indicates their formulaic character.

[90]*Sāmaññaphala Sutta, D.N.*, I, 49 (*Sutta* 2. 8).

to recite the *Mahāmangala*,[91] *Ratana*, and *Karaṇīya-metta Suttas* morning and evening. Moreover, when I asked him for some *yantra mantra* (apotropaic spells), the first one he recited to me was the Pali

Sabbapāpassa akaranaṃ kusalassa upasampadā
Sacitta-pariyodapanaṃ etaṃ Buddhānusāsanaṃ

to be repeated three times, with Dhamma and Sangha substituted for Buddha at the second and third repetitions. The verse means, 'To abstain from all evil, to do good, to purify one's mind, this is the teaching of the Buddha/Dhamma/ Sangha.' It is a famous verse from the Canon,[92] slightly misquoted: in the original it ends *Buddhāna sāsanaṃ*, 'the teaching of the Buddhas'. The reason for this misquotation is probably that in its original form the verse would require more change to accommodate the Dhamma and the Sangha, a variation which patterns the verse on such familiar models as the Three Refuges (p. 76). Examples of similar verses in spells could no doubt be multiplied by research. The question again arises whether the *Buduguṇa* and similar Buddhist formulae are mere spells, or whether their use can be rationalized: affectively they are surely a spell, but does their use involve a *cognitive* inconsistency? Perhaps not, because to recite the Buddha's qualities is to remind the evil spirits of his power and goodness, so that they will lose the will to attack. According to one monk, the Buddha himself recommended the practice, saying that even Śakra (who is addressed in the *Dhajagga Sutta*, one of the best known *pirit* texts) has passion, hatred and delusion (*rāga dosa moha*), 'so if you want anything just think of me (*mama sihi karagaṇṭa*)'. If the qualities of the Buddha fail, recite the qualities of the Dhamma; if that still fails, those of the Sangha. Recital of the Three Jewels will get rid of all fear

[91] = *Mangala.*
[92] *D.N.*, *Sutta* XIV.3.28 = *Dhammapada*, 183. In the former passage the verse is one of three stanzas given by the former Buddha Vipassi as part of the original *pātimokkha* (cf. pp. 372–3); on this see Dutt, *Early Buddhist Monachism*, p. 71.

and danger. This explanation touches on the belief in the power of truth, which will be discussed in the next chapter. However, Obeyesekere has told me of a twist in the use of *Buduguṇa* which defies even this type of explanation. Among villagers out on a hunt he heard the *Buduguṇa* muttered by a man to prevent his rival from catching anything. The qualities of the Buddha prevent violence—even when used with ulterior motives! Having found Buddhist texts used as spells, it will be less surprising to find a relic used as a talisman. I did not come across a case in practice; but I was told that someone who has a Buddha relic on his person is invincible at cards! But lest this be taken for a modern degeneration, let me refer to *Mahāvaṃsa*, XXV, 7, which tells us that Duṭugämuṇu had a relic put in his spear.[93] Nothing reported by any ethnographer in modern times approaches this flagrant violation of both the letter and the spirit of the doctrine. The use of spells and talismans characterizes what we are calling 'magic'. There is a gap here between our categorization and that of the Sinhalese, because where the spells are Buddhist texts or the talismans, Buddhist objects, the practices with which they are associated are generally considered to be part of Buddhist religion (*Buddhāgamaya*); in fact it is largely these practices which Buddhist modernists call Buddhist religion (*Buddhāgamaya*), as opposed to Buddhist philosophy (*Bauddha darśanaya*) which they consider the true, original Buddhism. While in this chapter I am mainly concerned with statements by Buddhists which interpret *pirit*, for example, as something other than magic, its resemblance to magic will strike the western reader; I will return to it in Chapter 5. At this point it is sufficient to point out that magic *per se* is not contrary to Buddhist doctrine, provided it serves only worldly ends. In this re-

[93] Geiger (note to his translation of the passage) says: 'the spear serves as a royal standard, which is always carried before the prince'. Duṭugämuṇu's use of the relic is thus reminiscent of Constantine's labarum. He was waging a 'holy war', leading the Sinhalese Buddhists to regain Anurādhapura and its holy places from Tamil Hindus, much in the manner of the Christian crusaders.

spect it is on a par with gods and other spirits; a picture of the world which includes these forces, and considers a spell of similar efficacy to a medicine or a poison, is not logically incompatible with a belief in *karma*.

Black magic is contrary to Buddhist ethics, not to Buddhist metaphysics: a sin, but not a heresy. White magic to secure worldly ends is contrary to neither. A monk who practises black magic is doctrinally on a par with one who drinks; a bad Buddhist, if you like, but bad in the sense of wicked, not of inconsistent. A monk who says *pirit* to cure sickness, whatever may be his theory to explain its efficacy, is a good Buddhist in every sense.

Although we have come across certain beliefs and actions which cannot be reconciled with the doctrine of the Canon, I would suggest that these are somewhat trivial and peripheral. They are also ancient; changes since ancient times even seem, oddly enough, to have been more towards than away from orthodoxy. In the ninth century King Sena II 'had the Ratana Sutta written on a gold plate and made offerings to it';[94] there is nothing like that today. Finally, are the 'deviant' practices so thoroughly unjustifiable? Only on one level. All can be explained by the Buddhist doctrinal belief in the power of human thought, to which we shall have frequent cause to refer in the next chapters. As a simple traditional monk remarked to me, diseases are usually curable by medicine or by *bali*, in which they use the *Buduguṇa*; the reason one gets better is because of one's own ideas (*tamangē adahasa*). Another monk said the same of all worship of gods, and specifically of *pirit*: it will only do you good if you have faith (*visvāsa*); *you are protected by your own belief*.

IV. Summary

> There are few or none zealous in their worship, or have any great matter of esteem for their Gods. And they seldom busie themselves in the matters

[94]Rahula, *History*, p. 100, referring to *Mhv.*, LI, 79.

> of their Religion, until they come to be sick or very aged. They debar none that will come to see the Ceremonies of their worship; and if a stranger should dislike their way, reprove or mock at them for their Ignorance and Folly, they would acknowledge the same, and laugh at the superstitions of their own Devotion, but withall tell you that they are constrained to do what they do, to keep themselves safe from the malice and mischiefs that the evil spirits would otherwise do them, with which they say, their Country swarm...
> It is a usual saying, and very frequent among them (if their Geraha [*graha*], which is their fortune, be bad) What can God do against it: Nay, I have often heard them say, Give him no Sacrifice, but shit in his Mouth, what a God is He? So slight an estimation have they of their Idol-Gods;...
> Knox, p. 132.

'Iti pi so' gāthā I have attempted to present the subject matter of this chapter analytically. To give a clear picture of local beliefs in a brief synthesis let me reproduce the opinions of the three men in Mīgala whom I knew best. Our neighbour, a very simple and uneducated man, had seen the *bali* with cockerel and arack, and said it was all false. Similarly, he said, all the stuff done by the *kapurāḷa* (K 1) was false (*boru*). These *kapuvō* ask for money, but why should a god need money? I asked if he believed in Piṭiya Deyyō. He did not answer me directly—plainly he took Piṭiya Deyyō's existence for granted—but replied with a vehement assertion that the gods need nothing but merit. I asked about tying on thread. No, that is not false, because that is *Buddhaguṇē*. *Yakku* only frequent the cemetery; if you go past there at midnight or twilight you may get a *bäluma* and get scared, and tying on the thread cures you of this fright. I found out that he himself had tied thread for someone so frightened. 'It is all in the mind (*okkoma hitē*)'; he meant not that *yakku* do not exist but that they only trouble those in a receptive state of mind. He too has seen *holman* near the cemetery, and heard their noise, but nowadays he is never troubled. I ask

if *holman* are people who sinned in previous births. No, *holman* are rightly called *yakku*.

Another villager whom we got to know very well, a share-cropper of very little education and no better than he should be, struck me as the perfect 'man in the street' of Mīgala. He did not go to the temple often, and had very few opinions on religious topics, but he did tell me that he doesn't go in for this *yakṣa* stuff. When he was seriously ill he did not get a *yakädurā* (exorcist), but had monks say *varu pirit*. On the other hand when his son was ill he made a vow to Piṭiya Deyyō, and gave the god a small weapon when his son recovered. Some people are frightened of the dark and hear footsteps behind them, especially near the cemetery, but he has never seen anything [and he lived fairly near it]. Some people in Mīgala have met Mahasōnā there and fallen ill of fright; a female cousin of his even died of fright one night; a year after her marriage she and her husband were asleep in the house when at midnight a bull lowed out at the back; when they went out they heard footsteps and her husband ran to look, but found no one. One may meet Hūniyam, but he is benevolent. A figure of a white naked man is a *holman*; his wife is frightened of these. Once she went out to the latrine at night and screamed to him that she heard footsteps, so he went out; there was nothing there, but he pretended to be shooing away a dog and so her fear was appeased.

Our landlord, a small cultivator in his fifties who had been a bus-driver, was in most respects a typical villager, but held some unusual opinions. It is possible that he had been influenced by spending some time at a mission school when a boy, but I would be inclined to discount this, as the same experience has not had the same effect in the other cases with which I am acquainted. He considered himself a devout Buddhist, but said he believed in no gods at all—it was all lies (*deyyō okkoma boru*). One of the village shrines was robbed of all its cash, and this caused him endless amusement, for, he said, if the god was so powerful why did he not stop the thief? He also refused to observe any of the tabus connected with the Sinhalese New Year celebrations and his wife served us a cooked meal at the time when the fire is supposed to be extinguished. He had been to Kataragama 'for fun' (*vinōdēṭa*), but Kataragama too was 'lies'; it was all for the *kapu* to make money: they rake in the coins (*pan̆ḍuru*) in the morning and drink toddy in the afternoon. Why should gods need money? One doesn't give rupees to the Buddha.

Such extreme scepticism, is, however, unusual. To conclude this chapter I reproduce my notes, taken almost on dictation, from an elderly monk who gave me in résumé a classic exposition of the Sinhalese view of the world—an anthropologist's dream.

He has never been to Kataragama—people go mainly for vows (*bāravalaṭa*), not to worship (*van̆dinṭa*). Kataragama was not a man but a god by birth (*utpattiyen deyyō*) and Ceylon is his sphere of responsibility (*bāramaṇḍalē*).

The gods have a system of government like the human world. Śakra is the chief of the gods, and he has a retinue of ministers (*amātyapirisa*), the four gods (Dhṛtarāṣṭra, etc.) who live in the Cāturmahārājika heaven. Below them are gods in charge of various countries. Ceylon is in the charge of four gods: Viṣṇu, Kataragama, Saman, and Vibhīṣaṇa. Each rules a quarter of the country; this part is under Saman. Pattinī is all over Ceylon in charge of one department (*eka aṃsēṭa pradhānē*). Däḍimuṇḍa is fierce (*caṇḍe*)—a *yakṣa*. Below these come the gods in charge of villages (*gambāra deyyō*) [here the monk wrinkled his nose], under the former as D.R.O.s are under G.A.s.[95] 'Those fellows are the bosses of tiny little parts (*Ē aya poḍi poḍi koṭasvala lokkō*).' The local D.R.O. equivalent is Piṭiya Deyyō.

There are three classes of beings, namely *deyyō, yakṣayō, prētayō*. The latter two groups are ruled by Vessavaṇa who is the boss of the *yakṣas* (*yakunnē lokkā*). He is very tough (*särayi*), and if someone breaks his laws he looks at them in a certain way and his gaze burns them to powder

[95]For District Revenue Officers and Government Agents see p. 213.

(*äsdṛṣṭiya piṭi piṭi piccenavā*).[96] Gods are pleased by the Five Precepts (*pan sil*) and *pinkam*, and like good people; *yakṣas*, on the other hand, break all the five precepts and like wicked people. But they cannot harm the good people, because they are scared of Vaiśravaṇa. *Yaksayō* and *prētayō* live on smelly foods like meat; to get people to make offerings to them they show them *holman*, which are just their own forms (*svarūpa*), apparitions (*avatāra*); these *holman* frighten people into making offerings. However, they may be exorcized by the recital of the Three Refuges (*tun saraṇa*), at which *yakku* and *prētayō* will flee for miles.

Astrology (*näkät śāstrē*) can tell only trends and dispositions, and give auspicious and inauspicious times. To say that it can predict the future in detail is contrary both to truth and to Buddhism.

The planetary deities (*grahayō*) are not a class of *yakṣa* (*yakku vargayak*); they are ways of effecting the good and bad *karma* which a man is born with. In other religions gods make creatures—but who makes the gods? *Karma* alone determines a man's birth, but *karma* is long-term (*diga*); it does not determine the details of one's life, but only those things which can't be helped—principally the condition of one's birth. To escape particular misfortunes may be possible by e.g. *bali* ceremonies, in which the planetary deities are propitiated (*śānti karanavā*). *Karma* is purely the result of one's own efforts and thoughts.

'All that we are is in the result of what we have thought' says the first verse of the *Dhammapada*.[97] To test whether this doctrine is still consistently upheld will be the purpose of the next chapter.

[96]Cf. *Samantapāsādikā*, II, 440.

[97]In Max Müller's famous translation, which is admittedly contentious.

5

Total Responsibility in Theory and Practice

AT the beginning of the previous chapter was stated the theory of *karma,* according to which a man's destiny depends on his own efforts. However, in the course of the chapter were mentioned certain beliefs which seem *prima facie* to contradict this. In this chapter we shall examine these beliefs and scrutinize their congruity with stated doctrine. Our principal topics are the doctrine of superseded *karma* (*ahosi kamma*), the religious wish (*prārthanā*) and the transference of merit (*patti* and *pattānumodanā.*)

Ahosi kamma is a Pali technical term, literally meaning 'has-been *karma*'. It refers to *karma* which is superseded by the course of events. Though doctrinally it can apply to deeds good or bad, the term is in fact used only in the context of *bad karma* which does not come to fruition. That even good *karma* may not bear fruit is logically implied by the very common expression 'Pin siddha vēvā' ('May the good deed be successful') which is said by the recipient of any good action, the monk who is reverently greeted or the beggar who gets a coin; but this cognitive implication is not felt affectively: the saying is rather an example of the type of religious wish which I categorize below (p. 256) as a 'mere expression of benevolence'. I here discuss only *ahosi kamma* in the sense of superseded bad *karma.*

If someone attains *nirvāṇa* he will not be reborn, so much of his *karma* will never bear fruit and becomes obsolete (*ahosi venavā*). Even an *arhat,* however, can never escape the consequences of (i.e. *ahosi karanṭa*) one of the five great sins: killing mother, father, or an *arhat,* causing schism in the Sangha, or shedding the blood of a Buddha. The venerable Mugalan, one of the Buddha's two chief disciples, suffered terribly at the hands of robbers long after he had attained Enlightenment. They surrounded his house, threatening to murder him, but he got out by his supernormal powers (*iddhi*). The same happened a second time. When he was in the same situation for a third time[1] he examined his past lives with the eye of wisdom (*ñāṇacakkhu*) which all *arhats* acquire, and realized that this was the result of his having killed his aged parents in a former life; so he submitted to his fate and was beaten up by the robbers who left him at the point of death. This story from the commentary to the *Dhammapada*[2] was told me by a monk. The circumstances under which he had killed his parents were these. They were very old and blind, and he was living with them and his wife. The wife said his parents were such a nuisance that he must choose between them and her. To deceive him she would throw the scum of the boiling rice on to the floor and then tell him his parents were spitting everywhere; similarly she simulated fallen white hair. Finally the son pretended to his parents that he had to take them on a journey through a dangerous forest. On the way he suddenly exclaimed that robbers were attacking. His parents told him to flee and save himself; he ran off and returned pretending to be a robber, and killed them. For this he came to be brutally murdered, *arhat* or no.

I questioned a monk in Mīgala about *ahosi kamma*. By doing some great act of merit, he said, one may anticipate the maturation of one's *karma* (*karmavipāka*) and reach *nivan* first. There are four kinds of *karma*:

(1) *dṛṣṭadharmavedanīya*: will bring results within this life (*mē ātmēma vipākē denavā.*)

(2) *upapadya*: will bring results in the next life (*īlanga ātmē dī vipākē denavā.*)

[1] Seventh, according to a monk, who alluded to the same story. See next note.

[2] *Dh.A.*, III, 65. The robbers were hired by jealous Jains. The story also occurs in the *Jātaka* book (*J.*, V, 126), with a few differences. Most of these are trivial, but the discrepancy that at the last moment he is moved by his parents and does not kill them seems to deprive the story of its *raison d'être*. Malalasekere, *Dictionary of Pali Proper Names* (Luzac, London, 1937), vol. II, p. 546, note 48, erroneously attributes this version to the *Dhammapada* commentary.

(3) *aparāpariyavedya*: there is no limit—will bring results when an opportunity arises (*simāvak nā—avasthāvak läbunōt vipākē denavā.*)

(4) *ahosi*: disappears (*nätivenavā.*)

For example, Duṭugämuṇu killed many Tamils in war, which is *pav,* but he did it to save Buddhism, and then he did so much for Buddhism (founding monasteries at Anurādhapura, etc.) that his *pin* so far outweighed his *pav* that he will stay in heaven (*divyalōkē*) till the time of Maitrī, the next Buddha, when he will be reborn as his right-hand disciple (*dakuṇat sav,* i.e. the equivalent of Säriyut for Gotama Buddha) and attain *nirvāṇa.* His *pav* will therefore never mature, there being no results (*vipākē*) of bad *karma* in heaven.

That my informant gave Duṭugämuṇu as his example is no accident, for apart from *arhats*[3] his is the only specific case of *ahosi karma* ever heard of. The prediction concerning him is contained in XXXII, so my informant was fully justified in saying that Duṭugämuṇu would never pay for the sin of killing. Even so the monks I interviewed were divided on this question: some concurred in saying that Duṭugämuṇu would get off while others asserted that at some point he must surely pay for his sins.

Although all the stories deal with the extreme case, it is not merely the attainment of *nirvāṇa* which can prevent the maturation of sin. Common sense suggests that it may not be possible to reap the recompense for every action. As an old *upāsaka* put it to me, though a man commit fifty murders he can only be hanged once. This was just an analogy fitted to my western understanding; if he is constantly reborn he can of course be hanged fifty times; yet if he persists in so murderous a course it becomes impossible for him to pay for all his crimes. This is the point of the above classification given by the Mīgala monk quoted above, as interpreted by his colleague. There are some

[3]Among *arhats* the classic case of *ahosi karma* is Angulimāla, who will be mentioned in another context later in the chapter. For his full story see the entry under his name in Malalasekere's *Dictionary of Pali Proper Names.*

sins [these would be the lesser ones] which are superseded (*ahosi venavā*) if you do not pay for them in this life or the next—'there is a time limit' ('Kālasīmāvak tiyenavā'). Some on the other hand may crop up any time there is a chance. Another analogy: if he (the speaker) wants to do me harm while I am in Ceylon but gets no chance before I leave for England, the matter lapses (*ahosi venavā*). [But killing is very bad, so] we cannot say about Duṭugämuṇu; finally he will be reborn as Maitrī's right-hand disciple, but we do not know what lives he will pass through before then.

I have presented *ahosi kamma* in a rather scholastic light for this was the only light under which it ever appeared to me. I never came across it as part of behavioural or 'actual' religion, and most laymen have no idea what it is. Obeyesekere, however, has come across a popular variant which by a small change runs clean counter to canonical doctrine. If sufficient merit can ensure that one will never pay for sins, it is not a big step to saying that merit can cancel out sin. Obeyesekere has met this argument in a remote area where villagers subsist partly by hunting, thus flagrantly violating the first precept not to kill; they hope that by becoming good *upāsakas* in old age they can nullify the effects of their past sins. This is a clear case of religious change on the cognitive level; its intellectual origin and psychological motivation are clear, but it is not, I think, widespread, and so is of limited interest. On the other hand it seems close—just a step over the line into doctrinal unorthodoxy—to the belief in the power for good of the death-bed wish, discussed in the next section.

Far more important and problematic, because a common feature of the life of every Buddhist, is the *prārthanāva* or religious wish. The same word is used by Sinhalese Christians to translate 'prayer'; I have avoided this translation in the Buddhist context, as it would prejudice a balanced exposition. The term 'prayer' implies a person who could answer it, and suggests that he could intervene in the course of events, thus interfering with the suppliant's *karma*. Neither implication is justified on the cognitive level, though affectively the *prārthanāva* does have some affinity to prayer of a very particular type. If a translation is required it would be best to use some such phrase as 'earnest wish', which is indeed the primary meaning of the Sanskrit word and of its Pali equivalent *patthanā*.

Prārthanā are made at the end of every *pinkama*. Most commonly they occur at the end of a sermon (however short): the monk expresses the hope that all beings may attain *nirvāṇa* (e.g. *siyaludenāṭama* or *siyalu sattvayanṭa nivan säpa läbēvā*) at which remark everyone present raises their folded hands to or above the head, if they are not there already (for this is the posture in which the pious listen to sermons), and exclaims, 'Sādhu sādhu sā', exactly like a Christian congregation saying 'Amen' at the end of a prayer. Notice that in this context the *prārthanāva* is always exactly the same, namely to attain *nirvāṇa*. The same *prārthanāva* is used at funerals, where *nivan säpa läbēvā* concludes the eulogies of the dead person which are printed and handed round, or at poor funerals merely recited, and the same words are printed on a banner at the entrance to the cemetery and perhaps elsewhere on the funeral route. In this context the *prārthanāva* is closely parallel to the Christian *Requiescat in pace,* with the difference that peace is requested for the Christian immediately in the grave, long before the Day of Judgement, whereas *nirvāṇa* is the Buddhist's long-term goal, certainly to be attained after further rebirths. Under Buddhist influence Ceylon Catholics have turned to consider their own long-term goal, and instead of R.I.P. their funeral banners read '*svargē säpa läbēva*'—'May he attain the bliss of Heaven'.

Another common occasion for *prārthanā* is in letter-writing and here I wonder whether there has not been western influence. It is customary to conclude a personal letter with a formulaic religious wish, usually to the effect that the recipient should find refuge in the Buddha or in the Three Jewels (e.g. 'teruvan saraṇa läbēvā kiyā patami'). There is nothing particularly uncanonical about hoping that someone will find refuge with the Three Jewels, in which he probably takes refuge daily, but these formulae are not used outside letter-writing, and the practice looks as if it is modelled on the Christian writing 'May God be your aid' or some such benediction.

The *prārthanā* already discussed are made for others, which makes it easy to explain them (as is done) as mere expressions of benevolence. But the remaining ones are made for oneself, which puts them in a different category, constituting a more serious doctrinal problem. If one posits, as I think one must, that *prārthanā* arose from an emotional need, one would expect the *prārthanā* for oneself to occur earlier than the *prārthanā* for others, and we shall see that such is indeed the case, only the former occurring in the ancient literature.

Our account above of the *prārthanā* for *nirvāṇa* was not quite complete. If the concept of *prārthanā* is mentioned to a villager he immediately thinks of the actual form which *prārthanā* usually take on public occasions. Only modernist monks confine themselves to the bald wish that all may attain *nirvāṇa* Traditionally (see for example the *pin anumōdana* in the Appendix) the form of such a wish is for the monk to hope that the donors, or all present, or those for whose sake the ceremony is taking place, may in their future lives enjoy human and divine bliss (i.e. be reborn as well-off men or as gods) till they are reborn in the time of Maitrī, and *then* attain *nirvāṇa*. All then say 'Sādhu', and by their assent make this *prārthanāva* for themselves. It is only a few fundamentalists who eschew this formula and condemn this postponement, urging the necessity of striving for *nirvāṇa* here and now. Their personal opinions deserve respect, but we shall see that even Buddhaghosa would have earned their censure.

The *prārthanā* for oneself may have originated with the dying wish, which—as we shall see below—is referred to in the Pali Canon. There is a belief that if a person on his death-bed aspires to be reborn in a particular state, his wish may well take effect. At first sight this may seem to run clean counter to the doctrine of *karma*; but on the cognitive level this is not so. A man's dying thoughts, so the argument runs, are necessarily conditioned by the life he has led, so that to say that they determine his fate after death is only to say that this fate is determined by his conduct in this life. Unless his life has been pure he will not be capable of making a *prārthanā* for *nivan,* but will aspire to some lowly form of existence. Conversely the good man on his death-bed will remember some former good deed of his which will help him to aspire to a good rebirth. Though this is doctrinally shipshape it sails very close to the breeze: a village girl told me that the man on his death-bed 'remembers according to his luck' (*tamangē vāsanāva anuva matak vennē*), and she had introduced this topic in the context of *ahosi karma*; though 'luck is *karma*' (p. 171) the connotation is different, and the clear implication of the girl's exposition was that a 'lucky' man on his death-bed will recall an act of merit and thus get a good rebirth, causing a host of minor sins, which but for his dying thought would have carried more weight, to become *ahosi*—inoperative.

Affectively here is an attempt to mitigate the rigour of *karma* by the possibility of a death-bed—not conversion exactly, but shall we say sudden improvement. From this situation (if I am right—I doubt whether the matter can be proved or disproved) there developed long ago the more general practice of making *prārthanā* for oneself, ideally to attain *nirvāṇa* but in fact probably for all kinds of satisfaction. To what extent *prārthanā* are made, and to what end, I cannot say, as they are for the most part a private affair, nor need they be made out loud. The usual occasion for *prārthanā* is some act of merit, typically at a *dānē*. On receiving a *dānē* a monk recites a Pali verse in thanks:[4]

Icchitaṃ patthitaṃ tuyhaṃ khippam eva samijjhatu
Sabbe pūrentu attasaṃkappā cando pannarasī yathā.

[4]Such an expression of thanks is called an *anumodanā*; these are discussed at length below (p. 266). When several monks are present all chant this verse in unison.

> May what you wish and desire[5] very soon be successful; may all your wishes for yourself be fulfilled like the full moon.

The content of this verse indicates that anything may be desired, not just *nirvāṇa*. (Indeed a reformist monk [not in my area] pointed this out to me as his reason for never using the verse.) The donor makes a wish and the monk hopes it will be fulfilled. This is not strictly in contradiction to *karma* theory, because it can be said that the wish will only be fulfilled if the *karma* is good enough, and the merit gained just before a *prārthanā* is made should ensure this. However, there is little doubt that affectively the donor feels he is achieving a certain result by a certain action in an automatic, magical way. Moreover, the explanation just given only avoids contradicting canonical doctrine in cases where the *prārthanā* is for something other than *nirvāṇa*. This is not because *nirvāṇa* cannot be achieved by mere wishing (for it can be argued that the *prārthanā* is only for an advance towards *nirvāṇa* through mental purification, not a direct means to *nirvāṇa* itself), but because the Buddha specifically condemned desire for *nirvāṇa*, as he condemned all desire; one should practice meditation for its own sake, in the spirit in which a hen sits on her eggs, and the results will follow. The later canonical literature shows us that this advice was soon disregarded, as might be expected, at least by the common run of Buddhists.

But before examining these ancient antecedents of the modern practice I must give the explanations of *prārthanā* offered by two monks. *Prārthanā* for *nirvāṇa*, they said, are merely expressions of one's desire for *nirvāṇa*, a reminder of one's ultimate goal. *Nirvāṇa* can only be attained by effort (*utsāha*) over many lives, so one has to keep oneself up to scratch. Success in the human world and in heaven (*mānuṣya sampat, diviya sampat*) come automatically when one has done merit, said one of them; but to attain *nirvāṇa* (*nivan sampat*) one must make a

[5] *Patthitaṃ*, from the same verb as *prārthanā*.

prārthanāva. This, he said, is because to attain *nivan* requires constant mindfulness and constant striving. If I may put this in a different, unSinhalese way: *prārthanā* for *nirvāṇa* are mere epiphenomena of the pure thoughts of a man who, by reason of those thoughts, is advancing spiritually. This explanation seems to me canonically orthodox in avoiding all suggestion that *prārthanā* are prayers and thus avoid *karma*; it fails only to satisfy the Buddha's injunction that one should not desire *nirvāṇa*—a text which is not, I think, widely known. However, it also comes close to saying that *nivan* is achieved by something other than *pin* (merit). *Nivan* is in fact, as explained in Chapter 2, attained by perfecting morality, meditation, and wisdom, all of which are *pin*; to say that anything else is necessary would be heretical.

This very heresy was put forward by a monk whom I shall call monk 6. I have so far not taken account of his opinions, because his is a very odd case: he is not a fully ordained monk, nor recognized by the other monks, and probably slightly crazy. He is a poor villager, most unlikely ever to have been exposed to external cultural influences; yet he has turned Buddhism into a devotional religion in the Mahāyānist style of such sects as Jodo-Shin—a genuine heretic by local standards. The monks just quoted said that no external help is possible in your quest for *nirvāṇa,* and every right-minded Theravādin would agree; but monk 6 expressed the directly opposite opinion: all *pin* is fruitless (*ahosi venavā*), and no one can attain *nivan* without the help of Maitrī. 'Only that man can be called a Buddhist (*Buddhāgam-kārayek*) who prays to reach *nirvāṇa* in the time of Maitrī.' Monk 6's opinions are more fully reproduced at the end of Chapter 7. Here we must return to the history of *prārthanā.*

Patthanā for oneself are found in the ancient Pali literature which I have taken as my basis for comparison with modern times; they are, however, restricted to commentatorial literature. In the Four *Nikāyas*, the main body of sermons, the *patthanā* practices described above do not occur, but the word is found in the same general senses.

In one text[6] it seems to be a synonym of *āyācanā*, which means 'request' or 'prayer'. The meaning 'prayer' is unambiguous in the *Nidānakathā*[7] (which strictly speaking is part of a commentary), when Sujātā makes a *patthanā* to a *yakṣa* that if she gives birth to a son she will make offerings to the banyan tree in which the *yakṣa* lives.

In other canonical passages[8] *patthanā* is a synonym for *paṇidhi*, a word which can be translated as 'earnest wish' or 'aspiration'. It seems to me that sometimes in the Canon *paṇidhi,* with its verb *paṇidheti,* is used to give the same sense as *prārthanā* today. *Paṇidhi* is the technical term for the vow to become a Buddha, i.e. someone who has made a *paṇidhi* is *ipso facto* a Bodhisattva. One monk said that a *prārthanā* is necessary to become a Bosat or just to see *nirvāṇa*; here he was using the word '*prārthanā*' as the translation of *paṇidhi* (which has no other Sinhalese equivalent); the use has, however, been slightly extended, so that it is made not only by those exceptional creatures who will become Buddhas, but by all seeking enlightenment—hoping to become *buddha* with a small *b*. (As mentioned in Chapter 3, anyone enlightened is *buddha,* nor is it peculiar to Mahāyāna (as is sometimes thought) to grade *buddhas,* the Bodhisattva being superior to the mere *śrāvaka*.)

The *paṇidhi* is also the canonical equivalent of the modern *prārthanā* in another context, that of the death-bed wish. In one story[9] a dying householder is advised by tree-deities to aspire to become a universal monarch ('*Paṇidhehi . . . rājā assaṃ cakkavattīti*'). They think that this aspiration will succeed as he is virtuous. But the householder says that kingship is impermanent, and instead recites the qualities of the Three Jewels, giving his relations faith (*pasādeti*) in them. It is perhaps notable that the householder does not make a *paṇidhi* (or *patthanā*) for *nirvāṇa,*

[6] *A.N.*, III, 47.
[7] *J.*, I, 68.
[8] *S.N.*, II, 99 and 154.
[9] *S.N.*, IV, 302–5.

thus preserving the pristine purity of the teaching; plainly, however, this is only a short step away. Before leaving the *paṇidhi* we may conclude that though the distinction between the spirit behind a *paṇidhi* to become a Buddha and a *patthanā* to attain *nirvāṇa* may be clear in theory, it is a nice one which is liable to become obliterated in practice.

The word *patthanā* occurs precisely in its modern sense in the commentary to the *Dhammapada*. Here are three examples, corresponding to the three main kinds of *prārthanā* for oneself described above as current. First the dying wish: a woman makes a *patthanā* to be reborn as a female *yakṣa* (*yakkhinī*), and her rival similarly achieves rebirth as a leopard.[10] Notice that these are wishes by sinful people for very low rebirths. Second, *patthanā* for some worldly end: a wrestling champion put two coloured banners on the shrine of a former Buddha and wished that all women who saw him, except only his relations, should fall in love with him; so in his future lives other men's wives on seeing him could not control their desire.[11] For this magical use of an act of merit to gain an immoral end I have no evidence today; I only suspect that it *may* occur—probably even the wrestler told no one of what he was doing. Thirdly, *patthanā* for *nirvāṇa* (and for lower grades of spiritual attainment) occur[12] in a story which could be describing procedure today. After feeding a *pratyekabuddha* with sugar-cane a man makes a *patthanā* for 'success among gods and men, followed by enlightenment', whereat the *pratyekabuddha* says, 'So be it' (*evaṃ hotu*), and recites *Icchitaṃ patthitaṃ*, etc.' What is more, he then 'forms the resolution that he [the donor] should one day comprehend the law' (*yathā so passati evaṃ adhiṭṭhahitvā*). This is wildly undoctrinal! Later, on hearing of the incident, the man's elder brother makes a *patthanā* for *nirvāṇa*.

We see therefore that though *patthanā* are foreign to the earliest Buddhism, they appear in their 'modern' form

[10] *Dh.A.*, I, 47–8.
[11] *Dh.A.*, III, 482.
[12] *Dh.A.*, IV, 200.

in ancient times. They do undoubtedly contravene the principle that one should not desire *nirvāṇa,* but they can be, and are, explained in such a way that they do not contravene the doctrines of *karma* and intentionality (*cētanāva*). At the same time it is clear that this cognitive congruence is achieved by a rather subtle argument which can bear little relation to the feelings of most participants. The man who gave the sugar-cane doubtless considered that the *pratyekabuddha* was granting his wish, and so did the story-teller. The notion that anyone, even a *pratyekabuddha,* can resolve on someone else's spiritual progress is a more flagrant deviation from doctrine than anything I came across in the field, and suggests the Mahāyāna. The elder brother probably felt that his own *patthanā* would produce its result automatically. The elder brother's affective beliefs suggest magic, the younger brother's theism. I shall return to this point in a moment.

The text in which the *patthanā* just quoted occur is mainly a collection of stories. But the most typical and 'popular' *prārthanāva,* the wish to be comfortably reborn till one finally attains *nirvāṇa* under Maitrī, occurs in the most serious and respectable ancient source outside the Canon itself. Here are the closing lines of Buddhaghosa's *Visuddhimagga.*

> *Yaṃ siddhaṃ iminā puññaṃ, yañ c'aññaṃ pasutaṃ mayā*
> *etena puññakammena dutiye attasambhave*
> *Tāvatiṃse pamodanto sīlācāraguṇe rato*
> *alaggo pañca kāmesu patvāna pathamaṃ phalaṃ*
> *Antime attabhāvamhi Metteyyaṃ munipungavaṃ*
> *lokaggapuggalaṃ nāthaṃ sabbasattahite rataṃ*
> *Disvāna tassa dhīrassa sutvā saddhammadesanaṃ*
> *adhigantvā phalaṃ aggaṃ sobheyyaṃ Jinasāsanaṃ.*

By the merit which has accrued through this < book > and by the rest which I have generated: may I in my next life rejoice in the Tāvatiṃsa heaven, delighting in the quality of virtuous conduct, and unattached to the five desires may I attain the first fruit; in my last life may I see that bull among seers Maitrī, the world's highest person, the Lord who delights in the welfare of all beings; may I hear his preaching of the true doctrine, attain the highest fruit, and beautify the religion of the Conqueror.

These lines are missing in Burmese editions, so they could be an interpolation. But no matter: the same idea is unmistakably alluded to in the body of the text (I, 135) and there ascribed to a monk called Mahāsangharakkhita, who may or may not be the same as the monk of that name whom Adikaram dates to the first century B.C.,[13] but must in any case antedate Buddhaghosa himself.

Before leaving the *prārthanā* I must mention a canonical doctrine which logically and affectively comes very close to it: the act of truth (Pali: *saccakiriyā*). It is believed that a solemn asseveration of one's righteousness in some particular respect can, by its truth, produce some desired result. Most of the canonical examples occur in the *Jātaka* stories,[14] but the *locus classicus* is in the *Angulimāla Sutta* in the *Majjhima Nikāya*. The former brigand Angulimāla, now a monk, sees a woman in a painful and difficult labour; on advice from the Buddha he says to her, 'Since being born in the noble birth [i.e. entering the Order] I have never intentionally taken life; as this is true may you and your foetus be well.' And it comes to pass. Angulimāla's words, known as the *Angulimāla pirit,* are still used in Ceylon to ease the pains of a woman in labour.

The 'act of truth' is today, not surprisingly, a matter of theory rather than of practice; perhaps no one alive is holy enough to bring it off. The last recorded 'act of truth' of which I am aware was by Duṭugämuṇu; when his soldiers in the confusion of battle mistook each other for the enemy he asseverated, 'Not for the pleasure of sovereignty is my striving, but always to establish the doctrine of the Fully Enlightened one. As this is true, let the armour on my soldiers' bodies acquire a blazing hue.'[15] And so it happened.

To harmonize the 'act of truth' with the doctrine of

[13]Adikaram, op. cit., pp. 68–9.

[14]For references see the P.T.S. dictionary *sub voce saccakiriyā*.

[15]*Mhv.*, 25, 18.

karma would not be logically impossible, as it could be claimed that truth is a natural force, which is here being harnessed to a righteous end; but this would be far-fetched. Affectively the 'act of truth', like the *prārthanā*, seems to be a short cut.

To the outsider it would seem that the *saccakiriyā* and the *prārthanā* might be grouped with *pirit* and other practices akin to white magic mentioned at the end of Chapter 4, in that all seem to be based on an implicit belief in the power of religious utterances. I was in fact told by a schoolmaster that the sound of the *Āṭānāṭiya Sutta*, which on a night of *pirit* is chanted in the small hours of the morning, produces vibrations which keep the *yakṣas* at bay. This explanation is reminiscent of Hindu theory and is unlikely to be traditional among Buddhists; but though untypical it is worth quoting, as it explicitly describes *pirit* as a spell of automatic efficacy. Moreover this is almost done by a *pirit* text itself. The *Mahā Jayamangala Gāthā*, verses which conclude the *mahā pirit*, begin

> *Mahākāruṇiko nātho hitāya sabbapāṇinaṃ*
> *Pūretvā pāramī sabbā patto sambodhim uttamaṃ*
> *Etena saccavajjena hotu te*[16] *jayamangalaṃ.*
>
> The lord of great compassion for the welfare of all alive fulfilled all the perfections and reached the supreme Enlightenment. By this statement of truth may the blessing of victory be yours.[16]

The last line recurs several times in the poem. The *saccavajja* (which literally means 'truthfulness') is plainly in the context a *saccakiriyā*, 'act of truth'; the text, the latest used in the *pirit*, thus gives this explanation of itself. Though this step has never, to my knowledge, been made by Buddhists, the most economical explanation of the *prārthanā* as behaviour would be to put it in the same category of white magic which works through the efficacy of religious utterance. It would of course be easy to describe the automatic use of prayer by a Christian in difficulties in similar terms; but we must remember that despite

[16]Or *me* 'mine', depending on the circumstances.

the prayer-like appearance and history of the *prārthanā* it is, at least nowadays, more akin to magic than to theistic religion, for even though the benediction of a monk or *pratyekabuddha* may somehow help it along, it is not considered to depend for its effect on the whim of any external agent.

The third contemporary belief which seems at first sight to run counter to *karma* theory is the transference of merit, usually called in Sinhalese 'giving merit' (*pin dīma*), a term which can be misleading. Giving normally implies that the giver parts with the thing given, but in giving merit one merely offers to others the chance to earn merit by rejoicing at one's own. It was several times explained to me that giving merit is like giving light when one lamp is lit from another. This disposes of the problem as far as the giver is concerned; what about the recipient? Can one acquire merit from an act one has not done oneself? Here I must refer the reader back to the list of good deeds on page 87. The fifth is *pattānumodanā*, rejoicing in another's merit (and the fourth is *patti*—giving someone a chance to rejoice in your merit, i.e. 'giving' it). If someone does a good deed you may earn as much merit as he does—or even more—by being really pleased about it. If this seems to the action-oriented westerner to be an easy way out, let me remind him that this doctrine is fully consonant with Buddhism's ethic of intention: it is the thought that counts, and merit bears fruit for the doer because of the pure thought that accompanies it; therefore if the thought of a spectator is purified too, so much the better for him. The high priest of Mīgala, having spent rupees on a *pinkama*, told me that a villager who took sympathetic joy in the merit he was earning might thereby earn more merit from it than he did himself, without spending any money. This seems to me a humane and rational equivalent of the New Testament story of the widow's mite. Theoretically indeed this could be an endless process, pleasure at the merit (and consequent spiritual progress) of others enhancing your own good *karma*, and their pleasure at your progress in turn enhancing theirs. All this is *patti* and *pattānumodanā*.

This ingenious and pleasant doctrine has a curious history, which well illustrates the interrelation between the cognitive and the affective which is a theme of this work. In this generalized form it is not a part of the original doctrine, and the terms *patti* and *pattānumodanā* in this sense arē not found in the Four *Nikāyas*. The verb *anumodati* is used in these early texts with two closely related meanings: 'to agree with'; or 'to receive with gratitude', i.e. 'to thank'. In the first meaning, Sāriputta says of a doctrinal debate:[17] *na me koci bhikkhu anumodati*: 'no monk agrees with me'. Parallel to the second meaning is the noun *anumodana*[18] 'gratitude' or 'thanks'. This word from the beginning[19] is mainly used as a technical term for the thanks uttered by a monk on being given alms. This usage has been preserved unchanged till today in the Sinhalese *anumōdan*. The passage in the *Vinaya Piṭaka*[20] in which the Buddha prescribes the utterance of the *anumodana* and says that it should be said by the eldest monk present does not specify the content of what is said: though the Buddha doubtless composed his thanks variously to suit the occasion, one may assume the early use of some such benedictory formula as '*Icchitaṃ patthitaṃ*. . . ' quoted above (p. 257).

Merit is typically transferred after a *dānē*. The donor (*dāyaka*) presents food (i.e. a *dānē*) to the monk. The monk then recites the Pali verse *Icchitaṃ patthitaṃ*, followed by a long formula in highly Sanskritized Sinhalese prose (see Appendix), telling the donor to transfer the merit to the gods. This the donor does, either by reciting the following Pali verse or by giving his assent ('Sādhu sādhu') when it is recited by a monk.

> *Ākāsaṭṭhā ca bhummaṭṭhā devā nāgā mahiddhikā*
> *Puññaṃ taṃ anumoditvā ciraṃ rakkhantu sāsanaṃ.*

[17] *A.N.*, III, 194.

[18] Rarer forms parallel to *anumodana* (neuter) are *anumodanā* (feminine) and *anumodanīya* (neuter).

[19] e.g. *D.N.*, II, 88, where the Buddha recites some verses.

[20] *Vin.*, II, 212.

> May air-dwelling gods and ground-dwelling gods,
> nāgas of great power, having rejoiced at the merit,
> long protect the Teaching.

The verse may be repeated, with 'me' substituted for 'the Teaching'. It is also used at the end of any *pinkama* or after private worship.

This transfer of merit to the gods is canonical. In the *Mahāparinibbāna Sutta* the Buddha receives a meal from two ministers. 'The Blessed One thanked (*anumodi*) them with these verses: Wherever a wise man dwells, he should feed the virtuous and restrained ascetics there, and dedicate the gift (*dakkhiṇaṃ ādise*) to whatever deities are there; when worshipped they worship, when honoured they honour him.'[21]

The text does not use the term *patti*, though the meaning expressed is the same; *patti*, however, is the commentatorial gloss:[22] *Tāsaṃ dakkhiṇaṃ ādise ti sanghassa dinne cattāro paccaye tāsaṃ gharadevatānaṃ apadiseyya pattiṃ dadeyya*. ' "He should dedicate the gift" means that when the Sangha have been given the four requisites one should dedicate, give the merit to those house-deities.' And the commentator significantly continues: ' "When worshipped they worship": they think, "These people are not even our relatives, and even so they give us the merit." '

Though the commentator is much later than the text, I think he is right about the implied origin of merit transference. We come here to a complex of ideas centring on those funeral feasts for dead relatives which are common to so many cultures. *Prima facie* they are perhaps an unexpected phenomenon in a Buddhist context, but Buddhism inherited them from its Indian Hindu background. Professor von Fürer-Haimendorf describes how Chetris, a high Hindu caste in Nepal, can gain merit by having brahmins recite sacred texts for a week (*saptāha*): 'If performed as a memorial rite the *saptāha* involved the gift of an entire set

21 *D.N.*, II, 88 (*Sutta* XVI. 1. 31).
22 *Sumangala-vilāsinī*, II, 542.

of household goods to the senior brahmin priest, and it is popular belief that as a result of this donation corresponding objects of personal use will be available to the departed for his life in the next world. The fact that such an idea is inconsistent with the belief in the immediate reincarnation of every human being in a shape conditioned by his earlier deeds does not seem to disturb the Chetris, who like other Hindus see nothing incongruous in the holding of apparently inconsistent views.'[23] Buddhists are more concerned with doctrinal consistency, so that this case affords a fascinating study of the interaction between behaviour and doctrine. But before reverting to ancient times let me describe what goes on today.

It is customary to feed monks, if possible in one's home, at certain fixed intervals of time after the death of a relative. The number and size of such *dānēs* depends mainly on the wealth and social status of the family; however, a *dānē* on the seventh day after the death is obligatory, and one three months after the death is almost equally common, while annual *dānēs* on the anniversary of the death are very common, especially for dead parents. (This practice is not confined to laymen: the chief monk in Mīgala gives two annual *dānēs* to commemorate the deaths of his parents, and a third to commemorate the death of the previous incumbent, his father in religion. *Sil māṇiyō*, who have more fully renounced the world, in some cases give up the rite (both for their parents and for their teacher), but do not seem to regard it as improper for them: it is not branded as worldly.) All these *dānēs* given for the dead are called *mataka dānē/dāna* ('dead' *dānē*) to distinguish them from *jīva dāna, dānēs* given by and for the living;[24] but the *dānē* after seven days is the *mataka dānē par excellence*. A *mataka dānē* should properly be *sānghika*, which means given to the Sangha as a body, not to individual

[23]C. von Fürer-Haimendorf, *Morals and Merit* (Weidenfeld and Nicolson, London, 1967), p. 168.

[24]Technically a *jīva dāna* is a special *dānē* given when someone expects to die soon; it is described by Dickson, op. cit., pp. 231–2

monks. The donor of a *sānghika dānē* must approach a monk (in fact the chief monk at his local temple) and issue an invitation by saying that he wishes to give a *sānghika dānē* for so and so many monks (at least five), without naming any particular monk he wishes to come. The monk who receives this invitation simply sends along the requisite number. Five is the minimum required for any official act of the Sangha (*vinayakama*). However, poor people who can afford only the seventh day *dānē* may even then feed fewer than five monks.

The *dānēs* for the dead vary in character. The seventh day *dānē* is a private affair for the family and maybe close friends. It is preceded by a sermon (*baṇa*) late on the previous evening.[25] The three month *dānē* (*tun māsa dānē*) on the other hand is an occasion for conspicuous consumption, and is usually preceded by *pirit*, to which all acquaintances are invited—though in the village explicit invitation is generally unnecessary. The annual *dānē* lies somewhere between these two. However, at *mataka dānēs* the ritual for transferring merit to the dead is the same, and takes place after the midday meal (*daval dānē*) which closes the whole *pinkama*, even if monks are also fed on the previous evening and at breakfast-time.

The meal is offered to the Sangha with the usual Pali sentence, repeated three times:

> *Imaṃ bhikkhaṃ bhikkhusaṃghassa demi.*
>
> I give this alms-food to the community of monks.

Sometimes a little food is thrown outside the house; it is variously said to be for the *pretas* or for the crows. When the monks have eaten (and, usually, been offered 'requisites' (*pirikara*), objects they are allowed to own such as pillow-slips), a small bowl or dish and a pitcher of water

[25]The Rev. Rahula has told me of a custom in some remote parts of Ceylon which suggests a linkage of exorcism to funeral feast. A monk will come to deliver the sermon in the evening, and then, on the pretext that it is too much trouble to return to the monastery after dark when he has to come back for the *dānē* the next morning, will spend the night in the bed of the dead man.

are set before them and the immediate relatives of the dead man come to the front. Everyone assumes a reverent posture and the head of the household slowly pours the water into the dish till it overflows, while the monks intone in unison:

Yathā vārivahā pūrā paripūrenti sāgaraṃ
Evam eva ito dinnaṃ petānaṃ upakappati[26]

As the full water-bearing [rivers] fill the ocean, so indeed does what is given here benefit the dead (*preta*).

Uṇṇame udakaṃ vaṭṭam yathā ninnaṃ pavattati
Evam eva ito dinnaṃ petānaṃ upakappati.[26]

As water rained on a height reaches the low land, so indeed does what is given here benefit the dead (*preta*).

When the water has overflowed the monks stop chanting and everyone says 'Sā'. The proceedings conclude with a short sermon on transitoriness (*anityatā*) to console the mourners, at the end of which, instead of the general formula transferring merit to the gods given above, the householder says (perhaps on prompting from a monk),

Idaṃ me[27] *ñātīnaṃ hotu. Sukhitā hontu ñātayo.*

May this be for my relatives. May my relatives be happy.

The doctrinal explanation of all this is rather complicated. It was explained thus by the Mīgala incumbent. The death is primarily an occasion for doing merit (*pina*) oneself; secondarily for offering it in case the dead man is expecting it. He can, however, only rejoice and benefit from the merit if reborn as a *perēta*, because if he is higher than that he does not need the merit, if he is lower, in hell (*apāya*), he cannot get it. [There is in fact a further refinement: only the top class of *preta*, 'those who live on merit

[26]My edition of *Bauddha Ädahilla* has *upakappatu* 'may benefit'. I emend on the authority of the Rev. Rahula and the P.T.S. text of the *Petavatthu*.

[27]Thus *Bauddha Ädahilla*. The P.T.S. text has *vo* for *me*; the meaning is unaffected, as *vo* agrees with *ñātīnaṃ*.

given by others' (*paradattopajīvin*) are able to sympathize with the merit of others.][28] But this does not mean, he said, that the relatives giving the *dānē* assume that the dead man is now a *preta*, for if we pay a call we take food along as a gift, but if the person is out we eat it ourselves; similarly, the *pinkama* earns merit for the living whatever the fate of the dead. The origin of the custom of offering it to the dead is this, he said. Once King Bimbisāra gave the Buddha a *dānē*, and his ancestors, who were *prētayō*, came to see it. He offered them no *pin*; so they were sorely disappointed. In the night there was a great noise round his palace, so next morning he went to the Buddha and asked if this boded ill for himself or his kingdom. The Buddha said not so, but explained what had happened. So to remedy his oversight Bimbisāra gave him a *dānē* that day too, and offered the *pin* to the *perētayō*. My informant added that to offer *pin* one has really to *think* of offering it while doing it—a mere form of words, or afterthought, will not do.

When introducing the *pretas* in Chapter 4 I dwelt on their ambiguous status throughout the recorded history of Buddhism, and the above statement illustrates this very well. It contains small but telling points of doctrinal inconsistency: it is not clear why *pretas* who have already come to the *dānē* (as in the story of Bimbisāra) should be unable to rejoice at the merit unless it is specifically offered; nor why gods, who in other contexts are always offered merit, are in this context said not to need it. However, the latter discrepancy can be removed by saying that while the gods are in no hurry for the merit the *pretas* need it urgently, because they are suffering in a state of woe, from which only *pattānumodana* can relieve them, because they have little or no opportunity for performing meritorious actions independently. Remember, moreover, that length of life is one of the things that decreases as one goes down the cosmic scale; the Rev. Rahula has told me

[28]Thus, e.g. *Milindapañha*, p. 294. The monk's explanation in the next four lines occurs on the same page of that text.

of a belief that *pretas* live only seven days, which makes it essential to catch them at the point before they sink further. He very plausibly connects this with a belief found in other schools of Buddhism (Mahāyāna and Sarvāstivāda) in an 'in-between state' (*antarābhava*) lasting seven days; during this period the person is suspended between death and rebirth, and any improvement in *karma* will of course make the next birth a better one. I must stress that this *antarābhava* is not a Theravāda belief; it goes towards explaining the seventh day *dānē* on the historical, not on the doctrinal level. From this historical angle it is also interesting to notice that in the Pali words just quoted the donor transfers merit to all his relatives, not just the recently dead man, thus reminding us that Hindu offerings are to ancestors (*pitaras*).

The *mataka dānē*, though not described in every ritual detail, is canonical in Theravāda Buddhism. In one *sutta*[29] a brahmin says to the Buddha that brahmins give funeral feasts (*śrāddhā*—Pali *saddhā*), praying that the gifts [given to brahmins on their behalf] may be enjoyed by their dead relatives, and he asks whether this really works. The Buddha at first replies that it does not work if the relative is reborn in hell, as an animal, as a human, or as a god, but works if he is reborn as a *preta*, in which case he lives on what his friends and kinsmen supply. In reply to further questions the Buddha says that if the particular relative the donor had in mind is not a *preta*, other relatives who are *pretas* will enjoy it, and it cannot happen that *no* relatives are re-born as *pretas*; but anyway no donor is without reward (*dāyako... anipphalo*). In this text no reference is made to the merit of the act; the gift is said to benefit (*upakappati*) the relatives and they to enjoy (*paribhuñjati*) it, so presumably the object passes to them direct. That all this is addressed to a brahmin points up the fact that the Buddhists were consciously adapting the Hindu custom.

There are many references to the custom in a canonical book, the *Petavatthu*, which consists entirely of poems

[29] *A.N.*, V, 269–73 (*Sutta* CLXXVII).

about *pretas*. The three verses cited above come from a poem[30] entitled the *Ñātidhamma Sutta* ('The Sutta of behaviour due to relatives').[31] (It also occurs under the title, taken from the first words, of *Tirokuḍḍa Sutta* as the seventh item in the nine-item canonical chrestomathy, the *Khuddakapāṭha*). Here is Bhikkhu Ñāṇamoli's translation of the whole poem.

1. Without the walls they stand and wait,
   And at the junctions and road-forks;
   Returning to their erstwhile homes,
   They wait beside the jambs of gates.
2. But when a rich feast is set out
   With food and drink of every kind,
   The fact that no man does recall
   These creatures stems from their past acts.
3. So they who are compassionate
   At heart do give for relatives
   Such drink and food as may be pure
   And good and fitting at these times:
4. 'Then let this be for relatives;
   'May relatives have happiness.'
   These ghosts of the departed kin
   Foregathered and assembled there
5. Will eagerly their blessing give
   For (plentiful) rich food and drink:
   'So may our relatives live long,
   'Owing to whom we have this gain;
6. 'For honour to us has been done,
   'No giver ever lacked the fruit.'
   Now there is never ploughing there,
   Nor any cattle-herding found,
7. Nor merchandizing just the same,

[30]Dickson reports (p. 234) that the monk reads out the whole poem in Sinhalese translation. I witnessed several *mataka dānēs* but never came across this.

[31]*Petav.*, I, 5.

Nor bartering for coin of gold:
The ghosts of the departed kin
Live there on giving given here;
8. As water showered on the hill
Flows down to reach the hollow vale,
So giving given here can serve
The ghosts of the departed kin.
9. As river-beds when full can bear
The water down to fill the sea,
So giving given here can serve
The ghosts of the departed kin.
10. 'He gave to me, he worked for me,
'He was my kin, friend, intimate'.
Give gifts, then, for departed ones,
Recalling what they used to do.
11. No weeping, nor yet sorrowing,
Nor any kind of mourning, aids
Departed Ones, whose kin remain
(Unhelpful to them acting) thus.
12. But when this offering is given
Well placed in the Community
For them, then it can serve them long
In future and at once as well.
13. The True Idea for relatives has thus been shown,
And how high honour to departed ones is done,
And how the bhikkhus can be given strength as well
And how great merit can be stored away by you.[32]

The verses cited above were, in order, the ninth, eighth and first half of the fourth. As Stede has remarked,[33] verses 11 and 12 (his 10 and 11) look like an addition. Moreover, till verse 12 there is no trace of Buddhism; dead relatives are to get food and drink, and benefit their donors in return. Not till the end is there mention of the Sangha or of

[32] *Minor Readings and Illustrator* (Luzac, London, 1960), pp. 7–8.
[33] Wilhelm Stede, *Die Gespenstergeschichten des Petavatthu* (Harrassowitz, Leipzig, 1914), p. 63.

merit, and they are not well integrated. In the context of the poem the 'this' which is given to the relative in verse 4 line 1 is food and drink; only in the ritual as now performed and explained is it merit, or rather the chance to rejoice at merit. It is this rather complicated explanation which has circumvented a doctrinal incongruity which originally must have been glaring. A vestige of the originally Hindu practice of actually offering food has, moreover, been preserved in the optional custom, noted above, of throwing a little food outside the house. Those who say this is for the crows are rationalizing, though in accordance with Buddhist ethics (kindness to animals); that it is for the *pretas* must be the ancient explanation. Note that the custom has persisted, with no logical congruity, throughout the doctrinal discussions about to be presented; but as their effect has been to shift the emphasis of the ritual entirely away from the food it is not surprising that the handful of food for the *pretas* has declined to a barely noticed, even an optional, detail.

The story of the origin of the *mataka dānē* told me by the Mīgala incumbent is taken from the commentary on this poem, Buddhaghosa's *Paramatthajotikā*. In the commentary the thing offered is still explained as the food, etc., not the merit; but this is perhaps not an important point, as the general interpretation is clearly the modern one: the king gives a *dānē* to the Buddha and dedicates it (*uddisati*) to the *pretas*. More important is the story of this event given in the commentary to the *Dhammapada*.[34] The Buddha explained to Bimbisāra that after he had given the first feast the *pretas* had made a row because 'when you gave the food they did not get the merit' (*dāne dinne pattiṃ alabhamānā*). When Bimbisāra therefore fed the Buddha the next day, 'he gave the merit, saying "Sir, may the divine food and drink from here accrue to those *pretas*." ' (*Bhante, ito tesaṃ petānaṃ dibbannapānaṃ sampajjatū ti pattiṃ adāsi*). They get the food, then show themselves to the king naked. The king therefore gives robes (*cīvarāni*)

[34] *Dh.A.*, I, 103-4.

the next day to the Buddha and his disciples, and the *pretas* accordingly are clothed in heavenly garments. At this they leave the condition of *preta* (*petattabhāva*) and become gods (*dibbattabhāva*). 'The teacher, giving thanks, used the words of thanks, "Outside the walls they stand", etc.' (*Satthā anumodanaṃ karonto: tirokuḍḍesu tiṭṭhantīti tirokuḍḍānumodanaṃ akāsi.*)

In this account the spirits are getting not mere merit, but more tangible benefits—food and clothes. However, they get the food and clothes as a result of getting merit—plainly an ambiguous situation. The question whether the *pretas* could actually eat the food was controversial in ancient times even though that they could is the natural interpretation of the *sutta* I have quoted. In Nyanatiloka's summary of the *Kathāvatthu*, a late canonical book (probably third century B.C.), question 69 is, 'Can alms which are given here be enjoyed by beings elsewhere (e.g. by the ... Petas)?' and we are told that two sects think that they can, but that Theravādins hold that 'the mind of the Petas might be favourably influenced, but the material food cannot be enjoyed by them.'[35] Though this seems to contradict the Theravādin commentaries just quoted, which in their present form are many centuries younger than the *Kathāvatthu*, it is very likely that the commentaries on this ancient custom are quoting an old story. But whatever the date of the final victory of orthodoxy, it is clear that sensible Theravādin monks decided that food being visibly consumed by a monk could not possibly be eaten by someone else, so that if people persisted in their habit of feeding dead relatives the custom required reinterpretation. What the relatives were really getting was something else—merit.

Though we saw above that the offering of merit to the gods occurs in the Four *Nikāyas*, the doctrine of *pattānumodanā*, the acquisition of merit by anyone through empathizing in another's merit, does not. According to modern doctrine such empathy can take place whether one

[35]Nyanatiloka, *Guide through the Abhidhamma-Piṭaka*, p. 71.

is 'offered' the merit or not. But the whole point of the story about Bimbisāra's ancestors was that they had to be offered the merit before they could get it, and the implication of offering merit to the gods is that they too cannot get it just by being present—which they are in any case (note that the reference in the *Mahāparinibbāna Sutta* is specifically to the local gods). Moreover even now in all standardized situations a verse or formula is recited offering the merit to specific benefactors. Why should the Pali verse be recited at the *dānē* offering the merit to the gods? The doctrinal answer (same monk) is that one is simply drawing their attention to the merit. The same reason can be given for the less institutionalized practice of carrying round among the laymen present an offering which one is about to make to the Buddha or the Sangha: the laymen fold their hands, touch or make to touch the offering with their fingertips, and then raise their hands to their foreheads in the gesture of worship: the person who is physically making the offering is drawing the attention of the others to his act of merit, and their gestures symbolize their participation. In this case the doctrinal rationale fits. It does not, however, adequately explain what goes on at the ritual for the dead.

The reinterpretation of the *mataka dānē* is the nub of this problem; it can be followed by tracing the evolution of the meaning of *anumodati* from 'thank' to 'empathize', 'rejoice in another's merit'. In the poem quoted above the verb *anumodati* is used of the *pretas* (poorly translated by Ñāṇamoli as 'their blessing give'). Then in the commentary the Buddha too does an *anumodana*. Now observe what happens. The Buddhist givers of funeral feasts have been told by the monks that their relatives are not getting the food, but are getting something else—merit. The whole point of the rite is to *give* your dead relative something, so the donors are satisfied, provided they still have the feeling they are *giving*. They give their merit away to the dead, like goods or cash, and the dead—presumably—say thank you (*anumodanti*). But no, say the monks; the doctrine of *karma* will not allow this; you cannot really give your merit away; you are just allowing the dead to improve their minds by expressing sympathetic joy at your good action in feeding us. So though the text used in the rite says that the *pretas anumodanti*, this does not mean that they thank you for a gift, for nothing passes between you; they are just rejoicing.

This is where the meaning of *anumodati* undergoes its crucial change: as part of the doctrinal response to undoctrinal behaviour. Once *anumodati* comes to refer just to a pure mental state, to empathy in doing good, it is of course open to anyone to do it at any time, without having to wait for an offer, and this is the modern position: the villagers could rejoice at the monk's fiftieth birthday celebrations without specific invitation.

But since *anumodati* was originally used both of the monk who gets the food and of the god or *preta* who gets the merit, the way is now open to linguistic confusion. That is indeed what we find in modern Sinhalese, for while what the monk recites at a *dānē* is still called the *anumōdana*, according to modern doctrine it is not he who *anumodati*, rejoices, but the gods—the third parties. We thus get the following table, which I owe to a conversation with the Rev. Rahula. In the table the three participants (or groups of participants) are on the left: in the centre are the actions they are performing in Pali, Sinhalese, and a literal English translation; on the right is the type of good deed (according to the Pali list of the good deeds) which the action represents. The lines from top to bottom are in chronological sequence.

Donor	deti	denavā	gives	dāna
Monk	anumodāpeti	anumōdan karavanavā	causes to cause to rejoice	desanā
Donor	anumodeti	anumōdan karanavā	causes to rejoice	patti
Gods	anumodanti	anumōdan venavā	rejoice	pattānum-odana

The Pali alone suffices to show that something has got twisted up here. In fact the double causative form *anu-*

modāpeti is not in the dictionaries, and the plain causative *anumodeti* is cited only once,[36] in the quite different meaning 'get the approval of'.

The popular understanding of what goes on—which I might also call the common-sense view—is rather different. It also corresponds to the historical view. The monk is understood to be saying 'Thank you', as indeed he was by original doctrine. The donor is then understood to be giving the gods his merit as a *quid pro quo*, as if he were buying their protection for cash.

This sort of transaction is only possible after the complete separation of the merit earned by a gift from the gift itself, a separation which we saw take place at the *mataka dānē*. In that context the 'transference of merit' was made in the *Kathāvatthu* to conform to *karma* doctrine by talking of the good intentions of all concerned. But this explanation becomes more strained in our next example, in which the merit of a gift is given retrospectively. In a *Jātaka* story[37] the Bodhisattva, born as a brahman merchant, has gained merit by feeding a *pratyekabuddha*; he is shipwrecked, and while swimming in the sea with an attendant is picked up by a deity whose duty it is to protect virtuous men in misfortune; she did not notice the attendant, so 'the brahmin gave him the merit of his good deed, and he received it gratefully' (*brāhmaṇo attanā katakalyāṇato tassa pattiṃ adāsi, so anumodi*) and was picked up.[38] Here we are very close to the idea of a fund of merit, like a bank account, to be drawn on at will. I stress that even this passage can be rationalized by reference to the doctrine of intention; but the more obvious interpretation of the passage would be to regard merit as a kind of spiritual money. And a characteristic of money is that when you have used it you no longer have it.

The equation of merit with money becomes virtually

[36] *Paramatthadīpanī*, VI (*Therigāthā Aṭṭhakathā*), 201, 1, 9. Even this is uncertain—there is a variant reading *anumānetvā*.

[37] *J.*, IV, 15–22.

[38] *J.*, IV, 21.

explicit in the story from the commentary to the *Dhammapada* about the two brothers and the sugar-cane (see p. 261). When the younger brother feeds the *pratyekabuddha* sugar-cane from his brother's field, he thinks, 'If my elder brother demands the price [of the cane] I shall give him the price, if the merit I shall give the merit' (*sace me jeṭṭhabhātiko mūlam āharāpessati mūlaṃ dassāmi sace pattim āharāpessati pattiṃ dassāmi*).[39] Of course this again is not a doctrinal treatise; but it is clear that the merit and the money are on an equal footing, and that the giving of the merit will have nothing to do with benevolence or purity of thoughts. Here the incongruity of the transaction with doctrine is not confined to the affective, and reaches the cognitive level.

In texts quoted so far the verb *anumodati* has only been used of receiving something offered, so that it has involved thanking for something, not just rejoicing at it. There is nothing especially meritorious about thanking someone for a gift; rejoicing at their merit, however, is a good psychological state, and thus meritorious. In our next example it is not yet clear whether the merit was offered or not, though I think the latter. Here[40] a monk talking to a *preta* says, 'You never gave anyone a gift with your own hands, but rejoicing at the gifts of others (*parassa dānaṃ anumodamāno*) stretched out your hand and spoke.' However, by this means the *preta* had acquired enough merit to be reborn in comfort.

In the next stage a man rejoices (*anumodati*) at merit, not just without being offered it, but without being present. He merely hears that there is going to be a *dānē* and expresses his joy. This is the modern doctrinal position.

Finally let me quote from a late commentary a passage in which both *patti* and *anumodana* occur. The words, though purporting to describe Visākhā and her friends after Visākhā has built a *vihāra* for the Sangha, could, translated into Sinhalese, be an exact transcription of modern

[39] *Dh.A.*, IV, 200,

[40] *Petavatthu*, 2, 9, 20.

procedure. Visākhā says to her companions,[41] ' "The merit I have earned, rejoice at it, I give you the gift of this merit."[42] With gladly trusting minds they all rejoiced. "Oh, it is good, oh, it is good." One good lady who was there concentrated especially on that gift of merit. Soon after she died and was reborn in the Heaven of the Thirty-Three.' (*Yaṃ mayā puññaṃ pasutaṃ, taṃ anumodatha, pattidānaṃ vo dammī ti. Aho sādhu aho sādhū ti pasannacittā sabbā pi anumodiṃsu. Tattha aññatarā upāsikā pi visesato taṃ pattidānaṃ manasā akāsi. Sā na cirass' eva kālaṃ katvā Tāvatiṃsesu nibbatti.*) This *anumodanā* of hers she describes[43] as a 'pure rejoicing' (*suddh' anumodanā*) and hence truly meritorious. (This is in the canonical text, not merely the commentary.) Though in this case the merit was offered, that 'rejoicing' and not 'thanking' is the appropriate translation is clear both from this passage and from the two previous passages cited.

We have traced here a correspondence between affective religion and an early behavioural deviation, appearing in Buddhist stories, but never explicitly accepted by doctrine; doctrine has then made a come-back and harmonized practice with canonical theory, though not without becoming exceedingly tortuous (and philologically barbarous). The stages through which behaviour evolved have been traced above; the behaviour represented in passages dealing with *patti* displays a gradual deviation from doctrinal orthodoxy, while the changed meanings of *anumodanā* and its verbs represent the rationalizations of doctrine to accommodate the behavioural deviations. On the behavioural level the passages first quoted for *patti* represent someone's giving their merit to another person, and that person's saying thank-you. As the idea that one can give away merit contradicts a fundamental doctrine, this clear implication has to be explained away, which is done, most

[41] *Vv.A.*, 188.

[42] The translation cannot convey the full ambiguity of *patti*, discussed in my text.

[43] *Vv.A.*, 189 = *Vv.*, 44, 9 (p. 40).

ingeniously, by changing the meaning of *anumodati*. Although I know of no passage which is quite explicit on the point, the identity of the last passage quoted with modern practice strongly suggests that the modern doctrine too had been evolved by the time it was written. For this it is significant that the good lady attributes her rebirth in heaven to the purity of her rejoicing (*anumodanā*). This comes not in the commentary, but in a canonical text, albeit a late one, the *Vimānavatthu*. The entire evolution of doctrine and behaviour with which we are concerned therefore took place, in all probability, within what for the purposes of this work I am calling the ancient period; and what I have called the 'modern' doctrine, though clearly different from the original doctrine, may be as much as 2,000 years old.

In the *mataka dānē* we encounter an especially striking case of incongruence between the cognitive and the affective. There is a very wide gap between the explanation of the ritual and what the chief participants feel about it. It is true no doubt that they are not calculating whether the dead person has been reborn as a *paradattopajīvin preta* so that he can benefit from their actions, but the reason is not one of subtle doctrine. They feel emotionally that they owe this ceremony to the dead man and that he will benefit from it; they would act in a very similar way without the doctrines to which they subscribe. Even the overflowing water may have been reinterpreted. The pouring of water in Sinhalese ritual frequently signalizes a solemn act (e.g. marriage); but here it seems most relevant to recall the libations poured to the Manes in other, older cultures.

The water-pouring ritual just described takes place at the funeral (*avamangalya*) itself. When the coffin has been placed in the pyre or over the grave, according to whether the body is to be cremated or buried, a white cloth is laid on it. One of the monks present—there may be any number, down to one—gives the Three Refuges and the Five Precepts as usual; then everyone present repeats three times after the monk,

> *Imaṃ matakavatthaṃ bhikkhusanghassa demi.*
> I give this corpse-clothing to the Sangha of monks.

At this the monks spread the cloth out across the coffin, and chant a Pali stanza:

> *Aniccā vata saṃkhārā uppāda-vaya-dhammino,*
> *Uppajjitvā nirujjhanti, tesaṃ vūpasamo sukho.*
>
> Impermanent indeed are compounded things,
> whose nature is to arise and pass away; having
> arisen they are destroyed; their being stilled
> is pleasant.

This couplet is supposed to have been recited by Śakra at the death of the Buddha;[44] its first words, *Aniccā vata saṃkhārā*, head the printed announcements of the death which are posted all over the village on the day of the funeral, and their general purport is probably understood by everyone. The monks then pick up the cloth, symbolically appropriating it, and someone takes it away. The water is then poured by a near relation as at a *dānē*, the monks reciting the same verses; as it is an outdoor ceremony the water is sometimes that of a young coco-nut, which is split at the appropriate moment. A monk then preaches. At a village funeral which I witnessed the monks then left, before the coffin was lowered into the grave, perhaps to avoid being present during the lamentations which naturally accompany the body's final disappearance.

The cloth given to the monks is known as *paṃsukūla* (literally 'dust-cloth'), a name which has also been extended to the ceremony of giving it. *Paṃsukūla* is the name of the first of the classical list of thirteen ascetic practices (*dhutanga*), optional for monks who wished to display more than the usual ascetic rigour.[45] A *paṃsukūla* monk dresses only in rags picked up at cemeteries. The modern *paṃsukūla* ceremony is a curious fusion of this with a *dānē*. By picking up the cloth from the coffin the monk is

[44] *D.N.*, II, 157.

[45] For the classical account of the *paṃsukūla dhutanga* (followed by the other *dhutangas*) see Buddhaghosa, *Visuddhimagga*, book II.

symbolically taking the winding sheet, or some other item of the corpse's clothing, and thus conforming to the letter of the *paṃsukūla* practice. On the other hand the dead man's next of kin are giving the cloth, which therefore is the best new white cloth, to enhance the value of the gift; they have made the funeral an occasion for transferring the merit earned by a gift to the Sangha, thus destroying the spirit of the *paṃsukūla* idea so that the original meaning of the term has been completely lost.

The doctrines discussed in this chapter avoid serious inconsistency with orthodoxy. Though some of them have been described as 'modern' they are so only in relation to the Four *Nikāyas*; in simple chronological terms they are ancient. (In our discussion of merit transference we have demonstrated development *within* the corpus of early Buddhist writings, an exercise not attempted elsewhere in the book.) The latter and more important doctrines discussed are rationalizations, or if you will Buddhicizations, of practices (the dying wish, the *mataka dānē*) which afford some psychological relief from the oppressive doctrine of man's total reponsibility for his own fate. Beliefs which these practices *imply* have never entered the mainstream of Theravāda Buddhism: the cognitive position has been maintained with remarkable tenacity. The canonical theory of *karma* survives intact—cognitively; affectively its rigour is sometimes avoided. Similarly, though the doctrine of *anatta* can be salvaged (see p. 85) by the claim that the personality continuing through a series of births has as much reality as the personality within one life, *prārthanā* for happy rebirths and the transfer of merit to dead relatives show that the *anatta* doctrine has no more affective immediacy with regard to the next life than with regard to this, and that belief in personal survival after death is a fundamental feature of Sinhalese Buddhism in practice.

6

The Ethic of Intention

IN the second chapter were listed the Five Precepts (*pan sil*), the Ten Good Deeds (*dasa kusala karma*) and the Noble Eight-fold Path (*ārya aṣṭāngika mārgaya*), three different ways of formulating the conduct expected of a Buddhist. How do these three formulations relate to one another? The first one which a westerner usually comes across is the Noble Eight-fold Path, for it is one of the Four Noble Truths and occurs in the Buddha's first sermon; but when a villager is asked about *karmaya* he will rarely volunteer information on the Eight-fold Path, and it is comparatively little known. The reader will recall that its eight factors have been grouped from the beginning into morality (*sīla*), concentration (*samādhi*) and wisdom (*paññā*). Although the impediments to lay meditation are practical, not doctrinal, they are, or are considered to be, so great that very few laymen in traditional Ceylon meditate before old age. Meditation and its peculiar prize, *nirvāṇa*, will concern us in the next chapter; they are the sphere of what Weber called virtuoso religion. The religious concerns of the normal Buddhist layman are centred on morality and merit-making (*pinkam*), which aim at a good rebirth, but rebirth none the less. To see the merit-making and meditation as a clear dichotomy, as has been done in sociological works, I do not find satisfactory in terms of doctrine or of analysis, but as a principle of arrangement it is convenient: this chapter will be concerned principally with merit-making.

The ways in which merit can be made are listed as the Ten Good Deeds. We notice immediately that the third of them is *bhāvanā*, meditation, which shows the difficulty of dichotomizing between merit-making and meditation if we are to use the Buddhists' own terms. The second of them is morality; so what is the relation of morality to merit-making? By *sīla* is meant the Five Precepts, which should be called the five abstentions, and these are negative. They are undertakings to abstain from killing, stealing, sexual misconduct, lying, and drinking intoxicants. From the point of view of the individual, to keep to these undertakings is a sufficient basis, as expressed in the Eightfold Path, for meditation and for the wisdom which attains *nirvāṇa*. Cognitively they are quite sufficient—but affectively perhaps they suffice only for the virtuoso, if even for him. A negative formulation sounds too cold-blooded and requires some supplement. The supplement can come from other canonical formulations, such as the four holy states (*brahmavihāra*) of loving-kindness (*mettā*), compassion (*karuṇā*), sympathetic joy (*muditā*), and equanimity (*upekkhā*); or simply from such an inclusive list as the Ten Good Deeds, which present a Buddhist's ideal behaviour—I hesitate to use the word 'duty' in the context of Buddhism, which says 'take it or leave it'—in a positive form. Moreover, the Five Precepts seem to concern a man in isolation; this is all very well for the virtuoso or the recluse, but an ordinary layman misses in them any allusion to such things as his interaction with the Sangha, which is his contact with organized religion. A final shortcoming of the Five Precepts from a practical point of view is that it is virtually impossible to keep to them, so if there is no easier goal the outlook becomes depressing. The Ten Good Deeds make the Five Precepts but one item in a list; if you fail to abstain from all sin you can at least compensate yourself by doing good in other directions. Weber called the Five Precepts an 'insufficiency ethic for the weak'.[1] It is quite true that Buddhism recognizes different stages of development, at which a man can legitimately make different demands of himself. These different levels of demand were summarized in Chapter 2. A monk has to do more than keep the Five Precepts; put in general terms, meditation and wisdom are necessary to attain the highest goal, but are expected of only a few people. Yet to call the Five Precepts an 'insufficiency' ethic seems to indicate a judge-

[1]Max Weber, *The Religion of India*, trans. Gerth and Martindale (Free Press, New York, 1958), p. 215.

ment that they are rather paltry stuff. On the contrary, being absolutes they are extraordinarily demanding. I am not alluding merely to the fact that nearly everyone lies. Even the first precept, not to take life, is necessarily broken by any agriculturalist, and the Sinhalese villagers are vividly aware of the fact that they are sinners (*pavkārayō*).

If anything deserves the name of an insufficiency ethic—a term I had rather avoid—it is the list of the Ten Good Deeds. To perfect them all is tantamount to attaining *nirvāṇa*, but at least one can make measurable progress by positive acts; unlike the black and white of the Five Precepts, they allow of shades of grey.

To sum up, the Five Precepts are negative—to do no evil—while the Ten Good Deeds are positive—to do good. For the Christian the latter is necessary for salvation; for the Buddhist only the former is absolutely required, but both the emotional needs of the individual and the practical needs of society seem better answered by the latter, broader formulation. I speak here only of ethical actions in the sense of actions affecting others, and disregard other recommended behaviour, notably faith (for the Christian) and meditation (for the Buddhist), to both of which I shall return.

Before discussing the substance of Sinhalese Buddhist morality I must draw attention to a critical difference between Buddhist and western moral philosophy. According to generally accepted western ideas an act may be good which is clearly not to one's own advantage: one may sacrifice one's life for another. According to traditional Christian ideas this is only a question of acting in one's own long-term rather than short-term interests, because the virtuous man will be suitably rewarded in Heaven. The prudent man will therefore do good, because it pays; this is called the *prudential* attitude in ethics. Ever since Immanuel Kant many people have considered this attitude somewhat base. Kant held that any act, of whatever apparent goodness, done with thought of reward, in this life or the next, was *ipso facto* not moral; all rewards were on a par with bribes. For Kant and his followers there is thus a fundamental opposition between prudence and true morality. To the Buddhist, however—as perhaps to the traditional Christian—this is a sheer nonsense. Buddhist doctrine agrees with Kant that what counts is intention, not effect. (This will be further discussed below.) *Karma* is nothing more or less than intention (*cētanāva*). But by the law of *karma* every intention good or bad will eventually be rewarded or punished, so prudence and true morality must necessarily coincide.[2]

It is therefore not surprising that prudential arguments in favour of moral conduct have a long and respectable history in Buddhism. When preaching to a lay audience the Buddha listed the five advantages of morality:[3] wealth, good repute, self-confidence in public, an untroubled death, and rebirth in heaven. The disadvantages of immorality are the converse. A mediaeval Sinhalese poet, Vīdāgama Thera, wrote a century of religious stanzas, the *Lōväḍa Saṅgarāva*,[4] which is read in the *daham pāsal*; nearly every one of these stanzas inculcates virtue under the threat of tortures in hell. What is perhaps more surprising is that the prudential attitude is often applied to this life with the mundane air of 'Honesty is the best policy'. I had a conversation with two monks which brought this out clearly. They asked me why I thought one should keep the Five Precepts. When I said that otherwise one would get a bad rebirth they said yes, but what about the results in *this* life? I suggested remorse, but this was impatiently brushed aside. If one breaks the precepts one will go to prison; if one kills a man one is hanged. I protested that for lying one does not go to prison, but one of them pointed out that one does go to prison for perjury, so I failed to make my point. The matter well illustrates the Buddhist belief in meeting the audience on their own level. Not only

[2]The argument of the above paragraph was clarified for me by a discussion with Professor Karl Popper, who is, however, not responsible for my formulation.

[3]*Mahāparinibbāna Sutta*, I, 23–4 (*D.N.*, II, 85–6)

[4]ed. Guṇadāsa Sōmasiri (Bastian Brothers, Colombo, 1955).

did the Buddha, of course, elsewhere produce far more elevated ideas on ethical motivation; I also found later that the monk who spoke on hanging held the pure canonical views on the supremacy of intention and the supreme importance of purifying one's thoughts.

In this chapter I shall concentrate on the first two of the Ten Good Deeds, *dāna* (giving) and *sīla* (morality), which are far the most important for the study of lay ethics. I shall focus on two theoretical problems: the problem of intentionality—whether the doctrine of pure intention is adhered to or is compromised by a utilitarian ethic of works; and the related problem of literalism—whether people pay more regard to the letter or to the spirit of moral precepts. A literalist interpretation of moral rules (pharisaism) is incompatible with an ethic of intention.

Giving comes first in the list of the Ten Good Deeds, and it is easy to guess why. The existence of the Sangha, and hence of Buddhism, depends, in theory at least, on the generosity of the laity. Since the Poḷonnaruva period many temples in Ceylon have owned lands which supply them with food and maybe additional income, but monastic landlordism was not part of the original scheme of things. There are, moreover, still many poor temples where the monks depend wholly or in part on the laity for their food, which is brought to the temple, and every now and again reformist monasteries or individual monks revert to the original practice of begging food from door to door. Beside these circumstances peculiar to Buddhism we may remark that all institutions seem to need cash, and that fund-raising is a prominent feature of all organized religion under the sun.

Here, however, Buddhism faces a difficulty. If generous intention is all that counts (and remember the monk who told me that a poor villager even without giving a cent might earn more merit than he from the *pinkama* on which he had spent 5,000 rupees), why should people give to the Sangha rather than to anyone else? This problem seems to have been acute from the earliest time, for already in the Canon we find the highly ambivalent doctrine of the *suitable recipient*. In the very formula describing the qualities of the Sangha (mentioned above, p. 243) it is described as 'the best field of merit in the world' (*anuttaraṃ puññakkhettaṃ lokassa*), which is to say that a good deed done towards the Sangha (especially a gift given to it) will bear more fruit for the doer than if bestowed elsewhere. In one sermon[5] the Buddha says that of the five timely gifts the most important is the gift given to a virtuous person at the time of the first fruits. In another[6] he says that even scourings thrown into a cesspool gain merit by feeding the creatures there, but gifts to the good are more fruitful (i.e. gain more merit) than gifts to the wicked. This was another question which I investigated in some of my interviews.

The fullest answer given by a monk went thus. There are two kinds of giving (*dan dīma*): that with thought of worship (*pūjābuddhiya*), which is motivated by respect (*gaurava*), and that with thought of favour (*anugrahabuddhiya*), which is motivated by pity (*anukampāva*). The former is exemplified by a gift to the Sangha, the latter by a gift to a beggar. For both, the accompanying thought is all-important (*cētanāva pradhānayi*), but the former is superior, i.e. brings more merit. [When I spoke up for the latter he showed no comprehension.] Merit varies with the virtue of the recipient, but only in so far as that virtue is known to the giver: if the monk practises secret vice this does not diminish the merit of his *dāyakas*. Someone practising the supreme quality of giving (*dāna pāramitāva*) [like Vessantara—see below] gives to everyone, regardless of their virtue; but for the best results one should find out about the recipient beforehand. 'The Buddha commended giving with discrimination' (*Viceyyadānaṃ sugatappasatthaṃ*—which is a Pali quotation).[7]

The other answers on this topic were all in substantial

[5] *A.N., Sutta iii*, 41.

[6] *A.N., Sutta iii*, 57 (vol. I, pp. 160ff).

[7] *Petavatthu*, II, 9, 75. The P.T.S. text has an inferior reading.

agreement with the above. One monk elucidated the point about the virtue of the individual monk. The Sangha is full of good qualities (*guṇasampanna*); when one gives to the Sangha, the virtues of the individual monk who receives the *dānē* do not affect the amount of merit, because he has virtues, as it were, inherited (*paramparāven*) from the Sangha throughout history, and the gift is made not to him, but to the Sangha as a whole. (Strictly speaking, as explained on page 269, a gift (such as a meal) can only be given to the Sangha if received by more than five monks, but in this context this would be considered too subtle a consideration.)

It already looks as if this doctrine of the suitable recipient is compromising the supremacy of intention, and another monk's answer makes this fairly explicit. The merit accruing from liberality depends on the intention, but it does vary according to the recipient: if the recipient has noble qualities (*uśas guṇa*) it increases. There is an analogy with sowing seed on fertile or barren ground. An elephant needs more than an ant, so it must be more meritorious to feed him. [Here I detected another element creeping in: to keep the argument on one track I pointed a choice between feeding an unhungry monk and a hungry beggar.] If one has to choose between an unhungry monk and a hungry beggar one feeds the beggar because of the exigency of the moment, but one gets less merit. Moreover, if with equally good intention one feeds a monk and a beggar, although the thought is the same (*hita eka vunāṭa*) it must be more meritorious to feed the monk.

The anti-utilitarian streak is interesting: one *would* feed the hungry beggar, but it would be less meritorious. The question of which is 'really right' cannot be put; the nearest one might get is to distinguish, as one monk did (see p. 300), between an action from the societal (*samājaya vaśayen*) and the religious (*āgama vaśayen*) point of view.[8] By dwelling on this we must, however,

[8]In commending to me the opinions of Professor Lévi-Strauss, a learned friend has written, 'You would agree, I think, that the Sin-

not forget that no Buddhist denies that one should *also* feed hungry beggars. A monk said that the main purpose (*paramārtha*) of the Sangha is religious progress, so it is best to give to them, but this does not mean that one should not give to the laity: one must help anyone in need; one has a duty to feed the hungry, and gains merit by doing so. In a truly Buddhist society the rich would give to the poor, and all would be well. Two other monks also spoke against social and economic inequality. However, this they seem to consider a question of politics rather than of religion. In the same way, one of them denied that capital punishment was contrary to the precept against taking life. 'That's politics' (*ēka desapālanē*), he said. The failure to apply the ethical standards of religion to politics seems to be universal.

But let us return to intentionality. It has been compromised by the variant of the recipient. The other variant is the size of the gift. Here, too, the evidence is highly ambiguous. In theory Buddhists believe in the widow's mite, but on closer inspection the picture is not so clear. For instance, one monk told me that the amount given is irrelevant, it is the effort that counts. But he went right on to say that a wealthy person like Mrs. Bandaranaike is lucky because she can give a lot, which is clearly inconsistent. Another monk also said that only intention (*cētanāva*) counted. To illustrate this he told me a story from the commentary to the *Dhammapada* about an ascetic who was very poor and so could give the Buddha nothing of value, but did his best, as a reward for which he was reborn in a very wealthy family and could thus give a great deal! Note that this ambivalent tale dates from classical times, so that this too is a dilemma of respectable antiquity.

I suggest that the ethic of intention has taken some blows because it is to some extent counter-intuitive: it

halese distinguish between something and something but that it would not be helpful to translate these somethings as "religion" and "society".' Sinhalese monks please note.

seems obviously better to do good, with whatever motive, than merely to mean well. I would connect this with my remarks above (p. 288) on the relation of the Five Precepts and Noble Eight-fold Path to the Ten Good Deeds. I said that if anything deserves the name of an insufficiency ethic it is the Ten Good Deeds, which offer a positive formulation psychologically more reassuring than the negative absolutes of the Five Precepts. I suggest that the list of Ten Good Deeds, which is post-canonical,[9] is the doctrinal come-back after experience had shown that the doctrine of pure intentionality was not fully accepted in practice. Just as the doctrine of merit transference which I discussed in Chapter 5 was an ingenious legitimation of the practices of those people (i.e. everybody, or nearly everybody) who could not accept a particular consequence of the intentionality doctrine, namely that they could do nothing for their dead relatives, so the Ten Good Deeds, with their blanket coverage of every potentially meritorious action, offer a general, though merely implicit, legitimation for the feeling that an act must surely be better if you have something to show for it. Historically and emotionally, though not logically, this preference for positive *pin* rather than mere abstention is linked to a general preference for a happy personal future existence rather than a 'blowing out' of the personality. Most Hindus have believed since before the time of the Buddha that good works, which they judge largely by effect, result in rebirth in heaven. (This course, the life of the householder, came to be contrasted to the ascetic's renunciation, which leads to his freedom from

[9] My search for the origin of the Ten Good Deeds has not been very successful. They seem not to occur in the Pali Canon. The earliest reference I can find is in a Sanskrit Buddhist text, the *Maṇicūḍāvadāna* (ed. Miss R. Handurukanda, *Sacred Books of the Buddhists*, vol. XXIV, London, 1967, para. 20, p. 26), which its editor says is close in style to another text, the *Divyāvadāna*, which Winternitz dates to the fourth century A.D.; but even there the deeds are not listed, and may be nothing but the opposites of the *dasa akusala karma*, a canonical list of ten bad deeds which is unrelated to ours. Our Ten Good Deeds are prominent in the *Upāsakajanālaṃkāra*, a Pali text composed in Ceylon which its editor dates to the twelfth century.

rebirth.) *Pinkam*, which include abstention from wrong-doing, meditation, and 'right views', but also easier and more specific goals, are thus the practical result of the affective ethics of people who hope that through some combination of good intentions and formally approved actions good works can ensure for them a pleasant rebirth.

But it would be a grave mistake to deduce from the above negative evidence that the ethic of intention receives only service, if that, and has little importance for the Buddhist ethos. English has the proverb, 'The road to hell is paved with good intentions', but I cannot see how to put this into Buddhist Sinhalese. Good intentions pave the road to *nirvāṇa*. Whether you use the Sanskritic word *cētanāva*, as my informants usually did in the religious context, or talk merely of thought (*adahas* or *hita*), it is the mind that counts. A canonical text says[10] that among the seven[11] motives for giving alms those alms bring the best results which are given 'for the decoration and equipment of the mind' (*cittālaṃkāraṃ cittaparikkhāratthaṃ*). Sinhalese speak of purifying the thoughts (*hita suddha kara ganṭa*) or mental progress (*hita diyuṇuva*)—terms which are applied equally to meditation and to other forms of merit-making. I have already mentioned (Chapter 3, p. 139) how the Mīgala incumbent told me that the point of offering flowers to the Buddha was to feel joy (*prītiya*). Professor Arnold Green has been given exactly the same explanation of the *dānē* (which in Chapter 7 I show to be ancient): the point of the *anumōdana*, the short speech which the monk makes on receiving the food, is to fill the donors with joy (*prītiya*), so that they do not think of how much it has cost them, but purify their thoughts and thus make mental/spiritual progress. In the *Dhammapada* commentary story of the two brothers and the sugar-cane, several times cited in Chapter 5, the elder brother, just before

[10] *A.N.*, IV, 60–3.

[11] The lowest motive is with thought of reward in the next life. Other motives which should be superseded include the mere thought, 'Giving is good', and the thought that giving will make one happy (i.e. any hedonistic calculation is not good).

making his successful wish (*prārthanā*) for *nirvāṇa*, is said to have 'his body suffused with joy' (*pītiyā phuṭasarīro*).[12] This religion which is founded on the premiss that the world is sorrow thus attaches great spiritual value, under the right circumstances, to the feeling of joy.

A corollary of these beliefs is the further belief in the *power* of the mind, a power we have already seen in operation with the religious wish (*prārthanā*) and religious resolution (*praṇidhi*). Another theory, which does not logically follow from this but seems to be connected, is the belief in the strength of mental impulse. On this again Professor Arnold Green has interesting information. He was told that someone who left valuables lying all around was as culpable as the thief if they were stolen, for no normal person can reasonably be expected to withstand such temptation. This was never expressed to me in so many words, but may help to explain the extraordinary insistence of the villagers that we keep our house locked. Corroborative evidence is the insistence of the chief monk that it is *natural* for the poor to envy the rich. Green was also told that one should not hesitate over difficult moral choices, but act on impulse. I would connect this value attached to impulsivity with the Buddhist theory of the mind as a rapid series of discrete impulses, not an uninterrupted stream of consciousness as we have thought of it in the West. For this, however, I do not have any evidence.

We must now attempt a discussion of 'morality' (*sīla*) in theory and practice. *Sīla* means the Five Precepts. These are the most obvious principles to examine *qua* Buddhist values: not to take life, steal, commit sexual misconduct, lie, or get drunk. They do not together add up to a whole ethos, because an ethos includes values of greater generality (e.g. kindness) and also contains values not of religious origin (e.g. loyalty) which may not be moral values. These values of secular origin, of which I judge the most important to be honour, lie outside the scope of this

[12] *Dh.A.*, IV, 201.

study, but they are there in the background, as it were; like other peasant societies, the Sinhalese villagers experience shame as well as guilt, and perhaps fear the former more than the latter. With this in mind we investigate the knowledge and practice of the Five Precepts.

The Five Precepts, preceded by the Three Refuges, are taken so frequently that they may be called the functional equivalent of the Lord's Prayer. They are repeated after a monk at the beginning of all *pinkam* and again at odd moments throughout. This raises the question in the mind of a spectator whether their recitation has not lost its meaning. Plainly any religious community anywhere in the world has not always got its mind on the texts it repeats; but how far has this gone? One monk told me that one always had the duty to keep the Five Precepts, whether one recited them or not; but would this be clear to ordinary villagers? I accompanied a group of some sixty villagers from Mīgala on a pilgrimage to climb Adam's Peak. At frequent intervals in our progress we repeated the Five Precepts after a *dasa sil upāsikā*, the person of highest religious status present. On the way back, being tired and impatient, I remarked to someone at a halt for such a recitation that I was not going to join in this time, because my last recitation of the Five Precepts had been so recent that I could not yet have broken them even had I wanted to. My remarks were passed on and discussed, and to my surprise it was soon decided—without any counter-argument—that I was right and another recitation would be pointless. The Five Precepts were not taken again for the rest of the trip.

The only systematic investigation of knowledge and interpretation of the Five Precepts of which I know was conducted by Obeyesekere and his research assistants in a remote Kandyan village. They asked twenty-two adults to recite the Five Precepts (in Pali, of course); all but one were able to do so. The informants who could recite the precepts were then asked for the meaning of each precept. The number who were able to assign meanings to the undertakings they had given in Pali can be tabulated thus:

Number of precepts understood	By how many people
5	5
4	3
3	5
2	0
1	2
0	6
	21

The precepts recited were thus understood about half the time. However, this question turned out to be of limited significance, a test rather of linguistic than of ethical knowledge; for when questioned in a different context everyone knew about the ideas expressed by the Five Precepts, and moreover identified them as Buddhist values. My own unsystematic observations would entirely support these findings; the Five Precepts are almost universally known by rote, and their meanings also are generally known and understood, though the specific meanings of the Pali words are often not known—but this knowledge is on the increase because of *daham pāsal* (Sunday schools) and religious instruction in state schools.

Before considering specific precepts a remark concerning their form may be in place. Obeyesekere has been at pains to stress, in accordance with Buddhist tradition, that the Five Precepts are not commands like the Hebrew 'Thou shalt not', but undertakings in the first person. Cognitively this is indeed a crucial point. Yet even here I doubt whether doctrine matches emotional reality. When monks in sermons allude to the precepts, as they very often do, they express them in the form of negative commands, e.g. 'Do not kill' (*maranṭa epā*). They can answer that strictly they are speaking to their audience, not *translating* the precepts; but I do not think that is the impression that they leave the layman with, and I strongly suspect, though he does not say so, that Obeyesekere elicited from his informants the meanings of the precepts expressed not as undertakings but as prohibitions.

It appears that Obeyesekere's informants have equated

sin (*pav*) with transgression against the letter of a precept. At first sight this looks like subscription to an ethic of works, not of intention; but it turns out that some things were said to be sins but nevertheless 'all right'. To explain this we must take a closer look at his data on the interpretation of the precepts.

The precepts against killing and stealing are unambiguous and their interpretation was not probed. Even a professional hunter said killing was always a sin. The precept against sexual misconduct (*kāmesu micchācāra*) has been variously interpreted in different Buddhist societies, which is quite in keeping with both its letter and its spirit. Everyone asked agreed that adultery was a sin (*pav*), though some said that it was much less sinful if committed with the knowledge of the spouse. Some said that premarital intercourse was a sin, though most of these added that it was not a sin if the parties subsequently married. A few said that adultery in secret was a sin but all right, and the same was said of premarital intercourse. One man, who admitted he was an adulterer, said adultery was a sin but all right. He went on to say of another man that he claimed to be a good Buddhist because he observed the Five Precepts, but he practised anal intercourse with his wife and therefore was observing the letter, but not the spirit —'a "good Buddhist" but a sodomist' (Obeyesekere's report of the statement).

Lying is sin, as it is against the fourth precept. Asked whether they would lie in court to protect a kinsman accused of murder some said that under those circumstances it would not be sin, others that it would be a sin but they would do it. Of the fifth precept against alcohol there was a more flexible interpretation: seven said that to take alcohol was always a sin; seven that it might be taken without sin for medicinal purposes; six that it was not a sin taken in moderation.

As the Pali words of the fifth precept can be taken to mean abstention from strong drinks *which* are the occasion of intoxication and carelessness or *when* they are the occasion for intoxication and carelessness I would not like to say which interpretation of it answers even to the letter of the law, let alone the spirit, so this evidence had best be disregarded. The case of the man who judged anal intercourse permissible according to the letter of the precept, but nevertheless wrong, is to some extent a red herring, because I think he misjudged the case: anal intercourse would come under 'sexual misconduct' no less surely than adultery if (as in the Sinhalese case) society disapproved of the practice. The quotation was worth including because of the insight it gives into how a villager thinks that *other people* interpret the precepts. These two cases apart, the problems raised by the (regrettably sparse) data are what is meant by 'wrong but all right' (said of secret adultery), and what attitude informs 'a sin, but I'll do it' (said of lying to save a kinsman). (In the context I take 'wrong' and 'sin' to be synonyms, as they would be in Sinhalese (*väradi* and *pav*).) The two statements seem to me to have quite different implications. Secret adultery may be all right because one will get away with it, or because 'what the eye doesn't see the heart doesn't grieve over', so nobody is hurt by it. The former reason embodies a prudential attitude taken by someone who does not really believe in *karma*, the latter a utilitarian ethic which judges actions solely in terms of their effects on others. It is rather the latter interpretation which seems to fit the case when premarital intercourse is said to be a sin but all right. The latter interpretation is, moreover, clearly the only one which fits the case of the lie to save a kinsman; here there is clearly added the notion that the morality of an action varies with its context so that literal adherence to moral precepts may not be the most moral course. (I prefer this to talking of 'the ends justifying the means', a phrase which may cover much confusion.) This idea of a higher morality behind the letter of the law is implicit in the whole doctrine of intention, and does not jibe well with the utilitarian ethic which measures an action by its effect on others.

Though killing is always a sin, is it equally bad to kill a man and a louse? After all, both are transmigrating beings who in a few years might change places; on the other hand, a man's life seems intuitively more valuable than that of a louse. As I mentioned in Chapter 4, there is depicted in a local temple a special hell reserved for people who kill lice; but I think you would have to go a long way to find someone who took this seriously. A monk explained the situation to me: the amount of *sin* (*pava*) varies with the intention (*cētanāva*). It is equally bad to kill an elephant or an ant, a good man or a bad, if the intention is the same; there is a different feeling about it in society, because of the different values of the things killed, but from the religious point of view both are the same (*āgama vaśayen dekama ekayi*).

One of the questions I frequently raised in my interviews was the morality of Duṭugämuṇu in making war on the Tamils for the sake of Buddhism. In considering the answers one must bear in mind that in the *Mahāvaṃsa*, where the events are recounted, Duṭugämuṇu is presented as the national hero and his actions are justified, so that to condemn him runs counter to tradition and requires an independent mind. Though the answers varied slightly, their general tenor is well illustrated by the reply of the monk just quoted, who said that Duṭugämuṇu's killing of Tamils was sin, but not great, because his main purpose (*paramārtha*) was not to kill men but to save Buddhism; he did not have full intention to kill. But to say that he will not pay for his sin (*ahosi veyi*) is wrong. This last point I have discussed in the previous chapter. The rest of the answer, which here concerns us, seems clearly to bring out two points already evident in Obeyesekere's village material. On the one hand killing is always, intrinsically, *pav*. On the other hand, what really counts is the intention; Duṭugämuṇu's intention was good, so his sin was 'less' (*pav aḍuyi*). This latter opinion can also be expressed by saying that his main purpose (*paramārtha*) was good. One monk actually quoted the *Mahāvaṃsa* to the effect that Duṭugämuṇu was told by *arhats* that it was right for him to fight the war; he *thought* (the monk said) that because of his ultimate purpose he was in the right, though the speaker disagreed with him. However, it is the intention that counts: what Duṭugämuṇu had in mind was not killing men, but the raising of religion (*āgama näga hiṭa vīma*).

This monk was the only one to say that in his opinion Duṭugämuṇu was wrong. Only two monks on the other hand went so far as to say that he did *not* sin. Most extreme in expression was the monk who said that Duṭugämuṇu did not sin in killing the Tamils, as they had wrong views (*mithyā dṛṣṭi*) [i.e. were not Buddhists]. It is always wrong to kill good people (*sīlavanta aya*), but not wrong to kill in order to save religion; killing in self-defence is also problematic. Though this sounds rather ferocious I should add that this monk seemed a kindly old person who went on to say that one must do one's best to spread loving-kindness (*maitrī paturuvanṭa*): he was, however, exceptionally unsophisticated. The other monk to say that Duṭugämuṇu did not sin brought the subject up spontaneously; though killing is a sin, he said, if Buddhism is in danger it is no sin to kill in its defence—as did Duṭugämuṇu.

This last answer exemplifies the ambiguity of the situation. Killing is *pav*—but sometimes it is not. Plainly the word is being used in two different ways; and these two ways correspond to the formalistic ethic of effect and the ethic of intention. According to doctrine it is only the ultimate purpose which counts, so that the intention must be the yardstick by which to measure right and wrong; but the word *pav* has come also—perhaps primarily—to mean 'sin' in the sense of transgression against the letter of the Five Precepts. The answers of my informants who merely said that Duṭugämuṇu did 'sin' do not therefore reveal whether the speaker thinks Duṭugämuṇu was right or wrong to act as he did. At the time I did not fully realize the ambiguity of the term '*pav*', so I did not probe more deeply, but to do so would have been very difficult because the double meaning of *pav* is not explicitly realized by the monks. In fact I think that they would have split about evenly for and against Duṭugämuṇu; but the results would have been tendentious, in that without my asking them they would never have considered the matter so deeply. (On the danger of 'pistol point' answers see Introduction, p. 44.)

Should any distinction between 'sin' and doing wrong seem too abstruse an extrapolation from the evidence, perhaps it will appear justified when we turn from the negative to the positive side of ethics. Here the accepted English translations of Buddhist terminology already seem to acknowledge a distinction between formalistic and intentional ethics, for *pin*, which is undeniably the exact opposite of *pav*, is translated not 'right' or 'good', but 'merit', and *pinkama*, or its equivalents in Sanskrit and Pali, is translated 'merit-making'. I contend that 'merit-making' has formalistic connotations which are in many circumstances quite correct; sometimes, however, the translation is unnecessarily pejorative and 'doing good' or 'doing right' would be more apt. Again, according to theory it is only 'doing good'—the pure intention—which counts; but in practice the performance of certain prescribed acts seems often to be held—in Buddhism as in other religions—sufficient to ensure rewards.

In the absence of statistical evidence for Ceylon and indeed of comparative data it would be invidious to attempt an assessment of the extent to which the Five Precepts are observed. Robert Knox, who lived about 20 miles from Mīgala in much the same cultural area, gave a character of his fellow-villagers which strikes me as quite up-to-date and applicable to my own experiences. He is so impressed by their mendacity that he makes three references to it within a couple of pages: 'For they make no account or conscience of lying, neither is it any shame or disgrace to them, if they be catched in telling lyes: it is so customary';[13] later qualified by '... approving lying in themselves, but misliking it in others'.[14] On the other hand 'Of all vices they are least addicted to stealing, the which they do exceedingly hate and abhor; so that there are but few robberies committed

[13]Knox, op. cit, pp. 101–2 (folio p. 64).
[14]Ibid., p. 103 (folio p. 65).

among them. They do much extol and commend Chastity, Temperance, and Truth in words and actions; and confess that it is out of weakness and infirmity, that they cannot practice the same, acknowledging that the contrary Vices are to be abhorred, being abomination both in the sight of God and Men. They do love and delight in those Men that are most Devout and Precise in their Matters. As for bearing Witness for Confirmation in any matters of doubt, a Christians word will be believed and credited far beyond their own: because, they think, they make more Conscience of their words.'[15]

The difficulty is, of course, that neither Knox nor I have been similarly exposed to other peasant societies for comparison. I did not have the impression that killing, stealing, sex crimes, or drunkenness were more prevalent than in any other community with which I am acquainted. Statistics do of course exist for serious crimes such as homicide, but these can only constitute a tiny part of the percentage of infringements of the precepts. The homicide rate in Ceylon is notoriously high, but it varies so much between different parts of the island (being quite low in the Central Province) that even this is not a sound basis for generalized judgements. Theft is very much feared by the villagers, as may be the case in all peasant communities; we were constantly being advised to lock up all our possessions, and thieves were spoken of with much vehemence and express disgust. The proximity of Buddhist institutions has no deterrent influence on thieves. One must enter a Buddhist temple barefoot, leaving one's shoes at the entrance; it is notoriously risky to leave shoes unguarded at the entrance to the Temple of the Tooth in Kandy. My own sandals —far too large, one would think, for Sinhalese feet—were abstracted from the entrance to a village temple during a *pinkama*; after a fruitless search the horror-stricken incumbent confessed to me that he himself had had a pair of new sandals stolen the previous week from his very bedroom in the *pansala*. I had the impression that sex crimes were

[15]Ibid., pp. 102–3 (folio p. 64)

infrequent; on the other hand Obeyesekere reported from his remote (and *ipso facto* untypical) village that nearly all the adult males there had committed adultery when opportunity arose. (We already saw that adultery was not very seriously considered by some members of the community). Drunkenness seems no commoner than in rural England, probably less.

But it will be thought that in one respect the conduct of Sinhalese Buddhists must differ very sharply from that of westerners: in the killing of animals. There is a prevalent misconception in the West that Buddhists are vegetarians. Yet there is no Buddhist country of which this is true on the societal level: vegetarianism is a minority practice freely chosen by individuals, both cleric and lay, much like abstention from alcohol in the West. The Buddha did not forbid meat-eating. In the *Vinaya* rules monks are forbidden ten kinds of meat, ranging from human flesh to lizards, but none of the creatures normally consumed are mentioned. The only rule is that a monk may not eat an animal killed specially for him; but if it is already dead, he may as well eat it. The Buddha himself is reported as eating meat, and it seems that his last meal was pork.

The result of this tradition is that villagers, especially in isolated communities, may occasionally boycott butchers' shops, so that no cattle or goats can be killed in the area; in this way they are directly saving lives. I believe that such boycotts tend to be organized by monks. Mere abstention from meat is, however, considered useless. Nor must one exaggerate even the reluctance to kill animals. To be a butcher is considered wrong for a Buddhist, and most of the butchers in Ceylon are indeed Muslims. Villagers in my area raised goats which in due course they sold to Muslims. That the Muslims happened to be butchers who then killed the animals they could regard as not their fault; on the other hand I encountered reluctance to admit to the situation and was told that the goats were raised as pets. Once again *pav* seems to be the literal transgression of the precept, but this interpretation does not satisfy the conscience. In remoter areas villagers go hunting, and I am sure they make no secret of it. As they themselves would say, they are forced to it by poverty; the extra twist which they give is that their poverty is due to sin in previous lives, so previous sin produces conditions for further sin, and they are caught in a vicious circle from which only the exceptional person is likely to escape.

Vegetarianism I found universally admired, but rarely practised. There are, moreover, degrees of vegetarianism. It is worse to eat beef than other meat (which in practice means chicken or goatmeat), worse to eat meat or fowl (*goḍa mas*) than fish (*diya mas*); eggs seem to be worse than fish, but not as bad as meat. A true Buddhist vegetarian eats no eggs; even educated people think that all eggs are fertilized, and when I tried to tell people that a hen could lay without prior assistance from a cockerel, I was never believed, but probably considered crazy. To break an egg is to take life, which means that in one way eggs are worse than any meat, because the 'killing' is committed on the spot by the cook. Bareau reports that eggs are not used in monastery kitchens; for similar reasons middle-class urban Buddhists tend to buy 'Buddhist eggs', which are already cracked. The hierarchy of value of meats appears to me to relate to the size, value, and apparent closeness to humanity of the animal slain, eggs counting roughly as chickens. This may also be part of the original reason for the special disfavour of beef-eating. In terms of immediate history this attitude is due to cultural contact with the Hindus; in 1815 the British found that among the Kandyans beef-eating was tabu, as it still is among orthodox Hindus. (This does not mean that either in Ceylon or in India beef was never eaten by poor and remote villagers.) Taking a longer historical view, the Hindu tabu on beef-eating owes something to Buddhist influence, for the Buddha drew attention to the plight of the cow when beef-eating seems to have been general. Explanations given by Buddhists for the dislike of beef-eating, where forthcoming, tend to be a mixture of the economic (buffaloes are useful) and the moral (cows give us milk, so we should not be so ungrateful as to kill them). (Goat milk is rarely drunk.) I have even heard the psychological argument that cows, in that they give us milk, are like our mothers. Villagers are well aware, however, that Buddhists may eat beef but Hindus may not; a lady told me that before visiting a Hindu temple to Kataragama one had to abstain from beef for a week, and ingeniously explained this by saying that Kataragama would be angry because a bull (Nandin) is his father's (Śiva's) mount.

In killing smaller animals Buddhist villagers seem to behave much the same as other villagers the world over, and they do not display the compunction or squeamishness sometimes found in the urban middle class. I came upon a monk who with the help of the young temple servant (*äbittayā*) was clearing out a storeroom. A cockroach ran out. 'Kill it' (*maranṭa*) he shouted. The boy, however, who was piously minded, swept it over a small precipice and thus saved its life. Monks will also slap at insects in a way scandalous to pious Hindus. Not that they would ever deny this to be a sin—they just don't care that much. The one animal which villagers have great compunction about killing is a cobra; as mentioned in Chapter 4, there is a belief that the cobra is an animal of special worth and dignity, and to injure one is considered unlucky.

We are now in a position to hazard some remarks on ethos, or at least on religiously inspired moral values. Ethos I take to be something on the affective level—sincerely held high-level values, whatever the *fable convenue*. Frequent failure to live up to an expressed ideal may make us suspicious whether that ideal represents an affective value, but is not conclusive: discrepancy between theory and practice may result simply because the ideal is so difficult. Truth I would hardly describe as a *major* value in fact—affectively—however much lip service is paid to it. The very frequency in villagers' conversation of the sentence 'Boru kiyanṭa hon̆da nǟ' ('Lying is bad'), usually uttered with a light intonation in the context either of mild accusation of a third party or of protestation of one's own sincerity (compare the English, 'To be perfectly frank...', which regularly precedes a lie), may be offered as evidence for the frequency of lying; while its tone suggests that the offence is not really considered heinous. Lying is bound to be frequent in a culture much concerned with the preservation of status (*tattvaya*) and dignity (*nambuva*)—saving face; the most trivial matter which might in any way appear discreditable to the speaker is concealed almost as a matter of course. Finally, although *religious* truth, the Dharma, is of course a matter of paramount importance, the idea of truth as an autonomous secular value, the truth which scholars seek or are supposed to seek, has no firm base in village society. The *Kalama Sutta* enjoins each man to seek the truth for himself, but here too the reference is to *religious* truth conducive to salvation, not to truth as an absolute value, and the passage is remarkable rather as a charter for tolerance and individualism—but in any case the *Kalama Sutta* and similar texts are not generally known to villagers. Truth is a value, certainly, in so far as *telling* the truth is enjoined by the fourth precept, and *seeking* the truth of a particular kind is an important aspect of meditation; but where truth comes into conflict with more important values—honour, loyalty, kindness—it can be lightly discarded.

Piety receives less lip service than truth, but affectively I would judge it to receive about equal weight: not a major value, but definitely admired. It is conceived as a character trait rather than as an attribute of a particular speech or action. The adjective used is *bhaktimanta*, derived from *bhakti*, 'religious devotion', the key concept of Indian devotional religion; besides *bhaktiya* the noun *sardhāva* (see p. 69) is used in a closely allied sense. Both nouns refer to the kind of faith, of loving trust, which is recommended by theistic religions, for all that according to some authorities this is supposed not to exist in Theravāda Buddhism. The sentiment in Sinhalese Buddhists is certainly a mild one compared to, for instance, the ecstasies of their Śaivite neighbours, and its focus is rather diffuse: the devotion and trust are chiefly directed towards the Buddha, but may include other religious characters such as the great disciples or good Buddhist gods like Vishnu, venerable objects such as Bo trees or books of scripture, or even particular monks. Though such veneration is accounted for in rational terms, as discussed in earlier chapters, the religious feeling shown by some pious laity—the sort of people who at funerals are accorded the title of *upāsaka* whether or not they took the Ten Precepts—goes beyond what reason or doctrine would warrant. Nevertheless, no one would *admit* to going beyond reason, in contrast to the Christian, whose faith beyond reason is specifically commended.

Christianity speaks about three cardinal virtues: faith, hope, and charity. Buddhists have no similar list of virtues in common use, but—in keeping with the tendency to negative expression—they have a very commonly used list of three vices. These are *lobha* (or *rāga*), *dosa*, and *moha*, commonly translated as greed (or passion), hatred, and delusion. One monk translated them into Sinhalese as *āsāva, taraha*, and *mōḍakama*, which are naturally translated as desire, anger, and stupidity. Of these three there is no doubt that the most cited and the most abhorred is desire. When a neighbour wanted to convey to me his disgust for another man he said he was *lōbayi* (greedy); there is no other single word which carries such a weight of moral disapprobation. When our chief monk heard that some men had gone out ploughing on Wesak—a day of all days on which one should avoid killing even worms—he got really angry. I suggested that it was just stupidity. No, it was desire (*āsāva*). Remember also the peculiar horror (noted by Knox) of stealing. Though the accusation of *lōba* on the lips of poor villagers often contains more than a modicum of jealousy, the coincidence with the second Noble Truth—that desire is the root of all evil—is striking. In practice Knox found the Kandyans 'near and covetous',[16] which he seems also to have been himself; and certainly it is hard for the poor not to care. Nevertheless I make bold to say that freedom from attachment to worldly goods is a true Buddhist value.

[16]Knox, op. cit., p. 102 (folio p. 64).

The question of anger is more complex. A harsh, irritable, or aggressive person is characterized as *särayi*. Like *boru*, the word *sära* is very frequently and lightly used. It may even carry a connotation of approval, like the English word 'tough'. This approval even became explicit in one interview: a monk told me that though one should generally be *śānta dānta* (mild and restrained—see below) there are times when threatening (*tarjana karaṇaya*) is necessary and one has to be tough (*särayi*)—though one should never carry this beyond words. This limitation is important: violence is certainly condemned; even the censorious Knox wrote, 'They are not very malitious one towards another; and their anger doth not last long; seldom or never any blood shed among them in their quarrels. It is not customary to strike; and it is very rare that they give a blow so much as to their Slaves;...[17] Moreover, the most highly esteemed form of human activity, meditation, is passive (however strenuous) rather than active. Passivity in the West carries rather negative connotations which it certainly does not possess in Sinhalese society, and children are brought up to behave even more passively than long physical dependence on the mother might warrant. Yet inborn human aggression cannot vanish without trace. Compared to western children, Sinhalese village children fight and hit each other far less; but in playing with smaller children or western children (mine), when it is doubly tabu to hit, they give them potential weapons such as sticks and stones and court attack; when duly attacked they then sometimes go and complain to authority. Such complaint of course provides vicarious satisfaction of aggressive impulses, also common in the West; but it is by no means always resorted to, and the courting of attack by others is clearly masochistic. This masochism seems to me to find expression in the gruesome scenes depicted in many temples. Not only are paintings of tortures in hell fairly common; a couple of famous temples have permanent exhibitions in sculpted tableaux of old-time Sinhalese tortures,

[17]Knox, op. cit., p. 102 (folio p. 64).

and these are visited by tourists from all over the country. One such torture shown in three-dimensional lurid colour is the impalement of a man on a sharp pole which enters the anus and comes out at the chest. The flimsy pretext for these displays, which are highly profitable, is that they illustrate the perils of wrong-doing. What chiefly distinguishes them, to my mind, from their western equivalents such as Madame Tussaud's Chamber of Horrors, is that in the West the audience is generally supposed to identify with the executioners who are giving the victims 'their just deserts', whereas the Buddhist shows explicitly identify the spectator—you miserable sinner—with the sufferer in hell or on the stake. The spectator's psychology need not comply with this prescription, but my own conclusion (which might be empirically tested by a researcher with a strong stomach) is that these horrible spectacles are outlets for suppressed aggression, but primarily in masochistic rather than sadistic form.[18] Aggression, in particular physical violence, is thus strongly condemned in Sinhalese society, and its absence is a high-ranking Buddhist value.

The word *mōḍa* means 'foolish' or 'stupid' and carries about the weight of the latter. The Indian cultural tradition, very alien to the western Christian, strongly associates intelligence with virtue. The highest of the three stages of ideal Buddhist conduct is *paññā*, wisdom, and this is given a fairly intellectualist interpretation in Sinhalese tradition: study of the *abhidharma* is these days generally considered the highest-level prerequisite for Enlightenment (see *vipassanā* meditation in the next chapter). Education and learning, however formalistically conceived, are thus not merely technical accomplishments but morally positive. In condemning a monk who was in fact disreputable for quite different reasons a man dismissed him as *ugat madi*, 'insufficiently learned'. Learning, too, is a Sinhalese Buddhist value.

[18]On the other hand, gruesome depictions of hell were probably just as common in mediaeval European churches; coming from a culture which in this respect has become more squeamish, I may be overreacting to a sight which natives take lightly.

I listened to people's judgements on their fellow men, and in particular to funeral orations. The two main values expressed seem to be kindness, especially as expressed in liberality, and above all moderation. There is no doubt that the most frequent phrase used to convey approbation of someone is *śānta dānta*, nor is there any doubt that this is a pure Buddhist value. *Śānta dānta* are two Sanskrit past participles for the roots *śam* 'to appease' and *dam* 'to tame'; together they express quiet self-control. Appeasement of the passions, taming of the senses—these were the Buddha's constant themes. The oldest and the most famous books of Buddhist religious poetry, the *Dhammapada* and the *Sutta-nipāta*, repeat these phrases and their synonyms so often that at times they seem to consist of little else. *Śānta dānta* continually occurs at every level of conversation. It is also a value in politics. Our village neighbours, who were supporters of the U.N.P., whose party colour is green, taught their children to sing,

> *Apē pāṭa koḷa, api nä kalabola.*
> Our colour is green, we are not rowdies.

The standard criticism of the other side which we heard from U.N.P. supporters was that they scolded too much (*baninavā väḍi*). The *śānta dānta* man (as they all conceived themselves to be) keeps a civil tongue in his head. *Śānta dānta* is non-aggressive (*sära nä*), but also something more. He is polite, in the fullest sense.

The other word most frequently used in praise of someone is *karuṇāvanta*, 'kind', 'compassionate'. This, too, is a truly traditional Buddhist value. I mentioned above the four holy states (*brahmavihāra*) in the Canon, of which this is one. Though scholastically *karuṇā* is differentiated from *maitrī* (loving-kindness) in that *karuṇā* applies only to people in misfortune, in Sinhalese *karuṇāvanta* governs both meanings, like English 'kind'; nor is it an accident that the most popular meditation among monks seems to be the meditation on kindness (*maitrī bhāvanāva*), in which one is supposed to suffuse the world with one's kind thoughts.

The clearest mark of kindness is generosity, and no one with any experience of Sinhalese villagers will demur at my saying that to westerners their generosity borders on the incredible. There are of course two sides to this, as I have already indicated: giving has become institutionalized to a high degree, not only as a means of making merit, but in more obvious forms of exchange and purely social relationships. A westerner is also struck by the preference, explained above, for giving to a wealthy temple rather than to a poor layman. Nevertheless sheer generosity of both goods and effort (known in a formal context as *śramadāna*) is abundant, and disregards the letter for the spirit. Westerners are not favourably impressed by the famous *Jātaka* story of King Vessantara. This was the last birth of the Bodhisattva before he became Gotama Buddha, and he was to achieve in it the supreme quality of liberality (*dāna pāramitāva*). To this end he gave away everything, even his wife and children. This strikes us as excessive. It strikes the Sinhalese in the same way. The two monks with whom I brought up the subject both said that Vessantara was *wrong*. Generosity is very well, but even there one must exercise moderation.

Is there then any difference between the ethos of Sinhalese Buddhists and that of other civilized communities? The moderation and self-restraint of *śānta dānta* are perhaps not very far from the Greek καλὸς κἀγαθός, with his μηδὲν ἄγαν and σωφροσύνη, or from the English gentleman ideal. But when we consider the three cardinal virtues of Christianity we come to a startling contrast. Faith we discussed above; the Christian ideal of faith beyond reason is certainly not a Buddhist virtue, and might even be considered a vice. What about hope? There is no Sinhalese word for hope. There are words for expectation, but none for the mixture of expectation with longing which we mean by 'hope,[19] The Sanskrit word usually translated 'hope' is *āśā*,

[19]Neither faith nor hope is listed in the index of Tachibana's book on Buddhist ethics, which is based on Pali materials (S. Tachibana, *The Ethics of Buddhism*, O.U.P., London, 1926). The narrow theo-

the very word that in Sinhalese is most commonly used for desire! In so far as hope is desire, it is the supreme Buddhist vice! Only charity—*karuṇāva/maitrī*—is a Buddhist value and that indeed is all-important.

logical meaning of Christian hope as confidence in God's goodness is, of course, inappropriate in a Buddhist context.

7

The Monastic Ideal and the Decline of Buddhism

ANY of the Ten Good Deeds may be performed by anyone, monk or layman. However, two of them, teaching (*desanā*) (which includes preaching (*baṇa*)) and meditation (*bhāvanā*), are more typical of monks; laymen may do either, but traditionally laymen only teach or preach when monks are unavailable, and they generally preach merely by reading or reciting the scriptures. I came across cases where monks through infirmity or laziness delegated their preaching duties to lay *upāsakas*, but this is not standard practice. Similarly, meditation is recommended for all, but it is recognized that in practice laymen will lack the necessary time and tranquillity. On *poya* days laymen who take the Eight Precepts are expected to meditate, and the principal goal of retirement late in life as a *dasa sil upāsaka* or *upāsikā* is also meditation. As the Eight Precepts are usually taken communally by a group of people up at the temple there is probably not much opportunity for meditation then; but as meditation is virtually the sole purpose of taking the Ten Precepts I have little doubt that *dasa sil upāsakas* meditate, probably more than most monks.

It is sometimes assumed that meditation is the ideal for monks, more active religiosity for laymen; but this is a misconception. Given that everyone should meditate if possible, both laity and clergy are in this respect divided into two groups of unequal size. Just as laymen are in practice divided into the small minority of meditating *upāsakas* and the large majority of people who do not meditate, so monks are divided into two categories with the primary duties of teaching and of meditation, and the former group is many times the size of the latter. Those who are primarily supposed to teach are called *granthadhura* (Pali: *ganthadhura*) (literally 'having books as their burden'), and the others are called *vidarśanadhura* (Pali: *vipassanādhura*) (literally 'having meditation as their burden'). These categories are first found in the commentaries, and the distinction probably does not antedate the Christian era.[1] In theory all are supposed to do some meditation, just as all are supposed to preach if requested, but what is theoretically a mere emphasis tends in practice to become an absolute distinction. There is another traditional distinction which might be supposed to correspond to that between *granthadhura* and *vidarśanadhura*, namely the distinction between village-dwelling (*grāmavāsin*) and forest-dwelling (*āraññavāsin* or *vanavāsin*) monks; however, the categories do not in fact correspond at all. The former division is still taken to mean what it says, while the latter dichotomy has for the most part lapsed into meaningless scholasticism. There are still a few monks who live in forests, while most monks live in villages (or towns), but village dwellers are often called *āraññavāsin*. The theory is that in the Siyam Nikāya, Malvatta monks are *grāmavāsin* and Asgiri monks are *āraññavāsin*. This ascription dates from the re-establishment in 1753 of these two monasteries and the branches (*pārśva*) they head; it continues the tradition of a dichotomy formalized by Parākramabāhu I when he unified the Sangha.[2] In fact, however, all Asgiri monks (so far as I know) live in villages just like Malvatta monks. At least within the Siyam Nikāya the status of *āraññavāsin* has thus become meaningless and is not really a matter of choice. On the other hand whether a monk is *granthadhura* or *vidarśanadhura* is largely a matter of individual choice, and I met a monk who was *vidarśanadhura* (= *bhāvanāmārgaya*) though living in a village as an ordinary parish monk. In theory monks are supposed to go through both stages, passing from book-learning to meditation, but this happens only in exceptional cases. The

[1]Rahula, *History*, pp. 159–60.

[2]Groups of monks are referred to as 'village-dwelling' and 'forest-dwelling' much earlier, without the implication of a formal organizational rift. See Rahula, *History*, p. 196.

meditating village-dwelling monk had entered the Sangha as an adult and had not received a monastic education; these circumstances, though unusual, are catered for in both theory and practice, and such a monk is not expected to undertake the *granthadhura*.

There is a conventional tripartite division of Buddhism into learning (*paryāpti*), practice (*pratipatti*) and realization (*prativedanā*). Each part is higher than the preceding but also depends upon them. *Paryāpti* means the preservation of the scriptures; though this is a lowly thing, it is the basis for everything higher, and thus indispensable. *Granthadhura* monks are the vehicle for *paryāpti*; their function is to hand on the doctrines by teaching other monks and preaching to the laity. (That they are also supposed to practise what they preach (*pratipatti*) and strive towards Enlightenment (*prativedanā*) goes without saying.) Some western authors have given the impression that Theravāda presents the 'selfish' ideal of attaining one's own Enlightenment and that a monk has no duty but to strive for his Enlightenment; according to them it would therefore be anomalous to speak of a monk's 'function'. Whatever happens in practice, they are right to the extent that a monk is not traditionally conceived as having pastoral duties towards the laity as individuals under his care; but monks—or at least most of them—do nevertheless have the function, formalized as *granthadhura*, of preserving religious tradition. It is with this same context in mind, incidentally, that *suti*, listening to religious teaching, is listed as one of the Ten Good Deeds.

I was interested in finding out the extent to which monks actually do teach and preach, at least in a formal context. The role of the village monk as a teacher of the next generation of monks has largely been superseded by monastic schools, the *piriveṇas*. Out of thirty-five monks I questioned on this point, only eight had received their education entirely from their teachers, i.e. the monks who gave them the lower ordination; the rest had attended a *piriveṇa*, all but one of them for more than a year, typically for the several years between entry into the

Order and the higher ordination (*upasampadā*) at the age of twenty or twenty-one. (I disregard any lay education received before entering the Order—this never amounted to more than a few years at the village school.) Most of the nine monks who had been educated entirely or nearly so by their own teachers were elderly monks of the Siyam Nikāya, but one was in the Amarapura Nikāya, nor does the practice seem to be entirely dead: one young monk, not interviewed and so not included in the above figures, whose higher ordination ceremony I attended, had been educated in his own monastery by a monk who had sent his previous three pupils to *piriveṇas*. The *piriveṇas* are new but not untraditional institutions, being modelled on monastic schools and universities of ancient times. The two most important (and two of the oldest) of the present *piriveṇas* are Vidyodaya and Vidyālaṃkara, founded in 1873 and 1875 respectively in suburbs of Colombo. These now differ somewhat from the run of *piriveṇas* in that they are devoted to higher education and have become largely secularized; though popularly known as 'Buddhist universities' they have no official religious affiliation and have for some years admitted laymen, and in 1966 Vidyodaya started admitting girls as well. A few of my informants had gone on to these universities (none had been to the purely secular University of Ceylon); the *piriveṇas* most of them had attended could, however, more aptly be described as monastic schools or colleges than as universities. Such *piriveṇas* have proliferated only in the last fifty years; before that education with the teacher had been the norm for several centuries, but it is now too late to catch more than the remnant of the last generation to be generally so educated. Monastic education has now become more standardized, and there can be little doubt that the general level has risen. One of the monks educated by his teacher made the unique admission (unique in frankness, not necessarily in ignorance) that he knew no Pali, and a couple of the others said they knew very little indeed; none of them had more than perhaps a smattering of Sanskrit. On the other hand all pupils at *piriveṇas* are taught Sanskrit and Pali and consequently say that they know them; of course I could not test the content of their knowledge, but at least a certain expectation of learning has become normal. Monks usually take a paternal interest (as the Buddha recommended)[3] in their pupils, and finance their education at *pirivenas*, or get the parents to pay half. When their education is complete most monks return to their villages; the rest for the most part become teachers, either at a *pirivena* or at a lay school, where they teach Buddhism and other subjects. The role of a monk as a teacher has thus not disappeared, but has changed with the times and become more specialized; monks who teach usually do so professionally, on the same terms (including salary) as lay school and university teachers.

Religious education is, however, not confined to *pirivenas* and ordinary lay schools: mention has already been made (see especially Chapter 3, p. 98) of the *daham pāsal* or 'Buddhist Sunday schools'. These are usually headed and organized by local monks, though the monks do not necessarily teach in them. Of the thirty-six villages for which I have data eleven had such *daham pāsal* (one had two); in another nine the monks said that there had been a *daham pāsala* which was now defunct, usually for lack of a teacher. These figures show, however, that many monks, even among the *granthadhura*, neither personally educate their own pupils nor teach in an institution, and so probably do not teach at all.

It is widely believed by westernized people in Ceylon that monks preach every *poya* day, just as the Christian clergy preach every Sunday. There is to my knowledge no good historical or doctrinal basis for this belief, and my investigations showed it to be ill-founded. During the ten months in which I was at Mīgala the resident monks never preached on *poya* days,[4] though on the most important full-moon *poya* days they arranged for other monks

[3] *Vin.*, I, 45 (cited in Tachibana, p. 140).

[4] They did preach on the more private occasions listed on the next page.

to come and preach. The amount of preaching in other villages I could not establish with accuracy, because once I asked about it there was a feeling that there *ought* to be preaching and so its actual occurrence was probably exaggerated. An indirect, though equally uncertain, way of estimating such preaching is to ask about *aṭa sil upāsakas* on *poya* days, as a monk would be very unlikely to preach unless there were several such *upāsakas* present, who would be his principal audience. Data given me on both preaching and attendance of *aṭa sil upāsakas* varied a great deal from village to village, a variation which my own observation confirmed. However, a survey of my data suggests that the average monk preaches at his temple on full-moon *poyas* and a few other big occasions, such as some opening ceremony, in all maybe fifteen to twenty times a year; the more conscientious monks preach also on the no-moon (*māsa*) *poyas*; and a few preach twice on the fortnightly *poyas*, or even preach every *poya* (two cases recorded), maybe twice (one case recorded). Those who preach frequently tend also to be in demand at other temples; our temple was visited at Wesak by three monks from the area, all of whom had several engagements to preach that day. On these festivals a large part of the village would attend to hear preaching, especially the sermons after nightfall; but normally the audience was more or less confined to the *upāsakas* taking the Eight Precepts at the temple. These varied in number from about a hundred at Wesak in temples with a large catchment area (such as mine), to a couple or even none on half-moon *poyas*; on a full-moon *poya* the average temple in the area probably has forty or fifty people taking the Eight Precepts, and about half that number on the *māsa poya*. Most of these are old people, especially women, who outnumber men taking *aṭa sil* by at least four to one; there are also a few school children, which I believe to be a modern development. Very few people indeed take the Eight Precepts between the ages of twenty and fifty, except perhaps at Wesak.

The above figures on preaching do not include *pirit*, which though technically a form of *baṇa* is in a class by itself, and is so irregular in its occurrence that any small-scale statistics would be worthless. Nor does it include the essentially private preaching which accompanies *dānēs*, especially the ceremonies connected with death. The sermons of a Christian priest follow not only the calendar but also the life cycle of the individual. Buddhism as such, however, lacks sacraments; there is no equivalent of baptism, no pubertal rite parallel to confirmation or the first communion, and marriage is solemnized by a secular ceremony. The only life crisis with which monks are traditionally associated is death. The grief and separation which death involves are a suitable occasion for the exposition of the *Dharma* of sorrow and impermanence; so monks, who were originally refugees from lay life, have become involved in it at this point. The ceremonies at the funeral and on subsequent commemorative occasions, described in Chapter 5 in connection with the transference of merit, are thus over-determined, providing occasion also for sermons on the fundamentals of Buddhist doctrine. Funeral sermons are usually rather short (e.g. ten minutes), and contain a eulogy of the dead person; the sermon which closes a *dānē* (after the monks have eaten and the merit has been transferred at the water-pouring ceremony) are similarly short; both categories inevitably consist mainly of reflections on the transitoriness of all worldly things. Only the *baṇa* which takes place in the evening a week after the death, or as a replacement for *pirit* at one of the subsequent commemorations, is a full-scale sermon, lasting perhaps an hour, and may range over wider topics.

Like *baṇa* on a public occasion, this sort of sermon commences, very much in the Christian style, with a quotation from the Pali Canon, which is then expounded and enlarged upon, largely with the help of further quotations; there is more quotation and less invention than is usual in Christian preaching, but in my experience a monk preaching never confined himself to a mere recitation and paraphrase of a canonical text. While preaching a monk sits on a special chair (*dharmāsana*) or at least on a chair covered with a clean white cloth, and holds a preaching fan.

He may hold the fan in front of his face, which serves, I was told, to depersonalize the sermon, but this is often neglected. A member of the congregation, usually an elderly man, takes it upon himself to act as respondent (*pratyuttaradennā*); he squats in the front row, hands folded, and every so often says 'Ehē hāmuduruvō',[5] which is as much as to say 'Amen' in church; in theory he may also interrupt and ask for clarification, but I never saw this done.

The types of *baṇa* were enumerated for me by one of my informants, a well-known preacher. All the commoner ones we have already covered: *mataka baṇa* is preaching in the house of a dead man; *paṃsukūlē baṇa* is preaching at a funeral; *sāmānya baṇa* (literally 'ordinary *baṇa*') is preaching on *poya* days. *Dharmasaṃvāda*, 'doctrinal discussion', is usually carried on in an informal context. *Āsana dekē baṇa* ('preaching from two seats') seems once to have been common;[6] there was none in my area while I was there, but one was scheduled for just after I left. In an *āsana dekē baṇa* one monk reads out or recites a text from the Pali Canon, and the other reads out the *sannē*, a close paraphrase in Sinhalese; my informant said that the usual text preached like this is the *Damsak pävatum suta*—the first sermon. In ancient times there were apparently three monks preaching in a full-scale *baṇa*, one reciting a text, one paraphrasing in Sinhalese, and one giving a sermon proper;[7] but I did not come across such an event.[8] My informant did, however, list an *āsana hatē baṇa*, 'preaching from seven seats', which he said was used for the *Brahmajāla Sutta*, the first sermon of the *Dīgha Nikāya*. I assume from the nature of that text that this was a kind of part-reading performance, one monk taking the role of the Buddha and the others reciting the arguments of his oppo-

[5]Thus in my part of the country; elsewhere other synonymous expressions are used.

[6] Geiger, *Culture of Ceylon*, p. 200, para. 194.

[7]Rahula, *History*, pp. 267–8.

[8]Perhaps what happened, in our terminology, was an *āsana dekē baṇa* followed by a *sāmānya baṇa*.

nents. This kind of *baṇa* he said was obsolete.[9] However, my informant was himself responsible for an even more vivid form of *baṇa*, a full dramatization of a canonical story in which the Buddha converts a man-eating *yakṣa* called Āḷavaka. The original version of this story is a short poem with prose preface in the *Sutta-nipāta*, but the version my informant had devised took about three hours to perform and was a veritable folk drama. It was called *Āḷavaka-yakṣa-damanē*, 'The Taming of the Devil Āḷavaka'. He told me that he had himself devised it with the help of five drummers (*beravāyō*) from his village who performed the other parts while he sat on a preaching-seat facing the audience, with the actors before him, and to convert the *yakṣa* gave a sermon exactly as he would have done had there been no play. Whether similar dramatizations of *baṇa* have taken place in the past I cannot say; this one has so far remained unreported, though it might be said to represent a distinctive genre of folk-art, and it may have unreported predecessors. The nearest thing to it in my experience is the *sūvisi pinkama*, which others called *baṇa* though my informant did not mention it in his list; but the *sūvisi* is highly stylized, as my account in Chapter 3 shows. This particular drama is, however, the spontaneous creation of a local monk and his parishioners.

The last kind of teaching (*desanā*) which must be mentioned is, like *pirit*, not idiomatically referred to as *baṇa*, because though logically a form of preaching it is highly stylized and specialized. This is the *pin anumodanā*[10] already referred to in Chapter 5; we saw then that the original meaning of *anumodanā* is 'thanks' or 'grateful acceptance'. In the commentary to the *Dhammapada*[11] the term is already paraphrased *anumodanā-dhamma-desanā*

[9]Such part-reading performances, given by any number of monks from two to eight as appropriate, are still regular forms of preaching in Thailand, which derives so many of its Buddhist traditions from Ceylon. Wells, *Thai Buddhism*, pp. 273–4.

[10]For the full English translations of two *anumodanā* see Dickson, op.cit., p. 209, and the Appendix.

[11]*Dh.A.*, I, 209.

(teaching the doctrine by way of thanks). In the old sub-commentary (*purāṇa-ṭīkā*) on the *Jātakas*[12] the word *anumodanā* is glossed 'teaching the doctrine to arouse joy in creatures' (*sattānaṃ pīti-janaka-dhamma-desanaṃ*). As Professor Arnold Green has pointed out to me, there is a popular explanation of what the monk is doing which similarly goes beyond the idea of mere thanks: he is said to be causing the donors to feel joy *prītiya*; he is actually doing them a favour, by causing them to forget the trouble and expense involved in offering a *dānē* and rather to feel unalloyed pleasure at having given, thus purifying their thoughts and advancing towards *nirvāṇa*. In this way his *anumodanā* is not mere thanks, but a *quid pro quo*. This explanation is of course compatible on all levels with the previously mentioned functions of the *anumodanā* as thanks and as an exhortation to share the merit gained; it provides yet another example of the over-determination of a ritual act.

Though the recitation of the *anumodanā* may look to a western newcomer like the saying of grace before a meal, it lacks even external resemblance in that it only happens when the meal is given; when the monks eat their own food, cooked in the monastery kitchen, nothing is said. The original practice was for monks to eat only what they had begged; but when monasteries acquired possessions this became unnecessary, and when they were extremely large it also became impractical. In Anurādhapura, we learn from Fa Hsien and Hiuen Tsiang,[13] vast numbers of monks and nuns were fed at a central kitchen supplied by the King, i.e. at public expense. In the tenth century the King granted villages to the monasteries of Jetavana and Abhayagiri to maintain their refectories.[14] Throughout ancient times, however, very many monks, perhaps all those outside the capital, customarily went on the daily alms-round (*piṇḍapāta*). The *piṇḍapāta* became excep-

[12] *J.*, I, 119.
[13] Quoted by Rahula, *History*, p. 175.
[14] *Cūlavaṃsa*, LII, 59.

tional presumably only when the landless monastery became exceptional, i.e. in the Kandyan period.

There are today no monasteries except the *piriveṇas* so large that it would be impractical for all the monks to beg locally; but few are so poor as to be quite dependent on *dāyakas*. Most monasteries own a little land, and a few old ones own a great deal. I had the impression, however, that the extent to which meals are supplied daily to the monastery depends far less on the monks' need than on more intangible factors such as the character of the monk and the degree of organization of the laity. A few really organized monasteries had a roster so that each household could see when it would be their turn to supply the *dāne*. Our temple had such a roster for four months of the year only, the three months of *vas* (see below, p. 326) and the following month, during which it is also customary for monks to remain at home; in this period every Buddhist household in the village had a turn, supplying either the midday meal (*daval dānē*), or the evening requirements (*gilampasa*) and breakfast (*hil dānē*) the next morning. Even this was economically unnecessary to the temple, which was rich, but it was explained to me that every family was thus given the chance to earn merit. This argument was, however, not applied the rest of the year, when the monks ate food provided from their own resources and cooked in the monastery kitchen, except when they were invited out to a *mataka dānē* or when there was some big *pinkama*. On these special occasions, e.g. Wesak and the head monk's fiftieth birthday *pinkama*, the food was supplied by the whole village, nearly every family supplying something; it was carried up to the temple in a procession (*perahära*), the rice arriving in a huge pot suspended on a pole borne by a man before and a man behind it in the traditional Sinhalese manner.

The alms round (*piṇḍapāta*) is practised nowadays only by modern fundamentalists, notably the famous Vajirārāma in Colombo; it is a difficult practice to maintain, because a monk who goes begging for his food is usually regarded as remarkably holy and everyone is so eager to give him food that a roster has to be set up. There is a forest retreat called Salgala where since 1932 some monks of fundamentalist persuasion, including at least one European, have retired to meditate in the style of the original forest-dwelling hermits (*āraññavāsin*); to give a meal to these monks you have to put down your name more than a year in advance. The fact that the place where they eat it is called a *piṇḍapāta śālāva* does not make it different from the ordinary *dāna śālāva* (monastery refectory). On the other hand a monk may still beg for alms in case of need. Monk 6 lived entirely by begging because he had no alternative. He was not fully ordained, but a mere *sāmaṇera*, who had entered the Order as an adult, and he was somewhat odd; actually I never heard anyone say either that he was crazy or that he was heretical, but there were complaints that he was not learned, and some held it against him that he had a family, although originally it was of course quite normal to become a monk when an adult with a family—as the Buddha did himself. Be that as it may, he lived in the direst poverty with no perceptible possessions, and every morning at about 6.30 would set off with begging bowl and sun-glasses, hoping to collect enough for the whole day so that he would not have to go out again later. In our village, to which he occasionally came as it lay less than two miles from his temple, he was received by only a few households, so far as I could observe by low-caste people, who probably felt sympathy with him against the *goyigama* (high-caste) monks of the Siyam Nikāya, who held all the temples in the immediate vicinity and would have nothing to do with him, though he was Siyam Nikāya (and therefore high-caste) himself. Although his was a very unusual case, I must mention here that the lot of a poor monk may be most undesirable. In one monastery which I came to I found an aged monk, quite blind and nearly deaf, living all alone in filth and neglect; he was kept alive by food brought by a local family who took pity on him, but seemed to have no other company or support. Both the children who brought the food and the monk at the next temple, which was very nearby, said that the old man was too bad-tempered (*sära vädi*) for it to be possible to deal with him; his pupil lived elsewhere and visited him about once a year; whether in fact other people ever visited him I cannot say, but I did not get that impression.

Sil māṇiyō likewise depend on charity. Often they live at or near temples and get food brought much like monks. Two such ladies who lived apart in a cave under a Bo tree near my village were differently organized: on full-moon days the senior one went round the nearby villages collecting goods and cash, on which they then lived, doing their own shopping and cooking.

Monks are generally most active as preachers during *vas*. *Vas*, which originally means 'rain', was the three-month monsoon period in north-east India when the Buddha told monks to desist from their wanderings and stay in one sheltered place. Though in Ceylon this period is not climatically so distinctive, monks still have to observe *vas* and stay in one place for the three months of *vas* and the next month.[15] 'Stay' means minimally that they should not be away for more than six consecutive nights. In fact *vas* is sometimes broken; and when a monk went on a pilgrimage to India during *vas* no one disapproved. Usually they stay in their own monastery, but sometimes in another, or a layman provides a special lodging. In the last case the monk is led in procession to his retreat. A shopkeeper in the village next to Mīgala who had built a new house invited a monk who was from another village but locally respected to spend *vas* there, thus earning much merit and giving his house an auspicious start. Under such circumstances a monk is especially likely to preach often; at the least he constantly has to preach *anumōdan*, as described above. *Vas* is also the only pe-

[15]Dickson (op. cit.) has good material on *vas*, which relieves me of the necessity of supplying many details. I witnessed the beginning of *vas* much as he describes it, though I did not hear the *Nidhikaṇḍa Sutta* preached, as he says it is on that occasion; I also saw in Mīgala temple the *kaṭhina pinkama* which takes place at the end of the fourth month.

riod during which monks of the Siyam Nikāya in my area meet on full-moon and *māsa poya* days for the *uposatha* ceremony. It is a basic *vinaya* rule that monks who live in the same *sīmā* (see Introduction, p. 32) should meet every fortnight and confess their transgressions when the oldest monk present recites the *pātimokkha*, the canonical list of 227 *vinaya* regulations. In practice the monks who so unite are the inhabitants of an informal group of up to about ten monasteries which acknowledge the same head monastery (e.g. Asgiriya);[16] and in my experience only monks of the Amarapura and Rāmañña Nikāyas (see Chapter 8) meet outside *vas*, this being the one tangible respect in which I found the Amarapura more orthodox than the Siyam Nikāya. The Rāmañña and Amarapura Nikāyas, so far as I could observe, only hold the *pātimokkha* ceremony once a month, on full-moon *poyas*. Moreover in practice the Siyam Nikāya monks (I cannot vouch for the other two Nikāyas) do not rehearse the whole *pātimokkha* but only the first section, which deals with *pārājika* offences, for which the penalty is defrocking. This confirms the ritual's purely formal character: no confessions ever take place. Monks who are notoriously guilty of a *pārājika* offence (typically sexual intercourse) may be refused recognition by other monks and by the laity, but this never seems to happen as the result of a confession. Sometimes such monks continue to wear yellow robes and even to live in their monasteries, though it is legally possible for rival claimants to displace them.

The extent to which meditation (*bhāvanāva*) is actually practised by monks is extremely difficult to ascertain, not because meditation practices are esoteric, as some western authors seem to believe, but because the question is so involved with a monk's prestige, possibly even with his self-respect, that honesty is hardly possible. The monks

[16]Even this is theory: in practice I have known a Malvatta monk to join a *pavāraṇā* ceremony (the *pātimokkha* at the end of *vas*) at an Asgiri temple.

in my area who answered my questions on meditation fall into three groups of roughly equal size: those who said, or as good as said, that they did not meditate; those who claimed that they did some but certainly do very little; and those who seem to meditate regularly. The statement of the monk who said that there was only one monk in the whole area (another of my informants) who meditated, was certainly a gross exaggeration. His implication that *granthadhura* monks could not be expected to meditate was, however, accepted by many; though no one denied that meditation is necessary for *nirvāṇa*, several said that the life of a village monk was too busy, or hinted that they hoped for better opportunities in the next life. Against this, one monk went so far as to say that it is no good becoming a monk unless you meditate—and doctrine is of course on his side; but another, who was also in the Rāmañña Nikāya, explained to me as a matter of course that as a *granthadhura* monk his knowledge of meditation was purely theoretical.

The subjects—and no doubt the techniques—of meditation closely follow the instructions laid down by Buddhaghosa in his *Visuddhimagga*. This is not necessarily a modern feature; it may go back to the eighteenth-century revival, when Siamese monks came to teach meditation (*vipassanā*).[17] However, the tradition must at least have been reinforced by monastic education.[18] When I

[17] *Mhv.*, C, 174.

[18] Bechert (op. cit., p. 50) holds that traditions of meditation were completely lost in Ceylon at the end of the nineteenth century. He bases this on statements by Copleston, Sangharakshita, and Woodward. Woodward, as Bechert himself states, was referring to a divergent tradition of meditation represented by the Sinhalese text, probably dating from the eighteenth century, published as *The Yogāvacara's Manual*. (The text is admirably summarized by Eliade (*Yoga*, pp. 195–7). Its discrepancies from the main tradition are specified by Rhys Davids in the introduction to his edition (P.T.S., London, 1896), esp. pp. xxix–xxx.) Whether Copleston is to be considered an authority of weight on such a point must remain a matter of judgement. Sangharakshita is reporting the view of Dharmapāla, which is an even unsteadier foundation. The monks I interviewed seemed un-

asked monks on what subjects they meditated their answers never went outside the list of forty objects of meditation (*kammaṭṭhāna*) and fundamental doctrinal principles listed by Buddhaghosa. Popular subjects seemed to be the meditation on kindness (*maitrī bhāvanāva*) and the meditation on the impurities of the body (*piḷikul/asubha bhāvanāva*).[19] One monk said he meditated every day on *maitrī*,[20] and quoted to me the *Karaṇīyametta Sutta*. The *piḷikul bhāvanāva* consists in recalling the list of the thirty-two constituents of the body[21] and then applying these thoughts to oneself and others. This is traditionally the main subject for meditation by the elderly *upāsakas* who take the Eight Precepts on *poya* days; a very old monk told me he meditated on it 'to get used to it for *saṃsāra*' (*sasaraṭa purudu venṭa*), by which he meant that he was now making a start on meditation which he could perfect in a future life. Similarly meditation on the Buddha (*Buddhānusmṛti*) centres on the '*Iti pi so*' *gāthā* mentioned in Chapter 4. The only other text which was mentioned to me (by two monks) as a subject of meditation was the

affected by Buddhist modernist ideas on meditation methods, which have been influenced, as Bechert says, by the *Yogaāvacara's Manual* and the so-called Burmese methods, which seem to be more emotional and ecstatic in character than the traditional methods. I am therefore not nearly as positive as Bechert that the central tradition of meditation practice was lost. Unfortunately this is unlikely to be a soluble question, as published sources tend not to dwell on what, though not esoteric, is essentially a matter of intimate behaviour.

19 Dickson (op. cit., p. 205) had similar information in 1884.

20 This meditation is described in *Visuddhimagga*, IX.

21 Included as item 3 in the *Khuddaka-pāṭha*. The *piḷikul bhāvanāva* is a conflation of two originally different meditations. The meditation on the thirty-two constituents of the body is called by Buddhaghosa *kāyagatā sati* 'mindfulness referring to the body', and is discussed at length in *Visuddhimagga*, Chapter VIII, 42–144. It is distinct from the *asubha bhāvanā*, which consisted of the contemplation of corpses in ten stages of decomposition (*Visuddhimagga*, Chapter VI). I have never heard of anyone contemplating actual corpses nowadays; as bodies are now buried or cremated, not left exposed, it would indeed be practically difficult.

Satipaṭṭhāna Sutta,[22] which contains a wide-ranging analysis of the individual; the popularity of this text is also traditional.[23]

I was told in Mīgala that the previous incumbent of the temple and his chief pupil, the present incumbent, used to enter the *vihāragē* on *poya* days at some point in the afternoon, sit down cross-legged on their leather mats near the main Buddha image, and meditate—on what is not known. No doubt this presented an edifying spectacle to the old people taking the Eight Precepts that day. But most of the meditation in Mīgala is undoubtedly done by the *dasa sil māṇiyō*; they usually meditate for a couple of hours in the afternoons, mainly the *piḷikul bhāvanāva*. They meditate by telling beads and muttering *gāthā* (Pali verses and formulae), which is not the manner of meditation prescribed or practised by monks, so it is perhaps no wonder that the lady I talked to seemed rather pessimistic about their meditation, declaring that even to be reborn in heaven was an impossibly high goal and that they only aspired to be reborn as human beings so that they could go on meditating. On the other hand she said that it is written in the scriptures that if you do the *Buddhānusmṛti* with perfect concentration for two or three hours you can see *nirvāṇa*; but such perfect concentration was beyond their powers. Her selection of the most devotional topic of meditation as the key to salvation is noteworthy.

According to Buddhaghosa and to some of my informants there are two kinds of meditation, *samatha* and *vipassanā*, tranquillity and intuition.[24] (In the texts *samatha* is often called or equated with *samādhi* and *vipassanā* with *paññā). Samatha* is similar to—and largely borrowed from–non-Buddhist meditation techniques of ancient India, while *vipassanā* is a distinctively Buddhist contribution. Buddhist interpretations of meditation have varied

[22] *D.N.*, II, *Sutta* 22.

[23] Rahula, *History*, p. 253.

[24] The most comprehensive modern work on meditation according to the texts is P. Vajirañāṇa Mahāthera, *Buddhist Meditation in Theory and Practice* (Gunasena, Colombo, 1962).

greatly, but the Theravādin interpretation at least since Buddhaghosa unequivocally equates practisers of *samatha* with what Eliade calls 'partisans of *yogic experience*' and practisers of *vipassanā* with his 'partisans of *knowledge*',[25] and asserts the superiority of the latter. The objects of *samatha* are the forty *kammaṭṭhāna*; the principal objects of *vipassanā* are the three cardinal Buddhist principles of *anicca, dukkha, anatta* (impermanence, sorrow, and non-self). It was interesting to find that these topics were those named as the objects of their concentration by the monk who had a reputation for meditation and by monk 6, who was a religious enthusiast, albeit heterodox and eccentric. As neither of these monks had ever attended a *piriveṇa* we can certainly speak here of a living tradition, though whether it has been resuscitated only recently it is impossible to judge.

There are in Ceylon today forest-dwelling monks who devote their lives to meditation; one group of these, that at Salgala just referred to, numbered ten in 1969; a few others dwell alone or with their pupils, in greater or lesser isolation, ranging from those who live near big cities and thus receive frequent visits to those in truly remote parts of the island such as the south-east coast. Some of these monks are Europeans, and their entire behaviour is intended as a revival (though to some extent it may be a pseudo-revival) of ancient practices which have long lapsed. They are part of the phenomenon which Heinz Bechert calls Buddhist modernism, to which I have alluded in the latter part of Chapter 1.

In some cases western influence is extremely indirect. A monk meditating with his five pupils on the eastern coastal plains, interviewed in 1969, told me he knew no Europeans and used no European publications; he had studied for four and a half years in Rangoon and then lived for three years and eight months in the jungle at the foot of Adam's Peak, not even going begging but living on roots and fruits. He is only accessible to visitors for two hours a day (as

[25]Eliade, *Yoga*, p. 191.

against four hours at Salgala), and he and his pupils certainly spend most of their lives practising meditation. As at Salgala, they use a skeleton for meditation on the body; the chief monk also has in his cell an earth *kasina*, a disc used for concentration, described at length in *Visuddhimagga*, IV. Like the Salgala monks he said he made much use of the *Visuddhimagga*, but unlike them practised the meditation on breathing (*āṇāpāṇasati*) according to the Burmese interpretation of the *Mahā Satipaṭṭhāna Sutta*, which method, he said, is not fully expounded in any publication, but must be learnt from a teacher.[26] In saying that meditation cannot be studied merely by following written instructions this monk sided with ancient tradition against the modernists including the Salgala monks.

The comparative rarity of meditation is closely connected with the widespread belief in the decline of Buddhism, a topic which I usually included in my interviews. Gotama Buddha is said to have predicted[27] that his *śāsanē* would last for 5,000 years (5,500 according to two informants); this belief goes back to the commentaries on the Canon.[28] (The figure 5,000 lends a certain poignancy

[26]For the controversy on the merits of this Burmese method of meditation see Bechert, op. cit., p. 80.

[27]One old monk, oddly, called it a *prārthanāva*.

[28]The canonical prediction (*A.N.*, IV, 278 = *Vin.*, II, 256) is that the *Dharma* will last five *hundred* years. The Buddha makes this gloomy forecast when Ānanda has prevailed on him to allow the formation of an order of nuns (*bhikkhunī-sangha*). Even the nuns outlived expectation. This was of course apparent to Buddhaghosa when he wrote his commentaries (or to one of the unknown commentators whose work he used). In his comment on the *Vinaya* passage on the founding of the order of nuns (*Samantapāsādikā*, VI, 1291) Buddhaghosa explains away the figures in the text in such a way as to make the *Dhamma* last for 5,000 years. He here equates *Dhamma* with *paṭivedha* (realization), which will disappear in five stages of 1,000 years each, and *pariyatti* (learning) will disappear with it, but *linga* ('external signs'—here the Sangha?) will last even longer. This is not the version that I was told, and I further deduce that it is not the one which has entered the mainstream of tradition, because it also explains why now, in the third millenium of the teaching, there should be no *arhats*, which is contrary

to the celebration held in 1956 to mark the 2,500th anniversary of Buddhism; we are half-way through, and a monk remarked that the assassination of S. W. R. D. Bandaranaike in 1959 signalized the beginning of the decline.) Only during a *śāsana* are normal men able to gain Enlightenment; between *śāsana* the only enlightened beings are the *pratyekabuddhas* (see Chapter 3, p. 97), who have a store of merit so immense that they can realize *nirvāṇa* under such adverse circumstances, and are accordingly unlikely to be sojourning among us now. The theory that a man attains Enlightenment purely by his own effort is preserved, but this is impossible without a knowledge of the religious truths which a normal man is incapable of ideating for himself, so that in practice one who has not heard a Buddha's teaching has no chance. A village girl said that in a Buddha-less period one must keep trying (*utsāha karanṭa*), but only limited progress is possible. A monk said that the Four Noble Truths always exist, i.e. are true, but between *śāsana* they exist undiscovered, like electricity before man discovered its uses. It is further believed by the majority of monks, at least of those whose general attitudes can be characterized as traditional, that this *śāsanē* has already declined so far that it is no longer possible for men to attain *nirvāṇa*. This opinion is very prevalent among the laity and, interestingly, was even strongly put to me by a *sil māṇiyō*. One monk even specified that till Maitrī came it was not even possible to become *sovan* (Pali: *sotāpanna*), a religious state in which one will attain *nirvāṇa* after seven more lives. The last *arhat* is commonly said to have been Maliyadeva, though most people are very vague about when he lived. (In fact he is men-

to what I was told by some informants, and would be a better rationale for the pessimism of others than the obscure story of Maliyadeva (see below). On the other hand I think that this must be where the figure of 5,000 started, as there is good reason for it in this context. The story was then elaborated into the form given below, according to which the five stages of decline are differently interpreted and the lack of *arhats* in the third millenium of the teaching, though implicit if one knows the former passage, is not clearly stated.

tioned in *Mahāvaṃsa*, XXXII, 30 and 49, as an *arhat* in the time of Duṭugämuṇu; there are several stories about him in commentaries.)[29]

Others say that there *may* still be human *arhats*, but it is unlikely and/or undiscoverable. (One monk pointed out that an enlightened person is not supposed to boast about it.) One monk compared the *śāsana* to a worn-out organism: very few can attain *nirvāṇa* now, just as a tree grows barren when its fruit is picked too often, and the seventh child is weaker than the first. Some said there might be enlightened beings still alive in one of the five 'pure abodes' (*suddhāvāsa*) at the top of the *brahmaloka*, the other part of the universe besides mankind in which Enlightenment is possible. The average view, perhaps, was that of the monk who said that it is not impossible to attain *nirvāṇa* now, but 'religious practice is weak; it is hard to believe that there is anyone alive who has become an *arhat*' ('pratipatti durvalayi, arhat vecca aya innavā kiyalā hitanṭa amāruyi').

On the other hand a monk who knew the Canon unusually well told me that it was a grave mistake to state that no *arhats* now exist, for the Buddha's relics still exist, and so do *paryāpti*, *pratipatti*, and *prativedanā* [see p. 316]; there must be some *arhats* left on earth, maybe in Burma.[30] The Buddha once told a brahmin that his teaching (*śāsanē*) would last so long as monks, nuns, laymen, and laywomen practised mindfulness (*satipaṭṭhāna*), and of these four groups only the nuns have disappeared. Another monk, also well-informed, put the matter precisely:

[29]See Adikaram, pp. 66–7, where it is shown that the belief that Maliyadeva was the last *arhat* is not ancient, and may stem from a misinterpretation of a (probably interpolated) remark in the *Jātaka* commentary (*J.*, VI, 30) that Maliyadeva was the last of the characters in a certain *Jātaka* story to leave the lay life.

[30]Burma enjoys in Ceylon a wide reputation for holiness, fostered no doubt by the Buddhist council held in Rangoon 1954–6 (see Bechert, op. cit., pp. 105–6). The monk being quoted is moreover a member of the Rāmañña Nikāya, which like the Amarapura Nikāya derived its ordination from Burma.

books tell us that it is not impossible for anyone to realize *nirvāṇa* now, but we know of no cases. The *śāsana* declines because it is subject to the universal law that there is nothing eternal ('sadākālika deyak nā'). A third monk utterly rejected the suggestion that there is a decline (*pirihīma*) in the *śāsāne*, but he seemed altogether to be on the defensive against the foreign intruder.

There was some disagreement over what will constitute the disappearance of the *śāsāne*. One monk said that the Sangha will die out, and that will be the end of Buddhism. A second, however, included the relics and laity as physical indices of Buddhism's existence. The formulation of a third was the widest: after 5,000 years will come the disappearance (*antardhānē*) of five things: relics (*dhātu*), realization (*prativedanā*) (which he glossed as 'the fruit of Enlightenment' (*rahat phala*)), monks and novices (*linga*) (which he glossed as 'monachism' (*mahaṇakama*)), practice (*pratipattiya*) (which he glossed as 'morality' (*sil*)), and religious learning (*pariyāptiya*) (which he glossed as '*Dharma*'). This keeps very close to the commentatorial text,[31] which is also the passage on which is based the doctrine of the paramount importance of learning. (See below, Chapter 9, p. 374.) The text says that practice and realization depend on the continued existence of learning.[32] The canonical texts will finally disappear in reverse order: first the *Abhidhamma Piṭaka*, beginning with the last book; then the four *Nikāyas* of the *Sutta Piṭaka*, beginning with the *Anguttara* and ending with the *Dīgha Nikāya*; then the *Jātakas*; finally the *Vinaya Piṭaka*. Last to go is the

[31] *Anguttara-Aṭṭhakathā* (*Manorathapūraṇī*), I, 87–93. There is a different version with only trifling discrepancies in the *Vibhanga-Aṭṭhakathā* (*Sammohavinodanī*), pp. 431–2. The ascription of both commentaries to Buddhaghosa may be correct, but in any case the *Vibhanga* commentary seems to be written after the other, and some manuscripts interpolate passages from it in the text of the *Anguttara* commentary (see vol. I, p. 91, notes 4 and 9).

[32] Cf. *Vibhanga-Aṭṭhakathā*, p. 432, l. 3: *Sāsanaṭṭhitiyā pana pariyatti pamāṇaṃ*. 'Learning is the criterion of the continued existence of the teaching.'

Uposatha-kaṇḍa. When a king offers a purse of gold to anyone who can recite a four-line verse of the Buddha's teaching, and there are no takers, learning will have disappeared.

For another version of what happens next, let a Mīgala monk take up the story.

The *sāsanē* of a Buddha lasts for 5,000 years, which period is called a *Buddhotpādakālaya* (time producing a Buddha), and is followed by an *a-Buddhotpādakālaya* (the opposite). During all this time men get wickeder and wickeder, and their life span gets shorter, till it is only ten years. In these ten years people become adults but remain like children. Then comes the *lokavināsa alias sattuvināsa* ('destruction of the world' or 'of living beings'). At that time a king comes down from the *Cātummahārājika divyaloka* ('Heaven of the Four Great Kings'), which is one of the *kāmāvacara* ('sensual sphere', i.e. lower) heavens. He beats a *bera* (drum) and announces that after seven days will start a heavy rain, the *Murugasaṃvarsāva* ('wild beast deluge'). 'Don't get wet,' he warns, but most men are so wicked that they don't believe him; only those with *pin* believe, and they prepare provisions and shelter in caves, etc. Then a light rain (*sirivässa*) begins to fall. All who get wet begin to look like game animals, so people start shooting each other for meat. In this way all the wicked kill each other till nothing is left but a great pool of blood. When the rain finally stops those who had some merit left in them emerge from their shelters, and on seeing the slaughter they feel compassion (*anukampāva*). This good thought (*hoňda adahasa*) produces a revulsion from killing, and they thus relinquish the first of the *pas pav* ['five sins', the subjects of the Five Precepts]. At this the maximum life-span (*paramāyusa*) goes up from ten to twenty. Men then relinquish each of the *pas pav* in turn, and the *paramāyusa* rises to thirty, forty, fifty, sixty. They then get rid of the *dasa akusal* ['ten bad actions', another list of sins: these lists are not mutually exclusive—the story is not strictly logical] and other bad things till in due course the maximum life-span rises to infinity [*sic*]. But this is not a suitable time for a Buddha to be born, as men witness no death or decay and so see no reason to do *pin*. It is when the *paramāyusa* goes down again to 80,000 years that the time is ripe. Then the Bodhisattva who is [just about] to become a Buddha (*buduvena bodhisattvayō*) is always born in the *Tusīpura divyaloka* [another of the lower heavens, called in Sanskrit the Tuṣita heaven]. Then the gods invite him to be born on earth saying

> *Kālo 'yaṃ te Mahāvīra uppajja mātu kucchiyaṃ*
> *Sadevakaṃ tārayanto bujjhassu amataṃ padaṃ.*[33]
>
> This is the time for you, great hero, to be reborn in your mother's womb, and saving the whole world[34] to realize the deathless state.

Thereupon the Bodhisattva looks out for a suitable occasion.

> *Kālam desaṃ ca dīpaṃ ca kulaṃ mātaram eva ca*
> *Ete pañca viloketvā uppajjanti Tathāgathā.*[35]
>
> Time, place, continent, caste[36] and mother—after examining these five are Tathāgatas (i.e. Buddhas) born.

Gotama Buddha was born when the maximum life-span was 120, and lived to the age of 80. The maximum life-span has now declined to 100 years.

The last part of this myth, which I recount exactly as I heard it, is the episode which in Chapter 3 I called 'The Gods' Invitation'. There seems to be a slight discrepancy in the myth as the monk recounted it, in that he says that

[33] *Buddhavaṃsa*, Chap. I, v. 67 = *Madhuratthavilāsinī*, p. 53 = ibid., p. 142 = ibid., p. 273 = *Dh.A.*, I, 84. The P.T.S. edition of the *Buddhavaṃsa* reads 'Kālo deva', which is corrected in the commentary (p. 153).

[34] For this meaning of *sadevakaṃ* in a similar context see *J.*, VI, 546, l. 7, l. 19, and note 3.

[35] *Dh.A.*, I, 84, note 14, where the last word is read as 'mahāyasā.' For comment on the origin of these two verses see Chapter 3, p. 121.

[36] The translation of *kula* as 'caste' is on the informant's instructions.

the appropriate time for a Buddha to be born is when a life span is 80,000 years, but Gotama was born when the life-span was 120. This can be straightened out by comparison with another account: it is Maitrī, the next Buddha, who will appear when the maximum life-span is 84,000 years. (This latter account gives the maximum life-span at present as 120.) Incidentally, that the Buddha did not live his full natural term agrees with the canonical account in the *Mahāparinibbāna Sutta*[37] of his voluntary renunciation of life.

This story of the decline in world morals leading to general destruction is found in the *Cakkavattisīhanāda Sutta* of the *Dīgha Nikāya*,[38] the text which also contains the prophecy of the future Buddha Metteyya (Skt. and Sinh.: Maitrī). It is generally believed that Maitrī will be the Buddha in the next world cycle (*antarakappa*), and people express the hope to be reborn as human beings in the time of his teaching. Chances of this are comparatively good, as after attaining enlightenment he will live and preach for 80,000 years. The monk said that his two chief disciples (corresponding to Säriyut and Mugalan for Gotama Buddha) will be Duṭugämuṇu and his brother Saddhātissa, and his parents will be Duṭugämuṇu's parents, Kāvantissa and Vihāra Mahā Dēvī. This prediction is found in the *Mahāvaṃsa* (XXXII, 81–2). The belief that Duṭugämuṇu will be Maitrī's right-hand disciple is general, but some say that his left-hand disciple will be Devānaṃpiya Tissa, the king under whom Buddhism came to Ceylon.

The general opinion is that Maitrī will be born after an extremely long time (3,000 years? (a village girl); 10,000 years? (a monk); ten million years? (another monk)), but we had better start now our preparations for that event, so that we shall then be in a fit state to receive and profit by his teaching. Mainly we must be sure to be born as

[37] *D.N.*, *Sutta* 16. 3.

[38] *D.N.*, *Sutta* 26. A young monk who was infected by western ideas told me that Maitrī Buddha was an import from Mahāyāna, but he was wrong. He also ascribed to Mahāyāna influence the belief that the Buddha prophesied the decline of his *śāsana*.

humans or higher at that time. (Answers at this point reflect the general disagreement over whether gods can attain *nirvāṇa.*) Some say vaguely that 'people who have done merit' (*pin karapu aya*) will hear him; others lay more stress on the difficulties. The village girl says that if one meditates now it will come easier in the time of Maitrī, but one also needs faith (*sardhāva*). One who in this cycle has committed one of the five great sins[39] will not see Maitrī. To accumulate enough merit not to be born in a hell (*apāya*) under Maitrī one must keep the moral precepts, do meditation, etc., and one must work out one's bad *karma* (*pav ahosi karanṭa*) by rebirth in unpleasant existences. However, if one misses Maitrī there will still be an infinite number of Buddhas after him under whom one can obtain release, though it is true (but perhaps not widely known) that after Maitrī there will be a particularly long gap. Monk 6 was the only person whom I ever heard speak of Maitrī with any fervour; generally I got the impression that monks regarded him with no more than academic interest, politely assumed for the occasion. Nor was he ever spontaneously mentioned to me by a layman.

To close this chapter I shall reproduce the eschatological opinions of monk 6, to whose eccentric doctrines and unusual poverty I have already alluded. The heterodox tenor of these opinions, with their strongly theistic flavour, makes it difficult to subsume them in the general scheme of this work, but even if the deviance that they represent should be no more than a quirk of personal psychology, the fact that I encountered them locally virtually obliges me to record them, and their vivid fervour makes me not sorry to do so.

The present state of religion is very low, he said. No one can now attain *nivan* until Maitrī comes. No laymen now observe the Five Precepts, while monks multiply pictures and clocks in their monasteries till they are smarter than hotels. The Buddha in Jetavanārāma lived in utter

[39]Killing father, mother, or *arhat*, causing a schism in the Sangha, and shedding the blood of a Buddha.

simplicity.

A man can only be called a Buddhist if he prays to reach *nirvāṇa* [in the time of Maitrī] (*nivan labanṭa prārthanā kalot Buddhāgamkārayek, nätnam nǟ*). Religion is the use of truth (*āgama ätta pāviccikirīmayi*). [What he meant by this is obscure.] *Nirvāṇa* is purity of thought (*hita pirisudu kirīma*). A man who has attained *nirvāṇa* is no longer liable to birth, decay, sickness, and death; moreover his body has no weight, so that he can fly through the air, and nothing will harm him: even if he treads on a snake, the snake will not bite him. If he takes the Three Refuges and observes the Five Precepts it is enough, for only sin weighs him down and makes him subject to mortal changes. But he cannot attain *nivan* without the help of Maitrī; and *pina* by itself is useless, for despite *pinkam* one may be reborn in some low state like a louse, and then what use is one's merit? So *pina* is *ahosi, nikam* (useless), unless accompanied by *prārthanā*. Even the merit acquired by hoping that a crow will drink the water you spit out after rinsing your mouth is sufficient basis for a *prārthanā*. We attain *nirvāṇa* by our *prārthanā* and earnest wish to reach it; as this wish grows more intense we go through the four stages on the path, till in the final stage we reach *nivan*, the supramundane good, which no termite or mouse, no accident can destroy (*lōkōttara kusalaṭa kisi vēyek, mīyek kanne nǟ, anaturak nǟ*).

Concerning Maitrī I was given many more details than I can reproduce; I believe they all derive ultimately from a post-canonical Pali text, the *Anāgata-vaṃsa*. He will be eighty cubits high, and live in a capital city, Ketumatī, a hundred times better than a city in one of the heavens nowadays. Its inhabitants, Maitrī's congregation, will be deities (*divyarājayō* and *divyānganāvō*) who did their meditation here on earth and so no longer need to. All their physical wants will be automatically supplied: divine trees will clothe them; when they are hungry or thirsty food and drink will spontaneously appear; and when they want to go outside a lavatory will be before them. These remarks—heretical in their depreciation of meditation—show that the prayers to be reborn under Maitrī are aimed at a goal more succulent than *nirvāṇa*.

Gotama Buddha has not yet completely seen *nivan*, in that he has three *nivan*. The first two are his original Enlightenment and his *parinirvāṇa*. The third will come at the end of the 5,000 years for which the *śāsana* (doctrine) will last. For these 5,000 years the Buddha is alive in the three worlds (*kāmaloka, rūpaloka, arūpaloka*). At the end of this period, all relics and images of the Buddha will reassemble and join into one. (*Arhats*' relics, etc., will not be affected.) In Ceylon every relic, every image, every picture of the Buddha will go to the Ruvanväli säya at Anurādhapura. From Anurādhapura all these will go to Rangoon, and at the Rangoon *caitya* the corporeal Buddha will come to life again. Simultaneously the branch of the Bo tree at Anurādhapura will rejoin the *Mahājaya bōdhinvahansē*, the original Bo tree. Then the Buddha will return to the foot of the Bo tree, and seated there will preach his last sermon, for seven hours, and all the gods will come to listen. At its conclusion the Buddha will finally enter *nirvāṇa*, and all trace of his doctrine will have disappeared from the earth.

The final paragraph of this account is based on the same Pali commentaries as the account of the disappearance of the scriptures quoted above. According to what is probably the later of these two texts[40] there are three stages in the disappearances of the doctrine: its existence (*ṭhiti*) (during which it continually declines), its withdrawal (*osakkana*), and then finally its disappearance. When the Sangha has died out the stage of 'withdrawal' has been reached. At this point the text, like monk 6, says that there are three *nirvāṇas* of the Buddha (*parinibbānāni*): his Enlightenment (*kilesaparinibbāna*—'extinction[41] of the defilements'), his death (*khandhaparinibbāna*—'extinction of the aggregates [constituents of the person]') and *dhātuparinibbāna*—'extinction of the relics'. All the Buddha's relics

[40] *Vibhanga Aṭṭhakathā*, pp. 432–3.

[41] In this context *parinibbāna* is clearly so to be rendered.

in Ceylon (here conceived only as the physical (*sārīrika*) relics) will indeed assemble at the Ruvanväli sāya (Mahā-cetiya), and then stop at Nāgadīpa, on their way over not to Burma, but of course to India. At the foot of the original Bo tree (*mahā-bodhipallanke*) they will join up with the relics from the world of the *nāgas*[42] and the various heavens, *devaloka* and *brahmaloka*. There, according to the other text[43], they will reconstitute the Buddha, complete with his thirty-two major and eighty minor distinctive features, and he will perform the miracle of the pairs. (There is no mention of preaching.) No human being will go there, but deities will assemble from the 10,000 world systems and lament the approaching darkness. The body will emit a flash, and disappear. The later text does not say that the relics will reconstitute the body, only that they will form a pile like a heap of gold, which will emit rays of the six colours, which will pervade 10,000 world systems. From all these world systems the deities (*devatā*) will assemble for a last look; then the flash from the relics goes up as far as the *brahmaloka*, they vanish, and 'the doctrine has truly disappeared (*sāsanaṃ antarahitaṃ nāma hoti*)'.[44]

[42]According to the verses at the very end of the *Mahāparinibbāna Sutta*, *D.N.*, II, 167, the *nāgas* have a tooth.

[43]*Anguttara-Aṭṭhakathā*, I, 91.

[44]As with the life of the Buddha (see p. 121), most of the material in the last part of this chapter is known not directly from Pali texts but from mediaeval Sinhalese classics based on the Pali. In the case of eschatology the most likely direct source is the *Saddharmaratnākaraya*.

8

Caste in the Monastery

> The structure of Sinhalese society was based on the institution of caste. Is caste in accordance with Buddhism?[1]
>
> Dr. G. C. Mendis.

ALTHOUGH in the Introduction I stated that my main interest was in religious change, the tenor of this work has rather been to demonstrate that Sinhalese Buddhism has been surprisingly conservative. Before summarizing those conclusions in a final chapter, I wish to discuss the most striking exception, a change certainly since the time of the Buddha and probably even since the time of Buddhaghosa, which has so far been our basis for comparison on most points. *Obiter dicta*—e.g. allusions to sectarianism and to monastic possessions—will already have suggested to the reader that I have found more evidence for change in the practices of the Sangha than in doctrinal belief—that change has been organizational rather than ideological. Anyone who approaches modern Buddhism in any Theravāda country after a study of 'primitive Buddhism' through canonical texts or such excellent secondary sources on the early Sangha as Sukumar Dutt's *Early Buddhist Monachism*[2] is immediately struck by these changes in monastic life. The most striking ones in Ceylon are: the holding of often considerable property by monasteries; the custom of passing pupillary succession to a relative, who thus effectively inherits the monastic property; the invasion of the Order by caste, and its division into parallel groups (Nikāyas) split mainly on caste lines; the virtual disappearance of the alms-round (*piṇḍapāta*); the entry of monks into politics; the employment of monks in salaried

[1] *Ceylon To-day and Yesterday* (Associated Newspapers of Ceylon, Colombo, 1957), p. 110.

[2] 2nd ed., Asia Publishing House, London, 1960.

positions. Of these six features the former three can properly be called organizational, while the latter three more strictly concern the conduct of monks as individuals. The disappearance of the alms-round has already been discussed in Chapter 7; I shall here discuss caste, which will involve some reference also to the first two features, but for further data on these questions I must refer the reader to works listed in my Bibliography. To the participation of my informants in politics I have devoted a separate article. I cannot here go on to the question whether such participation is justifiable, beyond remarking that whenever Ceylon has had Buddhist rulers monks have held political power. On monks' salaries I have hardly any data: no monks normally resident in my area were employed, though I interviewed one who was. Moreover, in all Ceylon only a small minority of monks hold salaried positions, while monastic participation in politics, ten years ago the pastime of a small minority, is still not universal. Similarly, not all monasteries hold property, and only a very few have any considerable wealth, while the passing on of such property to relatives is very far from universal. The pervasion of monastic organization by caste is, however, complete.[3] But this is not my only reason for choosing to talk about caste rather than any other feature of monastic change. Nor is my decision primarily determined by the fact that others of the features listed have recently been written on.[4] My main reason for choosing the caste question is that it has the greatest ideological significance. Unlike the customs concerning property and succession it is admitted by traditionalists to be doctrinally indefensible, and it is of course heartily attacked by modernists. Some modernists go so far as to say that the Buddha was

[3]I except a couple of 'modernizing' monasteries, which have no significance at all for a study of traditional Buddhism.

[4]Hans-Dieter Evers, 'Kinship and Property Rights in a Buddhist Monastery in central Ceylon', unpublished article, 1966; Heinz Bechert, op. cit., especially Chapters 25 (on the organization and legal position of the Sangha and its temporalities) and 29 (on monks in Ceylonese politics).

against caste altogether: this is not the case, but is one of the mistakes picked up from western authors. As their belief is so prevalent I shall give more space than has been my custom to examining the ideas on caste found in the Pali Canon, before describing the entry of caste into the Sangha and the opinions of my informants on the subject.

The standard work on the Sinhalese caste system is *Caste in Modern Ceylon* by Bryce Ryan;[5] Chapter 9 (pp. 196–238) of his book, *Caste in the Kandyan Highlands*, is especially relevant to my experience; indeed the section of this chapter called 'Caste in the Simple High Caste Village' (pp. 204–11) might almost have been written about Mīgala. The chapter on caste (pp. 58–95) in Nur Yalman's book, *Under the Bo Tree*,[6] and his paper 'The Flexibility of Caste Principles in a Kandyan Community' in E. R. Leach (ed.) *Aspects of Caste in South India, Ceylon, and North West Pakistan*[7] are based on field-work in an area not far from my own. These are more detailed and technical works; I shall present here only such facts about Sinhalese caste as are relevant for a discussion of the relation of caste to Buddhism; my picture, moreover, is based on my own field experience, and thus differs in some details from previously published materials.

The Sinhalese caste system is historically and conceptually related to the Indian; but there are fewer castes, and there is less scope for ritual pollution through the violation

[5]Rutgers University Press, New Brunswick N.J., 1953.

[6]University of California Press, Berkeley, and Los Angeles, 1967.

[7]Cambridge Papers in Social Anthropology no. 2, C.U.P., Cambridge, 1960, pp. 78–111. This interesting paper is more concerned to analyse than to describe behaviour; some of its main conclusions are convincingly queried by Leach in his introduction to the volume. A good succinct description of the manifestations of caste distinctions may be found on pp. 91–2 of the book. For the rest the chapter mainly repeats material from the paper, adding little or nothing of importance except for some solecisms so bad as to make one wonder: *dūrava* are not lime-burners (pp. 60 and 86) but toddy-tappers; how on earth can *bhikkhus* (who are mis-spelled throughout the book) be the top Sinhalese 'caste category', (p. 61)?

of caste tabus than in India. The social distances between most of the castes are very small, and indeed are so unobtrusive in their operation that casual visitors to Ceylon are hardly aware of caste, though the effect on attitudes, which find expression for instance in political activity, is more far-reaching. By comparison with India there is far less inequality. This is partly because among the Sinhalese, as they see it, both the top and the bottom strata of Hindu society are missing. Of the four classical Hindu classes of brahmins, warriors, agriculturalists with traders, and menial castes (*brāhmaṇa*, *kṣatriya*, *vaiśya*, *śūdra*), the Sinhalese lack the first two: their highest caste, *goyigama* or *goyikula*, consists of *goviyō* or rice cultivators. This top caste, in striking contrast to the Hindu situation, is by far the largest: in fact in the area where I worked, as perhaps in Sinhalese society at large, it had an absolute majority of the population. The *goyigama* is the only caste found in the hill country which contains sub-divisions, but in most contexts these are not important, and all *goyigama* are known among themselves as 'good men' (*hoňda minissu*), in distinction to the 'lesser castes' (*aḍu kula*). At the other end of the traditional social scale, the Sinhalese hardly have anyone to correspond to the vast array of Hindu outcastes (who among the Tamils in Ceylon may be as numerous as those within caste lines).

The *goyigama* have been equated with *vaiśyas*, and this has considerable historical justification. The Sinhalese words *goyi* and *govi* are derived from the Pali *gahapati*, which literally means 'householder'. Socially this means something like 'bourgeois'. In his study[8] of the society depicted in the *Jātakas* Fick showed that the word *vaiśya* was never used to describe actual people, but the term *gahapati* denoted those who stood in the social structure below the nobility and above the artisans, i.e. where we would have expected to find the *vaiśya*. All the Sinhalese castes below *goyigama* are considered, by those who bother their

[8]R. Fick, *Die Sociale Gliederung im Nordöstlichen Indien zu Buddha's Zeit* (Haeseler, Kiel, 1897).

heads about such matters, to correspond to Hindu *śūdras* (the menial castes), until we come to the *roḍi* at the very bottom. I have not heard the *roḍi* explicitly equated with modern Hindu out-castes, but they are regularly equated with the lowest class in ancient times, the *caṇḍālas* who occur in canonical texts and the *Mahāvaṃsa* as out-castes (i.e. below *śūdras*), so I think the equation could properly be taken a step further. The *roḍi* are beyond the pale of traditional Sinhalese society, the only caste to be 'significantly differentiated culturally';[9] they seem not even to have been allowed into Buddhist temples—a point to which I shall return. There are interesting myths about their origin, which all concur in claiming that the *roḍi* have been degraded from high (royal) status for some heinous offence, e.g. eating human flesh. Traditionally *roḍi* are itinerant beggars, and they are rarely if ever refused, because it is held that their curses are singularly potent. By an extension of this useful belief, *roḍi* are considered experts in black magic. However, their existence does not much disturb the comparative homogeneity of Sinhalese society, because they are extremely few, between 1,500 and 3,000. Most of them have now settled in *roḍi* villages (*kuppāyama*), and in fact I never saw one in my area, where their place at the bottom of the social ladder was taken by exceptionally depressed Tamils.

Before I give a brief description of the operation of caste distinctions in Mīgala, I would like to make a brief excursus into the history of the caste system in Ceylon. In this history different types of social stratification seem to have existed in different periods, all of them usually called 'caste' by European scholars; rather than use question-begging terms like 'caste' and 'class' we might do better to employ some such neutral term as 'status group'; but for simplicity I shall here keep to conventional terminology. The *Mahāvaṃsa* and *Cūlavaṃsa* preserve intact the old Pali terminology according to which society is divided into the four classes *brāhmaṇa*, *kṣatriya*, *vaiśya*, *śūdra*, and

[9]Ryan, op. cit., p. 16.

the out-castes beneath them; but, as in post-vedic India, this division seems to have been primarily theoretical, and there were in fact many more than four status groups. There were never many brahmins in Ceylon, but one village still has the name Bamuṇugama, which means 'brahmin village', and even a thirteenth-century text mentions that a certain monk was of brahmin descent.[10] *Kṣatriyas* were the nobles, the royal and potentially royal families, and they seem to have been divided into clans. The terms *vaiśya* and *śūdra* did not correspond to any clear-cut social units, even in the ancient period, but various groups were subsumed under each term, and possibly the *vaiśyas* were farmers and the *śūdras* artisans, as is theoretically prescribed, though I know of no clear evidence for this. In mediaeval times (say A.D. 500–1500), though society was still said to consist of the four classes, this classification seems to have become irrelevant, and the *Cūlavaṃsa* usually divides society into *kulīnā* ('people of family') and *hīnā* ('inferiors'), the former apparently being the nobility, the latter the common people. The modern caste groupings are never mentioned in the chronicles, which give very scanty information about the sixteenth and seventeenth centuries, supplying only a bare outline of their political and religious history; nor are there any other sources to supply us with data on Kandyan society till the European accounts.

The Kandyan system,[11] which is known to us principally from the account of Robert Knox (see p. 30) written in the late seventeenth century and, in more detail, from nineteenth-century official British observations and reports, was a centralized feudalism in which the king had a basic right to all land, and granted some villages to nobles, temples and shrines, while other lands were held directly under the crown by the village cultivators. But in all cases in return for the land which they cultivated villagers

[10] *Hatthavanagallavihāravaṃsa* (ed. C.E. Godakumbura, P.T.S., London, 1956), 1, 3.

[11] Ralph Pieris, *Sinhalese Social Organization. The Kandyan Period* (Ceylon University Press Board, Colombo, 1956) is the standard work on Kandyan society.

gave service (*rājakāriya*), either to the court, directly or through an administrative official, or to the nobleman or the religious institution which functioned as landlord. In the Kandyan period brahmins and *kṣatriyas* have completely disappeared from Sinhalese society, except in so far as the kings, who latterly were imported from South India, claimed *kṣatriya* status. Society was thus divided into two principal classes, *goyigama* farmers and the service castes, identified by the learned as *vaiśya* and *śūdra* respectively; but although *goyigama* people still call themselves 'good' (*hoňda*) and the rest 'inferior' (*aḍu*) this dichotomy does not correspond directly to the mediaeval one between the *kulīnā* and the *hīnā*, if only because, as far as we can tell, the *kulīnā* were a clear minority of the people, whereas the *goyigama* were and are an absolute majority. On the other hand there is not the slightest doubt that in the Kandyan period all castes, including the *goyigama*, were differentiated by occupation: in other words they were professional groups. I am not asserting that occupation was in all cases the original factor of demarcation between groups. Some of the castes were originally ethnic groups, bodies of immigrants from South India; but such groups adopted particular occupations, which came to characterize them. (The same phenomenon continues today; e.g. all Pathan immigrants seem to be money-lenders.) How groups came by their professions is not entirely mysterious, for we know of cases in which the king ordered certain groups to undertake certain professions. Ralph Pieris writes:[12]

> ...in Kandyan times it was considered the lawful function of the king to ordain appropriate functions to various castes: he could also degrade certain villages or families of high caste to a lower status, and there are certain degraded *gattara* villages [*gattara* are the so-called *goyigama* out-castes, the lowest sub-caste of *goyigama*] in existence to this day. The caste system thus acquired a certain flexibility, and certain groups of people performing specialized functions became, in effect, separate

[12]Op. cit., p. 180.

> castes—the *halāgama* people for instance [who became cinnamon pickers, and are now so known] were weavers imported from India some seven hundred years ago.[13]

I would add that we do not know how many of the Kandyan caste groups, which indeed survive today, existed as groups before the Kandyan period. Notice also that the social groups so created have long survived the disappearance of the Kandyan state. The caste system of the Kandyan feudal period is gradually being superseded by the class system of a more mobile and industrialized society, in which wealth, education, and power (especially association with the government) confer prestige, but this development has not yet had far-reaching effects on Kandyan village life.

Though the central government and its modern apparatus replaced the court in 1815, a few villages are still owned by nobles, temples, or shrines. The present government has announced its intention of finally abolishing the noblemen's feudal villages (*nindagam*), but vested interests on both sides of the House are in no hurry to pass legialation to this effect and the institution is likely to survive for some time. Moreover, the abolition of *nindagam* need not involve villages owned by *vihāras* (*vihāragam*) or by *dēvālēs* (*dēvālayagam*). Mīgala temple, for instance, owns and will doubtless continue to own most of the rice fields of a village higher in the hills. Such ownership means that the temple gets half the produce from a large block of rice fields; the other half goes to the cultivators, who in return also perform services for the temple, which nowadays are virtually confined to ritual drumming. Nowadays if you ask a monk whether his temple has *rājakāriyō* (feudal villeins) he will probably understand the term to mean drummers who are obliged to give their services (rather than hire them out as free agents), whereas formerly the term would have covered all service castes—washermen, smiths, jaggery makers, etc. There are in Ceylon, and have been at least since the seventeenth century, some two

[13] See also Ryan, op. cit., pp. 108–9.

dozen castes, but only about half of these are found in any number in the hill country. Most of the inhabitants of Mīgala (I estimate over 80 per cent) were *goyigama* (rice farmers), many of them of the *paṭṭi* (herdsman) sub-caste and one family of the noble (*radala*) subcaste, which owned a lot of the village rice fields; the only other castes indigenous to the village were grass cutters (*panna*), washermen (*radā*), and a family of drummers (*beravā*).[14] There also lived in the village, in descending order peripheral to its society, Tamils, Muslims, and Low Country Sinhalese; but my remarks apply to local, that is Kandyan, families. Living as I did in a village so predominantly *goyigama*, with washermen, who are the most leniently treated of the low castes, the largest minority group, I probably have a rather rosy picture of inter-caste relations among the laity. Ryan and Yalman record more discriminatory behaviour. But there are many Kandyan villages of caste structure similar to my own, so my experiences are unlikely to be completely atypical.

There is no visible difference between members of different castes. In the Kandyan kingdom there were distinctions of dress, but these were gradually outlawed by the British or eroded by western contact; for instance, it used to be forbidden for low-caste women to wear blouses, but this mark of social degradation now has no legal sanction, and is confined to itinerant *roḍi* beggars, rarely seen in the area, and low-caste Tamil women from the estates. There is free social intercourse between all the poorer Sinhalese members of the village; people are quite likely to drop in on members of another caste for a chat, although it is unusual to pass beyond the verandah. (Members of different castes do not pay on each other those formal calls which Ryan calls 'inter-family visiting', but such visits altogether hardly occur except on ritual occasions, i.e. maybe as lit-

[14]Robert Knox does not list *panna*, though it appears to be a fairly important Kandyan caste; perhaps his informants confused it with *padu* (carriers), as many of mine did. He and most modern sources rank *radā* above *beravā*, but John Davy and my local *goyigama* informants put the washermen lower.

tle as once a year.) The only houses definitely outside this social round are those of the two richest families in the village, one of them the *radala* mentioned above, the equivalent to the lord of the manor, the other an unpopular parvenu with a white-collar job in Kandy; both these houses are distinctive, in their very different styles, by their size and situation. Even among the rest of the villagers it might be found that social familiarity went more by wealth and influence, i.e. 'class', than by caste, although as most or all members of one caste in a given village are also relations, who naturally see more of each other, this is hard to assess. Within the framework of this ease in casual intercourse certain distinctions are unvarying and taken for granted. A lower-caste person must sit on a lower seat, someone lower still must stand: the drummer family, being the lowest caste in my village, stood in the presence of anyone else. The drummer had become comparatively wealthy by growing vegetables on temple lands leased to him and he rented out a house to a schoolmaster, who was *goyigama*; but the schoolmaster, a man who had spent a year in the West, told me he could not bring himself to offer his landlord a seat when he came to see him and so he avoided having him in the house at all. Yet he teaches pupils of all castes seated indiscriminately, and I never found children who sit together at school unwilling to do so elsewhere. A high-caste person will not accept food or drink from a low-caste person, though he will accept a chew of betel, which keeps things sociable: he may offer a lower-caste visitor refreshment, but in a vessel which he does not use himself, e.g. a chipped cup; most often tea, the standard drink, is offered in a coco-nut shell which is then thrown away. To what extent these distinctions are observed among the low-caste (non-*goyigama*) I cannot say; I am sure that they used to be, but nowadays low-caste people are becoming an articulate and often solid minority, increasingly opposed to caste discrimination, and their opposition may gradually extend to discrimination from their inferiors as well as from their superiors. Marriage outside the caste is still very rare; there was one case in Mīgala, a *goyigama* woman married a low-caste man, but he was from Colombo and worked far away, so that he was rarely seen in the village. He was also a communist trade union official—a typical syndrome. Predictably this girl was generally regarded as a bad lot, but to us, perhaps because we were westerners known to care little about caste, her badness was said to consist in her communism, which was purely marital, and her private life, which was subject to various unsavoury rumours, not all of which, I suspect, were untrue. However, this woman was not boycotted by everyone in the village, nor as far as I know was she considered to have lost caste, a leniency in striking contrast to custom under the kings of Kandy, where in theory at least marriage to a man of lower caste was punished by death. Her children would be ascribed to their father's caste, but will probably move to the anonymity of Colombo, or at least to a government post far away where their antecedents are not known.

Despite the paucity of easily identifiable forms of discrimination, it must not be thought that villagers are for a moment unaware of caste distinctions. My evidence is linguistic. There are in Sinhalese several personal pronouns of address and reference, graded by status, as well as various forms of address: for instance, an equal or superior is not normally addressed by name. A person's attitude to caste is thus discernible in the pronouns he uses. My experience here is alas rather limited, especially as I myself always used polite forms for low-caste people, so that my interlocutors might politely adopt my style; however, I think that *goyigama* adults rarely address, and among themselves never refer to, low-caste members of their village as equals. There are of course degrees of inferiority, and I have heard the lowest pronoun, 'ū', which is primarily used for animals, used to refer to a low-caste person, though it is very rude for anyone, however socially exalted, to use this form to another person's face. The only time I heard this done was by a young monk, avowedly a communist, to an old service drummer with whom he was annoyed, and it had a most unpleasant ring. This brings us back to Buddhism, and it is time for me to consider the

Buddha's own attitude towards caste, as manifested in the Pali Canon.

In the Buddha's environment (north-east India round 500 B.C.) the caste system was by no means so rigid and elaborate as it has become in India, or even in Ceylon, and so we must not expect to find in the scriptures pronouncements dealing with precisely the situation obtaining today. The theory of the four great classes of *brāhmaṇa*, *kṣatriya*, *vaiśya*, and *śūdra*, to which I referred earlier, as well as the out-castes below these, already existed. There were also a few domestic slaves (as was also the case in the Sinhalese kingdom) who could in theory come from any caste though I suspect that they usually came from low castes; what their caste position in servitude was is not quite clear, but from a reference in a slightly later Sanskrit text, the *Arthaśāstra*, which says that high-caste slaves could not be compelled to do defiling duties, it seems that like their later Sinhalese equivalents they were not necessarily degraded. The institution of slavery, a peripheral phenomenon in Indian civilization, should be treated with caste because the children of slaves were also slaves (unless specifically manumitted), so that their status was wholly ascribed, not achieved. There was neither intermarriage (though hypergamy seems to have been allowed after the first wife) nor commensality between all members of one class, and *a fortiori* not between members of different classes, so the modern system was beginning to appear, but we lack details. Hindu law-books, of a slightly later date but pre-dating the modern system, show that ideally people followed the profession of their fathers, but there was provision for a different way of life in misfortune (*āpad dharma*), by which for instance a brahmin could engage in trade without losing caste. In north-east India, the area where Buddhism arose, the major question of the day seems to have been whether *brāhmaṇa* or *kṣatriya*, priest or warrior, spiritual or secular power, was the higher caste. Further to the west the brahmins had already established their supremacy. The Buddha, however, came from a tribe in the Himalayan foothills, the Śākyas, who claimed *kṣatriya* status. There is a Buddhist tradition that Buddhas are born into either the *brāhmaṇa* or the *kṣatriya* caste, whichever is higher at the time. Most of the Buddha's sermons dealing with caste are concerned with the problem, 'Who is the true brahmin?' Some western interpreters have jumped too quickly to the conclusion that the Buddha ethicized the concept of caste and argued against all such social distinctions. He did ethicize the concept, but he did not argue against the continuing use of the social distinction within its own context; moreover, this ethicization is only half the story. In one text[15] a caste-proud young brahmin is insolent to the Buddha and disparages the Śākyas. The first half of the Buddha's response shows the brahmin that *kṣatriyas* are superior to brahmins, for they are more rigorous and exclusive; for instance, if we are to believe the text, a *kṣatriya* outlawed by his own caste would be ritually acceptable to the *brāhmaṇas*, whereas the converse would not hold. The second half then proceeds to expound the often-repeated doctrine that holiness is not inherited but acquired, that the true brahmin is not a born *brāhmaṇa*, but someone who has achieved enlightenment. Obviously the Buddha preferred to argue from strength; had he merely told the brahmin that birth was irrelevant he would have been open to the charge of 'sour grapes'. Similarly, in an amusing mythical account[16] of the origin of the social order, the Buddha heartens two young brahmin converts, who are being reviled by brahmins for associating with him and the other monks, by telling them that the *kṣatriya* order is top because it came first, from men selected to govern the rest; at the same time he is at pains to point out that they were chosen from among equals as *primi inter pares*. But in talking of laymen the Buddha does not go much further than saying:[17] 'Not by birth is one a brahmin, not by birth an out-caste; by deeds

[15] *Ambaṭṭha Sutta, D.N., Sutta* 3.
[16] *Aggañña Sutta, D.N., Sutta* 27.
[17] *Sutta-nipāta*, 136.

is one a brahmin, by deeds an out-caste.' Inter-caste behaviour is not mentioned in discourses on lay ethics, and there are certainly no exhortations to social equality. Indeed, caste is accepted as a fact of life on a par with other forms of status; to be reborn in a low and unimportant family is the result of demerit in this life, typically of failing to respect those of superior status.[18]

Questions of inter-caste ethics among laymen seem to have been confined in primitive Buddhism to rivalry between *kṣatriyas* and brahmins for the top position. In all Buddhist texts, contrary to practice elsewhere, *kṣatriyas* are mentioned first when the four classes are listed. Presumably the Buddha's repudiation of ritual, by denigrating the brahmins' religious importance, involved also a denigration of their social importance. Buddhist ethics show a general tendency to esteem wealth and power, rather than birth, as criteria of worldly success, and I see the raising of the *kṣatriya* above the brahmin as fitting into this pattern. However, those who lead the holy life are supposed to pass beyond such rivalries and distinctions. The Buddha draws the line: 'In the supreme perfection of wisdom and righteousness there is no mention of notions of birth, of lineage, or of the snobbery which says "You are as good as I" or "You are not as good as I". It is when there is marriage or giving in marriage that there is mention of such notions. For whoever are bound by notions of birth, of lineage, of snobbery, or of marriage ties are far from the supreme perfection of wisdom and righteousness. Only having got rid of the bondage of these notions may one realize this supreme perfection.'[19]

Monks and nuns could come from any caste. This was apparently not a Buddhist innovation, but traditional among those who 'went forth to the homeless life' and became hermits or wandering ascetics. In the aetiological

[18] *Cūla Kammavibhanga Sutta, M.N., Sutta* 135. Other texts dealing with caste, not here discussed, are the *Madhura Sutta (M.N., Sutta* 84) and the *Assalāyana Sutta (M.N., Sutta* 93).

[19] *D.N.*, I, 99–200 (*Ambaṭṭha Sutta*, 2. 1).

myth just referred to the Buddha says that members of all four orders became the first ascetics. In the *Jātakas* we hear of a potter[20] and a *caṇḍāla* (out-caste)[21] who became non-Buddhist ascetics.

That all castes were admitted to the Sangha is stressed both by the Buddhists and by their brahmin opponents, who call them menial, dark-skinned *śūdras*, or even address the Buddha himself as an out-caste,[22] which from their ritual standpoint he was, because of his contacts with out-castes. We know of several monks and nuns that they were low-born, and Upāli, the monk who was the greatest authority on the monastic rules (*vinaya*) had been a barber, one of the lowest occupations. As for their relations with the laity, monks were told to accept food from anyone[23] (the doctrine is ascribed to Kassapa, a former Buddha, but I see no significance in this) so they did not recognize ritual impurity in laymen any more than they did among themselves. The Buddha's last meal was a dinner of pork given him by a smith.

In no other respect has Buddhism in Ceylon come so far from its original state as in the invasion of the Order by caste, yet another testimony to the remarkable strength of that insidious institution. By most monks the contradiction is realized and admitted; it is not a subject on which they are happy to talk. This shame shows that doctrinally they have not changed, though I shall recount one remarkable piece of sophistry, a reinterpretation of a scripture just quoted. Behaviour, however, is now completely at variance with the original doctrine in all the points I have set out concerning the internal conduct of the Order, as well as in the conduct of many monks towards the laity.

There are two pieces of evidence to suggest that caste discrimination within the Sangha is ancient in Ceylon. The

[20] *J.*, III, 381.

[21] *J.*, IV, 392.

[22] *Sutta-nipāta, Vasala Sutta Vasala Sutta*, prose introduction l. 7.

[23] *Sutta-nipāta, Āmagandha Sutta*, 241.

introduction to a *Jātaka* story (I, 217) told by the Buddha says that the occasion for the story was a dispute when monks who had been *kṣatriyas* and brahmins claimed preferential treatment in the monastery. This introduction is commentatorial, and in its present form was written in Ceylon about the fifth century A.D., but the commentator surely did not invent it himself. At the same time I doubt whether the tradition goes back more than the 700 years which would take its origin back to India rather than Ceylon. The most likely conjecture is that this episode reflects conditions very early in the history of Ceylonese Buddhism. The other piece of evidence has more radical implications but is less certain. Two of the monasteries founded during Mahinda's mission were called in Pali Issarasamaṇaka and Vessagiri, which names mean respectively 'That which has ascetics who are lords' and 'The hill of the *vaiśyas*'. The *Mahāvaṃsa* (XX, 14–15) says that the former monastery was entered by men from noble families, the latter by *vaiśyas*. This would show caste differentiation on what we shall see is the modern pattern. I say that the evidence is uncertain because the *Mahāvaṃsa* was composed over 600 years after the events described, albeit on the basis of earlier materials, and its author may be conjecturing the origin of place names. If, however, he is right, this would suggest to me not merely that monks in Ceylon were always divided on caste lines, but that this was probably so in India at that time, some 250 years after the Buddha's death; for I cannot believe that Mahinda would have sanctioned so radical an innovation.

However, there is absolutely no clear evidence for subsequent caste discrimination in the Sangha during the Anurādhapura and Poḷonnaruva periods. The origin of the restriction of entry to the Siyam Nikāya to the *goyigama* caste is the subject of much learned controversy.[24] Though the Siyam Nikāya was founded in 1753, the custom has far older roots. The first reference to the problem occurs in

[24]For the bibliography on this question see Bechert, op. cit., note 739 (p. 216).

the Dam̆badeni Katikāvata,[25] dated 1266, which says that at the *upasampadā* (higher ordination) ceremony the ordinand is to be asked his caste.[26]

The Portuguese historian Queyroz wrote in the 1670s[27] that only men of noble birth (*appuhāmis*) became monks.[28] Knox in the same period reports likewise: the only people admitted into the Sangha are 'persons of the most noble birth, and that have learning and be well bred'.[29] These two passages suggest that only *goyigama* men became monks. However, at the great *upasampadā* ceremony in Kandy in 1753 ordination was not in fact restricted to members of the *goyigama* caste: among the ordinands were a member of the *durāva* (toddy-tappers) caste, Siṭināmaluvē Dhammajoti, who became incumbent of the famous ancient monastery of Mulkirigala in the Southern Province, and Vēhällē Dhammadinna, who by caste was a drummer (*beravā*). These two were both pupils of Välivița Saraṇaṃkara, and most leading monks in the Low Country Siyam Nikāya today trace their pupillary succession back to them. However, in about 1765 a royal decree, claiming that unworthy monks had been ordained, restricted the holding of *upasampadā* ceremonies to the monasteries of Malvatta and Asgiriya in Kandy. Such a restriction is contrary to the *vinaya* rules, but has been in force ever since. Though peculiar to Ceylon, it has been copied by the other Nikāyas; they all restrict ordination ceremonies to Nikāya headquarters. Its purpose must have been to tighten central control, in particular

[25]A *katikāvata* is a decree promulgated by a Mahāsanghasabhā, a council of monks, and (before 1815) approved by the king, which comments on or modifies *vinaya* rules, and has the force of ecclesiastical law within the Nikāya in which it is promulgated.

[26]Published in D.B. Jayatilaka (ed.), *Katikāvat saňgarā*, Colombo, 1922, p. 9.

[27]I am indebted to Dr. K. Malalgoḍa for almost all the information in the following paragraph.

[28]F. de Queyroz, *The Temporal and Spiritual Conquest of Ceylon*, trans. S.G. Perera (Government Press, Colombo, 1930), p. 114.

[29]Knox, op. cit., p. 117.

royal control, over the Sangha; whether caste had anything to do with it we cannot tell, but the fact that the king, Kīrti Śrī Rājasiṃha, issued a *katikāvata* repeating the above-mentioned extract from the Daṁbadeni Katikāvata inclines one to suspect it. Already in 1769 monks replying to a questionnaire from the Dutch governor of the coastal provinces stated that according to the *vinaya* any caste was allowed in the Sangha, but that in fact admission was restricted to high-caste men. John Davy, who was in Kandy from 1816 to 1820, reports that only *goyigama* men can become monks.[30] There are cases between 1773 and 1798 of novices from the fisher (*karāva*) caste which ranks second to the *goyigama* , receiving the *upasampadā*, but these seem to have been exceptions allowed on orders from the head (Mahānāyaka) of the chapter.[31]

It was in 1798 that Aṁbagahapiṭiyē Ñāṇavimalatissa, a member of the cinnamon-picking (*salāgama*) caste, went to Burma to be ordained; on his return in 1802 he founded the Amarapura Nikāya. He was soon imitated by members of the fisher (*karāva*) and toddy-tapping (*durāva*) caste. These three castes are virtually confined to the Low Country, and are there reckoned below only *goyigama* in status. The Amarapura Nikāya thus contains several ordination traditions (*paramparā*). In 1864 the Rāmañña Nikāya was similarly founded by Aṁbagahavattē Indāsabhavarañāṇa.

If the Amarapura Nikāya contains more than one ordination tradition, it may well be asked what it is that constitutes a Nikāya. The answer to this question is complicated, but only because the word *nikāya* has come to have two closely related but distinct uses. In the Introduction was described how throughout most of the Anurādhapura period there were in Ceylon three *nikāyas*, so that the term 'the three *nikāyas*' was locally synonymous with 'the

[30]John Davy, *An Account of the Interior of Ceylon* (Longman, London, 1821), p. 219.

[31]For exceptions to the *goyigama* rule in this period see the bibliography in Bechert, op. cit., note 740 (p. 219).

Sangha'. It may be this historical fact which has determined the modern usage of referring once again to 'the three Nikāyas', by which is meant the Siyam, Amarapura, and Rāmañña Nikāyas. (In this sense I am spelling Nikāya with a capital N, and not italicizing it.)[32] This usage is universal and has some organizational correlates. From the point of view of ordination tradition, however, none of these Nikāyas is a unity. Nor is its origin the crucial criterion for establishing what is a *nikāya* in the narrow, technical sense of the word. A *nikāya* is a body of monks with a head (*mahānāyaka*) which holds independent *upasampadā* ceremonies for its novices, whether the line of pupillary succession has been renewed from abroad or there has merely been a fissure caused by a group of monks stating their autonomy. A *nikāya* in fact can be said to exist when it has been recognized by the Registrar General.[33]

A list of the *nikāyas*, which is based principally on the report of the Śāsana Commission,[34] appears on pp. 263–5 of Bechert's book.[35] As Bechert remarks in his note 718 (pp. 212–13), there are also some monasteries in Ceylon which do not belong to any Nikāya: these are the creations of modernists, often Europeans, and need not concern us.

There are absolutely no differences in doctrine between the three Nikāyas, merely a few differences in customs. These are listed by Bechert on p. 215. The Siyam Nikāya, as he points out, carries on the old Ceylonese traditions, whereas the other two Nikāyas have imported some customs from Burma. The Rāmañña Nikāya, the most recently formed, has not entirely lost its original reformatory zeal, and its monks, like those of some small Amarapura

[32]Keeping these Nikāyas in roman letters has the further advantage of differentiating them from the four *Nikāyas* (*Dīgha* etc.) of the *Sutta Piṭaka.*

[33]This point was explained by Arnold Green at the conference held on Ceylon in Philadelphia, August 1967.

[34]*Buddha śāsana komiṣan vārtāva*, Colombo, 1959, pp. 29–49.

[35]Basic information on the formation of *nikāyas* in the nineteenth century and their caste connections has been assembled and presented with admirable clarity by Dr. K. Malalgoḍa in his thesis and book.

nikāyas with similar origins, observe the *vinaya* rules more strictly in certain particulars, also mentioned by Bechert.

The main principle of differentiation between *nikāyas* is, however, caste. In general this is well known both to western scholars and within Ceylon; but I found a state of affairs more extreme than that reported by Bechert, whose work on the subject is the most complete and up-to-date published.[36] Between the various branches of the Siyam Nikāya I know of no caste differences, though it is rumoured that certain monasteries in Malvatta and Asgiriya (which are really two groups of monasteries sharing certain facilities) admit only *radalas*, the top *goyigama* sub-caste. That the Amarapura Nikāya is divided mainly on caste lines was already stated by Ryan in a passage quoted by Bechert (pp. 219–20).[37] It does not normally recruit from the *goyigama* or the very low castes, though in this certain *nikāyas* are exceptional (see below). Bechert, following Ryan,[38] is wrong in stating that the Rāmañña Nikāya is casteless, even though this was its original intention. It is generally believed in Ceylon that the Rāmañña Nikāya occupies an intermediate social position between the other two Nikāyas, and this appears to be correct. I cannot confirm or refute the popular opinion that in the Low Country it recruits predominantly from the top two castes, *goyigama* and *karāva*; I was, however, told by all the Rāmañña monks whom I interviewed (and am sure it is true) that the Kandyan (*uḍa raṭa*) branch admits only *goyigama* men, just like the Siyam Nikāya. Indeed, caste has penetrated the Rāmañña Nikāya so deeply that one of their young monks tried to convince me that they are socially superior to the Siyam Nikāya, claiming (untruly)

[36] Professor Arnold Green has a vast amount of material on the organization of the Amarapura Nikāya, based on field-work in Ceylon, 1960–1, but this is unfortunately not published. See also previous footnote.

[37] Ryan's conjecture near the end of the extract that some of the Amarapura schisms were on doctrinal lines seems to be without foundation.

[38] Bechert, op. cit., p. 220, inc. note 743.

that the Siyam Nikāya admit some low-caste men while the Rāmañña does not.

In reviewing the answers I got to my questions about caste I must distinguish between the members of the three Nikāyas. The six Amarapura monks were themselves low-caste while the rest were *goyigama*, and the Rāmañña Nikāya has an official policy of castelessness while the Siyam Nikāya does not. Common to all, however, was a readiness to describe the differences between the three Nikāyas in terms of caste; a couple of monks delicately referred to varying 'customs' (*sirit virit*). The answers of Amarapura monks held no surprises: they were against caste altogether, and said they made no distinctions even against *roḍi*, and in support of their views even cited the passage given above from the *Vasala Sutta*: 'Not by birth is one a brahmin ...' Even they, however, made no bones about stating that the Nikāyas are mainly differentiated by caste. As might be expected, they were perhaps readier than the Siyam Nikāya monks to claim social intercourse (*āsraya*) with the other Nikāyas, if such a statement can be made on the basis of so small a sample.

The attitude of monks of the Siyam Nikāya towards caste ranged from the monk who thought all caste distinctions were false and wrong ('*boru väḍak*') to the unquestioning acceptance of many monks, especially the older ones, coupled perhaps with some dismay at the disappearance of caste barriers. A young westernized monk claimed to be against caste distinction (*kulabhēdaya*), but belied his statements by his conduct, addressing even an old man of the drummer caste by a very low pronoun (*ū*). Very few monks regard caste distinctions in lay society as something undesirable or troublesome to the conscience; it is a fact of life, and the scriptural position that low caste is the result of sin in a former birth is widely upheld. The origin of caste was referred to the canonical text on the subject, which tells of the first king (Mahāsammata) and how the four classes arose by a social contract. One monk slightly perverted this story by claiming that castes were created by kings to punish people for their bad acts—a reference perhaps to the origin of certain Sinhalese degraded castes. He then astonished me by interpreting the *Vasala Sutta* in this way: people are high or low caste 'not by birth', but by their acts—so it is the low castes' own fault! Even he, however, said that essentially all men are equal (*ātmē vaśayen ekayi*), by which he meant that men of all castes have the capacity for Enlightenment. This I think no Sinhalese Buddhist could be found to deny.

Siyam Nikāya monks are generally well aware that in the time of the Buddha the Order was open to all. Only one monk stated the opposite. One monk represented such freedom as exceptional, due to special circumstances in their former lives. As an instance he told the story of Upāli: six cousins of the Buddha went to join the Order and took along Upāli, their barber. In the forest they prepared themselves for ordination, and gave him their lay clothes. He thought that if he returned alone with the clothes of the six princes he would be assumed to have murdered them for their valuables, so he took fright and decided to join the Order too. The Buddha ordained him first so that he was senior to the other six and they had to worship (*vaňdinṭa*) him; he did this to ensure that they would not return to the lay life, because they would be so ashamed at having worshipped a low-caste man. Upāli had been born in a low caste because in a previous life he was haughty towards his inferiors; but he had good *karma* to get him into the Order because for innumerable ages (*kalpa lakṣayak*) he had wished to be a monk under the Buddha. My informant has related the story as it is told in the *Vinaya Piṭaka*,[39] with one twist: in the original text it is the princes who suggest, as a token of humility, that Upāli be their senior; but in the new version it becomes the Buddha's idea, to rub in the degradation of prostrating oneself before a barber.

The story which Siyam Nikāya monks will almost invariably tell when asked why they only admit *goyigama* recruits is, in view of the historical antecedents quoted

[39] *Vin.*, II (*Cullavagga*), 182–3.

above, presumably apocryphal. The king (often specified as Kīrti Śrī Rājasiṃha, or the last king of Kandy, Śrī Vikrama Rājasiṃha), who is of course ritually inferior to the meanest novice, was paying a call on a monastery, when a low-caste monk so far forgot himself as to rise from his seat at His Majesty's entrance. The king was so embarrassed by this breach of decorum that he decreed that henceforth only men of good birth could enter the Order. Monks explain that they are bound to obey the temporal power. I would suggest that the temporal power of today does not demand caste exclusiveness in the Sangha, and most had no answer to this, but one replied that the king's injunction is embodied in a *katikāvata*, and as it has never been rescinded it still has the force of *vinaya*. I asked several monks what would happen if they gave the lower ordination to a low-caste pupil, and all agreed that he would be refused the higher ordination at Malvatta or Asgiriya. At least half the monks questioned on this point seemed, however, somewhat ashamed of the state of affairs, and candidly admit that entry into the Order should be unrestricted. In strong contrast, one monk said that all respectable (*sälakiyayutu*) people joined the Siyam Nikāya; some *goyigama* joined the Rāmañña Nikāya, but this was not good [i.e. letting the side down].

As mentioned above, the three monks of the Rāmañña Nikāya whom I interviewed were also *goyigama*, and I gathered from them that locally, and probably in the whole of the Kandyan area, their Nikāya too was restricted to this caste. One of them, who went so far as to tell me that his Nikāya was purer caste-wise than the Siyam Nikāya, behaved very like a Siyam Nikāya monk in telling me that he personally disapproved, but his headquarters would not allow him to ordain a low-caste pupil.

Caste also plays a part in determining the behaviour of monks to laity. The extreme case is that of the *roḍi*, who were not admitted to monasteries or temples. One monk said that the Sinhalese kings prohibited it. John Davy wrote:[40] 'Prohibited from approaching temples, there is a solitary instance on record of a priest going and preaching to them, for which, having incurred his sovereign's displeasure, he replied, "Religion should be common to all".' That priest would nowadays find more approval but still few emulators. I believe that the settlements of the *roḍi* and the *kinnara* (the next lowest caste) lack monasteries, so that they do not normally hear preaching; but a famous monk from Vajirārāma, Nārada Thera, has gone and preached to them, and I doubt whether anyone now would censure him. Not surprisingly, the only monks who indicated that they would not allow *roḍi* in were three elderly members of the Siyam Nikāya. Another monk, who was generally reactionary on this subject, said they could go into the *vihāra* but not come into the *pansala*. One of the Rāmañña Nikāya monks said that of course *roḍi* could come if they wished, but they would normally not enter a *pansala*. Most monks, however, seemed to think that they both could and would come, and welcomed the change.

One Siyam Nikāya monk, an amiable character, went so far as to specify that *roḍi* could even give a *dānē*. Were such a situation ever to arise I wonder what would happen. The question whether *goyigama* monks (perhaps I should say Siyam Nikāya monks) will accept food and drink from a low-caste person is most curious. There is no doubt that according to doctrine they should, and I was always assured that they do; however, I witnessed a counter-example. A large group of Siyam Nikāya monks were invited to a washerman's home for their midday meal; they came and ate the food, but brought with them a lot of king coco-nuts, from which they drank the liquid instead of accepting ordinary water from the householder. Though no one would admit to there being any particular reason for this I cannot think that they were actuated merely by gormandize. They might take pork from a smith, but they refuse water from a washerman.

In considering the attitude of the laity towards monks

[40] Davy, op. cit., p. 131.

of different caste, we come perhaps to the nub of the problem. Brahmins reviled the Buddha and his followers for their ritual impurity, but they did not mind; their successors have proved less stoical. Davy brings up this point:[41] 'Only the Goewansè... can belong to the priesthood; not that religion excludes the rest, but pride—people of the first caste not being able to condescend to pay the respect due to a priest to a low-caste individual.' A *goyigama* friend of mine confessed to me that he still feels the same way. The Siyam Nikāya story about the king and the low-caste monk is no doubt an attempt to show this tension between high-caste layman and low-caste monk in another light. In the area which I have observed, the usual solution to this problem is avoidance: high-caste laymen just do not normally go to Amarapura monasteries. If they do for some reason have to go they fail, unless they are very religious individuals, to pay their traditional respects by kneeling and touching or making to touch the monk's feet. High-caste monks condemn this failure, but in fact they themselves seem to avoid formal contact with their low-caste brethren; a Siyam Nikāya informant had been invited by an Amarapura Nikāya informant to the *nētra pinkama* at his temple, at the other end of the same village, but had not gone and had never even been to visit him.

So long as this remains the prevalent attitude among *goyigama* laymen it is hard not to sympathize with the following argument. The monk who offered it was a *goyigama* member of the Rāmañña Nikāya, who amply demonstrated his own freedom from traditional prejudice by planning an alms-giving to be attended by members of all three Nikāyas, an event which would I believe be unique in that area; he said he had friends in the Amarapura Nikāya, and had no time for caste distinctions. However, he had taken only *goyigama* pupils. He lived, he explained, in a village which was almost solid *goyigama*; if he took a low-caste pupil they would find fault, and some of them might not

[41] Davy, op. cit., p. 219.

even bow down to him. Plainly—if I may expand on his statement—a low-caste pupil would be a disaster, as his parishioners would stop attending the monastery, which would deprive him of his subsistence; some would go to a monastery elsewhere, and some would stop going at all, which would deprive them of merit. In all practical ways the cause of Buddhism would suffer, merely to accommodate a young man who could always find a niche in the Amarapura Nikāya.

The involvement of monks in the caste system is the result of their active involvement in a caste-ridden society. The Buddha told his monks[42] to travel around 'for the public welfare and happiness, out of compassion for the world', i.e. to keep in touch with the laity. The major unintended consequence of this involvement was the evolution of the Sangha in the first centuries after the Buddha's death from a fraternity of wandering mendicants to a loose federation (or group of federations) of settled monastic communities with communal property. It was given some rationale by the decision in ancient Ceylon (ascribed by Rahula to the first century B.C.)[43] that learning (*pariyatti*) was of paramount importance, and therefore book-duty (*gantha-dhura*) was more essential than meditation-duty (*vipassanā-dhura*). In this decision was implicit the previous ethical decision that the preservation of the doctrine (Pali: *sāsanaṭṭhiti*) was of paramount importance, a social aim not necessarily compatible with the original doctrine of individual salvation. Although the preservation of the doctrine was seen largely in terms of the preservation of the Sangha, and book-duty meant preservation of the texts within the Sangha, a Buddhist laity is essential for recruitment to the Sangha and for its economic support; book-duty therefore necessarily involves preaching and other religious education, and therefore residence near the laity and considerable contact with lay society. Compared to this general abandonment of the wandering life, a

[42] *Vin.*, I, 21.

[43] Rahula, *History*, pp. 157–60.

development which began before Buddhism left India, the secularization of monastic organization in mediaeval Ceylon is of secondary importance. Monasteries became landlords and their incumbents (*vihārādhipati*) feudal lords, so that the monks added temporal power to their traditional prestige. An incumbency (*ayitivāsikama*) became hereditary, so that monks were tempted, not to put too fine a point on it, to keep wealth in the family, and passed their position on to relatives.[44] This tendency for the families of monks to acquire wealth and power, and the general approximation of the role of monk to that of feudal landlord, must both have worked towards keeping monasteries in the hands of the top caste; since the pattern of family ties and caste exclusiveness had been established it was difficult for other Nikāyas, although founded with reformatory ambi-

[44]In Sinhalese ecclesiastical law there are two kinds of succession (*paramparāva*) possible: *śiṣyānuśiṣya paramparāva* and *jñāti paramparāva alias sivuru paramparāva*. A given incumbency is handed down by one method or the other. By the latter a monk leaves his incumbency to a relative, who to ensure his rights has of course to be a monk too, but may only enter the Order on taking his inheritance. The former covers several procedures somewhat more in accordance with the spirit of the *vinaya* (there can be no question of accord with the letter of the *vinaya*, as no such thing as succession was originally envisaged). As explained to me, it means that a monk's first pupil succeeds him: according to printed sources (see end of this note) there are other varieties. In any of these cases, however, the heir to the incumbency may still be a relative; the difference is that in law he does not inherit *ipso facto*, but by reason of some other claim. When I did my field-work this distinction was not clear to me: I thought that *jñāti-paramparāva* meant succession by a relative *under any circumstances*. I suspect that my informants may have thought the same. I came across several cases of succession by relatives, but whether any of these were *jñāti-paramparāva* monasteries I cannot say. I owe my enlightenment on this point to Bechert (op. cit., p. 226). In two sections, on the legal condition of individual monasteries (pp. 224–30) and the administration of the Sangha's temporalities (pp. 230–44), he provides an excellent summary of the situation regarding ecclesiastical property in Ceylon since 1815. As usual, his footnotes contain an extensive bibliography on the subject.

tions, not to go the same way.

If I am right, the demands of modernists that monks should involve themselves still further in society, after the model (usually not expressed) of Christian priests, would tend to perpetuate rather than diminish caste in the Sangha. This would be an unintended consequence of their actions; their intentions are of course quite in the opposite direction, for like early reformatory movements (e.g. the Rāmañña Nikāya) they hope to restore the primitive castelessness of the Sangha, or even to restore an imagined primitive castelessness among Buddhist laity. My hypothesis is unfortunately unlikely ever to be put to the test, because the influence of the modernists is a puny force compared to the general trend towards modernization which is breaking down caste barriers and other traditional societal patterns. However, my observations may support this interpretation. The attitude monks have to caste among the laity, as exemplified in their attitude to *roḍi*, has become far more liberal, in conformity with general modern trends in society and also with the views of Buddhist modernists; but I found no signs that caste within the clergy is losing its grip, for here the ever greater involvement of monks in society works in the same direction as traditional pressures, and the economic forces which play so much part in breaking down caste in society at large have no influence.

It only remains to consider why caste should be so much less oppressive in Sinhalese than in Indian society. What has already been said of Buddhism must render the answer obvious. (See also Chapter 4, p. 215.) Pollution plays far less part in Sinhalese than in Hindu society. The Buddha did not recognize the existence of such a thing as far as he and his fellow monks were concerned. The only ethic with which he was concerned was a universalist ethic: there is no mention in the scriptures of caste *dharma*, no suggestion that an action which is right for one man may be wrong for another. According to Buddhist theory, caste originated as a matter of convenience and has no more ethical implications than wealth or beauty. It is part of Ceylon's Indian heritage; but in Buddhist society it has lost its rationale.

So although caste is not condemned it is de-emphasized. The traditions of Hinduism tend to stress the differences between men; the traditions of Buddhism lay the accent on their similarity.

9

Conclusion

> What this Niwanē is, is a religious mystery: priests are rather averse from answering questions on the subject; they say, it is forbidden to discuss its nature, and on the principle that if men understood it they would not like it but prefer worldly things, as flies do bad smells.[1]

AT the outset of this work I said I would distinguish what people say from what they do. At its conclusion I wish to emphasize what this means. It is not the same as the distinction made between behavioural and textual Buddhism; for that is a distinction, as I understand it, between what people do now and what they said (or wrote) a long time ago. My investigation centred on what people *say now*, as well as what they do now, and I found, as will not surprise anyone at all familiar with Ceylon, that there are discrepancies. What people say now has turned out, however, to be remarkably similar to what was being said about 1,500 years ago. But are we sure that in those days they really did what they said, that they practised what they preached? I doubt it. The evidence of the *Mahāvaṃsa* suggests to me that there were then discrepancies between Buddhist principle and Buddhist practice quite as gross as anything found today. Around 100 B.C. Duṭugämuṇu puts a relic in his spear (magic talisman!) to fight a holy war (counter to doctrine!) for Buddhism, makes a statement of truth (magic spell!) to protect his army, is told by monks that killing non-Buddhists is not killing (intolerance! ignorance of first precept!), puts up vast relic chambers with a statue of the Buddha (devotional theism!), makes Buddhism the state religion (Buddhism in politics!), etc. The monks in the fifth century who compiled the *Mahāvaṃsa*,

[1]Davy, op. cit., p. 216.

and predicted Duṭugämuṇu's rebirth as the chief disciple of the next Buddha, obviously thought his holy war fully justified. Not all my informants were so sure.

The Reverend Rahula, who knows as much about the subject matter of this book as anyone alive, likes to call all this 'popular Buddhism'. Duṭugämuṇu's Buddhism was presumably 'popular'. I find this term dangerously misleading. It implies, I think, a decline by most people, the *plebs*, from an ideal standard which is maintained by a few spiritual aristocrats, a relationship analogous to that between 'popular' and 'classical' music. By some it might even be understood to imply the religion of the laity as distinct from that of monks. To this latter assumption, which would be especially erroneous, I shall return below. To the former I would reiterate a request for demonstration of 'classical' Buddhist behaviour, outside the edifying stories in scriptures and textbooks which are inserted for didactic purposes. Monks fought in Duṭugämuṇu's army and sanctioned what he did. And how many Buddhists in Ceylon, even in this post-Dharmapāla era, never take part in *pirit* or transfer merit, practices they brand as 'popular'? I think the only sense in which it is accurate to describe these beliefs and practices as 'popular' is the everyday one of 'widely liked' or 'prevalent'. But if so used 'popular' no longer distinguishes merit transference from, say, the Four Noble Truths or alms-giving.

Gananath Obeyesekere in his lectures has pointed out that Weber too mixed up what the texts say and how people actually behaved. In *The Religion of India* he paints a picture of the passionless *arhat*, the materials for which are drawn (mainly at second hand) from Pali scriptures, deduces from this picture of the ideal Buddhist personality that the first Buddhists were in fact like that, and then from this draws conclusions about their social and economic behaviour. 'The mystic, acosmic love of Buddhism (*maitrī, mettā*) is psychologically conditioned through the euphoria of apathetic ecstasy... [The *arhat's*] temper...remains cool and aloof...'[2] Weber then has difficulty harmonizing this picture with the *Theragāthā* and *Therīgāthā*, the two canonical collections of religious poems composed by the monks and nuns themselves. 'The tone to which the hymns of ancient Buddhism are attuned is triumphant joy.'[3]

This should have brought Weber face to face with the issue which, however, he fudged, of whether the Buddhist ideal was really negative, as he contended, or positive, which he claimed to be a later development. The Five Precepts, like the ontology, are negatively formulated, but have they ever constituted the whole ideal? To put the matter more clearly, is the ideal self-restraint or love? Not only are there two ideal values, which can be characterized as negative and positive; there are two possible ideal goals, *nirvāṇa* and heaven, which can be similarly contrasted; and two possible courses of action which characteristically lead to these goals, self-restraint and the outward passivity of meditation, or active 'merit-making', typically giving alms.

It is in the light of these and related dichotomies that I would like to survey the material collected in this work. In Chapter 6 we saw that these two values, self-restraint and love, usually expressed by the adjectives *śānta dānta* and *karuṇāvanta*, are dominant among the Sinhalese today. The ideals are very different, and not necessarily compatible. The contrast—if you like, the tension—between them illuminates the history of Buddhism.

We saw at the end of the previous chapter that early in the history of Ceylonese Buddhism the question arose, 'Which is the basis of the doctrine, learning or practice?',[4] and that underlying this controversy, which foreshadowed the division of monks into book men and meditation men, was the essentially altruistic concern for the preservation

[2] Weber, op. cit., p. 208.

[3] Ibid., p. 212.

[4] *Manorathapūraṇī* (*Anguttara Aṭṭhakathā*), I, 92, quoted in Pali by Rahula, *History*, p. 158, note 3.

of Buddhism. The same dilemma, though perhaps unrealized, already underlay the Buddha's injunction to monks to keep moving among the laity. This conflict between self-restraint and love, between selfishness and altruism, between negative and positive ideals—put it how you will—can, I think, be traced back to the Buddha himself. In his biography, which though preserved in late versions, Frauwallner has shown to date from only about a century after his death, he hesitates on becoming Enlightened as to whether he should go forth and preach the truth. Only with difficulty is he persuaded to do so. By acceding to the gods' request that he preach he gives himself forty-five years of unnecessary trouble; but he acts from his universal compassion, and comes as near as anyone can in Buddhism to saving mankind. Of course, being already Buddha he has it both ways: he fulfils the ideals of both self-restraint and love. When he decides to preach he is already an *arhat*; by founding a *śāsana* he shows that he is a *samyak sambuddha*. What many scholars, especially the older ones on whom Weber relied, have failed to notice is that for *all* schools of Buddhism the *samyak sambuddha*, who has added love to self-restraint, is infinitely superior to the mere *arhat* who does not benefit others after achieving Enlightenment himself. Even those who regarded attaining *nirvāṇa* as the *summum bonum* did not consider it the *solum bonum:* for all Buddhists love is a great good.

For the Buddha there was no incompatibility between the ideals of self-restraint and of love; he could pursue both. Most people are not so lucky. In practice it usually comes down to making a choice. There is not much hurry, because we have many lives, but in this life which shall we make our goal—our own Enlightenment through self-restraint, or the service of mankind?

This tension between the two ideals seems to me fundamental to the distinction between Theravāda and Mahāyāna. To equate Theravāda with self-restraint and Mahāyāna with love is mistaken: it is a question of emphasis. Mahāyāna, which faced the difficulty more explicitly, generalized the ideal of the Bodhisattva, who postpones his own Enlightenment till the goal of his love, the Enlightenment of all others, has been reached. Theravāda too presents the Bodhisattva as a noble ideal—but he does not fit in very well. What is emphasized is not his postponement of his own salvation, but his determination eventually to become a *samyak sambuddha*, and thus to realize both more or less simultaneously.

It seems to me, from the logic of later developments, that in this respect Theravāda Buddhism has preserved what must have been a feature of Buddhism from the very beginning. If the original conception of the *summum bonum* was one's own salvation, there must have been immediate obstacles to the translation of this ideal doctrine into actual behaviour. Firstly, if the ideal is consistently carried out, the religion would have little chance of survival, depending purely on a host of individual conversions unaided by any organization. If the Buddhists were utterly consistent this would not matter. But the second obstacle must have been human nature. All the evidence shows that many Buddhists were neither so consistent nor so averse to the altruistic ideal as Weber suggests and, perhaps, as they were intended to be. Those who kept themselves to themselves as forest-dwelling *arhats* have departed unsung (except by themselves), and few of their names are recorded in history. But throughout the history of Theravāda Buddhism, by which phrase I would like to subsume nearly 2,500 years, there has been this problem: according to doctrine *nirvāṇa* is the *summum bonum* and self-restraint the main means to it; but in practice there has been no such clear hierarchy of values, but rather a preferential value system, which at the highest level comprises a choice between self-restraint and love.

It is, I think, this dilemma which has underlined many of the differences between doctrine and behaviour, between what I have called cognitive and affective religion. (My choice of the word 'affective', with its overtones of 'affection', turns out to be fortunate.) Again, I am certainly not suggesting that the cognitive religion should be equated with the ideal of self-restraint, the affective religion with the ideal of love—it is rather a question of which way they lean. Nor, I must repeat, should 'self-restraint' and 'love' be interpreted too narrowly: it is here a question of whole syndromes, the one negative and world-denying, the other positive and world-affirming. (My choice of words in this sentence is an attempt to connect my concepts to those of Durkheim and Weber.) Amplification will make this clear.

The cognitive religion regards withdrawal for meditation as the consummation of religious behaviour, and regards the utterly negative (and rationally inconceivable) goal of *nirvāṇa* as the ideal destiny. In fact most people, even monks, say that meditation is impracticable, offering some such excuse as the pressure of affairs or the decline of the doctrine, and they display very little liking for *nirvāṇa*. Accordingly, *nirvāṇa* has been postponed in the popular mind to the coming of Maitrī, in some remote future era; it is so difficult to attain, and we are not sure that we want it anyway. Most people, monks included, devote themselves exclusively to acts of merit (*pinkam*), the aim of which is a good rebirth in heaven or on earth. The aim is made conformable to doctrine by saying that it all counts towards *nirvāṇa* in the long run; the list of *pinkam* conforms to doctrine by including, as two of the Ten Good Deeds (*dasa kusala karma*), meditation and the negative 'morality' (*sīla*) of the Five Precepts; but if people really want to be sure of merit they do not sit around practising self-restraint: they go out and do something positive like giving alms, which is emotionally more satisfying. Cognitively *pin* and *nivan* are hierarchically associated as means to an end; affectively, however, the two complement each other, and the values are preferential.

Finally, it must surely be significant that the name of the next Buddha, Maitrī, *means* 'love'. By postponing meditation and *nirvāṇa* till the time of Maitrī people are thus rendering explicit, on the symbolic level, that they attach at least as much value to the positive as to the negative ideal.

In various parts of this work, especially Chapter 5, I have shown how doctrine has to some extent come to terms with these emotional needs. The history of parts of Theravāda doctrine can indeed be seen as a running battle between doctrine and sentiment. Formulations of ethical prescriptions have moved from the negative to the positive, as just mentioned, without sacrificing consistency. An even better example is the history of the transfer of merit, where the emotional need to do something for your dead relatives, which according to original doctrine was impossible, has been elaborately rationalized to make it compatible with the fundamental doctrinal principle of self-help. Again, self-restraint has accommodated to love.

Though one of the terms in my explanation is a component of human nature, I have come nowhere near to saying that human nature and human religion are everywhere much the same. The feature of Theravāda Buddhism which I find most striking is indeed the counter-intuitive persistence of the self-restraint ideal, and the victories of doctrine. The latter are achievements of the scholastic intellect; the former is exemplified in the prestige of meditation and the extraordinary veneration in which any self-styled hermit is still held in Ceylon. The phenomenon of Salgala has already been cited in Chapter 7. Here monks have retired to meditation in caves, but they are pursued by what Obeyesekere dubs 'the relentless piety of the masses', who cement the caves and book a year in advance to offer food. In Obeyesekere's words, 'The *arhat* ideal is still the index of religiosity.'

The fate of the monks of Salgala conforms to a pattern which recurs throughout Buddhist history: the few men who really wish to follow the *śrāvaka* ideal break away and retire to jungle caves, but as they are dependent on the laity for their food they do not break off all contact with the outside world, and so they or their successors run the risk of reverting to the state of an institution. Traditionally these hermits—Paṃsukūlikas, Āraññavāsins—have been members of the Sangha, but this need not always be so: recently the short-lived *tāpasa* movement[5] consisted

[5]See Bechert, op. cit., p. 258, and references there given.

of hermits who considered the Sangha corrupt and not worth joining. The recurrence of these movements shows that there is often (or always?) a small group of people for whom the unadulterated *śrāvaka* ideal is attractive and not as psychologically implausible as it is for most. We may conjecture that some of the Buddha's original followers were of this type.

This brings us to the whole question of the monk-layman dichotomy. The cleft between them is obvious and needs no denying. But writers on Ceylonese Buddhism tend to associate with the two groups in a one-one correlation the two different types of religiosity which I have typified by reference to the ideals of self-restraint and love. The monks are all supposed to be 'salvation-strivers', and the laity interested mainly in heaven attained by faith and good works. This finds some justification in the texts, but none in social reality. Many monks reject this view of themselves, and I think they are right to do so. They point out that they need *pin* as much as anyone else. Just like laymen they observe astrological recommendations at the New Year or when embarking on a journey, and they give *mataka dānēs* for their dead parents; on analogy with laymen they treat their pupils as sons, their fellow pupils as brothers, and give *mataka dānēs* for their dead teachers. (Such familial relationships are prescribed for the Sangha in the Canon.) Indeed, all the inhabitants of Mīgala monastery used to prostrate themselves every evening before the photograph of the dead incumbent. Some *pansal* display the picture of Sīvali, the symbol of aspiration to material prosperity. I found monks, as a group, very kind, hospitable, and worldly people. Ethically they are mostly like laymen—but the point is whether they are like *good* laymen.

It is perfectly true that this development is only to be expected when monks are selected in childhood, and therefore constitute, so far as concerns their personalities, a random sample of the population rather than a group with a religious vocation. Bechert suggests that this juvenile recruitment is bad for Buddhism, and prefers the system in other Theravāda countries by which most males enter the Order for at least a short period. Whichever is more beneficial for society, I am sure the Buddha would have found the latter system at least as surprising a development as the former. However, the point that I wish here to make is that under any system the majority of monks are not likely to be unambiguously devoted to the *arhat* ideal alone. Already in a canonical text we find references[6] to *puthujjana-kalyāṇaka-bhikkhū*, quaintly rendered by Mrs. Rhys Davids[7] as 'hoi-polloi-good-fellow-bhikkhus'. And, once again, this shift from the *śrāvaka* ideal has been officially accommodated: these monks are designated village-dwelling book men (*grāmavāsin* and *granthadhura*). It is doctrinally impossible entirely to abandon the self-restraint ideal, but it has been pushed right into the background, and these monks too are tacitly sanctioned in a course of making merit like the laity. If they do not leave the monasteries, either reverting to lay status or at least abandoning more *vinaya* rules than they do, it is because of the fear of disapproval, the material benefits of monastic life and the continuing demand and admiration for examples of self-restraint.

If we wish to observe where the self-restraint ideal voluntarily functions, apart from the sporadic hermits who furnish the extreme case, we must look not to the ordinary village-dwelling monk, but to the *upāsaka*. Though an *upāsaka* originally meant any Buddhist layman, the term is now used mainly for those who, usually late in life, renounce worldly ties. Like the early members of the Sangha, they choose their status rather than having it thrust upon them, and free choice is a prerequisite for the wholehearted pursuit of any moral ideal. Some old village *upāsakas* have a knowledge of scriptures and doctrines which would be remarkable in a person of monastic education. Approaching death, however kindly they may

[6] *Paṭisambhidā-magga*, i. 176, ii. 190, ii. 193.

[7] In her introduction to *Manual of a Mystic* (P.T.S., London, 1916), p. x.

be, they conceive *maitrī* primarily as an exercise in solitary meditation; their goal is unambiguously selfish. Might we here find Weber's Theravādin recluse, 'cool and aloof'? Obeyesekere interviewed such a man. An inhabitant of a remote village, he had been illiterate but could now read both Sinhalese and Pali; he led a very simple life, and was respected by the villagers, to whom he preached. One can also assume that he meditated. Yet while he talked of the foulness of the female body, he gave glowing descriptions of the damsels in heaven, which he envisaged as a paradise of sensual delight. According to doctrines which he had studied and accepted, the next life conditioned by his *karma* would be experienced by a new constellation of impermanent constituents (*anatta* doctrine); all rebirth is unhappiness, and *nirvāṇa* the only goal worth seeking; and pious works are in vain unless they are accompanied by freedom from desire, which constitutes the only true progress. But these doctrines are counter-intuitive. He would probably never have admitted it, or been able to see the discrepancy so apparent to us, but we can surmise that he was not interested in *nirvāṇa* so much as in the female inhabitants of a heaven with whom he felt that the renunciation and other good works of his old age entitled him to associate. He practised restraint now so that he could indulge later; action rationally based on premises inconsistent with those he professed. I do not belittle him. I find his principles noble and profound, his conduct virtuous. But the two are not related quite as he imagines. Though he would probably never have admitted that he was more interested in heaven than in *nirvāṇa*, that was plainly where he hoped to be reborn.

The *upāsaka*'s discordant aspirations exemplify the tension between the two ideals, as well as the dichotomy between cognitive and affective religion (rather than between belief and action, for here the action suits both the cognitive and the affective belief system, and the behaviourist would have nothing to go on) with which this work has been largely concerned. They neatly illustrate also the unintended consequences of the adoption by a whole population of a religion which teaches that total renunciation of life is the only final answer to life's problems. Those who cannot make that renunciation require something else, and another system, logically subsumable to the former but emotionally alternate, comes into being. Both my argument and my evidence suggest that this happened very early in Buddhist history, at least before Duṭugämuṇu, 2,000 years ago. The adaptation was excellent: the accommodated system has survived with little change to this day.

Early Theravāda was an uncompromising doctrine. It is continually difficult to be entirely responsible for your fate. 'For emotional mass religiosity there have been and are but two possible types of soteriology: magic or a saviour.'[8] Sinhalese 'mass religiosity' has accepted in deed, though not in word, a modicum of both: the saviour we met in Chapters 3 and 4, the magic in Chapters 4 and 5. These acceptances are as old as the commentaries, some of them far older. The words are hardly changed all. If this is popular Buddhism, could it be that

Vox populi vox Buddhae?

[8]Weber, op. cit., p. 237.

Appendix

I. *Contents*[1] *of my copy of* Bauddha Ädahilla.

Bauddha Ädahilla with plates, ed. Ven. Pundit Kiriällē Ñāṇavimala, pub. M. D. Guṇasēna and Co. Ltd., Colombo, 2nd impression 1957.

Table of contents

Formula of salutation [to the Buddha].
Section of instruction.
Manner of salutation.
Sentence for asking for the Five Precepts.
Formulation of salutation [to the Buddha].
Manner of obtaining the refuges.
Manner of violating the refuges.
Various ways of going for refuge.
Results of going for refuge.
Categories of moral precepts.
Poya or Eight-fold Precepts.
Manner of undertaking the precepts when alone.
The 32 forbidden kinds of talk.
Thieves of [i.e. breakers of] the moral precepts.
The Ten Precepts.
Recollection of the qualities of the Buddha.
Burmese worship by recollection of nine qualities.
Recollection of the qualities of the Dhamma.
Recollection of the qualities of the Sangha.
Paraphrase of the qualities of the Buddha.
Paraphrase of the qualities of the Dhamma.
Paraphrase of the qualities of the Sangha.
Paraphrase of the formula of initial salutation.
Obeisance to the qualities of the Three Jewels.
Results of going for refuge to the Three Jewels.
Mindfulness with reference to the body or meditation on the disgusting.
Meditation of mindfulness with reference to the body both forwards and backwards.

[1]The table of contents (pp. viii–xiv) has been translated literally, just to give an idea of its scope. I am grateful to Dr. K. Malalgoḍa for correcting my translation.

Meditation on the disgusting.
Meditation of recollecting the Buddha.
Meditation on kindness.
Another meditation on kindness.
A meditation on kindness in another way.
Meditation on impurity.
Recollection concerning death.
Eight matters for concern which should be recollected.
Things always to be considered.
Worship of the Buddha.
Verses of worship to the Buddha.
Worship of the twenty-eight well-gone [Buddhas].
Worship of the Dharma.
Verses of worship to the Dharma.
Worship of the Sangha.
Verses of worship to the Sangha.
Praise of the Three Jewels composed by King Vajirañāṇa of Siam.
Verses for obtaining pardon from the Three Jewels.
Worship of the sixteen-fold stupas.
Worship of Mahiyangana stupa.
Worship of Nāgadīpa stupa.
Worship of Kälaṇiya stupa.
Worship of Siripāda.
Worship of Divāguhā.
Worship of Dīghavāpi stupa.
Worship of Mutiyangaṇa stupa.
Worship of Tissamahārāma stupa.
Worship of the great Bo tree.
Worship of Mirisaväṭi stupa.
Worship of Ruvanväli stupa.
Worship of Thūpārama stupa.
Worship of Abhayagiri stupa.
Worship of Jetavanārāma stupa.
Worship of the Stone Stupa [Lankārāma].
Worship of the Milk Stupa [Kirivehera at Kataragama].
Worship of the Tooth Relic.
Worship of the four footprints at Siripāda.
Verses of worship to the Bo tree.
Salutation to be made to relics used by the Omniscient one.
Salutation to the eighty great disciples.
Worship of the places where the Omniscient one passed the

Seven Weeks.
Salutation to the Three Jewels.
Verses recited when offering flowers.
Offering flowers which are on the tree.
Offering incense.
Offering lights.
Offering food.
Verses offering water.
Offering medicaments.
Offering a sheaf of betel leaves.
Offering kinds of food.
Offering kinds of side-dishes.
Offering rice gruel.
Manner of making offering through the offering of practice [moral behaviour].
The Noble Eight-fold Path.
The seven noble riches.
The Ten Good Deeds.
The desert of *saṃsāra*.
The manner in which the Omniscient one crossed to the further shore of the ocean of *saṃsāra*.
The ten things to be given.
The manner of offering the eight requisites.
Giving (*dānē*) to the Sangha.
Giving the *kaṭhina* robe.
Kinds of donors of gifts.
The way in which the precepts must be carefully kept.
The goodness of making a gift of the Dharma.
The Five Precepts.
Factors and dangers of taking life.
Factors of taking what is not given.
Factors and dangers of sexual misconduct.
Factors and dangers of telling lies.
Factors and dangers of drinking intoxicants.
The ten bad acts.
Back-biting or malicious speech.
Frivolous chatter.
Covetousness or strong greed.
Malevolence.
False views.
The pentad of impeding acts.
The five [kinds of] bad conduct.

The five desires.
The thirty-two corpses.
Faults which must be suppressed by one who wishes for improvement.
Kinds of *karma*.
The sorrow of birth.
The sorrow arising because of conception in the mother's womb.
The sorrow arising through one's own agency.
The sorrow which grows up through the agency of others.
The sorrow of old age.
The sorrow of death.
The thirteen ascetic practices.
Keeping to the practice of 'one sitting'.
Undertaking the practice of 'alms bowl'.
The deportment of one who undertakes the ascetic practices.
The training of a novice.
The novice's questions.
The morality of four purities.
The thirty-seven things conducive to Enlightenment.
The thirty perfections.
The ten repentances.
The four conditions which are hard to obtain.
The roots of evil.
The roots of good.
Good deeds conditioning rebirth.
The characteristics of an *upāsaka*.
The danger of intolerance.
The advantage of tolerance.
Those who will escape from *saṃsāra* by seeing Maitreya.
Those who will not see Maitreya.
Verse of worship to one's mother.
Verse of worship to one's father.
Something to be remembered when relatives and friends have died.
Giving merit to dead relatives.
Recollection on seeing a corpse.
The religious wish which the Buddhist should remember.
A religious wish made by the best men of old.
Giving merit to the gods.
Another merit-giving.
A religious wish.
The *Mahā Mangala Sutta*.

The *Ratana Sutta.*
The *Karaṇīya-metta Sutta.*
The *Dhajagga Sutta.*
The golden bier verses.
The Victor's cage.
The victory *pirit.*
The *pirit* of the twenty-eight.
The *Jayamangala* ['auspicious victory'] verses.
The *Mahā Jayamangala* verses.
The horoscope of the Omniscient one.
The main dates of the Buddhist religion.
Auspicious days of the Buddhist religion.
The *pirit* of Sīvalī.
Meditation on Sīvalī [includes diagram for an amulet].
Meditation on Sīvalī to be meditated on morning and evening.
Amulet of the nine qualities.
Amulet of the Buddha's qualities.

II. *Sunday school primers (Daham pāsala pot).*

A. Translation of first two chapters, first part, first grade primer.

The Life of the Buddha
Worship to the Blessed *arhat* truly fully enlightened.

1. The Prediction of Dīpaṃkara.

A long time ago there was a city called Amaravatī. In this city there was a young brahmin called Sumēda. The young brahmin was a very wise man. He was as rich as he was wise. The young man left everything he owned and going into the jungle became an ascetic. From that day on Sumēda the ascetic ate the fruit he picked from the trees in the forest, the yams he dug up from the creepers, and the leaves from the trees. He drank water from ponds. Eating and drinking like this he kept the moral precepts very well.

At this time the Lord Buddha Dīpaṃkara had appeared in the world. The people of the city of Rammavatī prepared a *dānē* for the Lord Buddha Dīpaṃkara. People began to make a good road for the Lord Buddha and the Sangha to come to the city. Sumēda the ascetic too came to that place, and when he heard the news he requested and obtained a piece of road to make. The ascetic received a muddy place. At this he was very pleased, and began to take up earth in a basket and to make the muddy place dry.

Before he had finished making the muddy place dry, Sumēda the ascetic saw the Lord Buddha approaching. For the Buddha to pass without touching the mud threw himself on his face on the heap of mud. Lying there he thought, 'By this act of merit may I too attain Buddhahood.'

The Lord Buddha Dīpaṃkara came up to the puddle. When he had come up he showed the ascetic to the monks and said, 'This ascetic is the Bodhisattva who in future time will be a Buddha called Gotama.' Hearing this Sumēda the ascetic became very happy.

Questions

1. Who is Sumēda?
2. Why did Sumēda the ascetic throw himself on the heap of mud?
3. What did the Lord Buddha Dīpaṃkara say about Sumēda the ascetic?

2. The Birth of Prince Siddhārtha

After that the Bodhisattva Sumēda after many and various births was at last born in the Tusita heaven as a god called Santusita. In that heaven he long enjoyed heavenly bliss. Thus when some time had passed the gods assembled, and requested the most excellent god, the Bodhisattva, to be born in the world of men and become Buddha.

The god Santusita granted their request after considering five matters. These five were the right time, the right continent, the right region, the right family and the right mother for becoming Buddha. When he had thus considered, the divine Bodhisattva was conceived in India's middle region in the city of Kapilavastu in the womb of Her Majesty Mahāmāyā, queen to King Suddhodana. It was the full-moon *poya* day of the month of Äsaḷa. Therefore the queen had taken the precepts. That night Queen Mahāmāyā had a dream. A baby elephant holding a white lotus flower in his trunk entered her womb from the right side. When this was reported to the king he asked the experts in portents. They told the king that a meritorious child had been conceived in the queen's womb.

Ten months after this Queen Mahāmāyā was on her way to the

city of Devadaha with large retinue, and came to the Lumbinī grove of sal trees. The day was the full-moon *poya* day of the month of Wesak. The sal trees were full of blossoms. Queen Mahāmāyā grasped a branch of a sal tree in the grove. At that time occurred the descent of the noble child from the queen's womb. Afterwards they led the prince and the queen to the palace in the city of Kapilavastu.

Questions

1. When the gods asked him to be born in the world of men what did the divine Bodhisattva do?
2. What was the dream of Queen Mahāmāyā?
3. Where did Queen Mahāmāyā give birth to her noble son? On what day?

B. Tables of Contents

First grade, first book:

The Life of the Buddha

1. The prediction of Dīpaṃkara.
2. The Birth of Prince Siddhārtha.
3. The ascetic Asita's worship.
4. The name-giving.
5. Studies and demonstration of skills.
6. Marriage.
7. Life as a householder.
8. Seeing the four portents.
9. The great renunciation.
10. Enlightenment.

Dharma

1. Taking the Eight Precepts.
2. Formula of the qualities of the Three Jewels.
3. Giving merit.

First grade, second book:

Jātaka stories

1. The Sāma Jātaka.
2. The Dīghīti Kosala Jātaka.
3. The Sattigumba Jātaka.

4. The Tittira (partridge) Jātaka.
5. The Mahākapi (great monkey) Jātaka.

Religious Poems [from the Lōväḍa Saňgarāva]

1. I worship King Buddha.
2. I worship the blessed true Dharma.
3. I worship the great Sangha.
4. Achieving birth as a man.
5. Banishing the pains of *saṃsāra*.
6. Experiencing pain in hell.
7. Māra.
8. Not doing good.
9. Delay in doing good.
10. Laziness in good.
11. Dancing, singing, playing music.
12. Be energetic in doing good.

Second grade, first book:

The Life of the Buddha

1. The childhood of Prince Siddhārtha.
2. Seeing the portents.
3. Going to become an ascetic.
4. Seeking the doctrine.
5. Experiencing pain.
6. Acceptance of rice balls.
7. Enlightenment.
8. Spreading the doctrine.
9. Acceptance of the Bamboo Grove.
10. The Buddha's death (*Parinirvāṇa*).

Dharma

1. Worship of stupas.
2. Worship of the Bo tree.
3. Worship of the Buddha.
4. Offering flowers.
5. Offering water.
6. Offering food.
7. Offering medicaments (*gilan pasa*).
8. Offering medicine.
9. Offering betel leaves.
10. Offering lights.

11. Offering fragrant smoke.
12. Offering incense.
13. Religious wish.
14. Obtaining the Buddha's pardon.
15. Worshipping monks.
16. Obtaining monks' pardon.
17. Worshipping one's father.
18. Worshipping one's mother.
19. The verse of the young brahmin Chatta.

Second grade, second book:

Jātaka stories

1. The Sujāta Jātaka.
2. The Dadhivāhana Jātaka.
3. The Rājovāda (royal advice) Jātaka.
4. The Tilamuṭṭhi (handful of sesamum) Jātaka.
5. The Mahāsīlava Jātaka.
6. The Apaṇṇaka Jātaka.
7. The Cullaseṭṭhi (small guild-leader) Jātaka.

Religious Poems [from the Lōväḍa Saňgarāva]

1. Pleasure has no substance.
2. The faults of the five sense-desires.
3. Doing sin.
4. There is no pleasure in sense-pleasures.
5. Not knowing the way to escape from pain.
6. Being greedy for pleasure.
7. What is the result of pleasure?
8. Behaving righteously at an age when one can.
9. Collecting merit.
10. The body is a heap of pain.
11. Decrepitude and death.
12. Why does one not do good?
13. Do not desire power.
14. Why be late for merit?
15. This is the time to gain merit.

C. The books available while I was in Mīgala for use in the *daham pāsala* were: a primer in six grades, two volumes per grade; *Vandanā gāthā* ('*Verses of worship*'); *Śāsana Itihāsaya* ('*His-*

tory of Buddhism'); *Buddha-caritaya* ('*The Life of the Buddha*'); *Jātaka Sangrahaya* ('*Collected Jātakas*'—one for each of the ten perfections); *Abhidharmaya* part 1; and the following Pali texts, with Sinhalese translation and commentary: *Sigālovāda Sutta, Dhammika Sutta, Satipaṭṭhāna Sutta*, *Dhammapada* part 2.

III. *Translation of a specimen* puṇyānumōdanā vākyaya ('*statement of thanks for/empathy with an act of merit*').

Sāmaṇera Mūladharma ed. Mīgamuvē Ñānadhaja, Guṇasēkara Press, Alutgama 1968, pp. iv–v.

May what you wish and desire very soon be successful; may all your wishes for yourself be fulfilled like the new moon.

May the entire company of divine kings with their lotus thrones of great Indra, yellow clothes and so forth, by empathizing obtain the characteristics which make for all good and meritorious things, brought into being by making the pure Buddha offerings in respect of the blessed *arhat*, the truly fully Enlightened holy omniscient supreme king, who was the throat-roaring lion to ward off the elephant of death [Māra], and then by the gift accepted with the requisites by the Sangha, the gift set apart for the Jewel of the great and noble Sangha—Sāriputra, Maudgalyāyana, Ānanda, Rāhula, Mahā Kāśyapa, etc. who are adorned with the qualities of being of good conduct, upright, etc. May they [the donors] receive protection from the company of divine kings, whose minds are gladdened by the aforesaid empathy with merit. And may all the dead relations of that [the donor's] name—mother, father, son, wife, brother, sister, etc.—feel empathy and attain that divine bliss which is known as a good rebirth. And may all those [the dead] and these [the donors], by acquiring these good characteristics, not come to the pain of a rebirth in the four hells, which are pervaded with perpetual pain; may they experience divine bliss in the six heavens, beginning with that of the Four Great Kings, where all is of the greatest well-being; and if a time comes when they are born again in the world of men, may they dwell enjoying to their heart's content the best of the blessing of long life, like those best of men the world-rulers Mahāsammata, Roja, Vararoja, Uposatha, Mahā Mandhātu, etc., of the blessing of great wealth, like Jotiya, Jaṭila, Dhanameṇḍaka, Kākavalya, etc., of the blessing of profound wisdom, like the famous sages Vidhura, Guttila, Senaka, Mahauṣadha, etc., and, if in the next life they are born as women, of the blessings of beauty, wealth and retinue, like the noble ladies Viśākhā, Candrapadumā, Sumanā, Sujātā, Yasodharā, Anulā, etc., and after so living may they be born in the excellent capital city, fit for the gods, called Ketumatī, and see the holy king Buddha Maitrī, the Good Friend of infinite glory, and offer to a hundred thousand holy *arhats*, including Him, the four requisites of robe, etc., and hear the preaching of the Four Noble Truths of suffering, its arising, its destruction, and the Way, which would be preached by the holy king Buddha, and at the end of the preaching reach the four paths and the four fruits of stream-enterer, etc., and so attain eternal, auspicious, supreme, beautiful, tranquil, happy, exquisite, superior, final, immortal great *nirvāṇa*! So thinking, with joyful thoughts one should empathize in the merit.

IV. *Translation of the* Mahā Jayamangala Gāthā (*'Pali verses of the great blessing of victory'*).

1. The lord of great compassion for the welfare of all alive fulfilled all the perfections and reached the supreme enlightenment. By this statement of truth may the blessing of victory be yours.
2. Conquering at the foot of the Bo tree, increasing the Śākyas' delight—thus may victory be yours; win the blessing of victory.
3. Paying reverence to the Jewel of the Buddha, the supreme best balm, welfare for gods and men—by the Buddha's power in safety may all dangers be destroyed, may your sorrows be stilled.
4. Paying reverence to the Jewel of the Dhamma, the supreme best balm, the stilling of fever—by the Dhamma's power in safety may all dangers be destroyed, may your fears be stilled.
5. Paying reverence to the Jewel of the Sangha, the supreme best balm, worthy to be invited, worthy of hospitality—by the Sangha's power in safety may all dangers be destroyed, may your diseases be stilled.
6. Whatever jewels, many and various, exist in the world,

there is no jewel like the Buddha; therefore may you be safe and well.

7. Whatever jewels, many and various, exist in the world, there is no jewel like the Dhamma; therefore may you be safe and well.
8. Whatever jewels, many and various, exist in the world, there is no jewel like the Sangha; therefore may you be safe and well.
9. I have no other refuge, the Buddha is my best refuge; by this statement of truth may the blessing of victory be yours.
10. I have no other refuge, the Dhamma is my best refuge; by this statement of truth may the blessing of victory be yours.
11. I have no other refuge, the Sangha is my best refuge; by this statement of truth may the blessing of victory be yours.
12. May all calamities be avoided; may all disease be destroyed; may you meet with no obstacle; be happy and live long.

The following verses may be recited separately.

13. May every blessing come; may all the gods give protection; by the power of all the Buddhas may you ever be safe and well.
14. May every blessing come; may all the gods give protection; by the power of all the Dhamma may you ever be safe and well.
15. May every blessing come; may all the gods give protection; by the power of all the Sangha may you ever be safe and well.
16. By warding off constellations, *yakṣas, bhūtas* and evil planets through power of *pirit*, may they stop their oppression.
17. May the heaven rain in season and may there be a good harvest; may the world be prosperous; may the king be righteous.
18. All Buddhas, who have obtained power—and the power which *paccekabuddhas* have—and by the glory of the *arhats* I secure protection in all ways.

Throughout the poem the first person may be substituted for the second so that the blessings are invoked for the reciter.

Glossary of Religious Terms

(and a few others)

THE aim of this glossary is purely the practical one of aiding the reader and it does not attempt complete consistency. Most terms ocurring only once are omitted. The terms are listed indifferently in Sanskrit, Pali, and Sinhalese, as they occur in the text, and not necessarily in every possible form or spelling; see also the Note on Pronunciation and Transliteration. In *ardhatatsamas* (see below) I have preferred Sanskrit to Sinhalese diacritics, e.g. *deśanā(va)*. Bracketed letters mean that forms of the word both with and without those letters occur.

abhidhamma, abhidharma(ya)—the classical philosophy of Theravāda Buddhism, perhaps best characterized as a scholastic approach to ethics and philosophy of mind
äbittayā—monastery servant
aḍukku—first fruits of harvest, offered to gods
āgamaya—a religion
akusala—opposite of *kusala*: morally bad, sin
ahosi—'has-been'; superseded. For *ahosi kamma*, a special type of *karma*, see Chapter 5
anagārika—'homeless'; originally an epithet of a Buddhist monk, now also denotes a celibate layman who observes the Ten Precepts
anatta, anātma—non-self; one of the three basic characteristics of phenomenal existence (with *dukkha* and *anicca*)
anicca, anitya—impermanence; one of the three basic characteristics of phenomenal existence (with *dukkha* and *anatta*)
añjali—pan-Indian gesture of respect, in which the palms are placed together in front of the face or body, as in Christian prayer
antarābhava—'in-between state'; existence between death and subsequent rebirth
anumodana, anumōdanāva, anumōdan—thanks for merit, empathy with merit—see Chapter 5
apāya—hell
ap(h)alē—astrologically inauspicious period
ārāma(ya)—Buddhist temple; a synonym of *vihāraya* in its general sense, but in Sinhalese usually confined to proper names
āraṇyavāsin, āraññavāsin—forest-dwelling, hermitage monks

ardha-tatsama—word in a language which is a loanword from another language with just a slight change or addition to assimilate it: e.g. Sinhalese *yakṣayā, dēśanāva* or *dēsanāva* from Sanskrit *yakṣa, deśanā*

arhat, rahat—enlightened person, one who has seen *nirvāṇa*

āśā(va)—desire

asura—a Vedic class of bad gods or demons

ātma(ya), atta—self, soul—which is denied by the doctrine of *anatta.* In Sinhalese discourse *ātmaya* can also mean 'life', i.e. a life-span

aṭṭhakathā, aṭuvā—commentary, esp. a Pali commentary on a canonical text

āturayā—the patient, the person being exorcized

āvāsa(ya)—residence of a Buddhist monk or monks without the other features of a *vihāra*

avatāra(ya)—in rural Sinhalese a synonym for *holman*, an apparition

āvuda—weapons, esp. of a god

baliädurā—an exorcist of evil planetary influences

bali(ya)—a ceremony for exorcizing evil planetary influences; an image of a planet used in such a ceremony

bäl(u)ma—the gaze, esp. of a god or demon, or of a human affected by one

baṇa—Buddhist preaching, sermon

baṇa maḍuva, baṇa gē, baṇa gedara— building (sometimes temporary, in which case called *baṇa maḍuva*) used for preaching

baṇa pota—a book of Buddhist scriptures (not necessarily canonical)

baṇḍāra—a Kandyan title, preserved in the names of many local Kandyan gods

bāra venavā—to make a vow to a god that if he grants X you will do Y

bera—a long drum, tapering at both ends, much used in Buddhist rites

beravā—a Sinhalese caste, 'drummers'

bhakti(ya)—religious devotion

bhāvanā(va)—meditation, development of the mind; one of the Ten Good Deeds

bhikṣu, bhikkhu, biku—Buddhist monk

bhikṣuṇī, bhikkhunī—Buddhist nun

bhūta(yā)—a *preta* or other mean spirit

billa, plural *bili*—victim in a sacrifice
Bō gaha, bōdhinvahansē—'Bo tree'; tree of the type (*Ficus religiosa*) under which the Buddha attained Enlightenment
bodhi, bō—Buddhist Enlightenment
Bodhisatt(v)a, Bōsat—being who has undertaken to become a Buddha
brahmaloka(ya), baṁbalova—the seven heavens immediately above the *divyaloka*
brāhmaṇa—brahmin: the first of the four classes of society in classical Indian theory; ideally priests
brahmavihāra—'holy state'; there are four: compassion (*karuṇā*), loving-kindness (*mettā*), sympathetic joy (*muditā*) and equanimity (*upekkhā*)
Buddhacarita(ya)—the Buddha's life and works, his biography
Budubala(ya)—Buddha force, potency of a dead Buddha
Budu räs—the five- (or six-) coloured halo of a Buddha

caitya, cetiya— = *stūpa*
cetanā(va)—intention

dāgaba, dāgäba—'relic-container'; = *stūpa*
daham pāsala—Buddhist 'Sunday school', now held on *poya* days
dāna—giving, the virtue liberality; the first of the Ten Good Deeds
dāna śālāva—the refectory in a *pansala*
dānē—etymologically a Sinhalese form of *dāna*, particularized to mean the food given to monks, a monk's meal; *hīl dānē, daval dānē* and *gilampasa dānē* are the approximate equivalents of breakfast, lunch, and evening tea respectively
dāyaka(yā), Pali fem. *dāyikā*—donor, a person who gives to the Sangha in fact or presumptively: by being a Buddhist living in a community which uses a particular temple one may be considered a *dāyaka* of that temple
deśanā(va)—teaching, preaching; one of the Ten Good Deeds
deva, deviyō, deyyō—a god
devālaya, dēvālē—a Buddhist shrine to a god or gods
devatā(va)—a deity, i.e. a god, esp. a minor god
dharmāsana(ya)—special seat used for preaching
dharma(ya), dhamma, daham, dam—Buddhism as a religious doctrine or truth

dhātu(va)—a relic, of three kinds: bodily (*sārīrika*), objects used (*pāribhogika*) and reminders (*uddesika*). In Buddhist cosmology *dhātu* also means one of the three strata of the universe: sphere of desire, of form, and of no form

divyaloka(ya), *devlova*—the six heavens immediately above the human world

dola—offering of food, etc., to a mean spirit

doḷos maha pahana—'twelve-month lamp'; the lamp on temple premises which could in theory always be kept alight

dos—evil influence, = [1]*vas*

dukkha, duḥkha, duka—unsatisfactoriness, pain, ill-being; the first of the Four Noble Truths, and one of the three basic characteristics of phenomenal existence (with *anatta* and *anicca*)

dummala—incense used in the worship of gods

durāva—a Sinhalese caste, 'toddy tappers'

Eḷu, Heḷu—'Sinhalese'; esp. the mediaeval Sinhalese language

gam maḍuva—'village shed'; a communal village ritual, of different specific character in different parts of Ceylon—see Chapter 4

ganinnānsē—kind of quasi-monk who had not taken the higher ordination and was not necessarily celibate; the institution existed in the seventeenth and eighteenth centuries

gāthā—Pali verses, sometimes also Pali prose formulae

gati—state in which one can be reborn, e.g. god, animal

goyigama—the highest and largest Sinhalese caste, the cultivator caste

g(r)anthadhura—the duty of handing on the scriptures

graha(yā)—planet—nine are recognized by astrology

g(r)āmavāsin—village-dwelling (monk)

gṛhastha—home-dwelling, householder; in Hinduism denotes the station of life during which a man is economically and sexually active, but in Sinhalese Buddhism used mainly as an adjective qualifying a category of *dasa sil upāsaka*

hāmuduruvō—'lord'; common term for a Buddhist monk; prefixed by *poḍi* or *puñci* denotes a novice

hēvisi—drums; both a generic term and a particular kind of cylindrical drum

holman—an apparition

horanāva—Shrill wind instrument used in Buddhist ritual

Jātaka—story of a former life of the Buddha
jīva dānē—a *dānē* given for the merit of someone still alive

kannalavva—invocation, entreaty to a god
kapurāḷa, kapuvā—the priest of a *dēvālē*
karaňḍuva—a casket esp. a relic casket
karāva—the Sinhalese caste ranking second to *goyigama*; 'fishermen'
kar(u)ma(ya), kamma—action, deed; in Buddhism the law of moral causation
karuṇā(va)—compassion, kindness
kaṭṭadiyā—magician, exorcist
kemvara, kembara—day of the week suitable for worship of the gods; also, locally, a communal rite for the gods
kēndraya—horoscope
killa, plural *kili*—pollution
kiripiḍu—balls of rice cooked in milk, commonly used as ritual food
koḍiya—flag
kovil—Hindu temple
kṣatriya, khattiya—the second of the four classes of society in classical Indian theory, ideally rulers
kusala—moral good

laukika—of the world, as opposed to *lokottara*
lobha, lōba—greed
lokapāla—'world-protector'; one of the four canonical guardians of the four directions
lokottara, lovuturu—above the world, supra-mundane, i.e. to do with *nirvāṇa*

mahaṇa venavā—to enter the Order, to become a novice
mahāsthāna(ya)—'great place'; one of the sixteen (*soḷos*) places in Ceylon visited by the Buddha; there is also a list of just eight (*aṭa*) of them
maitrī, mettā—loving-kindness
makara toraṇa—the decorative arch, topped by the head of a monster, which usually surmounts the entrance to a *vihāragē*
mal āsanaya—'flower-seat'; altar for offering flowers, etc., before a Buddhist cult object or to a god

mantra(ya)—charm, spell
mataka dānē—a *dānē* given for the dead
māyam venavā—to become possessed by a god or lesser spirit
mithyā dṛṣṭi(ya)—wrong, heretical views
mokṣa(ya)—liberation, escape from rebirth—a term common to all Indian religions

nāga(yā)—a kind of demi-god, a super-normal cobra
näkät, nakṣatra—heavenly body, constellation
nānumura mangalya—ceremony of bathing and anointing a Buddha image
navandannā—the Sinhalese caste of craftsmen, also called *ācāri*
nētra pinkama—'eye ceremony'; the rite which consecrated a Buddha image—see Chapter 3
[1]*Nikāya*—one of the five subdivisions of the *Sutta Piṭaka*; the first four contain sermons, the fifth miscellaneous texts
[2]*nikāya*—as organizational grouping of the Sangha in Ceylon; in the particular sense in which there are said to be just three of them in Ceylon I have written Nikāya without italics.
nirvāṇa(ya), nibbāna, nivan—Buddhist enlightenment, which guarantees freedom from rebirth

padu—a low Sinhalese caste, 'carriers'
Pāli—a middle Indo-Aryan language; literally meaning 'text', the word denotes the language of the Theravāda Buddhist Canon
paṃsukūla—'dust-cloth'; the robe offered to a monk at a funeral
pan̆ḍuru—the coins, usually small change, which accompany an offering or request, esp. to a god
paṇidhi, praṇidhi—a religious aspiration
paññā, prajñā—wisdom, esp. intuitive wisdom
pansala—monastery: the building in which monks live
pantēru—tambourine
paramārtha satya—the ultimate truth (as opposed to *sammuti satya*)
pāramī, pāramitā—perfection, a virtue which a Bodhisattva has to develop to the uttermost on his way to Buddhahood; according to Theravādin doctrine there are ten
parinirvāṇa(ya), parinibbāna, pirinivan—the death of an enlightened person (esp. the Buddha); originally also used as a synonym of *nirvāṇa*

pārśva(ya)—an organizational grouping of the Sangha, nowadays a sub-division of a Nikāya
paryāpti(ya), pariyatti—learning the Dharma, Buddhist book-learning
pātimokkha, prātimokṣa, pāmok—Buddhist monks' confessional, the list of 227 rules for monks, classified according to the penalty for infringement, which is to be recited once a fortnight
pātra(ya)—begging-bowl
pattānumodanā—see *anumodanā*
patti, prāpti—'transfer' of merit—see Chapter 5
pav, pāpa—sin, demerit
pävidi—clergy, monks and novices
pēna kiyanavā—to tell someone's future
perahära—procession, often religious
pidēniya—offering of food, etc., to a *yakā*
piḷikul bhāvanāva—meditation on the foulness of the body
piḷimaya, pratimā, paṭimā—image, statue
pin, puṇya—moral good, merit
piṇḍapāta—monk's begging round
pinkama—'act of merit': any essentially public Buddhist performance
pirikara—'requisites': the eight personal possessions allowed to a monk
pirisa—retinue
pirit, paritta—ceremony at which certain texts from the Pali Canon are recited to avert evil—see Chapter 4
pirivara—retinue
pireveṇa—school or university for Buddhist monks
Piṭaka—'basket'; one of the three parts of the Pali Canon: *Vinaya Piṭaka, Sutta Piṭaka* and *Abhidhamma Piṭaka*
poya—quarter day of the lunar calendar; on the half days, i.e. full moon (*pasaḷosvaka poya*) and no moon (*māsa poya*) monks are to convene and hold a ceremony, also called *poya* or *uposatha* (the Pali word from which *poya* is derived), at which the *pātimokkha* is recited
poya gedara, poya gē—a ding in which monks perform *vinayakam*, esp. the *poya*
prārthanā(va), patthanā—religious aspiration, prayer—and see Chapter 5
pratipatti(ya), paṭipatti—practising the Dharma, leading a holy life

prativedanā(va), paṭivedha—realization of the Dharma, leading a holy life
pratyekabuddha, paccekabuddha, pasēbudu—one who reaches enlightenment without having had the advantage of hearing the Dharma from another, but then does not preach it
preta(yā), perēta(yā), peta—ghost; one of the *gatis*—see Chapter 4
prīti(ya), pīti—joy
pūjā(va)—act of worship, esp. an offering before a cult object in a temple, e.g. a Buddha image

radala—the highest sub-caste of *goyigama*
rājakāriyā—villein, leaser of land for which he pays by performing prescribed services
rākṣasa(yā), rakusa—demon (not a specifically Buddhist term)
ṛddhi(ya), iddhi—supernormal powers gained by meditation
roḍi—the lowest Sinhalese caste

śabda pūjā(va)—offering of sound: the playing of drums and *horaṇavā* before a Buddha image
saccakiriyā, satyakriyā—'act of truth'—see Chapter 5
sādhu—'good'; exclamation used to express participation in a *pinkama*
samādhi—meditation, enstasis—a term common to all Indian religions. A *samādhi piḷimaya* is a statue of the Buddha seated cross-legged in meditation
sāmaṇera—Buddhist novice, commonly called *poḍi/puñci hāmuduruvō/svāminvahansē*
samatha—meditation of the yogic type, enstasis; this is sometimes equated with *samādhi* as against *paññā*
samaya—sect
sammuti satya—conventional truth, which allows the usages of ordinary speech (e.g. 'I', although ultimately there is no such thing as 'I')
saṃsāra(ya)—phenomenal existence, the round of rebirth
samyak sambuddha, sammā sambuddha—truly fully enlightened: epithet of a Buddha (as distinct from an *arhat* or *pratyekabuddha*)
salāgama, halāgama—a Sinhalese caste, most of whom in the seventeenth century became cinnamon pickers
Sangha—the Buddhist monastic order

sannaya, sannē—a translation or close paraphrase in Sinhalese of a Pali text

śānti(ya), set—tranquillity, peace

śāsana(ya)—teaching; Buddhism as a historical phenomenon

śāstra(ya)—a text-book; a science

sat satiya—'seven weeks'; the seven weeks immediately following the Buddha's enlightenment

sätapena piḷimaya—'sleeping statue', which shows the Buddha lying down

sǟya— = *stūpa*

sil, śīla—precept, moral undertaking, esp. in the sets of five (*pan, pañca*), eight (*aṭa, aṣṭa, aṭṭhā*) and ten (*dasa*); also generally, the observance of the precepts (thus the second of the Ten Good Deeds)

sil mǟṇiyō— = *upāsaka mǟṇiyō*

sīmā(va)—boundary, all monks within which should assemble on *poya* days

siṃha seyyāva—'lion bed': lying on the right side, the pose in which the *sätapena piḷimaya* shows the Buddha

sittarā—'painter'; hereditary craftsman employed in building and decorating temples, a sub-caste of *navandannā*

sivura—monk's robe

skandha—five groups which together constitute the appearance of a person: body, feeling, perception, inherited forces, consciousness

śraddhā(va), saddhā, sardhāva—trust, confidence

śrāvaka, sāvaka, sav—disciple, esp. a personal disciple of the Buddha

sthavira, thera, tera—elder: Buddhist monk of ten years' standing

stūpa, thūpa—large conventionalized burial mound containing relics

śūdra, sudda—the lowest of the four classes of society in classical Indian theory; ideally artisans

suti—'listening' to the Dharma; one of the Ten Good Deeds

sutta, sūtra(ya)—classical Buddhist text, usually a sermon by the Buddha or one of his personal disciples

sūvisi—'twenty-four'; refers particularly to the twenty-four Buddhas before Gotama, starting with Dīpaṃkara

svāminvahansē— = *hāmuduruvō*

svarga(ya)—general term for heaven

taṇhā, tṛṣṇā(va)—thirst, craving, the desire which leads to continued existence
tāpasa(yā), tavusa—general term for an ascetic
tēvāva—worship of a Buddha image, esp. those rites and actions which were performed for Sinhalese kings
Theravāda—'doctrine of the elders': the kind of Buddhism surviving in Ceylon
tovil—a name for a *bali* ceremony
T(r)ipiṭaka(ya)—the Pali Canon—see also *Piṭaka*
t(r)iratna, teruvan—the Three Jewels: Buddha, Dhamma, Sangha
t(r)isaraṇa, tun saraṇa—the Three Refuges: Buddha, Dhamma, Sangha (i.e. = *triratna*)

upāsaka māṇiyō, upāsikā māṇiyō—woman who has taken the ten precepts and lives as much as possible like a Buddhist nun, given that there is no longer an Order of nuns in Ceylon
upāsaka(yā), feminine *upāsikā(va)*—Buddhist layman, esp. one of notable piety
upasampadā(va)—higher ordination ceremony, at which a *sāmaṇera* becomes a *bhikkhu*
uposatha—see *poya*

vāhana(ya)—mount, the animal which habitually serves as the vehicle of a particular god
vahansē—literally 'sandal-shadow'; an honorific frequently appended to titles, e.g. *Budurajānanvahansē* 'King Buddha'; *bhikṣunvahansē* 'reverend monk'
vaiśya, vessa—the third of the four classes of society in classical Indian theory; ideally agriculturalists and traders
vanavāsin— = *āraṇyavāsin*
vandanā(va)—worshipping, act of worship, e.g. *vandanā gamana* ('worshipping journey') i.e. pilgrimage
varama—licence, warrant, esp. one by virtue of which a god or demon has jurisdiction
varuva—half-day
[1]*vas*—evil influence, that which has to be removed by exorcism
[2]*vas*—'rains'; the ecclesiastical season during which monks are to stay in one place
vāsanāva—luck
vaṭāpata—Buddhist monk's fan

vehera— = *stūpa*, although etymologically the same word as *vihāra*

vidarśana, vipassanā—meditation on *anicca*, *dukkha*, *anatta*; sometimes equated with *paññā*

vidarśanadhura, vipassanādhura—the duty of meditating, *via contemplativa*

vihāragama—village owned by a monastery

vihāragedara, vihāragē—the building in a Buddhist temple compound which contains at least one statue of the Buddha and other religious art; also called *vihāraya*

vihāra(ya)—Buddhist temple, with a *pansala* and other features; see also *vihāragē*

vinaya—Buddhist monastic discipline

vinayaka(r)ma—corporate rite of the Sangha

vipāka—maturation, the fruition of a former deed (*karma*)

viśvāsa(ya)—trust, confidence

yakā, plural *yakku*; *yakṣa(yā)*, feminine *yakṣiṇī*; *yakkha*, fem. *yakkhinī*— sprite, often maleficent—see Chapter 4

yakādurā—exorcist of *yakku*

yantra(ya)—amulet

yātikāva—invocation to a god

yōga—conjunction of planets

Bibliography

Pali

Dīpavaṃsa ed. and trans. B. C. Law; published as *Ceylon Historical Journal*, vol. VII, no. 1–4, 1957–8.

Jātaka, ed. Fausbøll (Trübner, London, 1877–97. Reprinted Luzac, London, 1962).

Milindapañho, ed. V. Trenckner (Williams and Norgate, London, 1880).

Vinaya-Piṭakam, ed. Hermann Oldenberg, 5 vols. (Williams and Norgate, London, 1879–83).

Visuddhimagga, by Buddhaghosa, ed. H. C. Warren and D. D. Kosambi (Harvard Oriental Series, vol. 41); (Harvard University Press, Cambridge, Mass., 1950).

The other Pali texts and their translations are all cited in the standard editions published by the Pali Text Society, except that the references to commentaries quoted in Rahula's *History of Buddhism in Ceylon* are to the Simon Hewavitarne Bequest edition, which was not available to me.

Sinhalese

ANON, *Buddhadharmaya, Mul pota* (Education Dept., Colombo, 1965).

Bauddha Ädahilla, ed. K. Ñāṇavimala, (Gunasena, Colombo, 1955).

Buddha śāsana komiṣan vārtāva, Sessional Paper XVIII—1959 (Government Press, Colombo, 1959).

Galakäppu Sähälla (N. J. Kūrē, Anula Press (Ceylon), 1961).

JAYATILAKA, D. B. (ed.), *Katikāvat Saṅgarā* (Colombo, 1922)

RATANAPĀLA, G., *Siṃhala Vimānavastu Prakaraṇaya*; MS., 1770.

VĪDĀGAMA THERO, *Lōväḍa Saṅgarāva*; ed. G. Somasiri (Bastian Brothers, Colombo, 1955).

See also Appendix.

European languages

ADIKARAM, E. W., *Early History of Buddhism in Ceylon*, 2nd ed., (Gunasena, Colombo, 1953).

AMES, M. M., 'Buddha and the Dancing Goblins: A Theory of Magic and Religion', *American Anthropologist*, vol. 66, no. 1, pp. 75–82.

AMES, M. M., 'Magical animism and Buddhism: A Structural Analysis of the Sinhalese Religious System', in Harper, E.B. (ed.), *Religion in South Asia* (University of Washington Press, Seattle, 1964), pp. 21–52.

AMES, M. M., 'Ritual Prestations and the Structure of the Sinhalese Pantheon', in Nash, M. (ed.), *Anthropological Studies in Theravada Buddhism* (Yale University, Southeast Asia Studies, 1966), pp. 27–50.

ARNOLD, SIR EDWIN, *The Light of Asia* (Trübner, London, 1879).

BAREAU, A., *Les Premiers Conciles Bouddhiques* (Presses Universitaires de France, Paris, 1955).

BAREAU, A., *La Vie et L'Organisation des Communautés Bouddhiques Modernes de Ceylan* (Institut Français d'Indologie, Pondicherry, 1957).

BARNETT, L. D., 'Alphabetical Guide to Sinhalese Folklore from Ballad Sources', *Indian Antiquary*, Supplement 1916–17.

BASHAM, A. L. 'Background to Parakkamabahu I', *Ceylon Historical Journal*, vol. IV, 1954–5, pp. 10–22.

BECHERT, H., 'Aśokas "Schismenedikt" und der Begriff Sanghabheda', *Wiener Zeitschrift zur Kunde Süd- und Ostasiens*, vol. V, 1961, pp. 18–52.

BECHERT, H., *Buddhismus, Staat und Gesellschaft in den Ländern des Theravada Buddhismus*; vol. I, *Allgemeines und Ceylon* (Institut für Asienkunde in Hamburg, Frankfurt am Main/Berlin, 1966).

BENEDICT, R., *Patterns of Culture* (Mentor Books, New York, 1959).

BOSCH, F. D. K., *The Golden Germ* (Mouton, The Hague, 1960).

CARTER, C., *A Sinhalese-English Dictionary* (Wesleyan Mission Press, Colombo, 1924).

CHARPENTIER, JARL, 'Zur Geschichte des Cariyāpiṭaka', *Wiener Zeitschrift zur Kunde des Morgenlandes* vol. XXIV, no. 4, 1910, pp. 351–415.

CLIFFORD, SIR HUGH, 'Ceylon', in *Encyclopaedia Britannica*, 14th ed. (London and New York, 1929).

COOMARASWAMY, A. K., *Mediaeval Sinhalese Art* (no publisher, Broad Campden, Glos., 1908).

COPLESTON, R. S., *Buddhism Primitive and Present in Magadha and Ceylon* (Longman Green, London, 1892).

DAVY, J., *An Account of the Interior of Ceylon* (Longman, London, 1821).

DE SILVA, W. A., 'Note on the *Bali* Ceremonies of the Sinhalese', *Journal of the Royal Asiatic Society* (*Ceylon Branch*), vol. 22, no. 64, 1911, pp. 140–60.

DICKSON, J. F., 'Notes Illustrative of Buddhism as the Daily Religion of the Buddhists of Ceylon and Some Account of their Ceremonies before and after Death', *J.R.A.S.* (*Ceylon Branch*), vol. VIII, no. 29, 1884, pp. 203–36.

DUMONT, L., 'World Renunciation in Indian Religions', *Contributions to Indian Sociology*, IV, 1960, pp. 33–62.

DURKHEIM, E., *The Elementary Forms of the Religious Life*, trans. J. W. Swain (Collier Books, New York, 1961).

DUTT, S., *Early Buddhist Monachism*, 2nd ed. (Asia Publishing House, London, 1960).

ELIADE, M., *Yoga, Immortality and Freedom* (Routledge and Kegan Paul, London 1958).

ELIOT, SIR CHARLES, *Hinduism and Buddhism*, 3 vols. (Edward Arnold, London, 1921).

EVANS-PRITCHARD, E. E., *The Nuer* (Clarendon Press, Oxford, 1940).

EVANS-PRITCHARD, E. E., *Theories of Primitive Religion* (Clarendon Press, Oxford, 1965).

EVERS, H. D., 'Kinship and Property Rights in a Buddhist Monastery in Central Ceylon', unpublished article, 1966.

FERNANDO, P. E. E., 'The Rakkhanga-Sannas-Cūrṇikāva and the Date of the Arrival of Arakanese Monks in Ceylon', *University of Ceylon Review*, vol. XVIII, nos. 1 and 2, 1959, pp. 41–6.

FERNANDO, P. E. E., 'Tantric Influence on the Sculptures at Gal Vihara, Polonnaruwa', *University of Ceylon Review*, vol. XVIII, nos. 1 and 2, 1960, pp. 50–66.

FICK, R., *Die Sociale Gliederung im Nordöstlichen Indien zu Buddha's Zeit* (Haeseler, Kiel, 1897).

FRAUWALLNER, E., *The Earliest Vinaya and the Beginnings of Buddhist Literature* (ISMEO, Rome, 1956).

FÜRER-HAIMENDORF, C. VON, *Morals and Merit* (Weidenfeld and Nicolson, London, 1967).

GARDNER, J., *The Faiths of the World* (Fullerton, Edinburgh, 1858).

GEIGER, W., *The Culture of Ceylon in Mediaeval Times* (Harrassowitz, Wiesbaden, 1960).

GEIGER, W., *Etymological Glossary of the Sinhalese Language* (Royal Asiatic Society, Ceylon Branch, Colombo, 1941).

GEIGER, W., 'Hūniyam, Ein Beitrag zur Volkskunde von Ceylon', in *Aufsätze zur Kultur- und Sprachgeschichte...Ernst Kuhn...gewidmet* (Breslau, 1916), pp. 185–92.

GLASENAPP, H. VON, *Buddhism: a non-theistic Religion*, trans. I. Schloegl (Allen and Unwin, London, 1970).

GOMBRICH, R., 'The consecration of a Buddhist Image', *J.A.S.*, vol. XXVI, no. 1, 1966, pp. 23–36.

GOMBRICH, R., 'Food for Seven Grandmothers', *Man*, vol. 6, no. 1, March 1971, pp. 5–170.

GOONERATNE, D. DE S., 'On Demonology and Witchcraft in Ceylon', *Journal of the Royal Asiatic Society* (*Ceylon Branch*), vol. 4, no. 13, 1865–6, pp. 1–117.

HARDY, R. S., *Eastern Monachism* (Partridge and Oakey, London, 1850).

HARDY, R. S., *The Legends and Theories of the Buddhists* (Williams and Norgate, London, 1866).

HARDY, R. S., *A Manual of Buddhism* (Partridge and Oakey, London, 1853).

HOCART, A. M., *The Temple of the Tooth in Kandy* (Memoirs of the Archaeological Survey of Ceylon, vol. IV, London, 1931).

JARVIE, I., *The Revolution in Anthropology* (Routledge, London, 1964).

JAYATILAKA, D. B., 'Sinhalese Embassies to Arakan', *J.R.A.S.* (*Ceylon Branch*), vol. XXXV, 1940, pp. 1–6.

KNOX, ROBERT, *An Historical Relation of the Island of Ceylon* (MacLehose, Glasgow, 1911), reprinted as *Ceylon Historical Journal*, vol. VI, nos. 1–4 (Maharagama, 1958).

LAMOTTE, E., *Histoire du Bouddhisme Indien* (Bibliothèque du *Muséon*, vol. 43, Louvain, 1958).

LAW, BIMALA CHURN, *The Buddhist Conception of Spirits*, 2nd ed., (Luzac, London, 1936).

LEACH, E. R., *Pul Eliya* (C.U.P., Cambridge, 1961).

LEACH, E. R., 'Pulleyar and the Lord Buddha: an aspect of

religious syncretism in Ceylon', *Psychoanalysis and the Psychoanalytic Review*, vol. 49, no. 2, 1962, pp.80–102.

LUDOWYK GYÖMRÖI, Dr. E., 'The Role of the Miracle in Early Pali Literature', unpublished Ph.D. thesis, University of Ceylon.

MALALASEKERA, G. P., *Dictionary of Pali Proper Names*, 2 vols. (Luzac, London, 1937).

MALALASEKERA, G. P., *The Pali Literature of Ceylon* (Royal Asiatic Society, London, 1928).

MALALGOḌA, K., 'Sociological aspects of revival and change in Buddhism in nineteenth-century Ceylon', unpublished D.Phil. thesis, Oxford, 1970.

MALALGOḌA, K., *Buddhism in Sinhalese Society 1750–1900* (University of California Press, Berkeley, 1976).

MASSON, J., *La Religion Populaire dans le Canon Bouddhique Pâli* (Bureaux du *Muséon*, Louvain, 1942).

MENDIS, G. C. *Ceylon To-day and Yesterday* (Associated Newspapers of Ceylon, Colombo, 1957).

NARADA THERO, *The Buddha and his Teachings* (no publisher, Saigon, 1964).

NETHERCOT, A. H., *The First Five Lives of Annie Besant* (Hart-Davis, London, 1961).

NYANATILOKA, *Guide through the Abhidhamma-Pitaka*, 2nd ed. (Bauddha Sahitya Sabha, Colombo, 1957).

OBEYESEKERE, G., 'The Buddhist Pantheon in Ceylon and its Extensions', in Nash, M. (ed.), *Anthropological Studies in Theravada Buddhism* (Yale University Southeast Asia Studies, 1966), pp. 1–26.

OBEYESEKERE, G., 'The Great Tradition and the Little in the Perspective of Sinhalese Buddhism', *J.A.S.*, vol. XXII, no. 2, 1963, pp. 139–53.

PARANAVITANA, S., *The God of Adam's Peak* (Artibus Asiae, Ascona, 1958).

PARANAVITANA, S., (ed.), *History of Ceylon*, vol. I, parts I and II (no further volumes have appeared) (Ceylon University Press, Colombo, 1960).

PARANAVITANA, S., 'Mahayanism in Ceylon', *Ceylon Journal of Science*, section G, vol. ii, 1928–33, pp. 35–71.

PARANAVITANA, S., 'Pre-Buddhist Religious Beliefs in Ceylon', *J.R.A.S.* (*Ceylon Branch*), vol. XXXI, no. 82, 1929, pp. 302–27.

PARANAVITANA, S., *The Shrine of Upulvan at Devundara* (Memoirs of the Archaeological Survey of Ceylon, vol. VI, Colombo, 1953).

PARKER, H., *Ancient Ceylon* (Luzac, London, 1909).

PIERIS, P. E., *Ceylon and the Portuguese*, 1505–1658 (American Ceylon Mission Press, Tellippalai, 1920).

PIERIS, R., *Sinhalese Social Organization, The Kandyan Period* (Ceylon University Press Board, Colombo, 1956).

POPPER, K. R., *Conjectures and Refutations* (Routledge and Kegan Paul, London, 1962).

POPPER, K. R., *Logik der Forschung* (Julius Springer, Vienna, 1935).

POPPER, K. R., *The Logic of Scientific Discovery* (Hutchinson, London, 1959).

POPPER, K. R., *The Open Society and its Enemies* (Routledge and Kegan Paul, London, 2nd ed., 1952).

PRZYLUSKI, J., and LALOU, M., 'Notes de Mythologie Bouddhique: I Yaksa et Gandharva dans le Mahasamaya Suttanta', *Harvard Journal of Asiatic Studies*, vol. 3, no. 1, 1938, pp. 40–6.

QUEYROZ, F. de, *The Temporal and Spiritual Conquest of Ceylon*, trans. S. G. Perera (Government Press, Colombo, 1930).

RAHULA, W., *History of Buddhism in Ceylon* (Gunasena, Colombo, 1956).

RAHULA, W., *What the Buddha Taught* (Gordon Fraser, Bedford, 2nd ed., 1967).

RHYS DAVIDS, T. W., *Buddhism* (Society for Promoting Christian Knowledge, London, 1877).

RHYS DAVIDS, T. W., *Buddhist Birth Stories* (Trübner, London, 1880).

ROBINSON, Richard, *An Atheist's Values* (Clarendon Press, Oxford, 1964).

RYAN, B., *Caste in Modern Ceylon: The Sinhalese System in Transition* (Rutgers University Press, New Brunswick, N.J., 1953).

RYAN, B., *Sinhalese Village* (University of Miami Press, Coral Gables, Florida, 1958).

SARATHCHANDRA, E. R., *The Sinhalese Folk Play* (Ceylon University Press Board, Colombo, 1953).

SELIGMANN, C. G., 'Note on the "Bandar" Cult of the Kandyan Sinhalese', *Man*, vol. 9, 1909, no. 77, pp. 130–4.

SENEVIRATNE, H. L., 'The Äsala Perahära in Kandy', *Ceylon Journal of Historical and Social Studies*, vol.6, no. 2, 1963, pp. 169–80.

SINNETT, A.P., *Esoteric Buddhism* (Trübner, London, 1883).

SMART, NINIAN, *Doctrine and Argument in Indian Philosophy* (Allen and Unwin, London, 1964).

SPIRO, MELFORD E., 'Religion: Problems of Definition and Explanation', in Banton, Michael (ed.), *Anthropological Approaches to the Study of Religion*, pp. 85–126 (Tavistock Publications, London, 1966).

STEDE, WILHELM, *Die Gespenstergeschichten des Petavatthu* (Harrassowitz, Leipzig, 1914).

TACHIBANA, S., *The Ethics of Buddhism* (O.U.P., London, 1926).

TAMBIAH, S. J., 'The Magical Power of Words', *Man*, new series, vol. 2, no. 3, June 1968, pp. 175–208.

THOMAS, E. J., *The History of Buddhist Thought* (Routledge and Kegan Paul, London, 1933).

THOMAS, E. J., *The Life of Buddha as Legend and History* (Routledge and Kegan Paul, London, 1927; 3rd edition, 1949).

UPHAM, E., *History and Doctrine of Buddhism* (Ackermann, London, 1829).

VACHISSARA, K., 'Välivița Saraṇaṃkara and the Revival of Buddhism in Ceylon', unpublished Ph.D. thesis, London, 1961.

VAJIRAÑĀṆA, P., *Buddhist Meditation in Theory and Practice* (Gunasena, Colombo, 1962).

WALDSCHMIDT, E., 'Das Paritta', *Baessler-Archiv*, 17, 1934, pp. 139–50.

WEBER, MAX, *The Religion of India*, trans. Gerth and Martindale (Free Press, New York, 1958).

WELLS, KENNETH E., *Thai Buddhism: Its Rites and Activities* (new ed., Bangkok, 1960).

WILSON, BRYAN R., *Sects and Society* (Heinemann, London, 1961).

WIRZ, P., *Exorcism and the Art of Healing in Ceylon* (Brill, Leyden, 1954).

WOOLF, L., *Growing* (Hogarth Press, London, 1961).

YALMAN, N., 'The Flexibility of Caste Principles in a Kandyan Community', in Leach, E. R. (ed.), *Aspects of Caste in South India, Ceylon, and North West Pakistan*, pp. 78–111 (C.U.P., Cambridge, 1960).

YALMAN, N., 'On some Binary Categories in Sinhalese Religious Thought', *Transactions of the New York Academy of Sciences*, series 2, 24, 1962.
YALMAN, N., 'The Structures of Sinhalese Healing Rituals' in Harper, E. B. (ed.), *Religion in South Asia* (University of Washington Press, Seattle, 1964), pp. 115–50.
YALMAN, N., *Under the Bo Tree* (University of California Press, Berkeley and Los Angeles, 1967).

Index

Abayakōn Baṇḍāra Deyyō, 218
Abhayagiri, 34, 35, 36, 39, 129, 323, 382
Abhidhamma, 36, 48, 49, 51, 84, 276, 310, 335, 392
act of truth, 263, 264, 372
Adam's Peak, *see* Siripāda
Adikaram, E. W., 50, 52, 124, 263, 334
aḍukku, 144, 231
adultery, 298–9, 304
affective religion, 6, 10, 11, 72, 86, 98, 143, 171–2, 196, 255, 258, 262, 266, 283–4, 286–7, 294, 297, 306, 7, 383
Africa, 195
ahosi kamma, *see* superseded *karma*
Ajapāla(na), 104, 113
Āḷavaka, 322
alcohol, *see* intoxicants
Alutnuvara Deyyō, *see* Däḍimunda
Amarapura Nikāya, 41, 317, 327, 334, 360–2, 367–8
Ambatthala stupa, 155
Ames, M. M., 68, 180, 183, 186, 193, 198, 213, 224, 225, 233
Amusiri Deyyō/Yakā, 218, 219, 223, 225
Anāgata-vaṃsa, 340
Ānanda, 107, 114, 115, 157, 187, 240, 332, 392
Anāthapiṇḍika, 107, 115, 118
anatta, anātmavāda, *see ātma*
Anattalakkhaṇa Sutta, 85, 106
Angulimāla, 253, 263
Angulimāla Paritta, 237, 263
animals, 10, 28, 80, 127, 171, 183, 184, 186, 196, 197, 199, 213, 216, 272, 276, 304, 306, 306, 336, 353
Anomā River, 104, 111
Anurādhapura, 25, 32, 34, 36–8, 50–3, 91, 112, 117, 128, 130, 131, 133, 167, 245, 253, 323, 341
Anurādhapura period, 24, 29, 31–6, 109, 130, 155, 358, 360
apalē, 175–6, 243
Arahata Vandanāva, 150, 175, 176
āraññavāsin, *see* forest-dwelling monks
arhat, 76, 83, 91, 96, 97, 107, 123–6, 157, 197, 251, 252, 253, 300, 332–4, 339, 341, 373, 375, 377, 378, 380, 387, 392, 393, 394
Arnold, Sir Edwin, 61
Arthaśāstra, 354
Äsaḷa Perahära, 123, 127, 131, 203, 207
Asgiriya, 41, 122, 315, 327, 359, 362, 365
Asita, 102, 389
Asoka, 32, 33, 34, 47, 49, 50, 60
astrology, 81, 158, 172–6, 215, 226, 230, 250, 379
asura, 187, 196, 204
Āṭānāṭiya Sutta, 238, 240–1, 264
ātma, 9, 84, 85, 284, 331, 383
Augustine, St., 19
Avalokiteśvara, 109, 209
Ayurvedic medicine, 176, 226

bali, 191, 225, 233, 243, 246, 247, 250
bälma, 163–4, 221, 232, 247, 249
baṇa, *see* preaching, Buddhist
baṇḍāra, 188, 191, 216, 219, 222–4; *see also* Twelve Gods
Bandaranaike, Mrs., 123, 174, 292
Bandaranaike, S. W. R. D., 130, 188, 333
Bareau, André, 48, 241, 306

Barnett, L. D., 38, 213, 216, 219
Basham A. L., 38
Bauddha Ädahilla, 75, 135, 145, 270, 383
Bechert, Heinz, 31, 48, 66, 70, 328, 331, 332, 334, 344, 358, 360–2, 369, 379
beef-eating, 28, 306
begging by monks, 289, 323–5, 331, 343
behaviour, religious, 2, 5, 14–5, 53, 97, 146, 154, 168, 183, 268, 284, 372–3, 377, 383
'belief' in Sinhalese, 68–70
beliefs, religious, *see* cognitive religion
Benares, 105
Benedict, Ruth, 11, 13, 202
Bengal, 211
beravāyō, 147, 151, 226, 231, 322, 351, 359, 365
Besant, Annie, 61, 62, 64, 65
bhakti, 177, 204, 207, 307, 330
Bhalluka, 105, 113
Bharhut, 50, 189
Bhātikābhaya, 155
bhūta, 190, 194, 195, 394
billa, see sacrificial victim
Bimbisāra, 49, 104, 116, 271, 276, 277
black magic, 176, 215, 221, 233, 235, 246, 261, 347
Blavatsky, H., 62, 64
Bo tree, 29, 33, 90–1, 93, 101, 105, 113, 123, 124, 127, 128, 129, 133, 135, 136, 139, 146, 155 211, 308, 326, 341, 342, 345, 384, 390, 393
Bodhisattva, 17, 35, 36, 95, 100, 101, 104, 105, 109–11, 115, 119, 121, 168 185, 205, 206, 208, 209, 213, 251, 253, 258–60, 263, 266, 267, 271–2, 276, 277, 279, 283, 285, 288, 289, 291–4, 304, 306, 307, 311, 312, 318, 321, 325, 326, 338, 339, 341, 342, 376, 388, 389; *see also* Buddha, Gotama
Bosch, F. D. K., 91
Bradlaugh, Charles, 61
Brahmā, 104, 105, 111, 182, 185, 186, 199
Brahmajāla Sutta, 8, 321
brahmins, 37, 80, 102, 225, 267, 272, 346, 348, 349, 354, 355, 356, 358, 367
Buckingham Palace, 195
Buddha, Gotama, 8, 9, 31, 47, 52, 53, 55, 56, 58, 61, 71, 73, 76–85, 90, 91, 95–168 *passim*, 170, 174, 177, 178, 179, 186, 187, 189, 190, 195, 197, 199, 200, 201, 203, 206, 209–11, 213–5, 225, 226, 228, 229, 234–6, 239–44, 249, 329, 330, 332, 334, 336, 339–44, 354, 355, 356, 357, 358, 364, 367, 368, 370, 375, 380, 383, 384, 387–93
Buddha pūjā, 127, 135–49, 156, 165–6, 225, 229, 231, 385, 390, 392
Buddhadatta (commentator), 51, 118
Buddhaghosa, 33, 50–3, 67, 85, 117, 122, 130, 134, 135, 139, 143, 158, 256, 262–3, 276, 283, 328–35, 343
Buddhas before Gotama, 90, 95, 97, 101, 107, 109, 118, 119, 150–4, 384, 394; *see also* Dīpaṃkara, Kassapa, Paduma, Vipassi
Buddhavaṃsa, 95, 118–21, 338
Buddhist modernism, 63–6, 74–5, 245, 331–2, 344, 361, 370
Budubalaya, 167, 394
Buduguṇa, see 'Iti pi so' gāthā
Burma, 22, 37, 40, 41, 263, 329, 332, 334, 342, 360, 361, 383
Butsaraṇa, 121

Calvinism, 172

caṇḍāla, 347, 357
Canterbury, Archbishop of, 7–8
cardinal virtues, 17, 308, 312
Cariyāpiṭaka, 118–9
caste, 8, 80, 96, 127, 134, 147, 148, 151, 162, 185, 197, 214, 215, 225, 226, 232, 267, 339, 343–371 *passim*
Ceylon, Buddha's visits to, 106, 107, 116, 128–30, 195, 210
Channa, 103–4, 116
charisma, 15, 16
Charpentier, Jarl, 119
Chetris, 267, 268
Childers, R. C., 61
Chinese, 21, 36, 39, 133
Chiswick, 123
Clifford, Sir Hugh, 63, 66
cloth, offerings of, 145–6
cognitive religion, 5, 6, 7, 10–1, 14–5, 17–8, 44, 59, 70, 72, 81, 86, 96–8, 124, 134, 138, 143, 147, 165, 167, 169, 171–2, 192, 196, 251, 254–6, 262, 266, 268, 283, 284, 286, 297, 302, 372, 376–7, 383
Cohen, Percy, 11, 13
Coḷa, 37, 39,
Colombo, 24, 25, 31, 39, 43, 58, 61, 62, 65, 74, 75, 128, 150, 170, 195, 209, 210, 317, 324, 353
commentaries on the Pali Canon, 23, 32–3, 34, 48, 50–2, 117–21, 170, 240–1, 259–61, 267, 276, 281, 315, 332, 335, 341, 358, 384; *see also Dhammapada* commentary, *Samanta-pāsādikā*
Constantine, 245
conventionalism, 11
Coomaraswamy, A. K., 90
Copleston, Bishop, 23, 51, 58, 61, 66, 328
'corrupt' Buddhism, *see* 'popular' Buddhism
councils, Buddhist, 47, 334
  first, 48
  second, 48
  third, 32, 48, 49
Cūlavaṃsa, 30, 41, 54, 129, 158, 323, 347, 348; *see also Mahāvaṃsa*
Cunda, 107

Däḍimunda, 210–1, 213, 218–22, 228, 249
daham pāsal, 63, 77, 98–9, 100, 115–6, 121, 288, 297, 318, 387, 391
Dakkhiṇadesa, 34
Daḷadā Māligāva, 122, 126, 132, 136, 150, 158, 166, 203, 207, 220, 303, 384
Daṁbadeni Katikāvata, 24, 359, 360
Daṁbulla, 110
dānē (giving food to monks), 88–9, 93, 107, 127, 141, 143–4, 148, 159, 238, 257, 266, 268–9, 271, 272, 276, 277, 280, 294, 320, 323–4, 366, 385, 387; *see also mataka dānē*
Dāṭhāvaṃsa, 122
Davy, John, 43, 351, 360, 365–7, 372
dāyaka, 77, 107, 266, 291, 324
death-bed wish, 254, 256, 257, 260
deductivism, 12
De Lanerolle, Julius, 222
demons, 10, 31, 54–7, 81, 105, 172, 176–8, 183–6, 189, 190, 192, 193, 195, 198, 211, 215, 223, 228, 232; *see also yakṣa*
de Queyroz, F., 359
de Silva, W. A., 181
desire, 82, 308, 313, 383, 388, 391
Devadaha, 102, 103, 111, 389
Devadatta, 106

dēvālē, 122, 145, 178, 202, 204, 205, 206, 207, 208, 214, 216, 220–2, 225–31, 350
Devānaṃpiya Tissa, 32, 123, 133, 156, 213, 338
Dēvatā Baṇḍāra Deyyō, *see* Däḍimunda
devil-dancing, 191, 232
Devundara, 208
Dhajagga Sutta, 244, 387
Dhammacakkappavattana Sutta, 83, 106, 113, 116, 187, 321
Dhammadinna, V., 359
Dhammajoti, S., 359
Dhammakitti, 122
Dhammapada, 51, 52, 244, 250, 311, 322, 392
Dhammapada commentary, 121, 252, 261, 276, 280, 292, 294, 322, 338, 339
Dhammapāla, 51
Dhammaruci, 35
Dharma, 71, 76, 80–7, 96, 105, 180, 243, 307, 320, 332, 335, 370, 384–5, 389–90
Dharmapāla, Anagārika, 64, 79, 328, 373
Dharmapāla, Don Juan, 39
dhobi, see radā
Dhṛtarāṣṭra 199, 249
Dickson, J. F., 88, 238, 241, 268, 273, 322, 326, 329
Dīghavāpī, 129, 384
Dīghāyu, 242
Dīpaṃkara Buddha, 95, 100, 101, 109, 118, 119, 120, 387, 388, 389
Dīpavaṃsa, 122
District Revenue Officer, 19, 213, 249
Divyaguhā, 130, 384
Divyāvadāna, 293
Diyavadana Nilamē, 122
doctrinal inconsistency, *see* inconsistency, doctrinal
Doṇa, 107, 122
dorakaḍasnē, 175, 238
Doravaka, 213
Droṇa, *see* Doṇa
drumming, 92, 123–6, 147–8, 153, 160, 195, 231, 232, 241, 336, 350
Dumont, Louis, v, 58, 70, 215
durāva, 345, 359, 360
Durkheim, 4, 10, 13, 68, 183, 377
Dutt, Sukumar, 244, 343
Duṭugämuṇu, 25, 34, 134, 156, 193, 205, 213, 245, 253–4, 263, 300, 301, 334, 338, 372–3, 384

Egypt, 32
Eight Precepts, 78, 94, 124, 314, 319, 330, 383, 389
Eḷāra, 220
Eliade, Mircea, 190, 328, 331
Eliot, Sir Charles, 54, 55, 57
empathy in merit (*pattānumodanā*), 87, 151–2, 243, 251, 265–81, 392–3
Enlightenment, the Buddha's, 22, 29, 33, 58, 63, 78, 85, 91, 95–6, 101, 104, 105, 107, 112, 113, 115, 118, 127, 141, 144, 150, 190, 211, 213, 260, 264, 338, 341, 376, 389, 390, 393
eschatology, 124, 166, 169, 339–42
essentialism, 9, 11, 56
ethos, 18, 20, 294, 296, 306–12
Evans-Pritchard, E. E., 1, 4
Evers, Hans-Dieter, 206, 344
Exeter, Bishop of, 7
exorcism, 7, 59, 163, 176, 181, 191, 194, 225, 230–4, 248–50, 269
Fa Hsien, 133, 323
'faith' in Buddhism, 69–70, 307–8, 339, 379
falsification, 2, 11
fatalism, 170–1
Fausbøll, 110, 118

Fernando, P. E. E., 36, 40
feudal structure in Ceylon, 18, 147, 148, 200–2, 213, 215, 219, 348–50, 369
Fick, R., 346
fire-walking, 203, 204
Five Precepts, 77, 87, 93, 99, 153, 239, 250, 283, 285–8, 293, 296–8, 301–2, 336, 339, 374, 377, 383, 385
flower offerings, 90–3, 135–9, 146, 229, 233, 294, 385, 390
forest-dwelling monks, 315, 325, 331, 376, 378
fortune-telling, 230
Four Kōralēs, 150
Four Noble Truths, 81–3, 285, 333, 373, 393
Frauwallner, E., 48, 49, 95, 375
funerals, 255, 283–4, 308, 311, 320, 321
Fürer-Haimendorf, C. von, 267

Galle, 24, 62
Gandhāra, 133
gandharva, 189
Gañgē Baṇḍāra Deyyō, 218–20, 223
ganinnānsē, 40
Gardner, James, 60
gāthā, 76–8, 87, 93, 99, 112, 120, 124, 132–7, 141–2, 166–7, 244, 257, 262–4, 266, 269, 270, 273, 283, 311, 330, 338–9, 383, 387, 389, 391, 393–4; *see also 'Iti pi so' gāthā*
gattara, **349**
Geiger, Wilhelm, 30, 31, 34, 54, 69, 128, 129, 158, 222, 237, 245, 321
ghosts, 6, 7, 8, 59, 81, 184, 186, 188, 191–5, 199, 235, 244, 273, 274
giving (as a Buddhist virtue), 87, 101, 289–94, 312, 373, 374, 378
Goa, 122
gods, belief in by Buddhists, 9, 12, 54–9, 246–8, 266, 278–9
gods, Sinhalese, 56–8, 80, 90, 123, 126, 132, 136, 142–3, 176–8, 183, 191, 197, 232, 246, 250, 308
Gombrich, R. F., 162, 218
Gooneratne, D. de S., 180, 186, 192, 195, 211, 224, 228, 235
Gotama Buddha, *see* Buddha, Gotama
Goṭhaimbara, 193
Government Agent, 19, 213, 249
goyigama, 221, 225, 231, 325, 346, 349, 351, 352, 353, 358, 359, 360, 362, 364, 365, 366, 367
graha, *see* planetary deities
granthadhura, 314–8, 328, 368, 380
Green, Arnold, 294–6, 323, 361, 362
Gṛhya-sūtras, 190
Guruḷugomi, 130

halāgama, 350, 360
Halāgiriya, 150
halo, 112, 144, 342
Hardy, Robert Spence, 60
Hatthavanagallavihāravaṃsa, 348
heavens, Buddhist, 81, 101, 102, 106, 114, 182–6, 199, 249, 262, 281, 330, 336, 340–2, 374, 377, 379, 383, 392; *see also* Tusita heaven
hells, Buddhist, 81, 183–4, 186, 191, 196, 270, 272, 288, 300, 309–10, 339, 390, 392
Hēvāvitarana, Don David, *see* Dharmapāla, Anagārika
Hinduism, 21, 54, 56–7, 68, 81, 140–3, 145–6, 156, 162, 168, 185, 190, 192, 198, 202–5, 215, 225,

226, 264–7, 272, 276, 293, 306, 306, 346, 347, 354, 370
Hiuen Tsiang, 36, 323
Hocart, A. M., 135, 136, 158
holman, 192–6, 199, 221, 235, 247–50
Horner, Miss I. B., 120, 121
horoscope, 172–5, 212, 230, 387
Hūniyam, 218–9, 221–3, 248

image, Buddha, 35, 73, 90, 93, 98, 107–15, 121, 124, 125, 130, 132–8, 140, 142, 145, 146, 152–4, 157–67, 239, 330, 341, 372
impermanence, 82, 222, 260, 270, 283, 320, 331
impulsivity, 296
incense, 135, 136, 138, 141, 229, 385, 391
inconsistency, doctrinal, 6–7, 58, 81, 86, 97, 144, 155, 156, 166, 170, 191, 196, 244, 246, 268–71, 284, 383
Indāsabhavarañāṇa, A., 360
Indra, 199, 392
intention, 69, 138–9, 170, 242, 262, 265, 279, 287–95, 298–302
intellectualist explanation of religion, 13–5, 157, 167, 170, 191, 196
intoxicants, 77, 286, 298, 385
'Iti pi so' gāthā, 179, 194, 234, 247, 329, 383

Jaffna, 24, 128, 209, 225
Jains, 81, 252
Jarvie, I., 14, 20
Jātakas, 39, 52, 95, 100, 101, 108, 110, 116–9, 120, 121, 189, 211, 213, 240, 252, 263, 279, 312, 323, 334, 335, 346, 357, 358, 389–92
Jayamangala Gāthā, 108, 135, 387
Jayatilaka, D. B., 40, 359
Jayawickrama, N. A., 129
Jesus Christ, 4, 15, 21, 71, 72, 112
Jetavana Vihāra (in Anurādhapura), 35, 129, 323, 384
Jetavanārāma, 107, 339
Jodo-Shin, 259
joy (*prīti*) as a religious emotion, 139, 294, 323

Kaḍavara, 218, 220, 223, 225, 227
Kägalla District, 150
Kāḷa Devala, *see* Asita
Kalama Sutta, 262, 307
Käḷaṇiya, 128, 130, 210, 384
Kalinga, 122
Kaḷu Baṇḍāra Deyyō, 218, 220
Kaḷukumārayā, 218, 221, 223, 224
Kandakumāra, *see* Kandē Deyyō
Kandē Deyyō, 218–20, 223, 227
Kandy, 24, 25, 26, 35, 39, 41, 42, 43, 62, 65, 108, 108, 122, 123, 127, 131, 132, 135, 150, 155, 156, 202, 203, 206, 207–11, 220, 228, 352, 353, 359, 360, 365
Kandyan Convention, 42
Kant, 288
Kanthaka, 103, 104, 116
Kapilavastu, 101, 106, 111, 388, 389
kapurāḷa, 145, 204, 213, 214, 216–23, 227–32, 236, 243, 247
Karaṇīya-metta Sutta, see Metta Sutta
karāva, 360, 362
karma, 9, 71, 81, 84, 85, 86, 87, 96, 168, 169–71, 172, 174, 176, 179, 196, 226, 242, 246, 250, 251–284 *passim*, 285, 288, 299, 339, 364, 383, 386
Kārttikeyya, *see* Kataragama (god)
Kashmir, 123
Kassapa Buddha, 107, 357
Kassapa I, 158

Kataragama (god), 44, 57, 131, 142–3, 185, 187, 198, 200, 202–7, 210–15, 222–3, 226, 227, 228, 231, 249, 303, 306
Kataragama (place), 129, 131, 203–6, 218, 249, 384
Kathāvatthu, 170, 276, 279
kaṭhina pinkama, 326, 385
Kāvantissa, 338
Ketumatī, 340, 393
killing, as first of the Five Precepts, 76, 298–301, 308, 372
kindness, 110, 241, 276, 286, 296, 301, 307, 311–2, 329, 374–9, 384
kinnara, 366
Kiri Baṇḍā, H. M., 150
Kiriammā Deyyō, 218
kiripiḍu pātraya, 144–5
Kirivehera, 384
Kīrti Baṇḍāra Deyyō, 218, 227
Kīrti Śrī Rājasiṃha, 40–1, 220, 360, 365
Knox, Robert, 25, 30, 40, 134, 163, 228, 247, 302–3, 308, 309, 348, 351, 359
koḍi, see pennants, Buddhist
Kohoṁba Deyyō, 218, 223
Koṇḍañña, 102, 104, 106
Kotelawela, John, 64
Koṭṭē, 39
kovil, 145, 203, 215, 225, 226, 228, 230, 306
Krishna, 62
kṣatriya, 346–9, 354–8
Kumāra, *see* Kataragama (god)
kumbhaṇḍa, 189
Kusinārā, 107

Lalou, M., 189
Lamotte, E., 48
Lankārāma, 129, 384
Lankātilaka, 158
Law , B. C., 192
Leach, E. R., 26, 56, 186, 345
leading questions, 44, 302
Lévi-Strauss, C., 291
Lévy-Bruhl, 4
lime-cutting ritual, 212, 230–4
London, 123
Lord's Prayer, 296
Lōväda Saṅgarāva, 288, 390–1
love, *see* kindness
Ludowyk Gyömrői, E., 69
Lumbinī, 102, 389
lying, 77, 298, 299, 302–6

Macedonia, 32
Madhuratthavilāsinī, 118–21
Madurai, 41
magic, 11, 12, 174, 176, 177, 179, 180, 222, 226, 234, 237, 245, 258, 262, 265, 372, 384; *see also* black magic, white magic
Mahā Brahmā, *see* Brahmā
Mahā Jayamangala Gāthā, 179, 238, 264, 387, 393
Māhā Kassapa, 107, 114, 115, 392
Maha Oya, 221
Mahā Satipaṭṭhāna Sutta, 330, 332, 392
Mahābhārata, 190
Mahādāṭhikamahānāga, 155
Mahāmangala Sutta, see Mangala Sutta
Mahāmāyā, 101, 388
Mahānāma, 52
Mahāparinibbāna Sutta, 96, 117, 267, 277, 288, 338, 342
Mahāsammata, 365, 392
Mahāsangharakkhita, 263
Mahāsena, 35, 36, 72, 213, 222
Mahasōnā, 193, 194, 196
Mahāvaṃsa, 29, 32, 38, 49–53, 59, 91, 108, 117, 123, 128, 129, 133, 147, 156, 158, 198, 208, 220, 245, 253, 300, 334, 338, 347, 358, 372
Mahāvihāra, 32, 34, 35, 36, 39, 50, 51, 52, 117, 129

Mahāyāna, 17, 22, 35, 36, 38, 39, 47, 75, 93, 109, 167, 168, 213, 222, 259–62, 272, 338, 375
Mahī Kāntāva, 112
Mahinda, 25, 32–3, 50, 53, 123, 131, 358
Mahinda II, 37
Mahiyangana, 128–31, 158, 210, 214, 384
Maitrī, 93, 95, 101, 107, 109–10, 190, 209, 253–6, 259, 262, 333, 338–41, 377, 386, 396
Majjhantika, 123
makara toraṇa, 90, 107, 199
Malalasekere, G. P., 31, 38, 47, 52, 53, 252, 253
Malalgoḍa, K., 40, 210, 359, 361, 383
Malinowski, 4, 13
Maliyadeva, 333, 334
Malvatta, 41, 122, 243, 315, 327, 359, 362, 365
Mangala Sutta, 237, 241, 244, 386
Mangara Deyyō, 218
Manicūḍāvadāna, 293
mantra, see white magic
Manu, 22
Māra, 104–8, 111, 113, 115, 116, 213, 241, 390, 392
Marx, 13, 74
Masson, J., 9, 10, 184
mataka dānē, 149, 192, 268–79, 283–4, 320, 324, 379
Mātara, 98, 108, 227
Mathurā, 133
Māvanälla, 211, 221, 228
Māyā, 34, 200
meditation, Buddhist, 83, 87, 96, 102, 105, 112, 285–7, 294, 309–11, 314–5, 327–32, 339, 340, 368, 374, 377–8, 383, 387
Mendis, G. C., 343
merit transference (*patti*), 87, 192, 251, 265–81, 284, 293, 320, 373, 378, 386, 389, 391–3
methodological individualism, 14
Metta Sutta, 237, 241, 244, 245, 329, 387
Metteyya, *see* Maitrī
Mīgala, 44, 45, 67, 74, 85, 89, 99, 126, 131–2, 136, 137, 139, 140, 142, 144, 146–8, 159, 172, 174, 175, 193–5, 198, 203, 210–38, 242, 243, 247–8, 252–3, 265, 268, 270, 276, 294, 296, 302, 318, 326, 330, 336, 345, 347, 350, 352, 379, 391
Mihintalē, 123, 129, 155
Milindapañha, 124, 192, 271
Mirisaväṭi sāya, 129, 384
Moggallāna, 107, 114, 251, 338, 392
'monk 6', 259, 325, 331, 339, 341
Mucalinda, 113
Mulkirigala, 359
Müller, Max, 64, 65, 250
Muslims in Ceylon, 42, 203, 214, 304, 351
Mutiyangaṇa, 128, 384

nāga, 189, 197, 267, 342
Nāgadīpa, 38, 128, 131, 209, 342, 384
Nāgammā, 209
Ñāṇamoli, Rev., 273, 277
Ñāṇaponika, Rev., 65
Ñānatiloka, Rev., *see* Nyanatiloka
Ñāṇavimalatissa, A., 360
Nanda, 106
Nandin, 306
nānumura mangalya, 158, 162, 165
Nārada Thero, 67, 366
Nātha, 207, 208, 209, 210, 213
Ñātidhamma Sutta, see Tirokuḍḍa Sutta

Navagamuva, 209
navandannō, 134
Nepal, 267
Nerañjarā River, 104, 111
Nethercot, A. H., 62
nētra pinkama, 134, 148, 158, 162, 164, 165, 367
Neumann, Karl Eugen, 65
Nevill, Hugh, 53, 216
New Testament, 7, 265
New Year, Sinhalese, 158, 248, 379
Nidānakathā, 95, 117, 118, 120, 141, 153, 260
Nidhikaṇḍa Sutta, 326
Nietzsche, 202
Nikāya, 35, 343, 358, 359, 360, 361, 365, 365; *see also* Siyam Nikāya, Rāmañña Nikāya, Amarapura Nikāya
nirvāṇa, 8, 17–9, 20, 82–3, 87, 93, 96, 97, 100, 105, 106, 139, 147, 182, 184, 197, 251–63, 285–7, 294–6, 323, 328, 330, 333–5, 339–41, 343, 374–7, 383, 393
Noble Eight-fold Path, 9, 83, 285–6, 293, 385
novices, Buddhist, 29, 32, 40, 79, 89, 160, 386
nuns, Buddhist, 34, 37, 53, 79, 323, 332, 334, 356
Nuwara Eliya, 25
Nyanatiloka, Rev., 38, 65, 170, 276

Obeyesekere, G., 57, 59, 124–5, 129, 135, 174, 177, 181, 184, 193, 194, 198–202, 209, 231, 246, 254, 296–8, 300, 304, 373, 378, 383
Olcott, H. S., 42, 62–4, 137

Padre Pio, 193
padu, 225, 351
Paduma Buddha 109
Pali Canon, 9, 22, 32, 34, 47–56, 66, 67, 69, 88, 95–6, 117–21, 127, 141, 152, 157, 167, 174, 183–8, 191–4, 197, 199, 200, 223, 237–44, 246 256, 258–60, 262, 267, 272–6, 281, 284–6, 289, 293, 311, 320–1, 327, 332, 334–9, 345, 354, 373, 379
Pali verses or formulae recited, *see gāthā*
Pallebädda Deyyō, 218, 219, 223
paṃsukūla, 283, 284, 321, 378
pan̆ḍuru, 152, 227, 229, 249
Paṇḍukābhaya, 32
Pāṇḍya, 37
panna, 351
pantēru nätum, *see* tambourine dances
Parakkama-Bāhu I, 38, 315
Parakkama-Bāhu II, 39
Parakkama-Bāhu IV, 39, 158
Parakkama-Bāhu VI, 39
Paranavitana, S., 31, 35, 207–8, 210
parinirvāṇa, the Buddha's, 96, 107, 114, 115, 116, 128, 152, 283, 341, 390
Parker, H., 216, 221
Pathan, 349
pātimokkha, 244, 327
pattānumodanā, *see* empathy in merit
patti, *see* merit transference
patti (sub-caste), 350
Pattinī, 57, 199, 207, 209, 226, 227, 232, 249
pennants, Buddhist, 126, 127, 146
Pertold, O., 181
Petavatthu, 270, 272–4, 280, 291
Pieris, P. E., 40
Pieris, Ralph, 348–9
Pihiti, 200
pilgrimage, 93, 123, 127–32, 157, 203, 210, 214, 296, 326

pilgrimage, places of, in Ceylon, 123, 127–32, 384
piṇḍapāta, see begging by monks
Pingree, David, 174
pinkama, 88–9, 92–3, 123, 146, 149, 153, 255, 265, 267, 269, 271, 285, 289, 294, 302, 303, 324, 377, 385
pirikara, see requisites
pirit, 88, 93, 126, 148, 175, 179, 180, 226, 236–43, 244, 245, 246, 264, 269, 319, 320, 322, 373, 387, 394
piriveṇa, 89, 175, 183, 316–7, 318, 324, 331
Piṭiya Deyyō, 132, 213, 216, 219–20, 223–4, 227–9, 247, 248–9
planetary deities, 172–6, 225, 233, 247, 250, 394
Pocock, David, v, 70
political Buddhism, *see* Buddhist modernism
pollution, 125, 215, 219, 345, 357, 367, 370
Poḷonnaruva, 25, 37, 39, 91, 130
Poḷonnaruva period, 24, 36, 130, 206, 240, 289, 358
Popper, Sir K. R., 2, 9, 12, 14, 16, 288
'popular' Buddhism, 46, 53–60, 184, 246, 373, 384
Portuguese, 20, 24, 39, 42, 122, 210
Poson, 131, 214
possession by a god, 215, 221, 228, 230, 231, 232
poya, 63, 77, 99, 101, 122, 124, 135, 148, 228, 314, 318–9, 321, 326, 327, 329, 383, 388
poya gedara, 92
prārthanā, 46, 179, 251, 254, 255, 256, 258, 259, 260, 263, 264, 265, 284, 296, 332, 340, 386, 391
Pratyekabuddha, 17, 97, 261, 265, 279, 280, 333, 394
preaching, Buddhist, 87–8, 92–3, 151, 153, 154, 242, 243, 255, 269, 270, 283, 297, 314, 316, 319–22, 326, 342
preaching hall, 90–2, 153
preta, 186, 188–9, 192, 195–6, 199, 250, 270, 272, 276, 278, 280, 283
Prinsep, James, 60
prudential ethics, 153, 287–8, 299
Przyluski, J., 189
Pūjāvaliya, 121, 153
Pūrṇaka, 211

Queyroz, *see* de Queyroz

radā, 351, 366
radala, 351, 352, 362
Radcliffe-Brown, 4
Rāhula (the Buddha's son), 103, 106, 392
Rahula, Rev. Walpola, 31, 33, 34, 35, 36, 70, 84, 85, 123, 130, 133, 139, 142, 143, 158, 216, 237–42, 269, 270, 271, 278, 315, 321, 323, 330, 368, 373–4
Rājagṛha, 104, 240
rājakāriyō, 148, 350
Rājasiṃha I, 40
Rājasiṃha II, 30
rākṣasa, 189, 190
Rāmañña Nikāya, 41, 225, 327, 328, 334, 360, 361, 362, 365, 365, 366, 370
Rangoon, 331, 334, 341
Ratana Sutta, 237–41, 244, 246, 387
Ratanapāla, G., 40
rationality principle, 14, 18
Redfield, 181, 184
relics, 30, 34, 72, 80, 91, 93, 107, 112, 119, 121, 122–35, 138, 149, 155, 157, 164, 167, 197, 214, 246,

334–5, 341–2, 372, 384; *see also* tooth relic
'religion' in Sinhalese, 68, 71, 73–4, 292
requisites, i.e. Buddhist monk's possessions, 152–3, 159–61, 267, 269, 385, 392, 393
restraint, 309–12, 374–83
Rhys Davids, Mrs. C. A. F., 380
Rhys Davids, T. W., 61–2, 65, 119, 120, 122, 328
Robinson, Richard, 17
roḍi, 347–51, 365, 365, 366, 370
Rohaṇa, 34, 200, 202
rosary, 78, 94, 330
Ruvanväli Sǟya, 129, 130, 155, 167, 341, 342, 384
Ryan, Bryce, 59, 345, 347, 350, 351, 362

Sabaragamuva, 211, 228
śabda pūjāva, 147–8, 155
saccakiriyā, *see* act of truth
sacrificial victim, 234
Saddharmālaṃkāraya, 121, 153
Saddharmaratnākaraya, 342
Saddharmaratnāvaliya, 121
Saddhātissa, 338
Sāgala, 35, 331, 332, 378
Śaivism, 40, 202–7, 225, 307
Sakka, Śakra, 57, 104, 108, 110, 111, 185–9, 199, 201, 244, 249, 283
Śākyas, 101, 106, 355, 393
salāgama, *see halāgama*
Salgala, 325, 331–2, 378
Saḷumiṇi sǟya, 111
samādhi piḷimaya, 112–3, 133, 146; *see also* image, Buddha
Saman, 132, 202, 207–10, 213, 249
Samanta-pāsādikā, 33, 128, 129, 143, 250, 332
Sanchi, 50, 189
Sangha, 24, 33, 35, 38, 39, 77–80, 140, 142, 178, 239, 243, 244, 251, 267–9, 274, 277, 280, 283, 284, 286, 289–92, 315–6, 332, 335, 339, 341–4, 357–61, 365, 368, 369, 370, 378, 379, 380, 383, 384, 385, 387, 390, 392, 393, 394
Sanghamittā, 33
Sangharakshita Sthavira, 328
śānta dānta, *see* restraint
Śāntideva, 167
Saraṇamkara, Väliviṭa, 41, 359
Sarathchandra, E. R., 181, 238
Sāriputta, 107, 114, 253, 266, 338, 392
Sarvāstivāda, 272
śāsana, 33, 125, 244, 333, 334, 335, 338, 341, 361, 368, 375, 391
sat satiya, 107, 112, 150, 385
sätapena piḷimaya, 115
Satipaṭṭhāna Sutta, *see Mahā Satipaṭṭhāna Sutta*
self-restraint, *see* restraint
Seligmann, C. G., 216
Sena II, 246
Senanayake, D. S., 137
Senanayake, Dudley, 35
Seneviratne, H. L., 72, 136, 207, 211
Siam, *see* Thailand
Siddamulā Hūniyam Dēvatā Baṇḍāra, 218, 219
sil māṇiyō, *see upāsaka māṇiyō*
Siḷumiṇi sǟya, 104, 111
sīmā, 32, 33, 41, 201, 208, 327
Sinhalese language, 23, 38, 50, 69–74, 156, 225, 278, 353
Sinnett, A. P., 62
Siripāda, 128, 130, 132, 210, 296, 331, 384
sittaru, 77, 134, 162
Śiva, 202, 306
Sīvali, 107, 115, 197, 379, 387

Siyam Nikāya, 33, 41, 43, 315, 317, 325, 327, 358–67
Skanda, *see* Kataragama (god)
slaves, 354
Smart, Ninian, 9
Spiro, Melford E., 12, 55
Śrāvastī, 107
Śrī Vikrama Rājasiṃha, 365
Stead, William T., 62
stealing, 76, 171, 286, 296, 298, 302, 303, 308
Stede, Wilhelm, 274
stupa, 29, 34, 90–3, 104, 111, 122, 123, 125–6, 129, 132, 134, 144, 155, 156, 157, 341, 384, 390
Suddhodana, 101–3, 106, 388
śūdra, 346–9, 354, 357
Sujātā, 104, 111, 113, 144, 190, 393
Sumedha, 95, 100, 109, 118, 120, 387, 388
superseded *karma*, 251–4, 300
Suppabuddha, 103, 106
Sutta-nipāta, 237, 311, 322, 355, 357
sūvisi, *see* Buddhas before Gotama
sūvisi pinkama, 150–5, 157, 322
syncretism, 54–8, 66

Tachibana, S., 312, 318
Tambiah, S. J., 70, 224, 235
tambourine dances, 127, 150, 154; *see also sūvisi pinkama*
Tamils, 25–6, 34, 37, 42, 57, 73, 140–2, 203–5, 214, 224, 225, 235, 245, 253, 300–1, 346–7, 351
Tantrism, 36
tāpasa movement, 222, 378
Tapassu, 105, 113
Tārā, 213
Telapatta, 110, 240
Temple of the Tooth, *see* Daḷadā Māligāva
Ten Good Deeds, 87–8, 242, 265, 285–9, 293, 314, 316, 377, 385
Ten Perfections, 101, 105, 108, 110, 116, 118–9, 312, 386, 392
Ten Precepts, 78–9, 308, 314, 383
Tēvānī, 203
Thailand, 22, 41, 237, 322, 328, 384
theodicy, 169, 171
Theragāthā, 374
Theravāda, 8, 10, 12, 17, 22, 30, 32, 35, 36, 39, 46, 47, 48, 51, 59, 66, 84, 138, 162, 168, 178, 198, 222, 259, 272, 276, 284, 307, 316, 343, 375–80, 384
third Buddhist council, *see* councils, Buddhist
Thomas. E. J. 9, 49, 85, 117
thread, prophylactic, 222, 230, 234–40, 247
Three Jewels, 76, 80, 84, 244, 255, 260, 383–5, 389
Three Refuges, 77, 80, 99, 153, 167, 239, 244, 250, 283, 296, 340, 383, 394
Thūpārāma, 34, 128, 129, 384
Tipiṭaka, see Pali Canon
Tirokuḍḍa Sutta, 273, 276
Tissamahārāma, 129, 131, 384
tooth relic, 35, 37, 122, 131–2, 135–6, 150, 158, 166, 203, 207, 220, 303, 342, 384
Toṭagamuva, 208
transference of merit, *see* merit transference
tree worship, vestiges of, 146, 190, 214, 260
Turnour, George, 60
Tusita heaven, 101, 106, 110, 338, 388
Twelve Gods, 191, 213–24, 225–31; *see also baṇḍāra*
Tylor, 4, 13

undecided questions in Buddhism, 8–9, 125
unintended consequences, 14, 15, 18, 19, 20, 368, 370, 383
Upaka, 105
Upāli, 107, 357, 364
Upanishads, 21, 191
upāsaka, 105, 329, 334, 380, 383, 386
upāsaka māṇiyō, 79, 237, 268, 314, 326, 330, 333
upasampadā, 32, 37, 40, 317, 359–61, 365
Upatissa I, 239
Upham, E., 181
Uppalavaṇṇa, 57, 208

Vachissara, K., 41
Väddas, 31, 43, 216
Vaiśravaṇa, 190, 199, 213, 241, 250
vaiśya, 346–9, 354, 358
Vaitulyavāda, 35, 206
Vajirañāṇa, King, 384
Vajirañāṇa Mahāthera, 330
Vajirārāma, 64, 324, 366
Vajjiputra sect, 35
Valkōn Baṇḍāra Deyyō, 218
Vallī Ammā, 203
values, 15–7, 296–300, 306-11, 374–7
Vanniya Baṇḍāra Deyyō, 218, 219, 231
Varuṇa, 208
vas (liturgical rainy season), 324, 326–7
Vasala Sutta, 357, 365, 364
Vaṭṭagāmaṇī Abhaya, 34
Vedas, 21, 185, 189, 191, 196, 199, 208
vegetarianism, 304–6
Vesālī, 239–40
Vessantara, 101, 105, 108, 110, 290, 312
Vibhīṣaṇa, 207, 210, 249
Vīdāgama Thera, 288, 389–91
vidarśanadhura, 315, 368, 374
Vidyālaṃkāra, 317
Vidyodaya, 175, 317
Vihāra Mahā Devī, 338
vihāragama, 149, 350
Vijaya-Bāhu I, 37
Vimala Dharma Sūrya I, 40
Vimala Dharma Sūrya II, 40
Vimānavatthu, 283
Vinaya, 33, 48, 49, 51, 129, 266, 30a 4, 327, 332, 335, 357, 359, 362, 365, 369, 380
Vipassi Buddha, 244
Virūḍha, 199, 249
Virūpākṣa, 199, 249
Visākhā, 107, 115, 280, 281, 393
Vishnu, 57, 142, 185, 187–8, 198, 200, 206–9, 210–13, 222, 227, 249, 308
Visuddhimagga, 50, 262, 283, 328, 329, 332

Waldschmidt, E., 237, 238, 241
water-pouring in ritual, 270, 283, 320
Weber, 13, 15, 16, 21, 285–6, 373, 374, 375, 376, 377, 383, 384
Wells, Kenneth E., 22, 237, 322
Wesak, 63, 78, 101, 105, 107, 130, 136, 210, 308, 319, 324, 389
white magic, 176, 179, 226, 235, 243, 246, 264
Wijesinha, 129, 158
Wilson, Bryan, 21, 70, 174
Winternitz, M., 293
Wirz, Paul, 59, 60, 65, 181, 190, 193, 198, 216, 223, 224
wisdom, 83, 310, 331
Woodward, F. L., 328
Woolf, Leonard, 203
'worship' in Sinhalese, 71–3

Y.M.B.A., 99

yakṣa, 163, 186–96, 199, 205, 207, 211, 220, 223, 225, 228, 232–4, 242, 248–9, 260–1, 264, 322, 394
Yalman, Nur, 124, 181, 241, 345, 351
yantra, see white magic
Yasodharā, 103, 106, 393
Yogācāra, 36

LEWIS AND CLARK COLLEGE LIBRARY
PORTLAND, OREGON 97219

Lewis and Clark College - Watzek Library
3 5209 00628 3069